CW00922356

The Cambridge Companion to International Law

This intellectually ambitious introduction to international law encourages readers to engage with multiple aspects of the topic: as 'law' directing and shaping its subjects; as a technique for governing the world of states and beyond statehood; and as a framework within which several critical and reformist projects are articulated. The chapters situate international law in its historical and ideological context and examine core concepts such as sovereignty, jurisdiction and the state. Attention is also given to its operation within international institutions and in dispute settlement, and a separate section is devoted to international law's 'projects': protecting human rights, eradicating poverty, the conservation of resources, the regulation of international trade and investment and the establishment of international order. The diverse group of contributors draws from disciplinary orientations ranging from positivism to post-modernism to ensure that this book is informed theoretically and politically, as well as grounded in practice.

James Crawford is Whewell Professor of International Law and a Fellow of Jesus College, Cambridge and Professor of Law at Latrobe University, Melbourne. He was a member of the United Nations International Law Commission from 1992 to 2001 and Special Rapporteur on State Responsibility from 1997 to 2001. He has also been a member of the Australian Law Reform Commission. In addition to scholarly work on statehood, self-determination, collective rights and international responsibility, he has appeared frequently before the International Court of Justice and other international tribunals, and is actively engaged as expert, counsel and arbitrator.

Martti Koskenniemi is Professor of International Law at the University of Helsinki and Director of the Erik Castrén Institute of International Law and Human Rights. He worked as a diplomat with the Finnish Ministry for Foreign Affairs from 1978 to 1994, representing Finland in a number of international institutions and conferences. As member of the UN International Law Commission (2002–2006) he chaired the Study group on the 'Fragmentation of International Law'. He has written widely on international law topics and his present research interests cover the theory and history of the field.

The Cambridge Companion to

International Law

Edited By

James Crawford

and

Martti Koskenniemi

Assistant Editor

Surabhi Ranganathan

CAMBRIDGE
UNIVERSITY PRESS

CAMBRIDGE UNIVERSITY PRESS
Cambridge, New York, Melbourne, Madrid, Cape Town,
Singapore, São Paulo, Delhi, Tokyo, Mexico City

Cambridge University Press
The Edinburgh Building, Cambridge CB2 8RU, UK

Published in the United States of America by Cambridge University Press, New York

www.cambridge.org
Information on this title: www.cambridge.org/9780521190886

First published 2012

Printed in the United Kingdom at the University Press, Cambridge

A catalogue record for this publication is available from the British Library

Library of Congress Cataloguing in Publication data
The Cambridge companion to international law / edited by James Crawford and Martti Koskenniemi.
p. cm. – (Cambridge companions to law)
ISBN 978-0-521-19088-6 (hardback)
1. International law. 2. International law – History. 3. Globalization.
I. Crawford, James, 1948– II. Koskenniemi, Martti.
KZ3410.C35 2012
341–dc23

2011041594

ISBN 978-0-521-19088-6 Hardback
ISBN 978-0-521-14308-0 Paperback

Contents

Preface

This study was conceived and planned in 2008–2009 when we were colleagues at Cambridge, during Martti's tenure as Goodhart Distinguished Professor of Law. We were able to discuss some of the contributions in draft at a mini-conference held at the Lauterpacht Centre for International Law in February 2010.

In selecting authors for the *Companion*, we sought to incorporate a wide range of views, including interdisciplinary and critical approaches, as well as ensuring a reasonable coverage of the various sub-fields of international law. As the reader will observe, the discipline/profession of international law is approached in different ways by different scholars: the subject looks subtly (and sometimes unsubtly) different from India or the United States or Australia than it does from different parts of Europe or Africa. We would have wished for an even more catholic range of contributors, but the demands of space and time precluded this.

We are grateful to Cambridge University Press, notably the responsible subject editor, Sinead Moloney, for a judicious combination of support, encouragement and patience. Much of the editorial burden fell on our graduate student at NYU and Cambridge, Surabhi Ranganathan, to whom we owe a lot. Lesley Dingle produced an admirable guide to electronic sources of international law; the guide is also available at the website of the Squire Law Library* where the links will be periodically updated: they were correct when the manuscript was submitted to the Press.

JRC/MK

26 June 2011

* www.squire.law.cam.ac.uk/electronic_resources/international_law_research_guides.php – S2.

Notes on contributors

Hilary Charlesworth is an Australian Research Council Laureate Fellow and Director of the Centre for International Governance and Justice in the Regulatory Institutions Network (RegNet) at the Australian National University. She also holds an appointment as Professor of International Law and Human Rights in the College of Law, ANU. She is a graduate of the University of Melbourne and Harvard Law School.

B. S. Chimni is Professor of International Law, Centre for International Legal Studies, School of International Studies, Jawaharlal Nehru University, New Delhi. He has held visiting positions at Brown, Harvard, Cambridge, York and Tokyo Universities. His central research interest is to elaborate in association with a group of likeminded scholars a critical Third-World approach to international law (TWAIL). His other areas of research interest are international economic law and international refugee law.

James Crawford is the Whewell Professor of International Law, University of Cambridge and Professor of Law at Latrobe University, Melbourne. As a member of the International Law Commission he was responsible for its work on the International Criminal Court and for completing the Articles on State Responsibility. In addition to scholarly work on statehood, collective rights, investment law and international responsibility, he has appeared frequently before the International Court of Justice and other international tribunals.

Lesley Dingle has been the Foreign and International Law Librarian at the Squire Law Library since 1997. She is currently Chair of the Advisory Committee for the Index to Foreign Legal Periodicals and has acted as a consultant for the UK section of 'The Bluebook'. Her interests include research on the history of the Law Faculty at Cambridge, and she is founder of the Eminent Scholars Archive. She is a Senior Member of Wolfson College.

David Kennedy is the Manley O. Hudson Professor of Law at Harvard Law School and Director of the Institute for Global Law and Policy. He teaches and writes on international law, international economic policy, European law, legal theory, and law and development. He is the founder of the New Approaches to International Law project. He has practised law with various international institutions, including UNHCR and the Commission of the European Union, and with the private firm of Cleary, Gottlieb, Steen and Hamilton.

Benedict Kingsbury is the Murry and Ida Becker Professor of Law and Director of the Institute for International Law and Justice at New York University School of Law. He co-directs NYU's research on the History and Theory of International Law, Global Administrative Law, and Indicators and Global Governance by Information. His research reflects commitment to a broad, theoretically grounded approach to international law, closely integrating work in legal theory, political theory, and history. He writes widely on contemporary issues, including arbitration, trade-environment disputes and the proliferation of international tribunals.

Jan Klabbers is Professor of International Law at the University of Helsinki and Director of the Academy of Finland Centre of Excellence in Global Governance Research. He has taught at the University of Amsterdam and held visiting professorships in Geneva and Paris. His publications include *The Concept of Treaty in International Law* (1996), *Treaty Conflict and the European Union* (2008), *An Introduction to International Institutional Law* (2nd edn., 2009) and, as co-author, *The Constitutionalization of International Law* (2009).

Karen Knop is Professor at the Faculty of Law, University of Toronto. Her book *Diversity and Self-Determination in International Law* (2002) was awarded a Certificate of Merit by the American Society of International Law. She is the editor of *Gender and Human Rights* (2004) and co-edited a 2008 symposium issue of Law and Contemporary Problems on 'Transdisciplinary Conflict of Laws' with Ralf Michaels and Annelise Riles.

Martti Koskenniemi is Professor of International Law, University of Helsinki and Hauser Visiting Global Professor of Law, New York University. He was the Arthur Goodhart Visiting Professor of Legal Science at Cambridge (2008–2009), a member of the UN International Law Commission (2002–2006) and Counsellor at the Ministry for Foreign Affairs of Finland (1978–1994). His publications include *From Apology to Utopia. The Structure of International Legal Argument* (2nd edn., 2005) and *The Gentle Civilizer of Nations: The Rise and Fall of International Law 1870–1960* (2001).

Dino Kritsiotis is Professor of Public International Law at the University of Nottingham. He has held visiting professorships at Michigan and Melbourne, and he regularly teaches on the International Committee of the Red Cross annual summer school in Warsaw. He specialises in the use of force, international humanitarian law and the history and theory of international law. He serves on the editorial boards of *Journal of Conflict and Security Law*,

Human Rights Law Review, *Human Rights and Human Welfare* and *African Yearbook on International Humanitarian Law.*

Susan Marks is Professor of International Law at the London School of Economics. Her research is concerned with international law and human rights. She is the author of *The Riddle of All Constitutions* (2000) and, with Andrew Clapham, *International Human Rights Lexicon* (2005) and she edited *International Law on the Left* (2008).

Frédéric Mégret is Associate Professor at the Faculty of Law, McGill University and the Canada Research Chair in the Law of Human Rights and Legal Pluralism. He holds a PhD in international law from the University of Paris I-Panthéon Sorbonne and the Graduate Institute of International Studies (Geneva). His research interests focus on international law, international criminal law, human rights and the laws of war.

Andreas Th. Müller is Assistant Professor at the Department of European Law and Public International Law of the University of Innsbruck. He has studied law and philosophy at the Universities of Innsbruck and Strasbourg and holds a Master of Laws (Yale, 2009) and a Doctorate in Law (University of Insbruck, 2010). In 2009–2010, he was University Trainee to Judge Abdul G. Koroma and Judge Bruno Simma at the International Court of Justice.

Sarah Nouwen is the Mayer Brown Research Fellow in Public International Law at the Lauterpacht Centre for International Law and Pembroke College, Cambridge. She holds a PhD (Cantab.) and an LLM (Utrecht/Cape Town/Western Cape) in International Law and an MPhil (Cantab.) in International Relations. She was a visiting professional at the International Criminal Court and has worked as a consultant for foreign ministries, Ugandan and Senegalese NGOs and the African Union High Level Implementation Panel for Sudan.

Anne Orford is the Michael D. Kirby Professor of International Law and the Director of the Institute for International Law and the Humanities at Melbourne Law School. She was awarded an Australian Research Council Professorial Fellowship from 2007 to 2011 to work on a project entitled *Cosmopolitanism and the Future of International Law.* Her chapter in this volume is drawn from that project. Her most recent book is *International Authority and the Responsibility to Protect* (2011).

Sundhya Pahuja is Professor of Law and Director of the Law and Development Research Programme at the Institute for International Law and the Humanities, at the University of Melbourne. Her research interests lie in international law, development, globalisation, jurisprudence and postcolonial theory. Her most recent book is *Decolonising International Law: Development, Economic Growth and the Politics of Universality* (2011).

Thomas Pogge is Leitner Professor of Philosophy and International Affairs at Yale, Research Director at the University of Oslo Centre for the Study of Mind in Nature (CSMN) and a member of the Norwegian Academy of Science. He has published widely on Kant and in moral and political philosophy. Recent publications include *Politics as Usual* (2010) and *World Poverty and Human Rights* (2nd edn., 2008). His current work is focused on reforming the pharmaceutical patent regime to improve access to medicines for the poor worldwide (www.healthimpactfund.org).

Surabhi Ranganathan is a PhD Candidate at the University of Cambridge, a Gates Scholar and the J.C. Hall Scholar at St John's College. She has degrees from New York University School of Law and National Law School of India University. She was Institute Fellow/ Program Officer at the Institute for International Law and Justice, NYU and has clerked for Justice Brijesh Kumar of the Supreme Court of India.

Hélène Ruiz Fabri is Professor of International Law at the University of Paris I-Panthéon Sorbonne, Dean of the Sorbonne Law School, Director of the Institute of Comparative Studies of Paris and Director of the Master 2 Program in International Economic Law. She teaches and researches International law, WTO law and International Dispute Settlement. She has degrees in law and political science from the University of Bordeaux and the Institut d'Études politiques de Bordeaux and a Doctorate in international law.

Bruno Simma is Judge at the International Court of Justice, Professor (retired) at the University of Munich and William H. Cook Global Law Professor at the University of Michigan Law School (on leave during tenure at the ICJ). He is a former member of the UN Committee on Economic, Social and Cultural Rights and of the International Law Commission. He is the co-founder of the *European Journal of International Law* and of the European Society of International Law, and an associate member of the Institut de Droit international.

Gerry Simpson holds the Kenneth Bailey Chair of Law at the University of Melbourne, where he is Director of the Asia Pacific Centre for Military Law and Convenor of the Global Justice Studio. He is a Visiting Professor at the London School of Economics and an AFP/Open Society Fellow based in Tbilisi, Georgia. He has authored several books including *Great Powers and Outlaw States* (2004) (awarded the American Society of International Law's prize for Pre-eminent Contribution to Creative Legal Scholarship in 2005).

Introduction

James Crawford and Martti Koskenniemi

Purpose of the *Companion*

From an exotic specialisation on the fringes of the law school, international law has turned during the twentieth century into a ubiquitous presence in global policy-making as well as in academic and journalistic commentary. With internationalisation first, globalisation later, questions about the legality under international treaties or customary law of this or that action were posed with increasing urgency in the media and by citizen activists as well as by governments and international institutions. International law exited the chambers of diplomacy to become part of the debates on how the world is governed. With good reason, the last ten years of the old millennium were labelled by the United Nations General Assembly the 'Decade of International Law'. The decade saw such impressive developments as the establishment in 1995 of the World Trade Organisation (WTO) with a powerful system for settling trade disputes. In 1998 the Rome Treaty was adopted that led to the setting up of the International Criminal Court (ICC) to try suspected war criminals and those committing grave violations of human rights. The system of multilateral human rights and environmental treaties expanded and, as many said, henceforth needed more deepening rather than widening. The UN Security Council arose from its Cold War slumber to take action in many regional crises, sometimes with more, sometimes with less success, but always surrounded by much legal argument. Cooperation in development and in the organisation of international investment took a legal turn: the rhetoric of 'rule of law' penetrated everywhere. The same trends continued in the first decade of the new millennium. At the same time, however, new concerns emerged. Violations of human rights and humanitarian law kept occurring, especially in the Third World but also in Europe, while only little progress was attained in the eradication of poverty and global economic injustice. Some activities led by the Great Powers such as the bombing of Belgrade by the North Atlantic alliance

(NATO) in 1999 or the campaign to oust Saddam Hussein from Iraq's leadership in 2003 became the subject of heated debate. The relationship between the fight against terrorism and the protection of human rights divided opinions in Europe and elsewhere. While the number of democratic countries increased, democracy also brought popular restlessness and conflict out in the open. If international law was rhetorically ever-present, it was often hard to say what its actual impact in the various situations had been.

In the nineteenth and twentieth centuries, foreign policy 'realists' routinely claimed that international law had a role only in affairs of minor importance. When matters of vital interests emerged, exit the lawyer. This is plainly no longer the case. Law participates in practically every single important aspect of foreign policy and international government. In 2009, for example, the International Court of Justice (ICJ) gave an advisory opinion on the legal status of Kosovo and in 2011 the International Criminal Court indicted Colonel Ghaddafi for suspicion of having committed crimes against humanity against his own population. It has become part of the routine vocabulary through which not only lawyers but journalists, political activists and citizens generally view what is going on in the world and hope to determine what attitude to take in respect of some recent development.

In this *Companion*, the editors have sought to provide an introduction to international law directed not only to lawyers but to academic and professional audiences generally, including non-specialist readers keen to form an overall view of the subject or to explore some aspect of it perhaps related to their own work or, perhaps more generally, to form a reasoned opinion on some matter of international interest. By preparing a volume that goes beyond a mere repackaging of existing materials we have aimed at a politically and historically informed account of the role of international law in the world.

As editors, we have pooled our different orientations to and intuitions about international law to convey both traditional and critical understandings of the field. In our telling, international law may be understood as 'law', with the capacity to regulate relations between states as well as between states, peoples and other international actors, but it is also recognised as a language of government in certain contexts, as a bundle of techniques, and as a framework within which several (modern and post-modern) constructivist projects are articulated. We have consequently selected four general themes to operate as 'windows' from which to approach the substance of international law. Each of them brings into visibility some aspect that we regard as important. We have been lucky in receiving the assistance as authors of some of the most talented and innovative international lawyers active today, each bringing to this project their distinct interests, preferences and outlook on the materials they have been asked to treat.

The first 'window' is provided by the *contexts* in which international law operates – that is to say, the worlds of diplomacy and ideas as well as its being also 'law'. The second 'window' is opened onto *statehood.* International law, after all, undoubtedly arose with modern statehood and its operation has been linked with the expansion of the idea of sovereignty around the globe. At the same time, however, these linkages have been questioned as morally and functionally doubtful, and we have sought to highlight the relevant debates. But international law is also a professional technique that is operative in typical institutional situations or 'arenas', and accordingly a special section is devoted to those *techniques and arenas* as well. Last but not least, international law is a vehicle through which different actors push their political, economic, ideological and other '*projects*'. It is not just a neutral technology of government but involves sometimes passionate engagement by those who have recourse to it. The fourth section is an exploration of some of international law's most important projects today.

Contexts of international law

One of the ambitions of this *Companion* is to highlight the variety of the professional, practical and literary contexts in which international law appears, the many vocabularies in which it is spoken and the plurality of meanings it carries. Often less technical and more immediately connected with political ideas and forms of social contestation than other legal disciplines, international law is invoked in the settlement of inter-state conflicts as well as in philosophical debates about perpetual peace. It is invoked in human rights rallies as well as in expert meetings on the design of rules on deep seabed mining or geostationary orbits. Debates amongst members of the Security Council in New York are framed by international law, as are the themes and demands of anti-globalisation activists in Porto Alegre. It is hard to think of *any* international meeting where international law would not appear as a key part of somebody's agenda, at least as a mode of expression. Scores of conferences are held at any moment on questions such as the 'fight against impunity', 'human rights and terrorism' or 'trade and global governance'; in such circumstances international law is not limited to the concerns of academics or professionals. Everybody meets with it when reading a newspaper or listening to the news, thinking about the last war or the next, or engaging in a conversation in the local café about the rights and duties of one's country regarding the plight of migrant workers, for example.

The sense of international legal concepts and institutions depends on the context in which they are invoked, often in polemical juxtaposition to contrasting positions or views. The 'domestic jurisdiction' to which a state refers at some international institution is not the same as that which is debated at an academic conference or contested at a meeting of Greenpeace activists. To know its meaning, we should know what policy it is intended to support, or against whom or which kind of preference it is expected to operate. International legal concepts and institutions are in this sense intensely contextual. This is not to say that their meaning necessarily varies from day to day or from speaker to speaker. The language of the law structures and inhibits as well as enables. There are typical contexts and patterns of behaviour, cultural frames in which standard positions keep occurring and fixed understandings emerge. To know something about these contexts is a first step in coming to know international law.

One rather obvious context is that of diplomacy. This is where international law is expected to show its 'hard' nucleus. The rules, institutions and techniques of diplomacy have always been framed by international law: rules regarding the immunity of ambassadors are amongst the oldest ones in the field, and since the eighteenth century have shown considerable continuity. (The rules on diplomatic precedence adopted at the Congress of Vienna in 1815 were included, without material change, in the Vienna Convention on Diplomatic Relations of 1961.) Here law appears as a tool of statecraft, an instrument to organise cooperation across boundaries and through which states may channel their controversies into more peaceful avenues. The close historical linkage of the law of nations with the diplomacy of the (European) states-system is certainly responsible for much of what we know as today's international law: the system of territorial sovereignty, of treaties and bilateral and multilateral negotiations, the rightful conduct of inter-state politics in peace and war.

Even within diplomacy, however, there are disagreements about how to understand international law's intervention, as discussed by Gerry Simpson in Chapter 1. It is sometimes imagined that international law is an 'autonomous system' of concepts and institutions that may be used to oppose and limit state power. But equally (or perhaps more) often it appears as a dependent variable, largely or entirely conditioned by the vicissitudes of diplomatic power and strategy. One way to highlight international law's significance is to point to the way its rules provide the frame – the procedures – through which diplomacy is to operate, and is to some extent domesticated. In this sense, much about international law depends on state power. But the equation goes both ways: is not the 'state' itself a legal construction, a product of legal rules and procedures? Debates on the emergence and dissolution of states illustrate this dialectic. In principle, only *de facto* powerful entities are accepted as formal states. But not all power (for example, illegal power – the case of Southern Rhodesia) leads to statehood. And sometimes relatively powerless entities may be qualified as states if they appear to fulfil the formal criteria (the cases of Tuvalu and Kosovo, for example).

Stressing law's role in diplomacy has often been challenged as excessively 'idealist'. However, key aspects of the international system and state behaviour operate by reference to legal rules and institutions and law itself is empowering to the extent that it provides a garb of legitimacy over practices, such as the methodical killing of human individuals on the battlefield, that might otherwise seem morally impermissible. Here there is reason to avoid sweeping generalisation. Diplomatic cultures are distinct, and different states give differing emphasis to law in their activities. Hence Simpson is right to point to the way international law has been sometimes seen as virtuous, sometimes marginal, sometimes as only a passive reflection of state power and will, at other times a morally inspired antidote to them.

Instead of fixing the relationship between diplomacy and law in some general frame – especially a 'realist' or 'idealist' frame – Simpson finds it more useful to provide a historical sketch of their interaction. In such an examination we see international law emerge, together with European statehood, from the collapse of empire and then engage in a flux between more or less imperial or anti-imperial positions, aligning itself at times closely with the hegemon, at other times taking on an anti-hegemonic appearance. Like any cultural phenomenon, international law has had its ups and downs. While the most recent 'up' was constituted of the period of busy institutional construction during 1989–2001 (including notably the creation of the World Trade Organisation in 1994, and of the International Criminal Court in 1998), more recent times have perhaps shown the limits to which law can be understood as crucial to diplomacy. It is part of statecraft – but it cannot be reduced to statecraft and is often used in order to criticise what states do, notably in the 'war against terror' that followed the attack on the World Trade Center on 11 September 2001.

But diplomacy is only one context in which international law appears. Martti Koskenniemi's contribution (Chapter 2) examines its role in the world of ideas, in the context of imagining alternative futures, in sometimes theological or morally oriented debates from early modernity to the present. Alongside statesmen and diplomats, international law is also spoken by political thinkers and philosophers who often see in international law a privileged platform over which to debate weighty issues of global politics or morality. The conglomerate of projects and intuitions labelled 'cosmopolitanism' frequently takes a legalistic air. And sometimes ideas of a world legal order migrate from political utopias to the conference-table. Human rights certainly navigate between the world of normative ideas and their formal articulation in legal instruments, inhabiting a gray zone between philosophy and legal practice in a way that leaves many argumentative avenues open for enterprising lawyers and activists. As with the context of diplomacy, however, it seems impossible to pin down a distinct, definable role that international law plays here. Koskenniemi, too, has chosen a chronological approach to illuminate the appearance of international law in the intellectual contests of the successive periods of (Western) modernity.

A visitor in the contexts of diplomacy and philosophical and political ideas, international law's 'home' surely is the context of law. This is the genus of which international is a species – and it is not uncommon for experts on diplomacy or polities to neglect this. International lawyers are not only trained in specific techniques of international cooperation, but also, indeed first of all, as *lawyers*. If there is a legal 'mindset' then, for better or for worse, what makes international lawyers often incomprehensible for their colleagues is that they share it. But as Frédéric Mégret shows, 'home' itself has not always been terribly accommodating and the question whether international law really is 'law' continues to be posed by suspicious legal colleagues – and answered in a standard series of arguments, with little hope that this controversy can be settled in the foreseeable future (see Chapter 3).

It is true that international law differs in many ways from other branches of law – and this has given rise to a long-standing debate about its 'special character'. Clearly it is 'law' in some respects (for example, it has courts). Yet it appears less so in other respects (for example, because those courts do not have compulsory jurisdiction over states). Depending on which aspect emphasis is laid on and what attitude one takes towards those special features, one may be classified as either 'denier' or 'idealist', 'apologist' or 'reformist' or, indeed, 'critic', in Mégret's useful classification. The most conspicuous aspect of international law's speciality, however, may be its constant silent transformation, not as a result of legislative activities of formal law-making organs (indeed there are few such organs), but in response to the needs of its 'consumers'. It is that fluidity – its 'dynamics' – that ultimately accounts for the inability of any of the four or five standard theoretical positions to grasp it wholly. International law is what we make of it and here the connotation of the 'we' has no pre-established limits. Surely, a consensus about what international law is, how it operates and for whom, may arise in each of its contexts – but that view may be different between those contexts and one source of richness of the discipline is that they operate relatively independently and are in no hierarchical relationship to each other.

International law and the state

The term 'international law' was invented by Jeremy Bentham in 1789 and established itself in the nineteenth century in preference to the older phrase 'the law of nations', itself a translation of the Latin '*jus gentium*' of Grotius, the French '*droit des gens*' of Vattel (see Janis 1984). None of these phrases expressly limited international law to a law between states. But over time, as the state system became established to the exclusion of other authorities (local and supranational), international law came increasingly focused on the state and on inter-state relations. And that is still a major preoccupation, despite developments towards greater inclusiveness in such fields as international human rights. Even there the state is an ever-present partner. Human rights at the international level are articulated as rights against the state; they define what the state may or may not do, as much as what individuals may claim or expect. Part II of this volume is accordingly focused on some major features of international law as concerns the state.

There is an initial question of identifying the components of the system, states, governments and peoples – a task undertaken by Karen Knop (see Chapter 4). In modern international law, the most present of the three, the active ingredient so to speak, is the government. Senior government officials (head of state, head of government, minister of foreign affairs and some others) have inbuilt authority to represent the state, with correlative immunities while doing so (see *Arrest Warrant*, ICJ Reports 2002, 22–25). Such authority does not depend on any mandate from the people of the state: democractic legitimacy is so far a desideratum, not a requirement, and thus not a basis for claiming that transactions are beyond power (*ultra vires*). But the entity represented and thereby committed is not the government (which is not regarded as a legal entity in international law); it is the state. This so-called 'fictional theory' of the state is justified as a force for stability, an inter-generational transmission device (see Skinner 2010, 46). It is the source of the 'borrowing privilege' of which Thomas Pogge is so critical (see Chapter 17).

Knop duly notes that 'the state as territory–people–government is international law's main device for representing the world', but she stresses the diversity of representational mandates both within and beyond the state. Aspects of this include the way in which the principle of self-determination has been selectively applied in practice, while continuing to act as a driving force underlying claims for identity and representation within the state (e.g., indigenous peoples) and also, in aspiration and occasionally in reality, beyond it (e.g. Quebec, Kosovo). Similarly with the case of democratic rights: these are rather weakly reflected in current international law – as rights against the state – but they are not entirely absent. In particular, in post-conflict situations, international law has mandated particular, sometimes intricate and experimental, forms of representative government, reflecting the presence of different national, ethnic, religious or cultural groups.

Beyond the state, there is increased interest in other forms of representation, for example in the idea of 'international civil society' (see Keane 2005) and in the practice of international non-governmental organisations (NGOs) (see Lindblom 2005). But Knop detects a trend back to the state – '[t]he emphasis is no longer on actors and who has the right to participate, but on law and how it works or what it is, international law in particular'. If so, the state on which attention is refocused can be seen as more diverse, and in terms of its capacity for representation of groups and peoples, more resourceful than standard legal accounts allow.

Statehood once achieved, international law regards each state as sovereign, in the sense that it is presumed to have full authority to act both internally and at the international level. In Chapter 5, James Crawford explores in more detail what this sovereignty consists in as a matter of international law. He stresses its formal character: the equality of states is a reflection of their sovereignty vis-à-vis each other but it is consistent with great inequality in fact. Post-1945 international law assumed the new task of a collective guarantee of sovereignty which, combined with the principle of self-determination led in the subsequent sixty-five years to a great increase in the number of states, with many new creations and the extinction of almost none. It is common in international relations theory to belittle this equal, formal sovereignty. International lawyers themselves are divided in their approach to sovereignty, accepting or contesting it, seeking to subvert or reinvent it. But seen as sovereignty under the law rather than above it, it can be defended as a flexible tool for protecting the autonomy of states, large and small, and for projecting them, rights and all, into the future. As such it remains a 'basic constitutional doctrine of the law of nations' (Brownlie 2008, 289).

Continuing in this formal mode, Simma and Müller give an account of the jurisdiction of states, their scope of legal authority (see Chapter 6). In the first instance it is for each state to decide which transactions or activities it will regulate and on what basis. States are both territorial governmental entities and aggregates of individuals owing allegiance (if nationals, permanently; if residents, then for the time being). International law seeks to reduce the scope for conflicts of jurisdiction, and where these cannot be eliminated, to moderate their effects. For example, states may tax persons on grounds of residence in their territory (all income earned by persons considered as resident for tax purposes, irrespective of nationality) or on grounds of nationality (all income earned by nationals wherever resident), or some combination of these criteria. Both the territoriality and the nationality principle being valid grounds of jurisdiction, international law does not choose between them, so taxpayers face double or even multiple taxation which international law merely mitigates (a) by the negative principle that no state enforces the fiscal or penal laws of another, and (b) by a network of treaties reducing the incidence of double taxation.

Like some other traditional areas of international law, the law of jurisdiction is dominantly an inter-state matter – individuals and corporations being treated as 'objects' rather than right-holders. For example, the human rights treaties articulate the right not to be tried twice for the same offence (*ne bis in idem* or double jeopardy), but this is without prejudice to the jurisdiction of each state over crimes defined by its own legislation: article 14(7) of the International Covenant on Civil and Political Rights (ICCPR, 1966) refers to 'the law and penal procedure *of each country*'. Even in fields where the development of human rights has impinged on jurisdiction – e.g. the conferral of nationality – it has done so only to a limited extent; there is a strong international public policy against statelessness, but the relevant treaties do not exhaustively specify which state's nationality shall be conferred in any given circumstance, so that statelessness remains an open possibility; indeed, it is still quite common.

Beyond the jurisdictional principles of territoriality and nationality, there are other accepted grounds for regulation and enforcement, as well as a number of more controversial candidates. Amongst the former, Simma and Müller identify flag state jurisdiction (for ships, aircraft and spacecraft) and jurisdiction based on the protective principle; amongst the latter, the principle of universal jurisdiction, traditionally exercised over piracy on the high seas but also over certain crimes (see the Rome Statute for an International Criminal Court 1998, one of the consequences of which – in conjunction with the principle of complementarity – has been to expand the scope of *national* criminal jurisdiction over specified crimes). And this lesson can be generalised: in both the civil and criminal sphere the law of jurisdiction gives no priority to exclusive jurisdiction (except in relation to enforcement) and is increasingly the subject of cooperative international arrangements from which individuals may find it more difficult to escape.

A further asserted monopoly on which the modern territorial state is founded is the monopoly of legitimate force, including ultimately resort to war. Here international law's role is commonly portrayed as one of restraint and limitation, but as David Kennedy shows (see Chapter 7) the matter is by no means so simple. In its origins international law was intimately associated with late medieval just war theory, and despite appearances the linkage between law and war has never been broken. Thus, according to Kennedy, in place of an unsatisfactory 'image of a law outside war (and a sovereign power normally "at peace")', the reality is 'an image of sovereign power and legal determination themselves bound up with war, having their origin in war and contributing . . . to the ongoing, if often silent, wars which are embedded in the structure of international life'. Far from being set over and against war as its antithesis, war and law are seen as opposite sides of the same coin; law and legal claims not merely structure war and our waging of it but they are increasingly part of the weapons of war, especially in sophisticated, relatively more accountable armed forces. Lawyers are 'embedded' in modern armies and navies, at least as much as journalists.

Techniques and arenas

Turning to a third cluster of themes – which we have called 'techniques and arenas' – there is the core issue how international law is made, identified, used and enforced. This is considered here from four perspectives.

The first is how actually to identify the content of international law, often referred to as consisting of 'rules' and 'principles'. Here, for want of a better articulation, article 38(1) of the Statute of the International Court of Justice is taken as canonical, with its listing of treaties, custom, general principles of law and (as subsidiary) judicial decisions and doctrine. But as Hilary Charlesworth points out (see Chapter 8), article 38(1) 'obscures the fact that international law is generated by a multi-layered process of interactions, instruments, pressures and principles'; in this regard, and within limits dictated by state representatives and legal tradition, international law is dynamic not static. Thus while article 38(2) of the Statute – providing for a case to be decided by special consent *ex aequo et bono* (on the basis of equity and justice) – has never been employed, international judicial decisions are often framed in terms of the perceived equity of outcomes, and considerations of proportionality and reasonableness are taken into account, giving flexibility to the system – but at the expense of determinacy.

Two factors, to some extent pushing in opposite directions, are the notion of 'soft' law and that of a 'hierarchy of sources' in international law. As to the former, there has been a great growth in the number of bodies, public and private, producing drafts, documents and declarations seeking to influence the course or content of international law. As to the latter, while article 38 is not expressed as establishing a hierarchy, certain hierarchical elements have been introduced – notably the concept of 'peremptory norms of general international law' (Vienna Convention on the Law of Treaties, 1969, article 53) and such institutions as the International Criminal Court (1998, in force 2002). If there is a developing hierarchy, however – which is doubtful – it is not that reflected in article 38 but requires a much more detailed analysis of the provenance of and support for particular norms, such as the prohibition of state-sponsored torture.

As Charlesworth notes, a feature of modern law-making is the tendency in particular fields to develop specialised concepts and techniques, so that international trade law, human rights law or environmental law are seen as more or less 'self-contained', even self-sufficient. In certain cases, of which the European Union is the best example, a legal system originating in a treaty and dependent on standard international law techniques for its origin and development, may come to seem – may actually be – sufficiently distinct as to constitute a separate legal system, linked to the international legal system, participating in it, but with its own 'reserved domain' and its own rules of recognition. But even with the European Union this is only provisionally the case: the member states generally treat it as a special kind of international organisation, and as only by delegation exercising state authority.

The UN International Law Commission (ILC) has dealt with this issue under the rubric of the 'fragmentation' of international law and has proposed interpretative approaches aimed at reducing its impact (see ILC 2006). But international law, lacking central institutions with independent authority not emanating from member states, has never been a unified system. 'Fragmentation' in the international system is to some extent unavoidable, even – in terms of the capacity for development and experimentation – desirable.

Overall, the sources of international law may seem 'disconcertingly negotiable' to lawyers used to constitutional systems of law-making and law application. To this several replies are possible: first, that legal regulation in most societies long predated modern constitutions; second, that indeterminacy is a feature of all legal orders. But there is a further point. Although international law began as a system without institutions such as courts or law-making organs, these have developed and play some of the same roles as their domestic counterparts. Whether this means that international law is becoming partly constitutionalised may be doubtful – it is beyond question, however, institutionalised to a degree. The remaining chapters in Part III deal with different aspects of this development.

Standing international courts and tribunals are a relatively recent addition to the international system. The first arbitral institution was the Permanent Court of Arbitration, established in 1899; the first court the Permanent Court of International Justice, established in 1922 according to a plan first proposed (by the United States) in 1907. Since the 1980s there has been a great increase in the number of functioning permanent courts, civil and criminal, and a corresponding increase in the volume of international litigation. In the last twenty years most governments have been parties to or intervenors in international cases of one kind or another, including governments to whom such involvement was previously anathema. For example China is a major litigant before the WTO dispute settlement body (DSB), while Russia has been party to cases before the International Court, the International Tribunal for the Law of the Sea (ITLOS) and the European Court of Human Rights (ECtHR).

How far these undoubted developments in practice are leading to an increased 'juridification' of the international system is a question explored by Benedict Kingsbury (see Chapter 9). His answer, after a *tour d'horizon* which is also a *tour de force*, is – only selectively and only up to a point. After distinguishing no fewer than ten basic types of international courts, he notes their limitations: the largest numbers of cases involve specialist tribunals giving effect to 'a global legal order dominated by liberal interests', e.g. in the field of free trade and investment protection; many kinds of issues rarely if ever reach courts or tribunals, especially those involving military and intelligence issues or global financial governance; the new powers (India, Brazil, China) may not continue the trend, may even seek to reverse it. He concludes that while '[l]iberal legalism continues to have substantial reach and influence ... further judicialisation through global treaty institutions may be unlikely in the near term, particularly outside the broad fields of trade, investment and property claims'.

Jan Klabbers asks similar questions about the growth of international organisations since the first ones were created in the 1860s and notably since 1945 (see Chapter 10). Theorists have always had some difficulty in finding the appropriate place for different types of institutions alongside states in the international world. Straightforward theories of 'functionalism', for example, while they may account for the role and the task of some bodies, are incapable of covering others – often, as Klabbers points out, the 'function' of an organisation is in the eye of the beholder. Moreover, from being the kinds of faithful servants to the states that have established them, institutions tend to develop identities and a professional culture of their own and sometimes even objectives that can only with difficulty be referred back to the objectives of their founders. Another big question tends to relate to the relative formality or informality of the institution. The choice of course lies again with the states – but it is not clear they are always well aware of the consequences of the alternatives. Institutions are useful, sometimes indispensable instruments of international governance – but they can hardly compensate for political communities and debates that must set the objectives of governance and control the way it is carried out. By way of conclusion, Klabbers too qualifies the idea that world governance is coming to be exercised by committee. Yet there is no denying that international law 'has come to a large extent to be developed and formulated under the auspices of international organisations: it has become institutionalised'.

A vital aspect of institutionalisation at least since 1989, is the increased possibility of enforcement through external means of international obligations and decisions. This – the most recent of the three developments surveyed in these chapters – is explored in some detail by Dino Kritsiotis (see Chapter 11). Historically international law was enforced by war, reprisals, diplomacy or implemented on the basis of considerations of reciprocity and a desire for decent international relations. International relations scholars would have regarded these factors as listed in descending order of importance, even though these days there is a respectable case for the opposite view. But there are severe moral hazards inherent in a wholly non-coercive legal order, and in various domains – notably through the Security Council, but also in the context of various treaty regimes – the international system is slowly becoming less voluntarist.

The projects of international law

Unlike other legal disciplines, international law usually involves a commitment on the part of those who have recourse to it. It is seen as more than just a neutral arbiter between disputing states or other actors but as bearing in itself some blueprint for improving the world, or those aspects of the world where it operates. International law, as an ordering factor in international life, is seen as vital, as a 'good in itself'. So that it is customary to think that there should be *more of it* in a way that we rarely think that there ought to be more of family law or administrative law. What the 'good' is that is assumed intrinsic in international law has been conceived differently in different periods: Christianity, civilisation, modernity, peace, development, self-determination – these are some notions that have been regarded as the gift brought to the world with the expansion of international law's more technical rules and institutions.

Sometimes, however, international law's connection with such projects has turned it into a target of criticism by those who feel it operates like a Trojan horse for values or preferences they do not like to endorse. Towards the end of the eighteenth century, radical thinkers attacked the way the 'European public law' had been designed to support the external policies of absolutist states. That the civilising mission was merely a thin veil over international law's support for European colonisation has been stated regularly from the late nineteenth century onwards. Few people disagree when international law's projects are today formulated in terms of the advancement of 'peace', 'development' or a 'clean environment'. However, when those terms are translated into more specific institutional proposals such as, for example, 'peace in the Middle East', 'development through bilateral investment treaties' or specific emission reductions to deal with climate change, disagreement emerges; commitment to international law meets with the profoundly contested preferences that any introduction of a specific set of rules or institutions in a particular situation will engender.

In a world of many actors with conflicting preferences, international law's projects proliferate and have become the source of controversy and contestation. Because of international law's strong ideological pull, its operation cannot be understood without examining what projects it invites its practitioners to participate in and in what ways those projects are contested in the political world in which the law enters. Part IV of this *Companion* has been devoted to discussing these issues.

Anne Orford examines the way in which international law – like any law – is involved in creating and sustaining an orderly world (see Chapter 12). But whereas social order is usually the result of a hierarchical structure of rule, the international world is characterised by the absence of hierarchy. Its principal actors – sovereign states – are equal amongst themselves so that whatever order may arise between them must be consensually based and guaranteed in a decentralised fashion. In this sense, Orford argues, international law is indebted to Thomas Hobbes' view that reliable order emerges not from religious or moral consensus but from the *de facto* effectiveness of the state. Our duty to obey arises from the state's capacity to protect us. Yet as she also shows, this view has not gone unchallenged. Its intrinsic conservatism has been put in question by revolutionary movements leading up to decolonisation on the one hand,

and to an increasing emphasis on individual rights on the other. Today, the order-creating function of political states has been accompanied and perhaps challenged by the power structures of an international economy based on private ownership and contract and guaranteed by the worldwide policies of global economic institutions, as well as, more tentatively, the disciplining of the decolonised world by an emergent system of international administration.

Establishing the rule of law – in however basic a sense – is not unconnected to the order-creating function of international law. As B.S. Chimni shows in Chapter 13, alongside its undoubtedly welcome effect of binding those in powerful positions it also has a legitimating effect that solidifies present *de facto* hierarchies. The rule of law is always also rule by those who can authoritatively determine what the law says. It is a notoriously complex notion, and its role in society and its effects appear differently when analysed from different jurisprudential standpoints or depending on whether one's perspective is that of the system's centre or its periphery – as graphically illustrated today by the criticism by African elites against the principle of 'universal jurisdiction' under which it has so far been mainly Africans who have been indicted for crimes against humanity in European courts (see Kmak 2011, and further Nouwen in Chapter 15). Against the hierarchy-legitimating function of the rule of law Chimni would juxtapose an image of the Indian experience of living in a 'composite culture'. Such a culture might preserve the hard-won principles of sovereign equality and non-use of force but would go further so as to enable the emergence of a substantively (and not merely formally) pluralistic international world. All this is set against what he sees as on-going efforts to use international law to provide even more efficient informal support to Western-dominated global order.

One of the more successful post-1945 projects of international law has been that of turning human rights into an international political *lingua franca*. Begun in the aftermath of the Second World War, or perhaps as late as the 1970s (Moyn 2010), this process has often been captured, as Susan Marks shows, in a romantic narrative about how victory is won out of struggle and hardship. Having reviewed the impressive achievements – the creation of the treaty systems, the human rights institutions and agencies – she then suggests that there is something lacking in that story, namely how the human rights institutions look away from persistent structural problems in the global system that, for the great majority of humans, perpetuate or leave untouched massive injustices that never get articulated as problems in the human rights culture (see Chapter 14). The non-political character of human rights ideology hides from sight the need for renewed struggle in order to abolish those injustices, often caused by aspects of private law and activity, which are not touched by human rights work. In a profoundly unjust international world, to emphasise the 'neutrality' or 'impartiality' of rights is to take the side of those who benefit from the system against those who do not. The ubiquity and professionalisation of rights have made them – not always, not everywhere – aspects of the banal administration of existing polities, 'part of the problem', as Marks would suggest. The task is then not to have more rights, but to create contexts of contestation within which political engagement becomes possible so as to transform the structural injustices against which rights have remained powerless.

One of the most spectacular, and yet least well understood, of international law's projects is that of bringing international penal justice to populations scarred by war and large-scale violence. As Sarah Nouwen points out, while international criminal law is an attractive field for legal and humanitarian activism, it is also hugely ambivalent in its actual consequences and in its reception amongst the concerned communities (see Chapter 15). The attitudes of the Balkan populations towards almost twenty years of operation by the International Criminal Tribunal for the Former Yugoslavia (ICTY), established in 1993, have been anything but straightforward. Outsiders have often puzzled about the way these attitudes have oscillated between exaltation and rejection, and most frequently have been characterised by a total lack of interest. Why are not people everywhere rejoicing at the prospect of seeing bloody tyrants or human rights offenders indicted and sometimes brought to trial?

The 'fight against impunity' has been such a self-evident target of professional activism that asking for its justifications may seem almost sacrilegious. And yet, as Nouwen shows, when those justifications are examined in view of actual situations (and not just in an abstract way through the various treaties and reports), they turn out as indeterminate and sometimes contradictory; their specific objectives in concrete situations may appear unattainable or undesirable or both. That relentless pursuit of criminality may sometimes be destructive of peace is well known and societies may often have to balance between the two concerns in a way that calls for trust within the community and political leadership. But when an outsider is ideologically committed to employing criminal justice in a particular crisis, whatever the costs, how are the concerned communities to look upon it? When that justice is (as it inevitably is) selective, realised by foreign experts at often distant locations – is that really conducive to reconciliation? And what if the carriers of criminal justice come from those same directions where once upon a time came all kinds of missionaries, civilisers and colonists – how are the local communities to understand that *this time* their words emerge from love, and not a desire to dominate, that *this time*, they have shed their hypocrisy? It is a general problem of international legal activism that its commitment to particular institutional models – here, criminal trials, prosecutors, judges, and the imprisonment of some individuals – may often occlude the activists' ability to assess their real-life consequences. Nouwen's finely tuned account of the role of the International Criminal Court in on-going African crises compares the justifications of criminal justice with the response of the targeted communities with a view to enabling an enlightened assessment of the historical and political meaning of this project. The jury (a simile rather than a metaphor, since there are no juries at this level) is still out on this issue.

It is certainly an underappreciated fact that public international law emerged in the sixteenth century together with a global economy based on private property, contract and an international system of currency exchange; one of international law's 'projects' has been to see to their maintenance and expansion. Hélène Ruiz Fabri shows how the three parts of this global system (of trade, investment and money) have in the past half-century developed as elements of an allegedly autonomous economic logic (see Chapter 16). But she also shows how what she calls 'linkage issues' have more recently put in question both their separation from each other as well as their dissociation from (extraneous) concerns of environment and human rights, for example. Both trade and investment law developed from the Keynesianism of the 1950s to an increasingly liberal (and for a moment in the 1990s even 'ultra-liberal') direction. That the legitimacy of expanding free market principles outside trade in goods (to agricultural commodities, services, intellectual property) has today been put in question has not meant a turn (back) to the regulative approaches manifested in the UN Conference on Trade and Development (UNCTAD) in the 1970s. Instead, multilateralism has given way for the time being to piecemeal approaches under free trade areas (FTAs) and bilateral investment treaties (BITs). In over 2,400 BITs the rights and duties of investors and (largely Third-World) host states are unevenly balanced against each other, leading to limitations on the regulative capacity of the states parties that are not offset by the fragile efforts to support 'corporate social responsibility' within the United Nations and elsewhere. As Ruiz Fabri observes, linkage issues with important political repercussions have been channelled to judicial, quasi-judicial and arbitration bodies (such as the Appellate Body of the WTO and investment arbitration panels) not well suited for this task. Likewise the Bretton Woods institutions (the World Bank and the IMF) have largely given up attempts to regulate global currency exchanges in favour of assisting member states in economic distress. After the demise of the 'Washington consensus' in the 1990s, the financial crisis of 2008 initiated a new debate on the degree of supervision and coordination – perhaps even regulation – needed in the monetary system so as to prevent such collapse in the future.

Thomas Pogge's chapter continues the structural critique of the international human rights system inasmuch as it has failed to deal with global poverty – one of the most striking effects of structural injustice in the world (see Chapter 17). The fact, he points out, is that 'in 2000 the bottom 50 per cent of the world's adults together had 1.1 per cent of global wealth, while the top 10 per cent had 85.1 per cent and the top 1 per cent had 39.9 per cent'. This moral and political disaster, Pogge shows, has not emerged from natural causes against which international institutions have either done their best or which they have been powerless to prevent. In fact, he argues, these institutions (amongst them international law principles that enable the elites of Third-World states to bind their countries for decades to systems of resource extraction and debt management) are directly *responsible* for the creation and persistence of these injustices. Moreover, they are so in spite of the fact that significantly reducing or even ending massive poverty would require only marginal sacrifices by the citizens of the wealthier nations. Despite the current bleak picture, Pogge suggests that there is no reason to despair over the so far relatively ineffectual efforts at a reform of the international institutional system of wealth distribution. The huge number of existing international projects and aid programmes would pale into insignificance if compared to the foreseeable benefits of focusing on the eradication of just this one problem. It is hard to see any more worthwhile project for international law than achieving such reform.

Finally, Sundhya Pahuja examines the conflicts and compromises between two of international law's key projects, namely exploiting natural resources to attain 'development' and conserving them in view of the dangers to the global biosphere (see Chapter 18). That the tension between exploitation and conservation has been largely integrated into policy-making by international institutions almost automatically favoured those who have a leading role in such institutions. The compromise of 'sustainable development' froze the terms of the debate for a while but has not dealt with (nor was intended to deal with) the background conditions in which the negotiations take place. The origins of the way, as Pahuja puts it, we 'share the earth' inheres in geographically limited jurisdictions decided at the moment of the Western colonisation or decolonisation. That background determined the form of the global negotiations of exploitation and conservation at the time, in the 1970s, when Third-World states were proclaiming 'permanent sovereignty' over their natural resources and calling for the joint management of the 'global commons' situated in the High Seas and the deep seabed during the Third UN Conference on the Law of the Sea (UNCLOS, 1974–1982). None of this was very successful. On the contrary, the backlash against global regulation of resource uses took the form of the development of the international environmental law largely in response to concerns raised in the developed world, and the creation of a network of bilateral treaty arrangements to facilitate and protect Western investments in the Third World. The background allocation of jurisdictions, Pahuja argues, or the so far rather disappointing results of dealing with resource issues at a global level, should not prevent efforts to articulate anew the point of view of the 'global commons' as a theme and a platform over which contestation over 'how we share the world' could take place.

Bibliography

Brownlie, I., 2008. *Principles of Public International Law*, 7th edn., Oxford University Press

ILC 2006. *Fragmentation of International Law: Difficulties Arising from the Diversification and Expansion of International Law. Report of the Study Group of the International Law Commission*, finalised by Martti Koskenniemi, UN Doc A/CN.4/L.682, 13 April 2006

Janis, M. W., 1984. 'Jeremy Bentham and the Fashioning of "International Law"', 78 *AJIL* 405–418

Keane, J., 2005. *Global Civil Society?*, Cambridge University Press

Kmak, M., 2011. *The Scope and Application of the Principle of Universal Jurisdiction*, Helsinki: Erik Castrén Institute Research Reports

Lindblom, A.-K., 2005. *Non-governmental Organisations in International Law*, Cambridge University Press

Moyn, S., 2010. *The Last Utopia: Human Rights in History*, Cambridge, MA: Harvard University Press

Skinner, Q., 2010. 'The Sovereign State: a Genealogy', in H. Kalmo and Q. Skinner (eds.), *Sovereignty in Fragments: The Past, Present and Future of a Contested Concept*, Cambridge University Press, 26–46

Part I

The contexts of international law

International law in diplomatic history 1

Gerry Simpson

Introduction: three questions, three images

The relationship of international law to the practice of international diplomacy, or to global politics, is obscure and, sometimes, paradoxical. As a prelude, then, to sketching the structuring role international law performs in the present phase of globalisation, or may have played at different moments in diplomatic history (a history that, for these purposes, emphasises the formal institutions and semi-formal practices of diplomacy in inter-state relations but encompasses, also, the broader world of international political life), it is important to say something about the ways in which the relationship might be framed in general. Three questions seem pertinent. Does international law influence or found the diplomatic system, or is it largely an irrelevance or trifling preoccupation? Has international law been a force for good (or for global well-being) in diplomatic history? And is it possible to speak intelligibly of a single body of norms, or way of thinking and acting, called 'international law'? These questions might, in turn, generate (at least) three images or ways of thinking about the field: (1) international law as virtuous and marginal, (2) international law as constitutive and responsible and (3) international law as a combination of norm and aspiration. We can imagine other images, for example international law as substance and form or as change and stability or utopia and reality (Carr 1946), and other combinations: there are, no doubt, ways in which international law is constitutive and virtuous. I have chosen these three because of their ubiquity and influence, and for what I hope are the heuristic possibilities they offer.

Virtuous/marginal

Approached for the first time – by students, by state officials, by the intelligent, non-specialist reader – international law, as a body of principles or a way of doing things, might appear virtuous yet marginal. This, too, would be the self-description of many international lawyers. From this perspective, international law is a mostly frustrated project to civilise global politics, humanise war, tame anarchy, restrain the Great Powers and ensure fairer re-distributive outcomes.

As a result, international law tends to find itself aligned with a vaguely leftist, liberal, progressive politics or with a form of anti-politics. Correspondingly, as a general rule, political parties of the centre-left and left seem much more hospitable to international lawyers (frequently enlisted to fight poverty or to advance human rights or to end colonialism or to help refugees) than are parties of the conservative or radical right. But international lawyers are also prone to represent themselves as opposing or transcending politics altogether. At conferences to combat global warming (Copenhagen 2009) or create international criminal courts (Rome 1998) international law is cast in a heroic role: capable of providing the necessary tools or the language or, even, the substantive goals, if only politicians would get out of the way (Bassiouni 1997).

But, of course, they don't get out of the way. And so international law is understood, too, as a marginal enterprise; lawyers are regularly sidelined, and law ignored or depreciated, when matters of great political and economic moment arise. Even the advice of government lawyers or the arguments of international jurists can be thought of as worthy and intellectually sound but, ultimately, either disposable, displaceable or too plastic to supply binding constraints. This image of international law as marginal tends to get reinforced at moments of political crisis.

Dean Acheson, former US Secretary of State, adopted a variant of the disposability argument when he said, during the Cuban Missile Crisis:

> The power, position and prestige of the United States had been challenged by another state; *and the law does not deal with such questions of ultimate power* – power that comes close to the sources of sovereignty. (Acheson 1963)

More recently, the UK House of Commons Foreign Affairs Select Committee noted, in relation to the decision to intervene in Iraq:

> We gained the impression that established international legal standards would be of secondary importance compared with the need to take action. (Foreign Affairs Select Committee, 7th Report 2002)

And, at the beginning of 2010, during his appearance before the Chilcot Inquiry into the Iraq War, Sir Michael Wood, the Foreign Office legal adviser during that War, revealed that Jack Straw, the Foreign Minister at the time:

> took the view that I was being very dogmatic [Wood had told Straw that intervention in Iraq would be unlawful] and that international law was pretty vague and that he wasn't used to people taking such a firm position. (Norton-Taylor 2010)

More typically the domain of the letter-writer, pamphleteer or academic, public international law is an outside position offering the seductions and anxieties of powerlessness. Virtue and marginality, of course, work in tandem. By remaining marginal, international lawyers more readily can advance virtuous ends, adopt utopian projects or engage in outsider politics. The absence of responsibility brings with it an accretion of freedom. Equally, a non-conformist position of purity guarantees marginality. Always being right means never being held to account.

Constitutive

This first image of the relationship between law and diplomacy, though ubiquitous, is hardly unchallengeable. Indeed, it may be more productive to think of international law as constitutive of – and not always benign in its effects on – global politics. International lawyers have created a system without which international diplomacy would shrivel and international political life would be rendered unrecognisable. If this view is correct, international law has participated in, facilitated and established the conditions for many of the practices that are thought to be impediments to a just world order. For example, the doctrine of sovereignty and the society of competitive, occasionally warring, occasionally pacific, states with entitlements over their own citizenry and powerful claims to self-realisation, are creations of international law, not obstacles to its implementation.

To adopt a rough periodisation, running from Westphalian sovereignty through European colonialism to late-modern global capitalism, it could be argued that international law, at every step of the way, has established, legitimised and structured the defining relationships of the era. This is the case whether it be the project of colonialism (facilitated by international law rules on territorial acquisition or unequal treaties or trusteeship) or globalisation (reinforced by public compacts in international economic law or the private/public arrangements and associated forms of arbitration entrenched in bilateral investment treaties) or the original Westphalian sovereign ideal (buttressed by an international legal regime that authorised war and tolerated massacre). And international law supplies, too, a whole catalogue of argumentative techniques that prioritise some projects and obscure others, institutional processes that include one group of actors and exclude other groups, and technical resources that can be deployed only by diplomatically literate elites.

This less orthodox second image of international law holds it to account for both its achievements and its failures. In this story, it can be, and has at times been, both malign and powerful: a *force* for bad.

Law and aspiration

But all of this raises a final question: namely, can we speak of 'international law' as a coherent activity or an accumulation of texts that is somehow one thing or another (marginal, virtuous, constitutive, noxious)? Probably not, but a common, and largely misconceived, response to this question is to posit the existence of two international legal orders. This third image of international law's role in diplomatic life is built around a duality between 'real' law and speculative jurisprudence. State officials or political scientists, often, will concede the existence or force or 'normativity' of law in areas such as trade or civil aviation while at the same time dismissing as mere unenforceable aspirations, say, the laws on the use of force or human rights. At the same time, lawyers themselves think of some parts of international law as legitimate (norms possessing, for example, 'compliance pull' (Franck 1990) and others as ineffectual relics or insubstantial innovations.

This third image of international law goes back, at least, to Hans Morgenthau who contrasted 'two obviously different types of international law': a 'functional international law' based on 'deeper covenants' of cooperation or 'permanent or stable interests' and a 'political international law' that was opportunistic, i.e. the product of a transient confluence of circumstances or a response to an immediate and fluctuating situation (Morgenthau 1940 279), indeterminate (subject to 'contradictory interpretations (1940, 279)) and aspirational (failing to reflect the realities of the inter-state order (Jackson 1999, 123–124)).

All of this is a piece with another implicit contrast between Acheson's high politics (e.g. use of force or arms control) and the low politics of the everyday (e.g. trade regulation or maritime resource allocation) with only the latter susceptible to binding legal regulation. Others have distinguished, along similar lines, the superior norms arising out of classical international law (rules intended to shield sovereignty within a pluriverse of states) and a more recent and largely aspirational 'declaratory' tradition in which worthy moral ideals are transformed into worthless legal norms (Jackson 1999). The classical mode encompasses the standard rules of traditional international law, e.g. the laws of war, the right to make treaties, the immunities of diplomats and title to territory while the declaratory mode is said to include trading rules designed to alleviate inequalities between states, laws prohibiting gender discrimination, rules requiring that democracy be a condition for membership of international bodies and laws invoking a common heritage of humankind.

This image of a divided international legal order is pervasive but it is doubtful that it can survive close examination. To take an example (and one I shall return to) from diplomatic history, the Charter of the United Nations remains a key foundation of the international legal and political order and yet it was, of course, also an 'opportunistic' response to a particular and immediate situation (the consequences of German aggression in 1939). Indeed, it is difficult to see how international norms could develop at all if the absence of opportunism was a test for their legitimacy. Often, international societies are the product of post-traumatic constitutional architectures from Westphalia to Vienna to San Francisco. Meanwhile, the indeterminacy of international law's structure of argument has by now been well established. It is no longer possible to go back to a position whereby some rules are regarded as having a pre-interpretive 'essence'. After all, even so-called technical or functional norms, like all norms, will consist of a combination of indeterminate readings of the present and contentious prescriptions for the future.

To conclude, international law's relationship to diplomacy has been understood through, at least, these three images related to questions of virtue, influence or marginality, and character or status. Such images are constitutive in their own way and they offer a useful framing device for approaching the expanse of diplomatic history.

An episodic history of international law in diplomacy

Historically, international law's relationship to diplomacy is defined by the ways in which it has organised relations amongst the Great Powers (the problems of hegemony or balance of power), between the Great Powers and the peripheries (the problems of colonialism or domination or exploitation or 'outlaw states') and between the autonomy and independence of the sovereign state, and, at different times, the imperatives of international regulation, world order, globalisation, and humanitarianism. The remainder of this brief, inevitably impressionistic, essay will be organised around six episodes in diplomatic history in which these themes emerge and re-emerge. In the first episode, classical international law comes of age at Westphalia in the mid-seventeenth century with the transition from empire to sovereignty. These sovereigns then become empires as international law enters its colonial phase from the seventeenth to the mid-twentieth century. A third period begins with the Congress of Vienna in 1815 and the growing self-awareness of the hegemons as they form incipient institutions or 'regimes'. It ends with the Great War and the formation of permanent organisations at Versailles in 1919. The deepening bureaucratisation and juridification of international diplomacy and the resistance to these processes are the subjects of two final sections on the Charter era (1945–1990) and the present phase of globalisation, proliferation and diffusion.

Empire to sovereignty

In 2004, one year after the beginning of the Iraq War, then British Prime Minister, Tony Blair, gave a speech at his Sedgefield constituency in northern England (Blair 2004). In the midst of an otherwise unremarkable apologia for the war, the Prime Minister made a surprising reference to the Peace of Westphalia, calling for the abandonment of the Westphalian consensus on the inviolability of sovereignty (this, as a precursor to arguing for a reinvigorated doctrine of humanitarian intervention). Westphalia (in fact several treaties adopted at Münster and Osnabrück in 1648) has come to represent, then, a point of inauguration for modern international law and for the modern state, a moment when the core concepts of sovereignty, hegemony and balance became part of international law's official inventory.

No doubt, there is something arbitrary and clichéd about harking back to Westphalia in this way (Teschke 2003). After all, states existed prior to the seventeenth century (Gat 2006); international law can trace its origins to the Roman *ius gentium*, Cicero's cosmopolitanism (Cicero 54–51 BC [1998]), Aquinas on just war (Aquinas 1265–1274 [2002]) or the Salamanca School of the early sixteenth century; there may be more significant openings both earlier (the Peace of Lodi, 1454; the Peace of Augsburg, 1555) and later (say, the Treaty of Utrecht, 1713); and pre-modern history is dotted with examples of practices and norms that would be familiar to contemporary international lawyers as the 'laws of war' or 'diplomatic immunity' or 'treaty-making' (Bederman 2001; Mattingly 1955). Equally, international law, in the broad sense of a code of behaviour applied to cross-border relations, was found outside Europe long before Westphalia. There were, for example, Islamic laws, from the seventh century onwards, applying to relations between Muslim states and between Muslim states and heathens or infidels (Neff 2010, 5).

But Westphalia makes some sense as a cipher for the formation of the field. It coincides, roughly, with the work of three great post-Spanish School political philosophers of the international: Hobbes, Grotius (indeed, Hugo Grotius just missed out on a place in the Swedish delegation to Westphalia in 1643) and Pufendorf; it is a self-conscious effort to contractualise relations between European states (Bull 2002); it formalises a transition from empire to sovereignty in the European political order and, at the risk of anachronism, it might be described as one of the first examples of comprehensive, post-war, multilateral, treaty-making in the international system. As Charles Tilly has put it: 'War made the state, and the state made war' (Tilly 1975, 42). And war and state, at Westphalia, made a certain sort of international law.

In one sense, then, international law, at Westphalia, was ascendant. The Treaties confirmed the supplanting of centralised imperial power by a juridical arrangement of autonomous sovereigns. Medieval theocracy gave way to early modern legal-rationalism (for some time after, the Vatican continued to think of international law as a Protestant conspiracy), and religious authority to secular consensus. A small number of sovereigns within Europe were accorded legal equality in their external relations and, most importantly, in their internal political and religious arrangements. Indeed, the Treaties contain early examples of what came to be called the (legal) principles of non-intervention and self-determination. The Westphalian period, then, confirms the centrality of a language of law and legality that states deploy in their relations with each other.

But the moment is ambiguous, also. The affirmation of sovereignty can be thought of as a defeat for a particular conception of (international) law as the basis for a world society. The autonomy of political units within Europe becomes the foundation for a narrower idea of international community and a guarantee against projects that saw international law's destiny in federation, perpetual peace, an updated *res publica Christiana* or a future world government (Abbé de St Pierre 1713; Kant 1795 [1970]).

Indeed, the whole idea of law as a form of judgement standing over sovereigns was sidelined. It is true that declarations of war in the late seventeenth century frequently contained references to the 'righteousness' (England's 1652 Declaration of War against the Netherlands) or 'justice' (the Netherlands 1652 Declaration of War against England) of the cause (Neff 2005, 106–107) but Westphalia expressly rejected a structuring principle that was to become central from Versailles onwards: namely the idea that inter-state relations, and in particular war, can be organised on the basis of some sort of centrally enforced accountability for illegal acts. If international law began in 1648, it did so in a forgiving, agnostic mood, introducing us to sovereignty as a form of forgetfulness:

> That there shall be on the one side and the other a perpetual ... Amnesty, or Pardon of all that has been committed since the beginning of these Troubles, ... but that all that has pass'd on the one side, and the other ... during the War, shall be bury'd in eternal Oblivion. (Treaty of Münster, article II)

And so, Prime Minister Blair found Westphalia uncongenial to his political project of belligerent humanitarianism precisely because Westphalia rejected justice or righteousness as an organising principle of the international (European) order. Instead, sovereignty became its own justification; *ex post facto* justice was cast into oblivion and assertions of righteousness were relativised. International law might legitimately seek to prevent the recurrence of wars (Westphalia followed, after all, a century-long European bloodbath) but it had little role in judging them (it would take three hundred years for the diplomatic system to embrace this sort of retributive legalism at Nuremberg and Tokyo).

Sovereignty to empire

If international law was bound up with the transition from (Holy Roman) empire to sovereign state in 1648, by the nineteenth century it had spent at least three centuries organising relations amongst some of the same European states in their imperial mode, and between these European metropoles and their colonial territories. This relationship between international law and empire has been understood in two quite distinct ways. In the first, international law tempers empire, then dismantles it. In the second, international law facilitates or legitimises empire then obscures it.

It is not uncommon to think of international law as instinctively anti-imperial: one more liberal-left project capable of being deployed to resist empire. The doctrines of sovereign equality or human rights, say, are applied on behalf of colonised peoples in order to promote self-determination or national liberation or development. Historically, then, the traditions of naturalism, then humanism, then liberalism, in which many international lawyers were situated meant that some international legal writing and legal-diplomatic innovation was concerned to, if not oppose, then certainly soften the effects of, colonial exploitation. At the very least, progressive international lawyers pointed to passages in Vitoria (1532 [1991]), Suárez (1613 [1944]) and, though with less confidence, Grotius (1605 [2006]), to show that the field's founders had been uncomfortable with the wholesale absorption of non-European lands by the great European powers. The emblematic moment in international law's resistance to empire is a period of decolonisation running from the mid 1950s to the mid 1970s when General Assembly resolutions, legal scholarship and doctrinal innovation coalesced into a language of emancipation, and dozens of former colonies in Africa and Asia became states. Some of international law's anti-colonial reputation is staked on the UN Charter (with its Trusteeship System for colonised peoples) and the 1960 Declaration on the Granting of Independence to Colonial Peoples (with its more full-blooded rejection of colonial administration). There is a residue of this period found in the invocations of a Palestinian right to self-determination or a Kurdish claim to a homeland or, more tangentially, in attacks on neo-colonialism or uneven development or predatory global capitalism.

This once-standard account is associated, too, with a conception of international law as somewhat marginal to the economic and strategic imperatives of colonialism. According to this view, empire results from competition amongst the Great Powers, the manifest destiny of nation-building, the need to invest surplus capital or acquire raw materials, and personal ambition. International law's role, then, is to speak for the natives (Vitoria 1532 [1991]) or head off war by allocating colonial territory (General Act of the Congress of Berlin 1885) or establish some basic standards of human decency (anti-slavery protocols in the nineteenth century, trusteeship arrangements in the twentieth).

Compelling recent work has turned these orthodoxies on their heads by showing how international law was formed, or is implicated, in the European domination and exploitation of the non-European peripheries

(Anghie 2005). The writings of many classical international lawyers are re-read here as arguments *for* the extension of European rule to the colonies. Meanwhile, a host of euphemistic international legal doctrines (discovery, conquest, *terra nullius*, settlement, acquisition) is charged with permitting extirpation and war, and facilitating colonial expansion. The mid-to-late nineteenth century is regarded as a bleak time for international law; in that period international lawyers began to construct legal theories distinguishing civilised and uncivilised peoples (Gong 1984) or justifying the non-recognition of 'savages' (Lorimer 1883 [2001]). The Treaty of Berlin is the culmination of unapologetic empire: an effort to extend the balancing mechanisms introduced at the Congress of Vienna in 1815 to a non-European world. International legal techniques for claiming and disbursing territory facilitated the partitioning of Africa at the Berlin Conference of 1884–1885. Within two decades from 1875 to 1895 most of Africa had been appropriated to the colonial powers (prior to 1875 only one-tenth of African territory had been colonised). The Treaty of Berlin formalised empire and did so through the language and doctrine of international law.

The Treaty may have been adopted in order to save Europe from war by neutralising inter-imperial rivalry but Europe, in 1914, went to war in any case. After the Great War, empire was repackaged in the League of Nations Covenant, which contained, in article 22, the outlines of a system (the mandates) that seemed also to prefigure the slow recession of classic colonialism. Colonialism did not disappear but became a matter of international administration and oversight during the inter-war period and later in the UN trusteeship system. Even international law's anti-colonial peak in the 1960s, when it seemed to be at the vanguard of decolonisation, turns out to have been a much more equivocal experience. The independence of new states in the era of decolonisation was highly conditional. Many were subject to the economic stringencies of the World Bank and structural adjustment, many were recruited by the superpowers for bloody proxy wars and all were eventual participants in a global economic and political order that began as 'neo-colonialism' and later became 'globalisation'.

The deeper implication of all this is that international law is founded on colonial and neo-colonial exclusions and distinctions. These are subject to alteration with each generational shift. Languages and legal relations are modified and made palatable as each generation of enlightened empire-builders looks back on the vulgar imperialism of the previous one. *Terra nullius* becomes colony, colony becomes trust territory, trust territory becomes territorial administration. Discredited rhetorics of separation and exclusion (the nineteenth-century distinction between civilised and uncivilised peoples; earlier distinctions between Christians and infidels) are refurbished, de-racialised or secularised (their counterparts are found in the distinctions between democratic and undemocratic sovereigns or between developed and underdeveloped states) but, in the end, the spectres of empire are always present in new programmes, logics and orientations.

Hegemony to Concert

International law is a practice of administration and organisation (it organises sovereigns and it facilitates, then administers, colonial relations). The classic *telos* of the project is the international organisation itself and, more ambitiously, the promise of a global constitution. Establishing institutions is a negotiation, though, between the competing claims of hegemony, sovereignty and some concept of global authority. In Vienna in 1815, the great European powers initiated a public ordering project that was to culminate a century and half later with the UN Charter.

The Congress of Vienna in 1815 was a response to Napoleonic revolution, conquest and imperial ambition. It sought to restore Europe to some sort of equilibrium by institutionalising the balance of power, partially restoring the sovereignty of middle and minor powers and by introducing a novel form of Great Power management. The secret protocol, signed by the Four Powers (Austria, United Kingdom, Russia and Prussia) at Langres in 1814, affirmed that 'relations from whence a system of real and permanent Balance of Power in Europe is to be derived, shall be regulated at the Congress upon the principles determined upon by the Allied Powers themselves'. International law, or what was to be known as the public law of Europe, was intended to bind this arrangement together in a set of treaties and norms for the regulation of nineteenth-century Europe. This was the essence of the Concert system that was to operate, though with diminishing effect, until the Great War.

The Congress of Vienna, though, is not a particularly celebrated marker in the history of international law and the diplomatic system (see Chapter 2 in this volume). It seems distinctly pre-modern in its lack of an institutional architecture, in its failure to create any judicial organs, and in its overall lack of solidity. And, of course, it was, famously, 'the Congress that was not a Congress' (as Talleyrand put it: Palmer 1977, 139). Representatives of the smaller powers (principalities, fiefdoms and so on) danced and drank through a year-long social calendar but they did not form themselves into a general assembly. There was no legitimation from below. Vienna was Dumbarton Oaks (the elite Four-Power – United States, United Kingdom, the Soviet Union and China – meetings in 1944) without its San Francisco (the plenary conference in 1945 to draft the UN Charter). The Great Powers determined the future of Europe in secret protocols drafted prior to the Congress, in Metternich's apartment in Vienna.

Still, there are a number of important respects in which the Congress of Vienna and the subsequent Concert era foreshadowed twentieth-century innovations in institution-making. For example, the bureaucratisation of international law began here. The Congress was, in effect, two plenary committees and ten sub-committees (reporting to the plenary committees on matters such as diplomatic precedence, the slave trade and international rivers). In addition, the Vienna settlement concretised the victors' successes in war, endorsed particular internal government structures (in this case, hereditary rule) and introduced a doctrine of mild interventionism (designed to prevent further revolutionary outbreaks). Most of all, Vienna brought into being or, at least, juridified, the idea of an 'international community' acting as the guardian of peace, good government and the international rule of law.

This combination of technocratic, legalistic decision-making (the committees, the treaties, the plan for regular congresses) and political decision (the tendency to have treaties merely ratify the pre-determinations of the leading states, and the willingness of coalitions of these states to engage in extra-legal action when constrained by the existing institutional arrangements) was to prove archetypal when the great twentieth-century institutions were being founded.

Concert to League

As the Concert system began to wither towards the end of the nineteenth century, international law was undergoing a vigorous expansion in the technical (e.g. the establishment of the Universal Postal Union in 1874), humanitarian (e.g. the St Petersburg Convention in 1868) and colonial (the Treaty of Berlin in 1885) spheres. But the early twentieth century was a paradoxical moment for international law. On one hand, the discipline was newly invigorated by the entrenchment of whole new fields of regulation such as the law of war (at The Hague in 1899 and 1907), and collective security (at the League of Nations in Geneva throughout the inter-war years) and the inception of others (e.g. international criminal law at Versailles in 1919). On the other hand, the Great War, German revanchism, Bolshevik isolation and institutional paralysis combined to produce a sense that international law was, again, marginal to the central dilemmas and practices of war and peace. Not for the last time, productivity failed to guarantee relevance. And even international law's 'successes' were the subject of critique either shortly after (Schmitt 1950) or in retrospect (Jochnick and Normand 1994). A further problem was that these new legal regimes (whatever their merits) seem to work against each other in some not-yet-quite-fully-conceptualised way. For example, the humanisation of war (and the respectability juridification seems to afford the practice of war) sat uncomfortably with the effort to criminalise it at Versailles. The criminalisation of war, meanwhile, seemed incompatible with softer efforts to regulate war or preserve sovereign prerogatives in the League of Nations Covenant or, later, the Kellogg–Briand Pact of 1928.

In retrospect, it is possible to discern four views of international legality in this period. In the first, a bureaucratised, judicialised and institutionalised international law was posited as the solution to the problems of war, lawlessness, colonialism and clandestine diplomacy. This perspective has come to be associated with Woodrow Wilson (though he is an ambiguous figure in this regard) and the League of Nations Covenant. For Wilson, the First World War was caused not by German aggression but by the deformities of old-European diplomacy with its secret articles, its endless subterfuge and competition, and its roots in national vanity. All of this was to be substituted by an open, transparent, accommodationist ethic rooted in international legality and a diplomacy conducted through public assemblies and institutions. War would be tamed by collective security, empire would be transmuted into administration and politics would become law. This was the League of Nations ideal: international law as virtuous and constitutive. It is an ideal that continues to motivate a substantial cadre of international lawyers.

A second view, now associated with the German constitutional and international lawyer, Carl Schmitt, was sceptical of this turn to legalism and institutions. According to Schmitt, a nineteenth-century international legal regime founded on the balance of power, a rough formal equality amongst states and an agnosticism about the responsibilities of war was usurped at Versailles by a hegemonic and punitive legal order. Defeated states were no longer rehabilitated or reabsorbed into a new configuration of power (post-Napoleonic France's early readmission into the Quintuple Alliance in 1815 was the model here) but were instead subject to criminal sanctions and exile from the system (e.g. the reparations imposed on Germany and Turkey). Their leaders were made individually culpable for acts of aggression (article 227 of the Treaty of Versailles). What had once been mistakes of statecraft were now crimes. Meanwhile, war's winners were no longer merely the temporary beneficiaries of fate but the guardians and creators of a new legal order and hitherto provisional coalitions of particular interests were transformed into the 'international community'. 'Pest control' had displaced war; enemies had become criminals. International law, vesting legitimacy on these arrangements, was central to all of this but its effects on international diplomacy were malignant. Negotiation, diplomacy, the economic calculations of realism, the classic Westphalian assumptions about the equality of nations, and the sense that 'it must always be kept in mind that after a war we have sooner or later to live with our enemies in amity' (Hankey 1950), had all given way to the imperatives of punishment and retribution.

But not everyone wanted to either live with their enemies or embrace an 'international community' capable of repressing them. A third – and particularly hostile – response to the League of Nations was that of a largely rejectionist Bolshevism. Periodically, throughout history, revolutionary powers have emerged. These, usually dominant (contemporary Iran is an example of a middle-power revolutionary state) powers do not simply seek recognition as a Great Power or make classic territorial claims. Instead, the organising political ethos of such states makes them radically incompatible with the existing international order. Martin Wight associated such states with what he called catastrophic revolutionism: the desire to transcend the existing structures through violent action (Wight 1994). Philip II of Spain, Hitler, and (at least first-term) Reagan each fall into this category. The Soviet Union in its early fervent Leninist phase was a revolutionary power in this regard (by the 1940s under Stalin it had begun to behave as a more familiar alliance-building Great Power). For it, the League of Nations was a parliament of capitalists. Its refusal to join, and opposition to, the League was symptomatic of a distrust of accommodation or neutrality.

The post-war 'realists' – Reinhold Niebuhr (the American, 'Christian' realist), E.H. Carr (the English author of *The Twenty Years' Crisis*),

Morgenthau (see Chapter 2), post-war US Foreign Policy doyen, George Kennan – represented a fourth view on all this: one that regarded the political as constitutive and the legal as epiphenomenal. They thought the relationship between the diplomatic system and the legal order had become radically disjunctive throughout the inter-war period. For them, international law managed to be at once both supremely irrelevant and dangerously seductive. The League of Nations and Wilsonian diplomacy had been built on a fantasy about the motivations behind inter-state rivalry and the potential constraints law might impose on hegemonic or imperial ambition. The war-like would not be deterred much by declarations of war's criminality or illegality but the innocent might believe that by rendering war unlawful there was no need to take precautionary measures against it.

Perhaps, though, from this perspective, the greatest error made by international lawyers lay in their teleology of progress. The relationship between law and diplomacy was a relationship between a futile project or narrative of improvement and advancement, and a structure of international relations that is resilient, static and trans-historical. A later 'structural realist', Kenneth Waltz, remarked on the 'striking sameness in the quality of international life through the millennia' (Waltz 1979). In the absence of federation or world government, and given the proclivities of powerful sovereigns, Wilsonian international lawyers, on this view, were scheming, hopelessly, against history.

League to Charter

After the Second World War, the scheming intensified but this time, and to avoid the shortcomings of the League system, international legal institutions were to be more closely aligned to the realities of collective security and the balance of power and less punitive in their treatment of enemy or defeated states. The post-war era was built around three pillars and a decoupling. Bretton Woods, San Francisco and Nuremberg provided, respectively, the economic, social-political and retributive bases for the post-war diplomatic order. But this whole diplomatic and juridical order became unhinged as a result of the onset of US–Soviet rivalry and competition. The world's most elaborate and self-confident international legal order was imposed upon the strategic reality of mutually assured destruction (MAD). International law had entered its neurotic age. The ostensible vibrancy of law's institutions and norms masked an intense anxiety about the survival of humanity.

In many respects, though, the edifice was impressive. The Charter drafted at San Francisco seemed to offer a brilliantly realised and redemptive version of the Covenant. The Great Powers would no longer require balancing (after all they were allies now) but would act as a collective security force patrolling a largely disarmed world (this was Roosevelt's 'Four Policemen' model) in which enemy states would be slowly rehabilitated. There was a representative second chamber, the General Assembly, where middle and minor powers would be given a voice. Meanwhile, presiding over all of this was the force of international law. The classic legal principles of diplomacy (sovereignty, territory, equality) were to be joined to an invigorated new international law with an emphasis on human rights, decolonisation, disarmament and a tough prohibition on the use of force in inter-state relations. Bilateralism, secrecy, thin cooperation, threat and counter-threat, and *ad hocery* would be supplanted by a society of 'peace-loving' states engaging in powerful new forms of multilateralism and communal activity.

There were certainly successes. Human rights law grew out of its aspirational (the Universal Declaration of Human Rights) or interstitial (e.g. article 55 of the UN Charter) origins to become a system of legal rules (the International Bill of Rights) and institutional sites (Geneva, New York). The UN Charter was creatively re-read in order to permit 'peace-keeping' or, later, 'peace-building', decolonisation was transformed from administrative routine to moral–legal imperative within a decade and half of the San Francisco meeting and international law in general began to infiltrate virtually all aspects of international social and political life from civil aviation to space exploration to atomic energy to environmental protection.

In some respects, though, the diplomatic system and the ideological schism underlying it proved stubbornly resistant to all this innovation. The political seemed to offer a retort to every legal principle. Neither classic re-statements of sovereign equality or domestic jurisdiction (old diplomacy) nor refurbished doctrines of collective security (new diplomacy) sat comfortably with the strategic realities of superpower spheres of influence. Indeed, these spheres of interest or influence constituted the extra-legal norms that defined the initial phases of the post-war settlement; in Hungary, in the Dominican Republic, in Czechoslovakia and in Nicaragua, intervention was the rule not the exception. Similarly, collective security could only work where there was historical anomaly (the Chinese seat was located in Taipei until 1971) or diplomatic farce (the absence of the

Soviets from the Security Council during the vote on Korea in 1950) or *ultra vires* creativity (a brief constitutional overreaching on the part of the General Assembly at the time of the Korean crisis).

The post-war era could be configured, then, as familiar diplomatic manoeuvring built on pessimism and acted out against a backdrop of shiny but sometimes marginal legal institutions and texts. International legal initiatives in the area of disarmament were rendered nugatory by an intensifying nuclear arms race; the grand political gesture (Reagan and Gorbachev in Reykjavik) seemed so much more promising than the endless legal and bureaucratic wrangling around the Non-Proliferation Treaty. Meanwhile, the centrepiece of the UN system, article 2(4)'s prohibition of armed force, was undergoing an existential crisis provoked by the sheer persistence of war. The UN Charter seemed beside the point in a political environment defined by its incumbent insecurities, mad paranoias and cold-eyed strategising. The two other wings of the post-war settlement fared no better. The Nuremberg principles possessed only hortatory value. International criminal law was useful as a language of calumny but, in the absence of settled rules and enforcement machinery, there was not a single trial of an alleged war criminal before an international criminal court until well into the 1990s. With the field in recess, war crimes trials became local affairs: in Jerusalem or in Frankfurt or in Lyon. Bretton Woods, meanwhile, gave rise to institutions – the World Bank, the International Monetary Fund (IMF) – but not to the institution that international economic lawyers desired most dearly, a judicial tribunal to regulate, adjudicate and enforce economic relations amongst states.

There was a growing sense that, after an initial wave of optimism, international lawyers, unable to fully comprehend the nuclear threat, were rearranging the deck-chairs by retreating into 'positivism' (parsing texts or interpreting rules without much thought for compliance or structure) or by embracing sociology (bringing text into conformity with behaviour) or by reinvigorating naturalism (positing fundamental norms of human dignity against which 'law' could be judged) or by building institutions that seemed disassociated from the realities of superpower rivalry, colonial exploitation or economic cruelty. Unexpectedly, towards the end of the century, an opportunity presented itself; the Soviet bloc collapsed and this collapse seemed to promise a thoroughly re-energised international legal project and an end to the ideological struggles that had inhibited the formation of an authentic international law.

International law's future

What, then, has public international law become at the post-political terminus of democracy, globalisation, ecology and market? There are several possible answers. In one answer, international law has enjoyed a transient revival in the interregnum between two falls: that of the Berlin Wall and the Twin Towers. From 1989 to 2001, then, international law was in its pomp. The Nuremberg Principles were enshrined at Rome in 1998 with the establishment of a permanent international criminal court and activated a year later during the extradition proceedings in the United Kingdom involving General Pinochet. The architects of the post-war international economic order and trading regime finally established their World Trade Organisation (WTO) with its Dispute Settlement Body (DSB) and quasi-judicial Appellate Body, and the UN Charter's collective security norms, finally, worked in response to Iraq's invasion of Kuwait. International law had moved from the margins.

The period around the end of the millennium marks a sort of closing, then, after this period of triumphant legalism. International criminal law is coopted in the war on terror or mired in politics (neo-colonial or hegemonic or partial), international economic law gives way to new forms of protectionism or is sidelined by apparently lawless global financial crises, and the UN Charter is rendered obsolete by an increasing propensity on the part of the great powers to use extra-legal force to advance idiosyncratic conceptions of humanity (Blair) or security (Clinton), or to eradicate evil (Bush II).

A second answer might suggest that nothing much has changed and that international law's future will look very much like its past. The Great Powers will continue to dominate the system and compete (sometimes violently) over resources. International law might, from time to time, constrain the hegemons, or occasionally provide cover for their adventures but mostly it exists as a structuring mechanism to guarantee hegemonic power. Sovereignty, too, will remain constitutive. The great summits (Rome, 1998, Copenhagen, 2009) come and go but the sovereign prerogatives of states ensure that initiatives in the area of international criminal law or international environmental law will founder on expressions of national security or collapse in the face of insurmountable collective action problems. The old diplomacy, built around sovereign exceptionalism, diplomatic immunities and voluntarism, will form the core of international law (Morgenthau's 'functional' international law,

Jackson's classical norms) while newer multilateral initiatives in criminal law or environmental law fail. Or, to partially invert this picture, the split might work another way with the classical rules on the use of force or immunity subject to Great Power caprice or humanitarian corrosion, and the newer norms of international economic law being rigorously enforced to open markets or ensure investment security. Whatever the particular division it will remain the case and has always been the case that: 'international law is one more weapon in the pragmatic political calculations of the great powers' (Douzinas 2007, 216).

A third, and ultimately more convincing, thesis is that international law's attachment to global politics is now secure. Law has become – over the centuries and more than ever – an organising ethics of global life and a thoroughly embedded and irresistible language of statecraft and diplomacy. To talk about evil in international society is to invoke, in international war crimes tribunals, the categories of crime and punishment; to discuss the economic foundations of the system is to refer to institutional management undertaken by the WTO or to informal mechanisms such as the Basle Committee; to argue for the preservation of planetary life is to catalogue a series of legal landmarks (from Stockholm to Rio to Kyoto) or advance a set of universalisable legal standards; and to argue about war is to document the performance of war through codes of humanitarianism and, more generally, speak the lexicon of law (the debate over the Iraq War or the reconfiguration of humanitarian intervention as a 'Responsibility to Protect' being two obvious example of this normative and linguistic turn). Either one speaks the language of law or one self-consciously casts oneself in opposition to it. This became apparent at the beginning of the twenty-first century when a new US administration, allegedly unsympathetic to multilateralism and international law, came to power in Washington, DC. It turned out that even its most fervent manifestoes, were couched in the language of law. The Bush Doctrine, thought to exemplify his Administration's radical departure from international legality, was set out in a National Security Strategy as a successor to the nineteenth-century *Caroline* principles (elaborating on the law to be applied to cases of self-defence).

But if international law structures the way we talk, it cannot determine what we choose or how we act. In this sense, and to return to the themes at the beginning of the chapter, it can appear procedurally central and substantively marginal. Institutions are by-passed by sovereigns acting 'unilaterally' or deep principles can work against the progressive development or status of international law (the immunity accorded abusive heads of state can look from the outside like an extra-legal privilege) or it can look as if norms are ignored or neglected or violated without consequence by states acting in some strategic or selfish interest (think, here, of the allegation that Tony Blair had committed Britain to war in March 2002, long before the legal arguments were fully canvassed). And public international law appears marginal when set against the reach and power of private capital. To what extent did international law create the conditions for or ameliorate the global financial crisis? And does international law have any regulatory role in relation to a black economy that now constitutes a second economic global order? Indeed, international can seem marginal even when it is highly visible. In debates about war, ecology or poverty, something other than law seems to determine policy outcomes or life-chances. No doubt, public international law is open to progressive orientations around the environment or human rights. But the requirements of sovereignty, consent and hegemony also work against, and often neutralise, these agendas or international legal norms seem too ambiguous or elastic to force particular results.

The argument around the Iraq War is typical in many respects (of course, its very visibility makes it exceptional in other respects). For a while, international law was *the* language of argument about the war. Indeed, Charter and customary law were invoked to demonstrate that regime change would be illegal in the absence of either a credible threat from Iraq or Security Council authorisation. This position was rejected by senior government lawyers, and a minority of academic lawyers, who argued that there had been Security Council authorisation or, less convincingly, that Iraq did pose a genuine threat. This debate trundled on and for a while international law seemed central but inconclusive. But this apparent lack of determinacy or certainty in the legal material generated a sense that lawyers could not be relied upon to decide anything: that somehow international law was a game played by initiates but lacking relevance in the 'real world'.

But though international law may not mandate particular outcomes, this hardly disposes of the question of relevance or virtue. Any language or *technē* that absorbs political capital (particularly the political capital of progressive dissent) for a prolonged period of time has opened up particular ways of thinking about global politics or diplomacy and closed down others. The rhetorical strategies used to talk about global order (around dinner-tables, at cabinet meetings, in class-rooms, in international institutions) are now thoroughly infected with legalism. International diplomacy is unimaginable without international law (see, too, Chapter 2). The principles that structure international politics (sovereignty, immunity, territory), the institutional arrangements that facilitate it (the United Nations, international treaty conferences, regional organisations) and the norms that regulate it (prohibiting force, humanising war, organising trade) have become an indispensable part of diplomacy's repertoire. It is not clear whether the gains (a common tradition of argument, a language of critique and transformation, an association with fairness or openness in decision-making) outweigh the losses (a technocratic detachment from the conditions of life, the occlusion of redistributive outcomes, the finessing of hegemonic desire, a culture of expertise).

Bibliography

Abbé de St Pierre, 1713. *Projet pour rendre la paix perpétuelle en Europe*

Acheson, D., 1963. 'Remarks', *Proceedings of the American Society of International Law*, 57, 13–15

Anghie, A., 2005. *Imperialism, Sovereignty and the Making of International Law*, Cambridge University Press

Aquinas, T., 2002. *Political Writings*, R. W. Dyson (ed.), Cambridge University Press

Bassiouni, C. M., 1997. 'From Versailles to Rwanda in Seventy-five Years: The Need to Establish a Permanent International Criminal Court', *Harvard Human Rights Journal*, 10, 11–62

Bederman, D., 2001. *International Law in Antiquity*, Cambridge University Press

Blair, T., 2004. www.guardian.co.uk/politics/2004/mar/05/iraq.iraq

Bull, H., 2002. *The Anarchical Society: A Study of Order in World Politics*, New York: Columbia University Press

Carr, E. H., 1946. *The Twenty Years' Crisis 1919–1939*, 2nd edn., London: Macmillan

Cicero, M. T., 1998. *The Republic and The Laws*, J. Powell (ed.), Oxford University Press

Douzinas, C., 2007. *Human Rights and Empire: The Political Philosophy of Cosmopolitanism*, Abingdon and New York: Routledge-Cavendish

Franck, T., 1990. *The Power of Legitimacy Among Nations*, Oxford University Press

Gat, A., 2006. *War in Human Civilisation*, Oxford University Press

Gong, G. W., 1984. *The Standard of 'Civilisation' in International Society*, Oxford: Clarendon

Grotius, H., 2006, *Commentary on the Law of Prize and Booty*, M. J. Ittersum (ed.), Indianapolis: Liberty Fund

Hankey, M. B., 1950. *Politics, Trials and Errors*, Oxford: Pen-in-Hand Co.

Jackson, R., 1999. *The Global Covenant*, Oxford University Press

Jochnick, C. and R. Normand, 1994. 'The Legitimation of Violence: A Critical History of the Laws of War', *Harvard International Law Journal*, 35, 49–95

Kant, I., 1970. 'Perpetual Peace', in Hans Reiss (ed.), *Political Writings*, Cambridge University Press, 93–130

Lorimer, J., 2001. *The Institutes of the Law of Nations*, Edinburgh: Blackwood–Elibron Classics

Mattingly, G., 1955. *Renaissance Diplomacy*, London: Jonathan Cape

Morgenthau, H., 1940. 'Positivism, Functionalism and International Law', *American Journal of International Law*, 34, 260–284

Neff, S., 2005. *War and the Law of Nations: A General History*, Cambridge University Press

Neff, S., 2010. 'A Short History of International Law', in M. Evans, *International Law*, Oxford University Press, 3–31

Norton-Taylor, R., 2010. 'Chilcot Inquiry: Lawyers Expose Pressure to Give Green Light for War', *Guardian*, 26 January

Palmer, A., 1977. *Metternich: Der Staatsmann Europas*, Hamburg: Claassen Verlag

Schmitt, C., 1950. *Der Nomos der Erde im Völkerrecht des ius publicum Europaeum*, Berlin: Duncker & Humblot

Suárez, F., 1944. 'Tractatus de legibus ac deo legislatore', in *Selections from Three Works*, 2 vols., Oxford: Clarendon

Teschke, B., 2003. *The Myth of 1648: Class, Geopolitics and the Making of Modern International Relations*, London: Verso

Tilly, C. (ed.), 1975. *The Formation of National States in Western Europe*, Princeton University Press

Vitoria, F., 1991. *Political Writings*, A. Pagden and J. Lawrance (eds.), Cambridge University Press, 231–327

Waltz, K., 1979. *Theory of International Politics*, New York: McGraw-Hill

Wight, M., 1994. *International Theory: The Three Traditions*, Leicester University Press

2 International law in the world of ideas

Martti Koskenniemi

The relationship of ideas and practices

Of the different types of law taught at universities or practised in governments, commercial companies, or law firms, international law has always been the most open to moral or philosophical reflection. To engage in international law has been to involve oneself in contested ideas about legitimate government, justified forms of violence, universal rights and the direction of human progress. Ideas about the politically just and unjust are condensed in technical international law rules and institutions, giving them sharpness and actuality that has fed back as experience to the worlds of politics and thought. For example, occupation of territory, the movement of military forces or the rights of aliens are seldom discussed in fully abstract terms – without thinking of *this* occupation, *that* war, *those* people. Abstract legal debate and political engagement are almost always two sides of the same coin. Which is why themes such as 'sovereignty', 'just war' and the 'right to trade and extract resources' may be equally at home in philosophy departments, international courts, foreign ministries and political rallies. As a vocabulary and a practice, international law is deeply embedded in the creation of a global, economically and technologically driven culture. Leading ideas such as the 'universal' or the 'humanitarian' are used both to legitimise current developments and to challenge them. There are few international controversies where both sides would not regularly invoke international law in their favour.

International law revels in conflict. Legal advisors use it to argue cases before tribunals such as the International Court of Justice in The Hague or the European Court of Human Rights (ECtHR) in Strasbourg. Diplomats strategise about it in bilateral relations and at meetings of international institutions. Politicians invoke it to defend their policies or to attack their adversaries in public speeches and declarations, newspaper articles, pamphlets and manifestos. Even academics find it useful as an instrument to defend or challenge particular forms of international behaviour and to engage in controversies about institutional reforms. But it also carries large ideas about peace, social justice, human freedom and rational management. Most significant political thinkers have, since the seventeenth century, felt compelled to say something about how their abstract reflections might be reflected as international legal institutions. There has always been some disciplinary rivalry about the 'ownership' of themes such as world peace, good government, free trade or sovereign statehood. Are they best dealt with by theologians, as claimed by sixteenth-century Catholic thinkers in Spain, or should they instead be reserved for statesmen and their secular advisors as suggested by their seventeenth-century Protestant followers? The relationship between 'effective action' preferred by foreign policy 'realists' and the 'binding rules' invoked by jurists continues to arouse intellectual debate. Should proposals for 'perpetual peace', made by liberal philosophers such as Immanuel Kant in the eighteenth or Jürgen Habermas in the twenty-first century, be taken as blueprints for diplomatic action (Habermas 2004)? How should writings on the ethics and politics of human rights be reflected in the practices of UN human rights organs? What is the relationship between international law and ideas about economic development and social justice? And what about the 'realist', 'institutionalist', 'liberal' or other models produced by foreign policy think tanks and international relations departments (Besson and Tasioulas 2010)?

Because there is no world government or a world legislative process, such ideas enter into, and are for their part affected by, international law in a subtle process of learning and exchange. Although they open areas of cooperation, they also serve as themes for conflict. No legal system, least of all international law, is a homogeneous bloc in which abstract ideas turn into concrete action an automatic way. The *indeterminacy* of notions such as 'peace', 'security', 'human rights', 'humanitarian action', 'sustainable development' renders them fertile ground for controversy. International law certainly looks for 'peace'. But what 'peace' means, say, to the Israeli government is completely different from what it means to the Palestinians and their respective supporting groups. Ideas about the use of international resources or environmental protection have since the 1990s been expressed in principles such as 'equitable utilisation' or 'sustainable development' that are wide enough to cover contrasting environmental and economic interests – that is the secret of their success. But they also defer concrete measures to be decided only later, in some further deliberation conducted by technical and economic experts at international institutions that are often distant from political or legal control. That is the problem of universal rules. In order for them to be acceptable, they must be formulated in such a general way that they fail to give indications of concrete action. What they mean, in practice, must then be improvised along the way, often by precisely those whose operations they aim to control (Koskenniemi 2007). For example, the laws of armed conflict, based on the universally accepted Geneva Conventions of 1949 and the Additional Protocols of 1977, are acceptable to countries because they are permeated by abstract standards such as 'proportionality' and 'reasonableness' that indicate a willingness to compromise between civilian and military interests while leaving operational decisions to be worked out between the (military, legal and humanitarian) experts on the ground (Kennedy 2006). The pathways from large ideas to concrete institutional practices are often complex and hard to follow.

Human rights provide inspiration for a variety of international action – they set standards for foreign policy and governmental behaviour vis-à-vis citizens. In fact, they have been so successful that nearly all policies today push themselves forward in human rights terms. From advancing development to expanding free trade, from intervening in 'failed states' to regulating (or not regulating) the internet, the benefits offered by such projects have been described in terms of the 'rights' of the beneficiaries. Because there is no clear limit to such re-labelling, it often happens that both sides in a conflict invoke their 'human right', say, a right to 'freedom' or a right to 'security'. This is why the practice of rights application often takes place by 'balancing' between conflicting rights, by invoking legitimate exceptions or, as in the case of the European Court of Human Rights, leaving a substantial 'margin of appreciation' with the domestic authorities. Through such (and other) mechanisms, abstract ideas about human rights receive concreteness and applicability in the daily decision-making by international institutions (Koskenniemi 1999). To find out the role of an idea in international law is to look for the embedded preferences of the institution that will have jurisdiction over it.

International law in the history of European ideas: early developments

Like other manifestations of European law, international law finds its ideological origin in Roman ideas about the lawful use of power. The law of nations (*ius gentium*) of classical Rome was eminently practical, created in order to facilitate Rome's commercial relations with its neighbours (Kaser 1993). Simultaneously, Stoic universalism pushed philosophically minded orators such as Cicero to imagine a natural law that would coincide with the requirements of human reason and whose validity would be independent of time and place. The idea of a universal law was consolidated in the early years of the Christian era when the church fathers suggested that God had planted certain immutable principles in all humans, regardless of their faith – a view supported by the sixth-century codification of Roman law that included a definition of *ius gentium* as 'what natural reason has established amongst human beings'.

The most influential medieval view of natural law and the *ius gentium* was written into the *Summa theologiae* by St Thomas Aquinas (1225–1274) who supplemented an immutable, divinely created natural law with a law of nations that contained situation-specific conclusions from the former and dealt with historically contingent types of human relations. Aquinas' *ius gentium* contained not only principles of inter-state behaviour later associated with 'international law', such as sending and receiving envoys, but also general rules of social life concerning contracts, inheritance, family relations and slavery. He accepted that independent political communities were to be led by the prince for the common good and that this included the right to wage just war if only the prince had right authority, his cause was just and he pursued it with right intention (Aquinas 1265–1274 [2002]).

In the twelfth century, the Roman–Christian notion of a universal *ius gentium* entered in tension with another product of the European heritage, namely the idea of the Holy Roman Empire. The French King had been declared by the Pope to be 'emperor' in his realm in the thirteenth century. Soon he, as well as the city-republics in Italy, were waging wars and sending ambassadors to other communities in a way that led jurists such as Baldus of Ubaldis (1327–1406) from a view of mere *de facto* independence alongside the authority of the Emperor to full *de iure* statehood that was derived from the *ius gentium* (see further Haggenmacher 1986, 311–358).

The emancipation of the secular state from the overlordship of the Emperor and the Church raised the question of the nature of its statehood into a significant *topos* of humanist thought in the fifteenth century. If Machiavelli (1469–1527) left little room for law in the conduct of external relations, jurists who had grown up in a renaissance spirit such as the Italian Protestant refugee Alberico Gentili (1552–1608) highlighted the pacifying effects of diplomacy while reconfiguring the principles of the just war so as to include the balance of power and reasonable action to forestall its disturbance. Both viewed law as an instrument for order rather than justice. Their antagonists, sixteenth-century Spanish writers, responded by developing a comprehensive vocabulary of natural law and the law of nations within a divinely instituted rational world. Reacting to problems Spain had encountered in Europe and the New World, Dominican theologians from Salamanca such as Francisco de Vitoria (1485–1546), jurists such as Fernando Vázquez de Menchaca (1512–1569) and Jesuits such as Francisco Suárez (1548–1617) started to speak of the use of human power (*dominium*) in terms of universal principles of state authority, Christian and infidel, secular government and universal rights, slowly departing from a theocentric view of the world (Reibstein 1949). They understood the law of nations as a set of pragmatic conclusions from human nature that justified limited state authority, authorised the evangelisation of the 'Indies', and solidified the emergence of a universal system of private property, monetary exchanges and trade. A reworked theory of the just war would help enforce this system. The Spanish theory of the law of nations sought to accommodate Christian ethics of human equality, common property and peace in a world of emerging absolutism, capitalism and war. Gentili's support for absolutism in England was opposed by Suárez, assigned to defend the Catholic subjects of James I by a theory of the Pope's indirect intervention. Suárez also advocated a law of nations that would be based on the customs of nations and divided in two parts: principles of civil law that were uniform across the world and laws applying to the conduct of the relations of independent states *inter se* (Gentili 1612 [1933]; Suárez 1613 [1944]).

A law among states

'The Spanish origins of international law' (Scott 1928) emerged from an amalgamation of humanist and counter-reformation thought but were taken by Protestant jurists such as Hugo Grotius (1583–1645), Thomas Hobbes (1588–1679) and Samuel Pufendorf (1632–1694) in three different directions that still mark the alternatives for international legal theory. Each argued in the idiom of natural law but in a different direction. In his mature work of 1625, Grotius depicted international law as the slow unfolding of universal principles of justice that were innate in human beings and identifiable by the use of reason. These would support freedom of commerce and navigation while indicting warfare as essentially irrational. For Hobbes, writing in the aftermath of the English Civil War (1651), any innate natural laws were only a figment of the speaker's imagination. Human beings were wolves to each other and needed a firm central power to keep in check their destructive passions. The only reality of the law of nations lay in those interests that sometimes made states cooperate. Pufendorf's compromise between Grotius (natural love) and Hobbes (pure passion) proved to be immensely successful. Generations of international lawyers would follow him in raising the principles of the social contract at an international level, arguing that even if states were egoistic about their interests, their leaders were (or should be) also rational and would understand that those interests could only be realised in cooperation. Drawing on the experience of the fragmented structures of the Holy Roman Empire (of the German nation), and understanding human 'sociability' as a creation of reason and culture, he combined the writers of the *raison d'état* with a rather cheerful view of universal legality (Tuck 1999; Covell 2009).

While German thinkers elaborated the principles of sociability at enlightenment universities such as Halle or Göttingen, French *philosophes* were debating projects of 'perpetual peace' on the basis of themes set out by the Abbé de St Pierre (1658–1743) in 1713. The principles of European public law (*Droit public de l'Europe*) were for the first time collected alongside European treaty practices in a work by the Abbé de Mably (1709–1785). While sympathetic to St Pierre's proposal and critical of the diplomatic practices of the *ancien regime*, Jean-Jacques Rousseau (1712–1778) resigned himself nevertheless to defend the balance of power as the best instrument for a stable legal order in Europe. A revolutionary draft declaration on the 'rights of nations' was debated in the National Assembly in Paris in 1795. It was never adopted, however, as the French troops in Germany turned from liberators to occupiers, vindicating Rousseau's pessimism (Belissa 1998).

Immanuel Kant (1724–1804) rejected the idea that international law (or indeed any law) could be derived either from human nature or from anything empirical. There is no access to 'nature' that would be independent from its realisations in history. But Kant wrote of the ('pure') laws of universal reason that would be applicable regardless of time and place and that would unfold slowly with the progress of humanity. A 'world state' could not be immediately attained; instead, the principles of lawfulness ought to be written into national constitutions so that, with increasing civilisation, a peaceful world would emerge as a federation of (democratic) republics (Kant 1795 [1970]).

Kant's views clashed with the Great Power diplomacy of the nineteenth century. As domestic law stressed the independence of the nation, international law was often reduced to a series of bilateral treaties whose binding force might be doubted. With the conclusion of the first Red Cross Convention (1864), with increasing international cooperation in the technical and economic fields and with the establishment of chairs of international law at European universities, however, this view began to change. The debate on the 'basis of the binding force of international law' ended with the general acceptance amongst jurists of the view, initially put forward by the Austrian public lawyer Georg Jellinek (1851–1911), that this basis lay in the 'nature of the conditions of the international world itself'. No state could live in isolation; every state needed others. Of course, there was no system of enforcement of international law – but neither did there exist rules on the enforcement of domestic constitutional law. To the old problem about the basis of international law, Jellinek gave a response that resembled the one proposed by Pufendorf: it was binding because and to the extent it was socially necessary (Jellinek 1880).

In the last third of the nineteenth century, international law emerged as a practical craft, no longer deriving its rules from theological, philosophical or moral reflection. To be sure, leading lawyers invariably supported liberal ideas, freedom of trade, humanisation of warfare and domestic legislative reform. But they did not feel that these were in need of an elaborate defence and would anyway, with European civilisation, almost automatically spread all over the world. They saw their nationalism as fully compatible with an emerging international legal order and were instrumental in the convening of The Hague Peace Conferences in 1899 and 1907 (Koskenniemi 2001).

A colonial legacy

The history of international legal ideas is intensely Eurocentric. Until the twentieth century, the non-European world appeared to Europe predominantly as an object of colonisation, evangelisation and civilisation. From the Romans through to the nineteenth-century 'informal imperialism', European lawyers and political thinkers understood international law as being developed in Europe and providing for different rules for inter-European relations and relations between European and other entities, labelled *en masse* as 'uncivilised'. But the colonial legacy was never uniform and while its practical realisation usually involved ruthless disregard for colonised peoples and their interests, the official justifications varied from religious ideas to a secular paternalism, from efforts to eradicate 'unnatural' or heathen practices to more recent policies to direct the 'development' of the Third World or to inject it with 'human rights' and the 'rule of law'. Although long-standing diplomatic and treaty relations existed between European states and such non-European states as China, the Ottoman Empire, Persia, and Siam, amongst others, the only specific ideas that related to those relations had to do either with advantages provided to the Europeans (and the United States) or special procedures for carrying out the work of 'civilisation'. In the eighteenth and nineteenth centuries, international law's relationship with the non-European world was embedded in a philosophy of history that saw Europe lead the way to a universal organisation of humankind in some distant future. Only towards the end of the twentieth century has there emerged something like an effort to think about international law from the perspective of the colonised (Anghie 2005).

Twentieth-century controversies

After the First World War, debates about the nature, force and content of international law commenced anew. At this time, expressions such as 'positivism', 'naturalism', 'realism', 'sociological jurisprudence', 'idealism' and, slowly, 'functionalism' emerged to characterise typical positions. Because these positions were also dependent on each other in complicated ways, none of them was able to attain a hegemonic stance. The urgency of the debate was underlined by the collapse of the old diplomatic system and the creation in 1919 of the League of Nations as a completely new type of institution for peace-keeping and the friendly settlement of disputes. But the origins of the League Covenant in the peace treaty with Germany together with its operative weaknesses contributed to the continuation of a debate about the force of this new law.

That debate was conducted with most sharpness in Germany, where the powerful 'formalism' of Hans Kelsen (1881–1973) stood against a revival of natural law and the emergence of a sociologically oriented jurisprudence. Was international law binding because that was how we should logically think about it, because it embodied valuable goals of human association or because it was (and only to that extent) in the interests of states themselves? Political 'realists' used generalisations from psychological, sociological or existential facts against the very possibility that an artificial and history-less normative structure could ever become a reality. Some, such as the public law theorist Carl Schmitt (1888–1985), were arguing that the 'universal' principles underlying the League were in truth mere extrapolations from the interests of the Anglo-American elites. By contrast, in Britain, the Cambridge professor Hersch Lauterpacht (1897–1960) read the Covenant of the League as 'higher law' and lectured to his students during the war on the coming world federation (Kelsen 1928; Lauterpacht 1933; Schmitt 1950).

The Second World War did not end in a blueprint for a new international law. There was little discussion about international law 'ideas' – apart from dismissing them as utterly unreal or counter-productive. A pragmatic spirit accompanied the establishment of the United Nations and the outbreak of the Cold War. While Europeans focused on regional integration, political science departments in the United States produced sociologically oriented re-readings of legal and diplomatic materials. The view of law as an instrument for foreign policy was articulated by Myres McDougal (1906–1998) from Yale, perhaps fittingly so as to defend US interests in the Cold War. The German lawyer-refugee Hans Morgenthau (1904–1980) became extraordinarily influential in establishing 'international relations' on such realist premises as the balance of power and an extensive concept of the 'political'; but he also advocated a limited role for the law and speculated about the possibility of a world federation (Morgenthau 1948).

The rise of the Third World to prominence began by a call for a 'clean slate' in international law. After all, international law had provided many of the forms of the defunct colonialism. But Third World jurists soon realised that traditional ideas about statehood, self-determination and non-interference could be employed in their interest as they had once been employed in the interests of their colonial masters. In the 1970s and 1980s, welfarist themes about a new economic order, including nationalisation of foreign property on equitable conditions, technology transfer and redistributive justice took over international law's agenda of reform. These ideas became very visible in the United Nations and associated intergovernmental organisations until the 1990s when they were offset as the World Bank and the major capital exporting countries turned to neo-liberalism and structural reform.

Throughout the twentieth century, international lawyers have had a complex relationship with the idea of sovereignty. In the 1960s it became fashionable in the West to attack it as an obstacle to the protection of human rights, to securing the conditions of universal free trade, and to taking effective action to combat environmental degradation. In the mid 1990s, the critique of sovereignty turned towards advocating intervention and realising the criminal responsibility of national leaders accused of crimes against humanity. The collapse of real socialism and the predominance of the liberal ideology of the market supported the development of a robust system of free trade under the World Trade Organisation (WTO) in 1995 with a system of legal dispute settlement at its core; it also supported (though never unequivocally) the notion of an 'international community' that would take upon itself the reconstruction of 'failed states' and later, the 'fight against terrorism'.

Amongst the most conspicuous developments in the past decades have been the consolidation of international human rights institutions on a regional and universal scale as well as the emergence of international criminal law, both reflecting the turn to values such as 'good' and 'evil' as informing international action. The close relationship between the activities of human rights organs and international criminal trials with political questions has sometimes – for example with the prosecution by the International Criminal Court of parties in the civil wars in Uganda and the Sudan – raised the question of the appropriate role and jurisdiction of such bodies in on-going conflicts. In the aftermath of the increased activity of the UN Security Council in the 1990s, a debate on the extent of the Council's jurisdiction and its accountability under international law was briefly raised. Today, the front line in action under maintenance of peace and security has been taken by coalitions of 'likeminded' countries in a way that is not always easy to compress within existing legal institutions – though the attempt to do so is usually made (e.g. Calliess, Nolte and Stoll 2007).

In the twenty-first century, international law has been vigorously invoked by all in the controversies about globalisation. Is international law politically neutral or is it for such ideas as 'democracy', 'freedom' or 'security'? One predominant theme has been international law's 'fragmentation' – the emergence of specialised regimes with their own experts, preferences and agendas in fields such as 'trade law', 'human rights law', 'environmental law', 'international criminal law' and so on. This has often been accompanied by 'deformalisation', the replacement of formal treaty rules by informal and flexible standards ('regulation'), emerging from decentralised regimes of informal governance – a new kind of 'transnational law' that has elements of private and public law and that is often managed by technical experts and applied so as to receive economically optimal results. This has created problems of legitimacy that have been reflected in the anti-globalisation movement but also in the proposal for an international constitution or the creation of 'international administrative law' to provide for the transparency or accountability of this type of 'governance'. In these debates, old ideas about the relations of law and power have often been dressed in novel vocabularies borrowed from political theory or social sciences (Koskenniemi 2007; Klabbers, Peters and Ulfstein 2009).

Ideas and controversy

International legal ideas constantly interact with philosophical and jurisprudential debates, often in the context of on-going political controversy. Rather than showing any clear, linear progress, their history unfolds as a succession of debates in which new vocabularies often give expression to old themes sometimes in more or less self-conscious right- or left-wing versions (see, e.g., Goldsmith and Posner 2005; Marks 2008). The ideas typically come in pairs of opposites, reflecting contrasting ways to think about a problem. With this in mind, it is easy to identify five themes in international law that arise over again and in which contrasting approaches are used to give substance to disputed preferences or academic controversies.

The theme of the *international community* appears alternatively as a desired goal of international action or a negative utopia of hegemonic oppression. 'International community' is sometimes invoked to expresses human solidarity, universal rights or the homogeneous character of human experience. As such, it has supported utopian blueprints of 'perpetual peace' or 'world government' to which institutions such as the United Nations or the informal networks of 'globalisation' have given more or less successful expression. In its negative shape this theme has given rise to the critiques of empire or globalisation as a smokescreen for the advancement of the interests of those in powerful positions. Typically, 'humanitarian intervention' has been both celebrated as a manifestation of awareness of the unity of humankind and a sombre instrument for policing the world by those having the resources to do so (Orford 2003).

The theme of the *individual* is raised over and again in international law either in terms of 'belonging' (i.e. as citizenship, nationhood, diplomatic protection and, again, humanitarian intervention), or as desire for autonomy and freedom. The debates about jurisdiction are typically about the way individuals link to particular communities, while much of the law of human rights treats the individual as a counterpoint to community. The former perspective highlights human solidarity and the individual's participation in collective life as desirable; the latter emphasises the individual's need of distance from larger entities, stressing autonomy as an essential part of a fulfilling life. Debates about collective self-determination and individual rights often give expression to such contrasting pursuits, as do those concerning migration, indigenous peoples or desirable structures of the international economy (freedom versus regulation).

Sovereignty mediates between international community and the individual. Its persistence as a leading international law theme is an outcome of our wish to seek a middle-ground between world order (oppressive hegemony) and the individual (anarchistic egoism). In its positive shape, sovereignty comes to international lawyers as self-determination by a historically formed group, giving expression to shared experiences and faiths, and as independence from outsiders. Its dark side connotes exclusion, boundaries, entrapment of human groups under oppressive regimes or perpetuating the ineffective management of problems thought to be essentially 'international' (Kalmo and Skinner 2010).

Peace is an idea endorsed by all – and yet much of international law has always been about the lawful ways in which to engage in war. This is so because *peace*, although desirable in the abstract, may also connote oppression, or a moment when the enemy collects its forces to prepare for battle.

There has been no lack of efforts to appeal to formal peace so as to uphold some politically unacceptable regime – and no dearth of peaceful explanations for the necessity of war. Caught in this dilemma, the International Court of Justice in 1996 saw it necessary to state that it could not say definitely whether the use of nuclear weapons might be allowed in self-defence when the very existence of the state was at stake (*Legality of the Threat or Use of Nuclear Weapons, Advisory Opinion*, ICJ Reports 1996, p. 226, 263).

Finally, *welfare* often appears among international law's leading objectives. But does it mean freedom of trade or more regulation for balanced development? Does it call for international action for the purposes of environmental protection or more efficient use of national resources? And what is the relationship between economic development and political rights? As a positive goal, 'welfare' connotes prosperity, a clean environment and social benefits. Its negative image takes on the appearance of increased regulation, managerialism, absence of citizen initiative and expert rule (Jouannet 2010).

Much of international legal controversy turns around such themes. The protagonists employ the positive and negative images associated with each theme so as to support their desired rules or agendas. There is no closure to such controversies because the more one presses on the positive image associated with a theme, the more one's antagonist is able to point the inevitable emergence of its dark side. With this, it appears that international law is not a blueprint, still less a logical system, but a language within which contrasting interests and values may be presented, a habit in which they may be dressed. To engage in it is not to be part of some world-wide effort to construct a harmonious system of rules but to take part in controversies about how to prioritise matters of international concern, for example, whether to prefer the private right of a foreign investor or the economic needs of the host state, the effectiveness of an occupation regime or the rights of those living under occupation. There are no 'final' answers to such questions. Often the good answers are intensely contextual: a compromise between opposing parties that can work only where it has been attained. International law does not contain a ready-made blueprint for a better world that could only be 'applied' so as to bring about peace and justice. Instead, it contains arguments and positions, precedents and principles that may be employed to express contrasting interests or values in a relatively organised way. To extract international legal ideas from their uses in actual controversies is the surest way of failing to understand their actual operation.

Structure of international law: between normativity and concreteness

This is not to say, however, that it would be impossible to extract patterns in recurring controversies about international law. There is a structure in the system of opposing pairs of legal concepts that can be depicted in the tension between the demands of international law's *normativity* and its *concreteness*. The normativity of a legal idea – say, a rule or an institution – has to do with its 'oughtness', the way it does not merely describe some aspect of reality but poses requirements for it. This accounts for international law's 'idealistic' aspect, the way its rules and institutions do not simply accept some political facts – occupation of territory, say, or pollution of the marine environment – because they happen to take place. International law seeks autonomy from such facts and, instead, aims give expression to (normative) ideas such as 'peace' or 'clean environment' whereby the present (unacceptable) facts may be changed.

However, international legal ideas cannot simply live as abstractions. They must also have concreteness; they must reflect what actually takes place in the political and economic world. This is important for two reasons. First, if they did not reflect what takes place in reality, we would be at a loss about where they come from. But when we assume that they 'reflect' the wills and interests of important actors, then we do know where they originate, and that origin – we assume – reflects a justifiable basis for applying them. And second, they must also link to verifiable facts because if they did not so do, then they would look like political or philosophical abstractions under which any policy might seem defensible. This is precisely why we look at treaties, customs and decisions of authoritative international institutions. They are the external surface – the 'canvas' – that is provided to lawyers by international facts, the content of which can be professionally verified (Koskenniemi 2005).

Now 'normativity' and 'concreteness' seem both necessary: an idea that lacked normativity would seem merely a sociological description. It would merely tell what people (or states) do, and not what they *should* do. It would be an *apology* for power. An idea that lacked concreteness would appear like a mere (philosophical) abstraction. We would have no way of explaining where it comes from or what it means in practice. It would seem a mere *utopia*. The critiques of 'apology' and 'utopia' are constantly used to contest the validity or application of particular legal ideas: either they are 'only hypocritical servants of power' or 'abstract expressions of idealist imagination'. To avoid such critiques, legal rules or institutions should be both 'normative' and 'concrete' simultaneously. But that is difficult. The more normative an idea, the less it can be defended by what actually takes place in the world of practice. And the more concrete an idea, the more firmly it is embedded in the sociological substratum of the international world, the more it comes to seem a mere apology for state power. Normativity and concreteness cancel each other out: the more normative an idea, the less concrete it is, and vice versa. But the tension between the two requirements may now be used to explain the dichotomous character of international law, the way its ideas always come in pairs, and the way it helps to structure international controversies, though it does not provide an independent resolution to them.

International law is an aspect of the world of philosophical, historical, political and even religious ideas. It expresses large aspirations for a better world. But is also a professional technique for pursuing and (sometimes) settling disputes. It is part of human desires and human practices, those two relating to each other in complex but relatively predictable ways. The tension in international law between the needs for normativity and concreteness explains at least in part why its ideas always appear in pairs, one side of which represents international law's idealist aspiration, the other its realist awareness. Because neither can be preferred in a general way, international legal practice constantly pushes towards the particular case, or the technical and contextual solution.

This is not to say that international legal ideas would be useless. They have a considerable historical, intellectual and emotional pull. They engage citizens, diplomats and lawyers to reflect on the problems of the world in a relatively structured way. But they do not themselves resolve those problems. They give a voice to demands and interests and facilitate the articulation of controversies – and thus also their resolution – by showing how alternative acts bear upon larger aspirations. They work as critique of power and as instruments of power. As ideas, they are a necessary aspect of thinking about the world but deeply unsatisfactory in trying to find ways of dealing with it.

Bibliography

Anghie, A., 2005. *Imperialism, Sovereignty and the Making of International Law*, Cambridge University Press

Aquinas, T., 2002. *Political Writings*, R. W. Dyson (ed.), Cambridge University Press

Belissa, M., 1998. *Fraternité universelle et intérêt national (1713–1795): Les cosmopolitiques du droit des gens*, Paris: Kimé

Besson, S. and J. Tasioulas (eds.), 2010. *The Philosophy of International Law*, Oxford University Press

Calliess, C., G. Nolte and P.-T. Stoll, 2007. *Coalitions of the Willing: Avantgarde or Threat?*, Cologne: Heymanns

Covell, C., 2009. *The Law of Nations in Political Thought: A Critical Survey from Vitoria to Hegel*, New York: Palgrave Macmillan

Gaurier, D., 2005. *Histoire du droit international: Acteurs, doctrines et développement de l'Antiquité à l'aube de la période contemporaine*, Presses universitaires de Rennes

Gentili, A., 1933. *De iure belli libri tres*, 2 vols., J. C. Rolfe (trans.), Oxford: Clarendon

Goldsmith, J. and E. Posner, 2005. *The Limits of International Law*, Oxford University Press

Habermas, J., 2004. 'Hat der Konstitutionalisierung des Völkerrechts noch eine Chance?', in *Der gespaltene Westen*, Frankfurt: Suhrkamp, 113–193

Haggenmacher, P., 1986. *Grotius et la doctrine de la guerre juste*, Paris: PUF

Jellinek, G., 1880. *Die rechtliche Natur der Staatenverträge*, Vienna: Hölder

Jouannet, E., 2010. *Le droit international libéral-providence: Une histoire du droit international*, Brussels: Bruylant

Kalmo, H. and Q. Skinner (eds.), 2010. *Sovereignty in Fragments: The Past, Present and Future of a Contested Concept*, Cambridge University Press

Kant, I., 1970. 'Perpetual Peace', in *Political Writings*, Hans Reiss (ed.), Cambridge University Press, 93–130

Kaser, M., 1993. *Jus gentium*, Cologne: Böhlen

Kelsen, H., 1928. *Das Problem der Souveränität und die Theorie des Völkerrechts*, Tübingen: Mohr

Kennedy, D., 2006. *Of War and Law*, Princeton University Press

Klabbers, J., A. Peters and G. Ulfstein, 2009. *The Constitutionalisation of International Law*, Oxford University Press

Koskenniemi, M., 1999. 'The Effect of Rights on Political Culture', in P. Alston (ed.), *The European Union and Human Rights*, Oxford University Press, 99–116

Koskenniemi, M., 2001. *The Gentle Civilizer of Nations: The Rise and Fall of International Law 1870–1960*, Cambridge University Press

Koskenniemi, M., 2005. *From Apology to Utopia: The Structure of International Legal Argument. Reissue with a New Epilogue*, Cambridge University Press

Koskenniemi, M., 2007. 'The Fate of Public International Law: Between Technique and Politics', *Modern Law Review*, 70, 1–30

Lauterpacht, H., 1933. *The Function of Law in the International Community*, Oxford: Clarendon

Marks, S. (ed.), 2008. *International Law on the Left: Re-examining Marxist Legacies*, Cambridge University Press

McDougal, M., 1953. 'International Law, Power and Policy: A Contemporary Conception', *Recueil des cours de l'Académie de droit international*, 82(I), 137–259

Morgenthau, H., 1948. *Politics Among Nations: The Struggle for Power and Peace*, New York: Alfred A. Knopf

Orford, A., 2003. *Reading Humanitarian Intervention: Human Rights and the Use of Force in International Law*, Cambridge University Press

Reibstein, E., 1949. *Die Anfänge des neueren Natur- und Völkerrechts: Studien zu den 'Controversiae illustres' des Fernandus Vasquius (1559)*, Bern: Haupt

Schmitt, C., 1950. *Der Nomos der Erde im Völkerrecht des ius publicum Europaeum*, Berlin: Duncker & Humblot

Scott, J. B., 1928. *The Spanish Origin of International Law: Lectures on Francisco de Vitoria (1480–1546) and Francisco Suárez (1548–1617)*, Washington, DC: Georgetown University, The School of Foreign Service

Suárez, F., 1944. 'Tractatus de legibus ac deo legislatore', in *Selections from Three Works*, 2 vols., Oxford: Clarendon

Tuck, R., 1999. *The Rights of War and Peace: Political Thought and the International Order from Grotius to Kant*, Oxford University Press

3 International law as law

Frédéric Mégret

Introduction

What is the character of international law as a legal system? How different is international law from municipal law? Is this difference significant or is it made into more than is justified? What consequences flow from international law being a distinct legal system in terms of its practice and prospects?

International law as a discipline has exhibited an unusual propensity to ask such questions, perhaps because, historically and politically, this has often seemed less a matter of course than for domestic legal orders. In truth the debate about international law as law covers three distinct though related questions. The first deals with what type of legal system international law is. It is immediately quite clear that international law operates differently from domestic law. But to what extent is it a *sui generis* legal system? Second is the rather more ominous question of whether, on the basis of its defining characteristics, international law can even qualify as 'law' properly so called. Confronted with widely publicised and spectacular violations of international law, popular opinion is often tempted to give up on the idea, yet international law is routinely treated as law by its practitioners. Why this disjunction? Third, one of the difficulties in determining what sort of law international law is, or whether it is law at all, is that it is a constantly evolving legal system that has seemingly taken many different shapes over time. Is international law so changeable that it lacks the minimum stability a legal order should have, or is it instead remarkably constant over time despite the appearance of constant renewal?

Characteristics: a classical view of international law as a legal order

International law is most often understood as a law that is fundamentally different from domestic law because it operates between equal and sovereign collectivities. Yet perhaps what more aptly characterises international law is its quality of being a law 'in between': both irreducible and inter-state on the one hand, and profoundly influenced and even tempted by the domestic law model. As we will see, these tensions manifest themselves in terms of international law's subjects, its ethical tenor, its organising social principle, its epistemological outlook, its normative structure, its relationship to domestic law, and its functional *modus operandi*.

Subjective dimension: between states and non-states

Perhaps the defining characteristic of international law traditionally is that it is a law of states rather than individuals. This was not always clearly so: the idea of the '*droit des gens*' or '*jus gentium*' suggested a law that applied to the relationship with foreigners rather than between equal, self-governing units. To modern ears, however, the very word 'inter-national' suggests a system geared towards the organisation of relations between self-governing collectivities. Statehood comes with a bundle of unique privileges including a monopoly of internationally legitimate violence (whatever that may be at any one time) and the ability to bring international claims. International law is in the first place that legal system which confers full legal personality only on states. Much of international law is devoted to protecting what one might call this 'monopoly of subjecthood', and the sovereignty that is its basis (see also Chapter 2). For example, the law of immunities ensures that states can for the most part not be sued before domestic courts and that certain agents of the state cannot be the object of any measure of execution (e.g. an arrest or a freezing of accounts).

What it means to be a state in this context is typically presented as an objective notion, indifferent to the particular political or ideological make up of states. A state is supposed to be no less a state in that it is federal or unitary, dictatorial or democratic, liberal or illiberal. At the same time, international law has always been associated with processes of excluding certain entities from statehood. Colonisation was, for example, justified by the fact that non-European political entities did not satisfy the demands of sovereignty and could not be expected to abide by the rules of international law. In a deeper sense, the world of states has perhaps always been defined by an 'other' that is incapable or unworthy of sovereignty.

Moreover, even as states are recognised as the principal subjects of international law, the international legal order has long witnessed the emergence of non-state actors with at least limited international capacity. Beginning in the late nineteenth century, international organisations were created that have increasingly been seen as endowed with international legal personality. In addition, a number of non-state actors – public corporations like the East India Company, national liberation or rebel movements, multinational corporations – had a more or less recognised status in international law. The Nuremberg tribunal made it clear that individuals too can be 'subjects' of international criminal law, and the growth of international human rights protection systems has given individuals the right of petition before at least some international bodies.

However, these non-state actors have only derivative or partial status as subjects of international law. They do not challenge the primacy of states as the only subjects partaking of the full range of rights and privileges conferred by international law. For example, international organisations can only do that which they have been mandated to do by states. Yet this recurrent recognition of non-state actors deeply influences international law's physiognomy.

Ethical dimension: between pluralism and cosmopolitanism

International law represents more than just the legal system of inter-state relations; it can also be said to classically express a certain ethos of pluralism. That ethos is deeply embedded in European history: the shattering of the aspiration to a single Christian realm following the Reformation and the traumatic wars of religion. The Treaty of Westphalia entrenched the principle *cujus reo, ejus religio* – essentially the idea that the global system would be a safer place, after three decades of devastating war, if each country were governed according to the monarch's religion. The idea also embodied a grudging respect for difference. Against the claims of a universal Holy Roman Empire, the emerging system of states, complete with a rudimentary system of minority protection in the form of internal religious tolerance, was one that promised to resist the urge to impose a single vision of the common good globally.

In this view, international law is based on a belief in the incommensurability of beliefs, and the impossibility of operating under a single unifying formula of the 'good life'. It is an intellectual extension of liberalism, and as a system is dedicated to protecting a diversity of beliefs. However, the system is certainly not beyond considering that certain ethical values transcend borders and are, or should be, common to all societies. The prohibitions on torture and on certain other atrocities are typically mentioned as minimum foundations of a common ethical project. Indeed, even as international law promotes a pluralist concept of international society, it also serves to suppress ways of life seen to be incompatible with those common values. The 'standard of civilisation', for example, long served as the arbiter of whether certain societies were fit for international life.

Social dimension: between anarchy and hierarchy

The fact that the principal subjects are states leads to a view of international law as a law operating between equals and without a superior authority. It is often said that the international system is an 'anarchical society' (Bull 2002). Anarchy, which is quite different from chaos, refers to the fact that the system is without superiors. Indeed even the most forceful international organisations are poor candidates for 'superiority' given that they exercise their usually quite limited powers only at the behest and tolerance of states. As a result of this anarchical structure, classical doctrine asserts that no international law can be imposed upon states except of their own choosing. International law tends to start from a position of complete freedom of states that it then attempts to curtail, rather than from a position of obligation from which zones of liberty might emerge (*S.S. Lotus*, Advisory Opinion, PCIJ (1927) Ser. A No. 10, p. 4). Moreover unlike domestic projects, the international legal project is largely procedural rather than purposive; it is about coordination rather than subordination, a system aimed at protecting coexistence rather than some common substantive goal (Oakeshott 1991; Nardin 1988). International law gives states the tools to achieve certain outcomes, rather than telling them what outcomes they should reach.[1]

Yet, for all its concern to express a principle of coexistence, the international system's 'anarchy' has long been premised on the idea that there is such a thing as an 'international society'. This is reflected in, for instance, the idea that there are norms of general customary international law applicable to all states. (For more on sources, see Chapter 8.) Being a sovereign typically involves a duty to respect the sovereignty of others, and this is in itself a recipe

[1] For example, rules regarding diplomatic representation or even the conduct of war do not tell us what diplomatic representations should be geared towards and whether wars should be fought, but only *how* these activities should be conducted.

for certain obligations of care and good faith. The idea of state responsibility has long reflected the idea that states may be made to account for their acts. In other words, even an anarchical society can be quite an ordered society. Aside from specific international organisations, there is also a considerable sense of attempts at global regulation – in Wolfgang Friedman's words, a move from an international system of coexistence to one of cooperation (Friedmann 1964).

Moreover, the international legal system has always been less anarchic than it seems, underwriting vast empires that were strictly hierarchical, and behaving very much as a 'centre projecting a periphery' (Korhonen 1996).

Epistemological dimension: between positivism and naturalism

The birth of international law is intimately linked to thinking from within the tradition of natural law. For many of the so-called 'Founding Fathers' of international law, the law of nations was a corpus whose authority lay in divine law and whose content could be ascertained following the dictates of 'right reason'.

This faith, that international law could be dictated by natural law, evaporated with modernity. At the heart of the modern international legal project is the notion that international law has successfully abstracted itself from ethical, particularly metaphysical and natural law, thinking, to the point where a law does not cease to be law even if all were to agree that it was immoral. This is justified on the basis that in a deeply divided society, what is needed is an international law that can be determined through recognised professional procedures, distinct from the political or moral values that it may, more or less accidentally, embody.

The ideology of international legal positivism is based on the idea that international law is 'observable' from the practice and custom of states, that it can be inferred rationally from their interactions. For example, a feature of traditional international legal work is the practice of documenting state practice (e.g. in nationally published '*recueils*') as an indication of where the law stands. International lawyers are consummate treaty interpreters, and the Vienna Convention on the Law of Treaties (1969) as well as jurisprudence of the International Court of Justice (ICJ) suggest strict ways of construing the intent of drafters. Finally, much scholarly work in international law is 'doctrinal' in nature – seeking to expound fundamental legal principles coherently and according to analytical tools that are themselves taught as part of 'the law'. These various 'tools of the trade' help to distinguish the discipline as one grounded in technocratic rationality and a distinct *savoir faire*.

At the same time, international law finds it difficult to abstract itself entirely from any reference to higher-order norms of morality or justice (Koskenniemi 2005). 'Positive' norms that would entirely clash with deeply held beliefs are resisted. Occasionally, international law directly incorporates references to a quasi-metaphysical residue (e.g. the Martens clause in the laws of war). A certain humanism permeates its value system – international law as the 'gentle civilizer of nations' (Koskenniemi 2001), rather than merely the nations' blunt instrument of self-interest.

Normative dimension: between horizontality and verticality

From a normative point of view, international obligations are norms that apply between equals. International law is 'contractual' rather than 'legislative', an assortment of bilateral and multilateral engagements, each in principle voluntary. Obligations are often presented as synallagmatic in nature, involving an exchange of reciprocal promises. This means that they apply primarily in the sphere of state-to-state relations and there is little pressure by international law to make its norms part of domestic law (for example, states can opt for quite 'dualist' arrangements, wherein international law only becomes part of domestic law if it is incorporated legislatively). Moreover, international law cannot be enforced against foreign states before domestic courts because of sovereign immunities.

Within international law there is little hierarchy between norms, since in theory states can agree to virtually anything. One characteristic of a horizontal system is that, in dealing with the consequences of breaches, it only knows of the equivalent of 'contractual' (i.e. treaty violation) or 'extra-contractual' (violation of a non-treaty obligation) responsibility. There is no delictual, still less criminal, responsibility because, all norms being 'equal', the consequences of their violation are also essentially the same. In terms of adjudication, this is manifested by the fact that litigation traditionally occurred only when one state sued another. Moreover, the system was reluctant, with a few exceptions, to allow a state to sue in the exercise of a sort of '*actio popularis*', acting in the public interest (*South-West Africa* cases, *Second Phase*, ICJ Reports 1966, p. 6, 47).

Yet these dimensions are also quite contingent. International law can hardly be said to have always operated on a level ('horizontal') playing field, and 'unequal treaties', in various guises, have long been a characteristic of the international legal order. Although agnostic about modes of implementation, international law does consider that states' domestic legal arrangements are no defence to a violation of their obligations under international law, thus creating some pressure to incorporate these obligations into domestic law when appropriate. Moreover, the international legal system is prone to its own internal push towards making its norms and enforcement more vertical. There has long been a debate on the possibility of the 'criminal' responsibility of the state. Even if that debate led nowhere, the idea that certain norms apply *erga omnes* means that third states which cannot show a direct interest may nonetheless be justified in complaining about their violation. Moreover, the case of individual criminal responsibility suggests that the system already considers that certain violations fundamentally endanger international existence and should be marked by particular stigma.

Functional dimension: between decentralisation and centralisation

Finally, and perhaps most significantly for practical purposes, international law can be said to traditionally lack some of the key hallmarks of a functioning domestic legal order: a centralised legislative body, a compulsory court system, and centralised enforcement. More than that, one could argue that these functions are not strictly separated in the international sphere, and that what counts as legislation or adjudication or enforcement is at times hard to distinguish.

The absence of central legislative structures is typically seen as less problematic than the absence of compulsory jurisdiction or centralised enforcement. It reflects the fact that international law's mode of emergence was traditionally highly peculiar, and had more to do with the diffuse and bottom-up crystallisation of norms over time, than the adoption of a clear centralised legal framework, a feature that was seen as problematic by newly independent states who had not existed when the norm supposedly came into existence. It also explains the classically central role of custom as a source of international law, emerging from consistent practice and *opinio juris* (see Chapter 8). As a result, the work of international lawyers has often been qualitatively different from that of domestic lawyers in that much time and energy are devoted to elucidating the authority of sources and the content of norms. These typically have to be gleaned from custom or general principles of law, whereas domestic lawyers can count on constitutions, codes, laws and a wealth of judicial decisions.

At the same time, international legal work is often seen to move towards greater centralisation and institutionalisation. Starting from the great diplomatic congresses of the nineteenth century to the emergence of modern global conferences, the rise of international organisations equipped with deliberative fora has given a distinctly quasi-legislative tinge to much international norm production.

For a long time, the international system lacked permanent international courts; thus states, if they were so inclined, had to turn to forms of *ad hoc* settlement of disputes. Voluntary mediation or arbitration was the most that international law offered. This began to change with the establishment of the Permanent Court of International Justice (PCIJ) in 1922 and the International Court of Justice in 1946. The ICJ's lack of compulsory jurisdiction no doubt significantly limits its ability to act very differently from arbitrators. International courts also have limited powers of enforcement, even though their judgments are formally binding. Yet the permanent character of these international judicial institutions and the creative uses to which they are put,[2] alongside a number of regional courts with more compulsory arrangements, means that the international legal system is no longer one that can be defined by a total absence of judicial settlement.

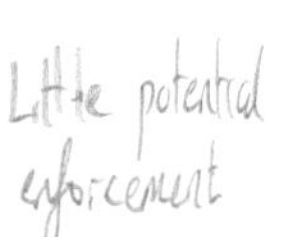

The international legal system has traditionally had little enforcement capability in the form, for example, of an international executive. This fundamental weakness of international law is all too well known, and has been exposed time and time again, particularly in relation to the unlawful use of force by powerful states (e.g. the invasion of Iraq in 2003). Short of a reliable sanction, there may be few concrete legal consequences that will flow in practice from violating certain norms of international law. The system does nonetheless rely routinely on a degree of decentralised

[2] These have included solicitation of significant advisory opinions by international organisations (on the *Legality of the Threat or Use of Nuclear Weapons* of 8 July 1996 or on the *Legal Consequences of the Construction of a Wall in the Occupied Palestinian Territory* of 9 July 2004), and attempted exploitation of undervalued compromisory clauses (e.g. the *LaGrand* and *Avena* cases on the basis of the Vienna Convention on Consular Relations, or the *Georgia* v. *Russia* case on the basis of the Convention on the Elimination of Racial Discrimination).

enforcement. The traditional focus in international law is on non-execution, counter-measures and even reprisals as remedies for breaches of international obligations. The most spectacular form of 'self-help' is self-defence, as anticipated in article 51 of the UN Charter. Moreover, elements of centralisation of sanctions are perceptible. Although tasked principally with maintaining international peace and security, the Security Council has increasingly incorporated elements taken from international law and justice to define its core mission, to the point that some see it as at least an occasional enforcer of international law.

Ontology: is international law 'law'?

As the above discussion shows, the classical characteristics of international law are themselves problematic and contentious. There is a perception that the lack of centralised organs weakens international law. Indeed some are driven to make the radical claim that international law does not deserve to be called 'law'.

The debate about international law's 'law-like' nature was initially spurred in the nineteenth century in the English realm by John Austin's statement that international law is 'law improperly so-called' (Austin 1832 [1995]). It provoked a long series of responses and counter-responses, evidence that, if anything, international lawyers were piqued by the suggestion. Indeed, international law is a law that seemingly cannot much rely on 'habitual obedience' nor do without the constant invocation of arguments as to why it should be respected.

Nonetheless, there had also long existed the opposite perception, that the critique of international law is excessive and misguided, and that the debate about its 'law-like' nature had been futile. According to this view, these doubts largely arise from a definition of law solely informed by domestic concerns, and such a definition is both reductionist and claims too much (Williams 1945). Even constitutional law in most countries is self-enforcing, but this does not give rise to questions about its 'legal' character. Moreover, it is important to note the ideological motives behind debates on 'international law as law': when some argue that international law is or is not law, they might be making a point about the (il)legitimacy of the international legal order, or about the primacy of the local over the global.

At a certain level, whether international law is law is also a matter of 'belief', or 'sentiment' and thus the debate about whether it is 'really law' can be retold as a debate about whether it has 'really been thought of as being "really law"'. Of course, the sentiment that international law exists – or does not – is likely to wax and wane depending, for example, on international events that seem to confirm or deny its existence (wars signal the breakdown and weakness of law; major institutional advances herald its renovation); or the level of ideological divisions (Soviet jurists during the Cold War would gladly have done away with bourgeois international law or rewritten it entirely; the end of the Cold War seemed to briefly herald a new international order); or whether any combination of actors sees it as a worthwhile project and invest significant resources in it (the Versailles Conference, the few years that followed the Second World War, decolonisation and the end of the Cold War come to mind as eras that have been defined by international legal imagination).

But the belief about whether international law is 'law' does hinge partly on the theoretical and doctrinal debates and it is to these that we now turn. What differentiates thinkers on this crucial question is that for some international law's weak decentralised features make it less of a legal system; for others, international law's decentralised features are irrelevant to its legal character; and for yet others, these features are a reason to change international law, to turn it into something more resembling domestic law. Finally, there are those who believe that we should simply strive to better understand international law as a different type of law, and those who find the whole debate to be a misguided effort that prevents us from asking the real questions about the ends of international law. For the purposes of discussion, these stylised positions can be roughly represented as five currents: the 'deniers', the 'idealists', the 'apologists', the 'reformists' and the 'critics'.

The 'deniers'

The deniers, going back to Hobbes, challenge the proposition that international law is law and are sceptical that a law between equals can be anything other than 'morality'. Generally, this analysis is based on a perception of what international law lacks, namely some form of centralised and systematic enforcement. For John Austin, for example, international law was not law because it lacked 'command backed by force', which Austin identified as the defining characteristic of law (Austin 1875, 86). After the Second World War, political 'realists' often emphasised that only national interests could account for how states behaved, and that international law was a system ill suited to the social reality it was supposed to preside over (Carr 1946). According to them, international law functioned only when no significant national interest was involved, and otherwise provided a normative gloss on decisions taken for other reasons. In our era, this critique has been renewed by scholars in law and economics who tend to see state behaviour as informed by rational 'economic' calculations (Goldsmith and Posner 2005). International law is thus either the name given to what states actually do for other reasons that have little to do with the pull of norms or, again, is a largely irrelevant body of symbols.

Deniers particularly criticise international lawyers for thinking that international law is the cause of that of which it is only the consequence. For example, if states do not go to war it is not because an international norm prohibits them from doing so, but because they deem it not to be in their national interest. The 'norm' that emerges as a result of the factual exceptionality of war is merely the appearance of a norm – it has significance only as long as states deem it in their interest to respect it. Even if states superficially engage in patterns of normalised legal interaction, what matters is that they do so for their own reasons, they will not commit to doing so in matters of life and death, and resort to a flagrant violation of 'international law' always remains an option. The lack of compulsory international jurisdiction is also a favourite target of the deniers. They point out that the fact that states can join at will, and withdraw more or less at will, from arrangements requiring them to submit their disputes to adjudication makes international law at best into a tool (to be used based on its usefulness) rather than a framework (binding and determinative).

For these reasons, deniers are often *radical* deniers in that they do not see that international law could *ever* become fully law and, as political realists, posit the primacy of force and the national interest (even endowing it with a measure of moral respectability) in international relations. They reject the idea that an anarchical society is a society at all in that it cannot impose or enforce obligations on its members. They emphasise the priority of the sovereign over any notion of international society. At best, international law is only the sum of self-imposed limitations by states, a mere 'system of promises' that can come unwound at states' discretion.

The 'idealists'

At the other end of the spectrum, the 'idealists' (understood as those who believe in the power of ideas rather than ideals) consider that international law is law because it is somehow mandated by some higher source. According to them, not everything is derived from sovereign consent. International law, even as a law for sovereigns, has its own sources of authority. Where the deniers see international law as 'only' morality, some idealists refuse to draw a neat distinction between morality and law, and argue that international law is law *because* it is moral or because it is moral for it to be so. Early modern theologians and lawyers such as Vitoria, Grotius and Pufendorf considered that what they called the law of nations (*jus gentium*) was mandated by natural law (both of divine origin and as ascertainable through 'right reason').

Although such ideas gradually became less popular, they continued to exert a significant residual pull; the idea that international law can be rooted in something higher than itself remained an object of deep fascination. Immanuel Kant, for example, established a strong connection between his *a priori*, transcendental method (practical reason) and the idea of international law. Hans Kelsen, perhaps the lawyer most associated with this current of thought in the twentieth century, considered the existence of the international legal order to depend on an *a priori Grundnorm* (basic norm) – although he was ambiguous about its precise content (Kelsen 1967). For thinkers in this tradition, international law can be derived from an 'ought' rather than an 'is' and is therefore impervious to the facile critique that it is not systematically respected. International law is, in a sense, because it must be. The role of international lawyers is thus to be true to the idea of international law as a legal order. Where the deniers problematise international law's legality, the idealists hypothesise it.

One classic idealist argument is to deny, against all appearances, the centrality of sovereignty, in that there must be some norm antecedent to it that tells us what sovereignty is, and what its proper usages are, since the sovereignty of any within the system must involve others treating it as such. Sovereignty cannot logically be its own legal source, or reveal itself as nothing else than circular force. This idea that there is something prior – and, unmistakably, higher – than the state is the defining mark of idealism, and is particularly apparent in contemporary discourse that emphasises the importance of human rights, for example, as a basic precondition of legitimate

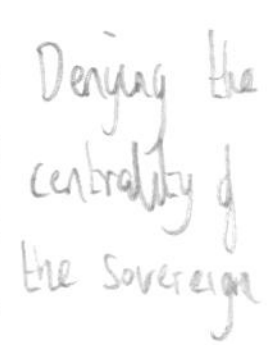

statehood. A similar structure of argument is sometimes used in relation to the law of treaties. For example, it is not, despite appearances, consent that is the basis of the obligatory nature of treaties but the maxim *pacta sunt servanda* (treaties are binding), a principle that is itself prior to any explicit consent of states and provides states with a conceptual roadmap to understand what the consequences of consenting are. The maxim itself may flow from the very need of having treaties or some higher moral inclination that says that promises should be honoured, but it cannot itself be the result of an 'original' treaty.

Idealists also make much of the connection between the idea of international law and the notion of justice. They may for example argue that international law exists because it embodies a particular concept of justice. That concept need not be substantive and may rather, in the tradition of Lon Fuller, represent some inherent property of the law's fairness or legitimacy (Brunnée and Toope 2010).

The 'apologists'

The apologists, as a loosely defined school of thought, reject both the deniers and the idealists. They start from the reality of the social practice that describes itself as international law, and infer from some of its characteristics a *sui generis* legal character. Although they are not necessarily hostile to the improvement of international law's mechanisms, they usually see international law as 'not all that bad', and stress the need to see what works rather than constantly seeking to reinvent the system. Some apologists even see some of the claimed deficiencies of a decentralised system to be 'necessary evils'. Rather than applying a theoretical definition of law taken from the domestic experience, they tend to scrutinise international law to identify its '*génie propre*'.

There are many scholars who fall in this rich, intermediary vein which is often informed by the experience of international legal practice; they are less interested in language games and note that most international lawyers do not pause to ask whether international law is really law but simply apply it as such. The starting point is typically one that stresses, for all the absence of sanctions, the extent to which international law is – in fact and contrary to realist claims – more often respected than not. Apologists insist that 'almost all nations observe almost all principles of international law and almost all of their obligations almost all of the time' (Henkin 1979).

They allow for the possibility that there exist various shades of legality and illegality, rather than adopting a strict 'conformity/violation' polarity. If nothing else, in a sort of homage paid by vice to virtue, states rarely boast that they have violated international law – instead, typically arguing that they did not, or that the law does not say what their adversaries say it does. This, surely, is evidence that law matters. The legal affairs departments of Foreign Ministries typically spend a lot of time advising governments of their obligations in advance, and this advice tends to be taken seriously. The overall image is one in which violations are not 'quite as bad as they are made out to be', and international law is more often honoured by respect than in the breach.

Why this is so is a puzzle to which apologists have no dearth of answers. Sociologically inclined international lawyers from Westlake to Abi-Saab stress the deeply social nature of international law (*ubi societas, ibi jus*) and the primacy of the social over individual units (Abi-Saab 1996). International law must exist since (although this seems to beg the question) international society exists.[3] That society is shaped by values and processes that are tailored to its aims, however limited, and evidenced by a considerable degree of non-hostile interaction. Constructivists emphasise how international law is not imposed from the outside upon preconstituted sovereign subjects, but powerfully shapes this subjecthood (Wendt 1999). This idea of international society as the basis for international law is given more credence by the development of many international institutions in the modern period.

Many have pointed out that, in such a social system, there are other reasons to respect law – including municipal law – than fear of force. Some reach for psychological analysis to reveal a general 'propensity to comply', or adduce a greater propensity to comply in certain regimes (e.g. liberal democratic ones) (Slaughter 1995); or focus on the role of 'norm entrepreneurs' domestically in encouraging compliance (Koh 1998). International law is complied with on a regular basis through soft means. Diplomacy, reporting, informal dispute settlement of various sorts, and increasingly mechanisms such as conditionality all have a role in maintaining at least a semblance of regularity and law-abidingness in international society.

[3] In this, defenders of international law's foundation in the social nature of international interaction have a proximity with scholars of international relations (e.g. the so-called 'English school') who, because they recognise the existence of an international society, are inclined to take international norms seriously (e.g. Bull 2002).

Indeed some apologists may seek to blur the distinction between interest and obligation, finding that the credibility of international law as law lies in the fact that it corresponds to a deeper structure of state interest.[4] For example, reciprocity is both a property of international legal rules and an inbuilt reason to respect them. Moreover, even if enforcement is at times insufficient (which apologists concede may sometimes be the case), the argument is that enforcement is not as central to the definition of law as it made out to be. In seeking to show how a legal order is compatible with substantial decentralised enforcement, they invoke the precedents of primitive societies, in which law is enforced through retaliation by victims against offenders. They point out that the high incidence of crime in domestic legal systems does not generally lead people to question its legal character. Instead, they propose more refined formulas of what constitutes law and, consequently, international law. For example, Franck has drawn attention to the 'power of legitimacy' of certain norms and institutions as a crucial factor in encouraging compliance (Franck 1990).

In redefining international law as something other than constraint, while avoiding the critique that it is nothing other than morality and arguing for its usefulness, apologists emphasise the extent to which international law provides guidance and tools to deal with problems – the extent to which it is, for example, a useful 'process' (Higgins 1995). In this view, international law provides an indispensable tool of communication that enables social life by limiting misunderstandings, stabilising expectations, and increasing transparency; it leads to mutually satisfying outcomes that are compatible with at least a long-term view of the national interest and may even satisfy a certain sovereign aspiration to international morality or justice.

As a result, apologists are prone to view with more indulgence what others have sometimes seen as congenital deficiencies of international law. For example, they may find virtue in modes of law-production such as custom, which may be slow and indeterminate but are also evolutive, flexible and adapted to the needs of international society. Even decentralised enforcement is reconcilable with international law's character as law. For example, the recognition of self-defence in the UN Charter can be seen as a way of outsourcing enforcement in exceptional circumstances by a system that can never rule out that it will be dysfunctional and thus allows states to

[4] In this they see the genius of international law – its ability to closely chart an underlying social structure – where deniers see its fundamental irrelevance.

'take things in their own hands'. An interesting 'apologetic' argument, in this respect, is George Scelle's idea of 'dédoublement fonctionnel' (Scelle 1956). Although Scelle deplored the bluntness of 'self-help' as an instrument of international law enforcement, he also suggested that in pursuing their national interest, states might at least at times be doing international law's work for it. Some go so far as to consider that 'war' is part of international law enforcement (or at least just wars are). In other words, a state that defends itself against an act of aggression is obviously doing so largely for itself, but it also, in the process, vindicates the international norm against unlawful attacks.

The 'reformists'

A distinct and often vigorous current, that has always existed, expresses an aspiration to 'reform' international law. The 'reformists' do not deny that international law as it exists is better than no law, but they are frustrated with its primitiveness and with the apologists' rationalisation of its particular legality. A long line of reformist commentators have tended to see 'apologists', in particular, as 'sorry comforters' (Kant 1970, 103). Taking direct aim at their rationalisations, van Vollenhoven, for example, once deplored the 'servile science of jurisprudence, *ancilla potestatis*' which 'instead of directing attention all the time to the shortcomings of a "law" possessing no sanctions or guarantees ... contracted the habit of pleading that a law of peace which is continually ignored was none the less a "law" of spotless character and beyond reproach' (van Vollenhoven 1932 [1936]).

Reformists are wary of a state-centred international law that they see as ultimately incapable of transcending egotistical national interests. In other words, they consider that 'international law would be more law if only it were different' and typically militate for international law to shed its anomalous specificity and become more like domestic law. As Hersch Lauterpacht, a reformist and one of the twentieth century's most influential international lawyers, once put it, 'the more international law approaches the standards of municipal law the more it approximates to those standards of morals and order which are the ultimate foundation of all law' (Lauterpacht 1932, 318). The reformists' is an evolutionary conception of international law, essentially biding its time until the conditions of international interdependence are such as to make the *civitas maxima* a reality. The 'domestic analogy' may not be a good way to analyse the current international system, but it is put forward as a good programme for international law.

Reformists typically argue for a 'purposive' concept of international law. Asserting the commonality of basic values, they discredit the idea that international law is necessarily a law of coexistence or at best of cooperation deprived of *telos*. They focus on the promotion of such values as human rights, free trade, and a clean environment. Theirs is a faith in the possibility of determining common ends for the global community and in the power of international law to articulate these (Lasswell and McDougal 1992). Arguably, they support the elimination of some of international law's foundational features, including the very idea of international law as a law between states – i.e., what may be called the 'normalisation' of international law. Collective security, for example, is an essential building block in a world in which decisions regarding the use of force are outside the purview of sovereign discretion. The reformists thus subscribe to more or less federalist ideas about 'world government', and see international law as imperfect but with the dynamic potential to evolve into a system like domestic law.

The 'critics'

A fifth view in the debate on 'international law as law' takes issue with the very premise of this debate. It sees it as either a distraction or a thin veil to cover the reality of international law as a system of exclusion and oppression. 'Critics' are not simply impatient with the debate, as apologists may be. Rather, they see the debate as part of an omnipresent and professionally narcissistic structure of legitimisation, of portraying international law as something else than it is, and of defending the status quo. In fact, they see the problem as badly posed: the question is not whether a 'horizontal' international law is really law, but whether international law is really 'horizontal' in the first place. Where classical international lawyers see it as pluralistic, horizontal and decentralised, critical theorists, especially those coming from the Third World, have long argued that whatever conditions prevail between European powers certainly do not apply in their relations to non-European entities.

To them, the question whether 'international law is law', begs the question who is asking and of whom? The debate as currently structured has largely occurred, for example, between European or Western theorists and seeks to understand the particular jurisprudential anomalies that result from a law between equals. However, for most of its history international law has not been a law between equals. It has, rather, been a law that defines who is equal and therefore enjoys subjecthood – i.e. rights and obligations – in law, and who is unequal and therefore a mere 'object' of the law (Anghie 1996). The debate on 'international law as law' fails to acknowledge that many of the founding concepts of international law are derived from this process of exclusion (Anghie 2005). Critics particularly take issue with the idealists' notion of international law as law irrespective of the real conditions of its operation. They also express disquiet with the apologist theme of international law as a law that operates within an unproblematised 'society of nations', when that 'society' is precisely the source of exclusion.

The critics share some affinity with the deniers, but they are less committed to a strong view that 'international law is not law properly so-called'. Rather, they see that metaphysical debate to be secondary. They caution against making a fetish of the question of 'what is law' irrespective of the social relations within which it is embedded. International law may well be some sort of law and, indeed, it is because of its ability to define certain areas of law that it can circumscribe spaces for non-law. The critics may also share something with the reformists in thinking that international law should be other than it is, except that theirs is an insistence on making good international law's original promise of protecting the pluralism of international life.

Dynamics: international law as a system on the move

The debates on 'international law as law' focus on international law's perceived characteristics, but it would be a mistake to treat these as constant. International law is constantly evolving as part of an essentially dynamic and unstable international system, so that even the question of international law's character must be answered against changing reference-points. For example, the debate was a different one during the Cold War or in the context of decolonisation, and has of late been considerably influenced by globalisation and what that portends for our understanding of law (Mégret 2008). It is also a debate that is shaped by its actors, of which there are an increasing number with divergent views about what international law should be.

In this respect, the popular linear view of international law as progressing from coexistence to cooperation to possibly integration may be dangerously simplifying. International law also 'regresses' periodically. Moreover, there is no reason to think that international law as it has been must of necessity remain that way. Rather than being stagnant or straightforwardly headed towards progress, international law is perhaps better conceived as a legal system which permanently oscillates between four tendencies: its own surpassing, absorption, dissolution and renewal. International law's peculiar nature as a legal system emerges from the problem of maintaining a *via media* between those tendencies.

Surpassing: centralising hopes and resolving contradictions

Perhaps one of the most enduring images of international law is that which represents it as leading, through fits and starts no doubt, to the centralisation of the system, i.e. to world government or something quite like it. International law, in other words, is destined to become much more like domestic law. This is the reformists' dream become reality and it suggests an exit route for international law 'from above'. This vision is currently popular; the advent of a more centralised global legal system is a recurrent theme in international legal discourse.

While even in the past international law was tempted by centralisation, it effectively avoided becoming so centralised as to no longer be international at all. Increasingly however, the line between cooperation, integration and some form of federalisation is becoming unclear. This is evident in the emergence of strong regional organisations, particularly the European Union (as seen through the debate on whether EU law is still 'international law', de Witte 1994). It is also quite clear from the rise of international judicial institutions such as international human rights and criminal tribunals that seem to significantly by-pass state sovereignty. The increasingly legislative role of international organisations and conferences not only in policy-making but also in administrative rule-making is also part of a trend that suggests substantial transfers of sovereignty to the supranational. States have also begun to trust international adjudicatory mechanisms to the point where decentralised means of enforcement (e.g. non-execution, counter-measures) are frowned upon (see further Kingsbury, Chapter 9).

This willingness to enforce its norms more forcefully is in turn revealing of an increased tendency to see respect for certain norms as crucial to international order. Ideas of *jus cogens* and *erga omnes* norms have gone from being doctrinal curiosities to being taken seriously, as evidenced in the rise of an 'international public order' and ideas of international criminal responsibility. Characteristically, a whole school of thought has emerged that seeks to think in 'constitutional' terms about the international legal order, and in so doing takes international law a step further towards becoming like domestic law: international law is both 'constituted' by certain international values and 'constituting' of an international order (Klabbers, Peters and Ulfstein, 2009). At a certain level, 'values' almost become more important than formal positive arrangements, so that, for example, states should occasionally be willing to step in to protect threatened populations even when the Security Council does not authorise them to do so (e.g. NATO's intervention in Kosovo) (Cassese 1999).

This tendency towards hierarchy is also revealing of a trend for international law to become more 'substantively committed'. International law's subject matter has grown considerably (trade, the environment) and incursions in matters that were traditionally the exclusive province of states have become increasingly marked (human rights). This produces significant overlaps between international and domestic law and puts at the forefront of international legal thinking issues of 'vertical' integration that used hardly to arise. Implementation becomes all important, as does the possibility of individuals invoking international law directly before domestic and, ultimately, international courts. International law increasingly becomes a 'law of laws' that prescribes the content of domestic legal regimes and oversees their operation rather than simply safeguarding the conditions of their independent existence.

Although the system may still acknowledge pluralism as one of its defining values, states are increasingly asked to subscribe to a minimum core of values, most notably those centring on international human rights. The latter are often presented as representing only a thin consensus, but typically prejudge a number of issues that would have traditionally been left to the sovereign. Human rights is increasingly committing states to a certain view of the 'good society', as evident in the increasingly explicit disparagement of societies that fail to attain that ideal domestically. Sovereignty remains but is so riddled with caveats and under such constant scrutiny that it can no longer be described as the ordering principle of the international legal order.

Little by little, given the breadth, depth and seriousness of commitments that states are supposed to undertake as part of the package of being a member of the international community, the impression emerges that the idea of an international law of coexistence does not do justice to the increasingly purposive nature of international association. Through increased interdependence and solidarity, yesterday's society of 'indifferents' is giving way to a 'community' (Simma and Paulus 1998) of, if not friends, at least broadly likeminded and neighbourly 'citizen-states'. In some regional contexts, coexistence has perhaps most clearly been transcended for the benefit first of cooperation, then of an integration that significantly blurs the distinction between the international and the domestic. International law becomes a global law of mankind, a cosmopolitan law displacing the sovereign as the ultimate community of reference.

Absorption: imperialism and the decline of international law

Contrary to the relatively rosy scenario of an international law pulling itself by its own bootstraps out of irreducible plurality, a darker scenario lurking in the background is that of international law falling prey to its old nemesis: imperialism (Cohen 2004). At regular intervals (Westphalia, Versailles, decolonisation), international law's genesis and rejuvenation have been profoundly linked to the breakdown, both conceptual and practical, of empires. Conversely, the rise of empires has often put international law in a delicate situation in which it risks being instrumentalised, sometimes for its own subversion. Herein lies the paradox: although international law may well express an ethos that is fundamentally at odds with that of imperialism, it has also proved very capable of justifying imperialism. And whilst horizontal anarchy may well be an apt description of the relations prevailing between some states, it has often in practice been complemented by vertical hierarchy vis-à-vis others (Keene 2002).

To parallel a question that Richard Rorty once put at the heart of his thinking about human rights (not 'what are human rights' but 'who is human?') (Rorty 1993), what matters is not 'what are the rights and duties of states?' but 'who is a state?' In that respect, a long tradition, from nineteenth-century colonialism's claims that non-European lands are '*terra nullius*' to the vision of 'collapsed states' incapable of discharging their functions or of 'criminal states' whose populations are in need of saving has sought to deny statehood or full statehood to a certain states (Simpson 2004). The world according to imperialism is separated between 'civilised' and 'uncivilised', 'democratic' and 'non-democratic', 'law abiding' and 'rogue'. There are deep continuities between the formal colonialism of yesterday, and post-colonial enterprises of informal economic domination or cultural subjugation. At the very least, the traditional principle of the equality of states is severely put in question.

Rather than simply a rejection of sovereignty, this logic is often based on an assertion of the *über*-sovereignty ('imperial sovereignty') of some and the denial of the sovereignty of others. Legitimate war, for example, becomes a monopoly of imperial powers, whilst rogue states' exercise of self-defence is presented as a violation of the international order. Obligations are owed to the empire that it does not owe to its subjects. The support of the international legal project by the hegemon, then, is obtained at great cost to international law including the ultimate price, the fact that the hegemon itself is not susceptible to that law. International law becomes a law of domination, subjugation and homogenisation, whose discourse of universalism thinly masks its logic of unipolar power, its role limited to giving the subjects of domination 'clear indications of what is expected of them' (Vagts 2001).

Dissolution: the new transnationalism and the waning of the state

An alternate tendency for international law is not one in which it is absorbed from above by the logic of empires or resolves its contradictions through centralisation, but one in which it is taken over by developments that 'bite' at its very foundation 'from below' (Mathews 1997). The challenge here is not only to the internationalism of international law but also its very publicness, and to the monopoly of states on the formulation and development of international law. To use an image, rather than transcending its ceiling, international law sees its conceptual floor collapse. Rather than an excess of centralisation, international law is rendered brittle by an excess of decentralisation. Rather than specific, territorially determined empires, the international legal real becomes suffused with the logic of 'Empire', an a-territorial and a-temporal structure of global domination profoundly implicated in the production of legitimate violence (Marks 2003).

This idea of an international law transcending the state altogether has had precedents such as the *lex mercatoria*, the famous medieval transnational law of merchants. It is anchored in a periodic distrust of the state that is perceived as corrupt, sub-optimal, inefficient or unjust. The new transnational law occasionally seeks to circumvent the state entirely by reaching its regulatory arm all the way to non-state actors (corporations, armed movements, individuals, non-governmental organisations (NGOs)). At best the state serves as a sort of conveyor belt for instructions coming from above; at worst it is seen as an irrational impediment to a work of global regulatory homogenisation facilitating, most notably, the operation of the world economy. Infra-state actors may even conspire in hand with supranational ones to unhinge the last remnants of sovereign resistance.

International law thus increasingly operates in the interstitial space between the public and the private, becomes hybridised and eventually even fully privatised. Law is produced by the actors themselves (self-regulation) rather than the sovereigns (e.g. the Global Compact),[5] traditional intergovernmental relations are replaced by occasionally shadowy horizontal regulatory networks that link governmental officials in communities of expertise (e.g. the Basle Committee); 'governance' (the G7 or G20, the IMF Board of Governors) replaces diplomacy (Slaughter 1997); networks take over formal international organisations; vertical relationships (for example, international organisations to civil society, international courts to individual petitioners) substitute for horizontal state-to-state relations; accountability replaces (international) responsibility; adjudication is replaced by arbitration; constitutionalism stands in for democracy; lawyers give way to technocrats.

Under this scenario, international law becomes virtually indistinguishable from domestic law except through its broad, ubiquitous character. Fragmentation is the order of the day, one in which functional logic dominates public integration. A bizarre new legal geography emerges, one made up of islands of law in a sea of regulation. Territory becomes secondary as an ordering principle as the logic of law increasingly follows persons (e.g. the law of foreigners) or the exercise of power (e.g. occupation) or operates entirely in de-territorialised realms (e.g. the internet). Demands against the system manifest themselves in the form, at best, of 'global administrative law' (Krisch and Kingsbury 2006).

With the fall of the sovereign, it is also the positive and centralised character of international law that is challenged: whereas public international law adopted a formalist stance focused on sources, global regulation draws its inspiration from law and economics, rational choice and institutional

[5] The Global Compact is a UN initiative to encourage corporations worldwide to accept certain sustainable and socially responsible commitments.

design theories. Establishing the pedigree of norms whilst refraining from evaluating their substantive content is seen as *passé* since 'we' know what the 'optimal' norms are. Characteristics that were once thought to be flaws of the system (e.g. its *ad hoc* character) are glorified. The venerable international society of states is replaced by a global system of states, individuals, corporations and networks, in which no actor stands necessarily above any other. The legal system that emerges is one that is perhaps best suited to what has sometimes been described as the 'new medievalism' (Friedrichs 2001).

Renewal: appeal and limits of the *via media*

Finally, there remains the possibility of a more fundamental renewal of the international legal project. 'Restoration' of a mythical classical international legal system made up of jealous and absolute sovereigns is perhaps the least likely scenario, given the contrary pushes of both centralisation and fragmentation. However, there would seem to be room for both an extension and a deepening of the international legal project that is perhaps best conceived as international law living up to its promise.

In many ways, especially in its classical form, the project was never fully realised, and excluded many who sought to partake in it. Rather than seeing decolonisation as a 'moment' in the history of international law, one might see it as a never-ending process of resistance to rampant domination of some states by others, opening up the way for a more equitable sharing in international affairs. Perhaps paradoxically, it has often been those forces that were excluded from sovereignty yesterday that have become some of the international legal system's most ardent defenders. In that respect, international law can count on the support of the many who consider that the value pluralism implicit in sovereignty is one of the better protections against the temptation of Empire. The decolonisation of international law is fundamentally an epistemological rather than a simply territorial project, one that would seek to emancipate fully the international legal order from its indebtedness to patriarchy or racism.

Against the formalism and intellectual grandiloquence of ambitions to transcend international law from above, international law could emerge as a renewed locus for classical cooperation, prompted by ever-increasing challenges to global life, particularly the increasingly erratic functioning of the world economy or the threat to the environment illustrated by global warming. This 'Grotian' route to international law is one that is frequently announced by international lawyers under different guises (Lauterpacht 1946). Although it has perhaps never been as challenged as it is today, it may become attractive precisely because of the way it can cancel out some of the more dramatic consequences of alternative routes: neither world state, nor Empire(s), nor private free-for-all.

However, the system will also be increasingly urged to defend its authority against challenges for greater participation, more equitable distribution, and more systematic enforcement. In particular, it will need to be better understood (and better understand itself) as one that, despite its claimed neutrality, has had and continues to have significant distributive impacts. A better understanding of how international law also manufactures exclusion and domination might emerge as an antidote to some of the hubris associated with the discipline. At the same time, international law as a broadly inclusive social project may need to become more imbued with debates about the conditions of an internationally just society (Buchanan 2007; Rawls 2001 and see Pogge, Chapter 17). The difficulty will be for the system of international law to adapt to some of these challenges without disowning itself, or falling prey to the accusation that it is merely a cover for something else.

Conclusion

International law's peculiar approach to law can perhaps best be described as that of a law that is 'in between', characterised simultaneously by what it seeks to escape from (e.g. wars of religion), what it is not (e.g. domestic law), and what it aspires to achieve (perpetuation, surpassing, transformation, etc.). This quality is a precarious one that relies on a particular conjunction of historical forces, preferred subjects, a certain ethos, a concept of society, legal constructs and a functional architecture.

The debate on international law's 'legality' reveals many connections between competing views. In terms of understanding the international-law-as-law debate, idealist contemplativeness, apologetic rationalisation, reformist ambition all share a certain basic faith in the reality of international law; apologists and idealists may find common ground in the idea of 'international society' as the basis of international law – the former seeing it as a basic fact, the latter tempted to idealise society based on a concept of the innate sociability of humans. Apologists can, in their rush to rationalise what is, end up conceding too much and thus come close to the deniers of international law's legal character; apologists and reformists alike tend to share a displeasure with the existing state of international law and a desire to make it more like domestic law; critics, in their displeasure with the emphasis on ontological questions dissociated from the practices of power, can be both deniers and reformists.

The debate, finally, must be understood as a dynamic and constantly evolving one. Many connections exist between different visions of what international law might turn out to be: for instance, the hailing of a global constitutional order in-the-making can serve the powerful by allowing them to dress their exercise of power in universalistic garb (references to 'humanity' in particular may serve interventionist agendas). There is a certain paradoxical affinity between the effort of completing the international project from above and the undermining of the state from below: humanitarian intervention and the *lex mercatoria*, for example, share a diagnosis about the obsoleteness of the state; both the centralising project and that of transnational law may at times be tempted into dangerous alliances with the hegemon to provide credible enforcement. Perhaps more often than not, the system will infelicitously combine aspects of all these: the zealous ordering drive of the centralising aspiration; the willingness of its more powerful subjects to mistake their national interest – or at least *Weltanschauung* – for that of the system; the general sense of chaos and dislocation that comes from the fragmentation of the state.

By the same token, however, these alternative views of global order may also keep each other in check, so that none is ever fully realised. The reformists know that international law's areas of integration are really only pools of regional or sectoral cooperation, where states have a particular interest in creating strong regimes, and that sovereignty is much more resilient than regular announcements of its demise suggest; there is a deep moralising thrust at work in the international system and an ingrained resistance to hegemony that always seems to counterpoise attempts to hijack international law for purely domineering aims; the movement to de-publicise and de-territorialise international law is regularly upset by reassertions of the public sphere and the considerable residual military, economic and symbolic resources of states.

Restoration of a 'classical' international law based solely on a society of states may be unlikely, but so are various scenarios announcing the demise of international law. The tension between models of stasis, change, autopoiesis, reform, progress, and eternal returns is almost palpable. At the intersection of these forces, international law so far remains as the appealing default position of the international system. International law is a legal regime which, despite the best attempts to reform, instrumentalise or dissolve it, best expresses a mixture of diversity and community, power and idealism characteristic of the global system.

Bibliography

Abi-Saab, G., 1996. 'Cours général de droit internationale public', *Recueil des cours de l'Académie de droit international*, 207(I), 1–463

Anghie, A., 1996. 'Francisco de Vitoria and the Colonial Origins of International Law', *Social & Legal Studies*, 5(4), 321–336

Anghie, A., 2005. *Imperialism, Sovereignty and the Making of International Law*, Cambridge University Press

Austin, J., 1875. *Lectures on Jurisprudence, Or, The Philosophy of Positive Law*, R. Campbell (ed.), New York: Henry Holt

Austin, J., 1995. *The Province of Jurisprudence Determined*, W. Rumble (ed.), Cambridge University Press

Brunnée, J. and S. Toope, 2010. *Legitimacy and Legality in International Law: An Interactional Account*, Cambridge University Press

Buchanan, A., 2007. *Justice, Legitimacy, and Self-determination: Moral Foundations for International Law*, New York: Oxford University Press

Bull, H., 2002. *The Anarchical Society: A Study of Order in World Politics*, New York: Columbia University Press

Carr, E. H., 1946. *The Twenty Years' Crisis 1919–1939*, 2nd edn., London: Macmillan

Cassese, A., 1999. 'Ex iniuria ius oritur: Are We Moving towards International Legitimation of Forcible Humanitarian Counter-measures in the World Community?', *European Journal of International Law*, 10(1), 23–30

Cohen, J. L., 2004. 'Whose Sovereignty? Empire versus International Law', *Ethics & International Affairs*, 18(3), 1–24

Franck, T., 1990. *The Power of Legitimacy Among Nations*, Oxford University Press

Friedmann, W., 1964. *The Changing Structure of International Law*, New York: Columbia University Press

Friedrichs, J., 2001. 'The Meaning of New Medievalism', *European Journal of International Relations*, 7(4), 475–501

Goldsmith, J. and E. Posner, 2005. *The Limits of International Law*, Oxford University Press

Henkin, L., 1979. *How Nations Behave: Law and Foreign Policy*, New York: Columbia University Press

Higgins, R., 1995. *Problems and Process: International Law and How We Use It*, Oxford University Press

Kant, I., 1970. 'Perpetual Peace', in *Political Writings*, Hans Reiss (ed.), Cambridge University Press, 93–130

Keene, E., 2002. *Beyond the Anarchical Society: Grotius, Colonialism and Order in World Politics*, Cambridge University Press

Kelsen, H., 1967. *Pure Theory of Law*, New York: University of California Press

Klabbers, J., A. Peters and G. Ulfstein, 2009. *The Constitutionalisation of International Law*, Oxford University Press

Koh, H., 1998. 'How is International Human Rights Law Enforced?', *Indiana Law Journal*, 74, 1397–1417

Korhonen, O., 1996. 'Liberalism and International Law: A Centre Projecting a Periphery', *Nordic Journal of International Law*, 65, 481–532

Koskenniemi, M., 2001. *The Gentle Civilizer of Nations: The Rise and Fall of International Law 1870–1960*, Cambridge University Press

Koskenniemi, M., 2005. *From Apology to Utopia: The Structure of International Legal Argument. Reissue with a New Epilogue*, Cambridge University Press

Krisch, N. and B. Kingsbury, 2006. 'Introduction: Global Governance and Global Administrative Law in the International Legal Order', *European Journal of International Law*, 17(1), 1–13

Lasswell, H. and M. McDougal, 1992. *Jurisprudence for a Free Society: Studies in Law, Science, and Policy*, Leiden: Martinus Nijhoff

Lauterpacht, H., 1932. 'The Nature of International Law and General Jurisprudence', *Economica*, 37, 301–320

Lauterpacht, H., 1946. 'The Grotian Tradition in International Law', *British Yearbook of International Law*, 23(1), 1–53

Marks, S., 2003. 'Empire's Law', *Indiana Journal of Global Legal Studies*, 10(1), 449–466

Mathews, J. T., 1997. 'Power Shift', *Foreign Affairs*, 76(1), 50–66

Mégret, F., 2008. 'Globalisation', in R. Wolfrum (ed.), *Max Planck Encyclopedia of Public International Law*, online

Nardin, T., 1988. 'Legal Positivism as a Theory of International Society', in D. Mapel and T. Nardin (eds.), *International Society: Diverse Ethical Perspectives*, Princeton University Press, 17–35

Oakeshott, M., 1991. *On Human Conduct*, Oxford University Press

Rawls, J., 2001. *The Law of Peoples: With, The Idea of Public Reason Revisited*, Cambridge, MA: Harvard University Press

Rorty, R., 1993. 'Human Rights, Rationality and Sentimentality', in S. Shute and S. Hurley (eds.), *On Human Rights: The Oxford Amnesty Lectures 1993*, New York: Basic Books, 111–135

Scelle, G., 1956. 'Le phénomène juridique du dédoublement fonctionnel', in W. Schätzel and H. Schlochauer (eds.), *Rechtsfragen der Internationalen Organisation: Festschrift für Hans Wehberg*, Frankfurt am Main: Vittorio Klostermann, 324–342

Simma, B. and A. Paulus, 1998. 'The "International Community": Facing the Challenge of Globalisation', *European Journal of International Law*, 9(2), 266–277

Simpson, G., 2004. *Great Powers and Outlaw States: Unequal Sovereigns in the International Legal Order*, Cambridge University Press

Slaughter, A. -M., 1995. 'International Law in a World of Liberal States', *European Journal of International Law*, 6(1), 503–538

Slaughter, A. -M., 1997. 'The Real New World Order', *Foreign Affairs*, 76(5), 183–197

Vagts, D., 2001. 'Hegemonic International Law', *American Journal of International Law*, 95, 843–848

van Vollenhoven, C., 1936. *The Law of Peace*, London: Macmillan

Wendt, A., 1999. *Social Theory of International Politics*, Cambridge University Press

Williams, G., 1945. 'International Law and the Controversy Concerning the Word "Law"', *British Yearbook of International Law*, 22, 146–163

de Witte, B., 1994. 'Rules of Change in International Law: How Special Is the European Community?', *Netherlands Yearbook of International Law*, 25, 299–333

Part II

International law and the state

Statehood: territory, people, government 4

Karen Knop

Introduction

Statehood has long been the central organising idea in the international system. Although there is no generally accepted legal definition of statehood, the best-known formulation is found in the 1933 Montevideo Convention on Rights and Duties of States: defined territory, permanent population, government and capacity to enter into relations with other states. Paradigmatically, territory, people and government coincide in the state to produce international law's map of the world as a jigsaw puzzle of solid colour pieces fitting neatly together.

Although the state as territory–people–government is international law's main device for representing the world, the intersection of this definition with other doctrines of international law complicates the picture. As this chapter shows, the result is a diversity of representational mandates: some states are made to carry one meaning, others another. From different conceptions of the state, the chapter moves next to different models of its centrality. The story it tells about international law scholarship proceeds from the state's twofold significance as the international system's main organising idea. First, on the analogy between states in international society and individuals in a society, states are like individuals. The accent on the state–individual analogy is basic to traditional international law, in which states are central in the sense that they are the only full legal subjects. But are states like individuals in a state of nature, as Thomas Hobbes famously thought, or are they like individuals in a state? Insofar as they tend toward the latter – or the domestic state even serves as the comparator for the international system – then ideas of the state fundamentally organise international law in a second sense. The international system is held up to the domestic state, whether in a concrete analogy or in some more abstract search for appropriate principles or a style of approach. And on this international system–domestic state comparison, the actors in the international system need not be limited to states.

In the 1990s and early 2000s, concerns about identity and difference were reflected in international law's shaping of states and also in thinking about international civil society and forms of representation beyond the state. The breakup of the Soviet Union and Yugoslavia was accompanied by more demanding guidelines from the European Community and the United States for the recognition of new states in that part of the world. The Rwandan genocide, along with humanitarian crises in Somalia, Bosnia and Herzegovina and Kosovo, prompted the development of the 'responsibility to protect' doctrine. Transnational feminist activism galvanised the prosecution of sexual violence in war. The Conference (now Organisation) for Security and Cooperation in Europe (OSCE) established a High Commissioner on National Minorities to identify and seek early resolution of ethnic tensions that might endanger peace, stability or friendly relations between states. Indigenous representatives played a key role in the decades-long development of the 2007 United Nations Declaration on the Rights of Indigenous Peoples, and there is now a UN Permanent Forum on Indigenous Issues, composed of members selected half from nominations by state governments and half in consultation with indigenous organisations. With the rise of a multidisciplinary literature on global governance has come increased attention to a variety of 'non-state actors' – Bill Gates, Osama Bin Laden, Amnesty International, De Beers – and how to model their positions relative to that of states.

Whereas the international law of this period thus pursued forms of identity and difference not captured by the state, this chapter suggests that in the international law literature, the state has more recently made a somewhat unacknowledged return as the central organising idea along both of the dimensions introduced above. Its centrality in the first sense, as actor, has been reinforced by the emergence, particularly in North American scholarship, of an interdisciplinary research agenda with international relations. Although this agenda does not preclude consideration of other actors, when studied they are most often treated empirically as influences on state behaviour, rather than as actors in their own right. A variety of other contemporary work on the global system returns to the centrality of the state in the second sense: it implicitly invokes the domestic state as a repository of ideals for the international system that are most fully theorised and are closest to being realised in the context of domestic states. Unlike in the 1990s and early 2000s, the recognition of non-state actors is less often argued for or against directly in this literature, but instead follows indirectly from ideas about what law is: whether non-state law should be understood as law, whether informal law-making by states has become more important than formal law-making, and so on. These propositions about law, in turn, encounter or anticipate objections that implicitly reintroduce the state as 'the best-stocked normative reservoir from which [responsible politics] may draw and the most persuasive medium in which it may be articulated' (as Neil Walker said of the tradition of constitutionalism, Walker 2001, 57).

The state

Multiple outlines

International law is traditionally based on a simple representational structure: a state speaks for its people in international law by virtue of controlling its territory. But even on the territory–people–government formula, the state is clearly a more complex device for representing the world's inhabitants.

While the paradigm is the territorial state, it goes without saying that not all individuals live within the borders of their state. Hence, the state's work of representation may be done through people as well as through territory. The operative concept here is nationality. International law has historically extended the ambit of the state through the legal implications of nationals abroad. For Francisco de Vitoria, the sixteenth-century Spanish theologian writing on natural and international law, there was a right to visit, in particular to trade with and proselytise to, indigenous peoples in the Americas which, if denied, was grounds for terminating indigenous title to territory and enabled Spain to use whatever force seemed necessary to enforce its rights (Vitoria 1991, 278–286). Indeed, the international law on the treatment of aliens has a longer and more controversial lineage than international human rights law. The protection of nationals can even extend to the use of force, post-UN Charter examples being Israel's 1976 raid on Entebbe and US interventions in Grenada in 1983 and Panama in 1989.

A state can also exercise jurisdiction outside its territory on the basis of nationality, thereby producing a jurisdiction that overlaps or sometimes even replaces that of the territorial state. Perhaps the most striking instance is the historical regime of capitulations established by a system of treaties (the name deriving from the word '*capitulo*' or chapter of a treaty). The rationale for early capitulations was to facilitate trade, and in addition to preferential economic treatment, capitulations gave foreign traders the right to remain under their own state's jurisdiction in recognition of differences in their laws and customs. As the capitulations regimes expanded and the context and dynamics of power changed, they came to symbolise the unjust extension of sovereignty by Western states over non-Western states including China, Egypt, Japan, Morocco and Turkey (formerly the Ottoman Empire). Certain current practices have been criticised as analogous to capitulations, including the immunity granted to foreign nationals serving as peace-keepers or working for international organisations and that granted to foreign private contractors in Iraq (see Bell 2009).

In the leading international case on nationality, decided by the International Court of Justice (ICJ) in 1955, Judge Read wrote, 'To my mind the State is a concept broad enough to include not merely the territory and its inhabitants but also those of its citizens who are resident abroad but linked to it by allegiance ... In the case of many countries ... the non-resident citizens form an important part of the body politic' (*Nottebohm Case (Liechtenstein* v. *Guatemala)*, ICJ Reports 1955, p. 4, 44). He had in mind the imperial powers (France, the United Kingdom and the Netherlands) and also China. Contemporary contexts would include the global movement of labour, corporations operating abroad and, on the horizon, climate change refugees. To illustrate, in 2006, an estimated 150 million migrants world-wide sent some US $300 billion home to their families in developing countries, typically in amounts ranging from $100 to $300 at a time (International Fund for Agricultural Development, 'Sending Money Home').

Judge Read, however, was in dissent. In *Nottebohm*, the Court held that Liechtenstein could not sue Guatemala on behalf of Nottebohm, a naturalised national of Liechtenstein who lived in Guatemala, because his nationality was not based on a 'genuine' or 'effective' link to Liechtenstein; it was not 'the exact juridical expression of a social fact of a connection' (p. 24). 'At the time of his naturalization', asked the Court, did 'Nottebohm appear to have been more closely attached by his tradition, his establishment, his interests, his activities, his family ties, his intention for the near future to Liechtenstein than to any other State?' The Court's answer was 'no'.

As Judge Read's dissent suggests, the Court's judgment in *Nottebohm* had and continues to have a mixed reception. Prior to *Nottebohm*, effectiveness was the test applied when a choice had to be made between two or more nationalities, whereas the Court transformed the test, controversially, into a question of the essence of nationality in international law. Read broadly (which not all do), the case stands for the proposition that while each state determines under its own law who are its nationals, other states are only bound to recognise that state's determination if it represents the person's strongest organic link to a territory – an idea described as belonging to 'a romantic period of international relations' by the Advocate General in the *Micheletti* case decided by the European Court of Justice in 1992 (*Micheletti* v. *Delegacíon del Gobierno en Cantabria*, Case C-369/90, European Court Reports 1992, p. I-04239, para. 5). *Nottebohm* would thus exclude most individuals living outside their state, whether expatriates, immigrants whose lives span old state and new, or citizens of the world. At the same time, the Court did not follow the logic of the genuine link all the way through and treat Nottebohm as a national of Guatemala or alternatively of Germany, his original state of nationality. Not permitted to return to Guatemala to deal with the fifty-seven separate legal proceedings aimed at expropriating all of his property without compensation, Nottebohm was left with no state to take up his claim.

If *Nottebohm* effectively aligns nationality with territory, the opposite is true of international law's greater receptiveness to multiple nationality. Amongst the developments responsible for this change as reflected in the 1997 European Convention on Nationality are 'labour migrations between European States leading to substantial immigrant populations, the need for the integration of permanent residents, the growing number of marriages between spouses of different nationalities and freedom of movement between European Union member States'. In addition, whereas nationality laws used to operate such that a woman upon marriage to a man of a different nationality would automatically lose her own nationality and acquire his, it is now recognised that women should have the same right as men to acquire their spouse's nationality and to transmit their nationality to their children (Explanatory Report, European Convention on Nationality, para. 8; 1979 Convention on the Elimination of All Forms of Discrimination Against Women, article 9). Related to this dissociation of nationality from territory, citizenship scholars are increasingly focused on representation and other issues relating to diasporas, such as whether nationals living abroad can or should be able to vote in elections in the state where they live, the state of their nationality, both or neither (see Spiro 2006). Similarly, sociologists of globalisation are studying other means of political participation, including political initiatives by undocumented workers.

In a certain respect, international human rights law can be seen as picking up where the Court in *Nottebohm* left off by attaching foreigners to the territory with which they have a connection. On the one hand, international human rights law is generally not about membership in a state, but about the entitlement of all individuals everywhere to rights based on a common humanity. The 1966 International Covenant on Civil and Political Rights (ICCPR), for example, explicitly conditions only two categories of rights on nationality or immigration status: political rights, which belong to 'every citizen' (article 25), and freedom of movement, which pertains to persons 'lawfully within the territory' (articles 12 and 13). On the other hand, some human rights respect and protect a connection to territory or to people in a territory. Notably, the rights of indigenous peoples include rights to their land, territory and resources, and the right of persons belonging to minorities, including non-citizens, to enjoy their culture, practise their religion or use their language extends to the exercise of the right in community with other members of the group (article 27). Similarly, international human rights law may attach foreigners to the state with which they have, to put it in *Nottebohm*'s terms, a genuine link. In particular, under certain circumstances, the right to family life has prevented the deportation of a non-national with close ties to family in the deporting state.

Much as the 'people' element of the territory–people–government formula for the state may not coincide perfectly with its borders, so too the other elements may extend beyond the edges of the puzzle piece. Colonisation and occupation can each be understood as the 'government' element by itself; the people and territory governed are not part of the state. States administering colonies were subject to a 'sacred trust': they governed not as the sovereign, but as a trustee bound to act in the inhabitants' best interests. The eventual exercise of self-determination by the people of an overseas colony did not breach international law's prohibition on disrupting the state's territorial integrity because these colonies had a separate legal status. Under the law of occupation, the occupying state governs, but does not acquire, the occupied territory. Israel's occupation of the Palestinian territories exemplifies control over people and territory not part of the state both because the Palestinian people are recognised as having a right of self-determination that has yet to be realised, and because the territories are recognised as occupied by, not as belonging to, Israel (see, for example, *Legal Consequences of the Construction of a Wall in the Occupied Palestinian Territory*, Advisory Opinion, ICJ Reports 2004, p. 136). As opposed to clear-cut puzzle pieces, then, the state as organising idea in the international system is messier, overlapping, with gaps here and there.

Multiple meanings

On the definition of the state as territory–people–government, there is no necessary correspondence between a state and a people. International law does not underwrite the state as authentic, or vouch for some original social compact, or build in democracy. (The right to democracy in the ICCPR is an obligation of, not prior to, the state.) People means 'permanent population', not a community defined by a shared characteristic experienced as objective like ethnicity, race or language (*ethnos*), or one united subjectively by choice (*demos*). The state is defined in terms of power: effective control by a government over a population and territory.

As the discussion of nationality has already suggested, however, there is more to international law's conception of the state. It is not enough to say that the state is the unit of representation in the international system simply because its leadership exercises effective control. International law is actually highly varied in the representational work it has required the state to perform. First, an alternative foundation for the state exists in the principle of self-determination of peoples, incorporated into the 1945 UN Charter and later as a right in the ICCPR and the companion 1966 International Covenant on Economic, Social and Cultural Rights (ICESCR). It is commonplace to describe the principle of self-determination as Janus-faced. In its stabilising mode, self-determination simply repackages the existing principles of sovereign equality and the prohibition of intervention. But in its destabilising mode, it requires the creation of a state to rest on something more than the establishment of order. International law lacks a clear definition of both 'self-determination' and 'people', right and right-holder, but the contrast with representation purely as a function of control is clear.

The partial uptake of the political principle of self-determination into international law – with a contradictory intellectual heritage that includes Johann Gottfried von Herder, Vladimir Lenin and Woodrow Wilson – produced arbitrariness. Some states in international law represent the exercise of self-determination by a people, others do not. Some peoples have their own state, others do not.

International law has limited the revolutionary potential of self-determination in several ways. The right of self-determination was routinised only in the process of overseas decolonisation, specifically of mandate territories under the 1919 Covenant of the League of Nations and trust territories and non-self-governing territories under the UN Charter. Mandate and trust territories were those detached from defeated states after the First and Second World Wars. Non-self-governing territories extended self-determination to all 'territories whose peoples have not yet attained a full measure of self-government' (UN Charter, article 73), narrowed in practice to those geographically separate from and ethnically or culturally distinct from the states administering them (UN General Assembly Resolution 1541 (1960), principle IV). On the dominant approach, self-determination developed into a right in certain categories of cases. In addition to that of overseas colonies, these categories include cases in which a people is subject to alien subjugation, domination or exploitation; and, possibly, relying on the 'safeguard clause' found in the 1970 Declaration on Friendly Relations and on statements in judicial decisions on Quebec, Katanga and Cyprus, when a people is denied any meaningful exercise of its right to self-determination within the state of which it forms a part. The recognition by many states of Kosovo's unilateral declaration of independence has raised the question whether this precedent establishes the possible third category or some new category, or whether it is better understood in legal terms other than self-determination – a question studiously avoided by the International Court of Justice in its advisory opinion of 2010 (*Accordance with International Law of the Unilateral Declaration of Independence in Respect of Kosovo*, Advisory Opinion, 22 July 2010).

The dominant approach to the scope of self-determination does not rest on some underlying normative idea that unifies the established categories, such as the taking of territory, consent to the state or denial of participation in government. It is irrelevant to the interpretation of self-determination, for instance, that the situation of an indigenous people in a settler state or a historical minority may be comparable to that of an overseas colony. This inconsistency drew strong criticism during the drafting of the Declaration on the Rights of Indigenous Peoples (13 September 2007). In the non-binding Declaration, the right of self-determination of indigenous peoples was ultimately expressed in the same language as the right of self-determination of peoples in the two International Covenants, and expanded to provide that 'indigenous peoples, in exercising their right to self-determination, have the right to autonomy or self-government in matters relating to their internal and local affairs, as well as ways and means for financing their autonomous functions' (articles 3 and 4). However, the Declaration also provides that nothing in it may be construed as 'authorising or encouraging any action which would dismember or impair, totally or in part, the territorial integrity or political unity of sovereign and independent States' (article 46(1)).

The main alternative approach to self-determination seeks to render the categories coherent by finding some common normative thread, and thereby extends self-determination further. For example, if the fundamental idea is taken to be the freely expressed will of the inhabitants (Cassese 1995, 128, 319–320), then the right of self-determination of peoples would be operative any time the status of territory is in question. But the rejection of the categories-based approach in favour of coherence means that these scholars struggle with the question of limits on the right.

Some critical scholars have argued that the revolutionary potential of self-determination is contained by the construction of a distinction between normal and abnormal, and the application of self-determination only to the latter situations (Berman 1988; Koskenniemi 1994). For instance, in the 1920 *Aaland Islands* matter, dealing with whether the Swedish-speaking Aaland Islanders had the right to separate from Finland and join Sweden, an international commission of jurists presented self-determination not as a right in international law, but as a fundamental principle that only comes into play when organised state sovereignty is disrupted. In the International Court of Justice case on Kosovo's unilateral declaration of independence, Finland took this position, arguing that an abnormal situation was created by factors including the violent breakup of Yugoslavia and the establishment of an international security presence in Kosovo following the government's persecution of ethnic Albanians, requiring the complete withdrawal of all its military, police and paramilitary forces from Kosovo, and that this abnormality supported granting self-determination special force in respect of Kosovo (Statement of Finland, April 2009).

On any of these approaches (categories, coherence, abnormality), the principle of *uti possidetis* requires that the exercise of self-determination take place within existing borders, whether they are international borders or internal borders such as those between the primary subdivisions of a state. A principal theme of many 1960s critics of self-determination, particularly as applied to Africa, was the contradiction between self-determination understood as the right of colonial peoples to choose their political status freely and the requirement that the resulting configuration preserve the existing colonial boundaries – drawn largely 'with little consideration for . . . factors of geography, ethnicity, economic convenience or reasonable means of communication' (*Territorial Dispute (Libyan Arab Jamahiriya* v. *Chad)*, Separate Opinion of Judge Ajibola, ICJ Reports 1994, p. 6, para. 8; see also paras. 7–12; compare Touval 1966). In a 1986 case involving the Burkina Faso–Mali frontier, the International Court of Justice concluded, though, that the conflict between the two principles was more apparent than real (*Frontier Dispute* (*Burkina Faso* v. *Republic of Mali*), ICJ Reports 1986, pp. 554, 567). The Court characterised the adoption of *uti possidetis* by African leaders, particularly in the Organisation of African Unity's 1964 Cairo Declaration on Border Disputes, as promoting the stability essential for post-colonial states to survive and hence for peoples to consolidate the gains of their struggle for independence. Scholars of nationalism have shown that, over time, even boundaries originally established by force, imperial administration or other outside imposition may become internalised as the parameters of the community, and hence their maintenance is not necessarily in tension with self-determination (Anderson 2006). However, political crises in Africa during the 1980s and early 1990s brought fresh criticism of the neglect of pre-colonial identifications. According to one argument, the artificial borders imposed by colonialism have helped set the continent on a road to ruin, and the map of Africa should instead be redrawn in accordance with a legitimate exercise of self-determination; that is, an exercise undertaken by entities defined along pre-colonial lines (Mutua 1995, 1118).

A second variation amongst states is that although international law is far from furnishing a collective guarantee of democracy (see Chapter 5), it has nevertheless required certain new states or post-conflict states to adopt particular, sometimes intricate and experimental, forms of representative government. In principle, each state is free to choose its form of government – this is the other face of self-determination. However, the recognition of statehood in certain cases has been crafted to reflect the presence of different national, ethnic, religious or cultural groups. (On whether the act of recognition brings the state into being or simply declares the fact of its existence, see Chapter 12.) In the context of new states in Eastern Europe and the Soviet Union, the rights of national and ethnic minorities figured in the US and European Community guidelines for recognition. In a series of opinions delivered in the early 1990s on major legal questions raised by the breakup of Yugoslavia, a Community Arbitration Commission for Yugoslavia created what has been described as a new geometry of identity for the former Yugoslavia: 'une dissociation très remarquable entre la nationalité et la territorialité' (Pellet 1991, 341). In response to the question whether the Serbian population in Croatia and Bosnia and Herzegovina had a right of self-determination, the Commission held that while the borders could not be changed, the Serbian population had minority rights within each state and possibly also, flowing from the broad principle of self-determination, the right as individuals to choose Serbian nationality and thus membership in a trans-border Serbian *ethnos* (Opinion No. 2, 1992). The inter-war system of minority treaties in Central and Eastern Europe, which gave certain minorities the ability to appeal directly to the League of Nations, is a historical precedent for this sort of innovation.

In a 1998 reference on the secession of Quebec, the Supreme Court of Canada raised another way of particularising statehood through recognition, namely, by factoring in compliance with the constitutional process for secession, where one exists. The Court observed that if Quebec acted unilaterally in breach of the constitutional duty to negotiate its independence and to pursue those negotiations in accordance with underlying principles of the Canadian Constitution – which include the rights of minorities – then its claim to statehood might not be accepted as legitimate by the international community. This having been said, international law does not give the former sovereign a veto over independence. And, indeed, the Court also noted that if the federal government or other provincial governments did not respect the Constitution in responding to Quebec's request for secession, then, by the same token, their own positions might be weakened internationally (*Reference re Secession of Quebec*, [1998] 2 SCR 217, para. 103).

Third, the most extensive specifying of statehood by international law has been in the design and implementation of complex politico-legal structures for post-conflict societies that have sometimes occurred under the international administration or military occupation of a state or territory. The 2003–2004 occupation of Iraq is a prime example of what has been called 'transformative' or 'humanitarian' occupation: the Coalition Provisional Authority enacted a set of comprehensive reforms overhauling the country's political, legal, economic and regulatory institutions to conform to familiar Western models. These reforms provoked debates amongst international lawyers about how such state-building initiatives can be reconciled with the law of occupation – which severely limits the occupier's capacity to modify local laws and change state institutions – what constraints international law imposes on such enterprises and who represents the affected population.

Although often portrayed as novel undertakings, these sorts of social engineering projects are not new to international law. The post-Second World War Allied administration of Germany and Japan are forerunners of Iraq, and the League of Nations' fifteen-year administration of the Saar Basin, a coal mining region disputed between France and Germany, is amongst the earlier instances in which a territory was administered by an international organisation in the wake of a conflict. In the legal framework for decolonisation, similar licence was granted by the 'civilising mission' reflected in the mandate system under the Covenant of the League and the systems of trust and non self-governing territories under the UN Charter. The Charter, for example, obliged states administering trust territories 'to promote the political, economic, social, and educational advancement of the inhabitants ... and their progressive development towards self-government or independence' and 'to encourage respect for human rights ... without distinction as to race, sex, language, or religion' (article 76).

The end of the Cold War saw the rise of post-conflict reconstruction missions, including UN missions to Cambodia, Haiti and Somalia, and the institution of full international governance in cases such as Bosnia and Herzegovina, Kosovo and East Timor. On the one hand, the mandates for these missions are particular arrangements more or less willingly consented to by the state or specific peace plans authorised under the UN Security Council's powers to intervene when international peace and security is at stake, as opposed to new international norms for what a state must be. On the other, their significance has also been seen more broadly, whether positively, as progress toward a normatively fortified account of the state in international law, or negatively, as a return to the 'civilising mission'. In the case of territories that aspire to statehood, some commentators perceive a notion of 'earned sovereignty' at work: to establish its entitlement to statehood, the territory must internalise the elements of government introduced by the international administration (for an overview of the broader notion, with bibliography, see Public International Law and Policy Group, 'Earned Sovereignty').

The structures of representation implemented by international administrations range from democratisation and human rights, including women's rights, to multi-ethnic politics and minority rights (Wilde 2008, 216–225, 227). In Kosovo, for example, the key UN Security Council resolution directed the interim international administration to establish 'provisional institutions for democratic and autonomous self-government' (UN SC Resolution 1244 (1999), para. 11(c)), and the Secretary-General called more specifically for 'multi-ethnic governmental structures' (UN Doc. S/1999/779 (1999), para. 55). With regard to gender, the UN Interim Administration Mission in Kosovo adopted a quota for candidates in the elections in order to ensure that a critical mass of those elected (28 per cent) were women (Wood 2001). And in East Timor, a gender affairs unit within the UN transitional administration focused on issues including women's participation in decision-making, the establishment of a gender-sensitive legal system and the development of an inclusive constitution (see Whittington 2000; but compare Charlesworth 2005, 12–13).

Beyond the state

Given these varied designs for the state under international law, the idea that the state is the formal agent for its population internationally takes on different shades. In some cases, international law certifies no more than the state's effective control over its population. In other cases, the creation of the state through an exercise of self-determination makes the state an agent chosen freely by a people. In yet others, international law engineers democracy and even differentiated forms and rights of representation for certain groups within the state.

In addition to whatever international law may require of the state by way of representation, individual international institutions may have guidelines for the composition of national delegations (for example, the Constitution of the International Labour Organisation (ILO) requires tripartite government–employer–workpeople representation), criteria for granting consultative status to non-governmental organisations (NGOs) (for example, UN Economic and Social Council Resolution 31 (1996)) or positions on whether NGOs can submit *amicus* briefs (for example, that taken by the Appellate Body of the World Trade Organisation (WTO)); and may establish bodies such as the UN Permanent Forum on Indigenous Issues and the UN Forum on Minority Issues. The resolution creating the Forum on Minority Issues, for instance, requested the High Commissioner for Human Rights 'to provide all the necessary support to facilitate, in a transparent manner . . . the participation of relevant stakeholders from every region in the meetings, giving particular attention to ensuring broadest possible and equitable participation, including, in particular, the representation of women' (UN Human Rights Council Resolution 6/15 (2007), para. 7). In general, international civil society has become larger and more democratic, and, as fora such as the 2009 UN Climate Change Conference in Copenhagen demonstrate, sub-state, international and transnational forms of representation may be layered over state representation. However, international law provides no general principles for the construction and regulation of 'civil society', international or other.

The international law literature of the 1990s and early 2000s reflects the growth of interest in 'international civil society' and arguments about forms of representation other than the state. Amongst the alternatives proposed by scholars were complex forms of cosmopolitan democracy (Held 1995) and the replacement of the existing international 'unsociety' of state representatives by a genuine international society of humankind (Allott 2001, xxxv–xxxvii). Others advanced arguments about particular groups. Feminist advocacy led to gender mainstreaming taking hold in international institutions (see Charlesworth 2005). Unique arrangements emerged for the representation of indigenous peoples within the UN system and elsewhere, such as within the intergovernmental Arctic Council, which has a category of 'permanent participant', distinct from the observer status accorded to NGOs, for arctic organisations of indigenous peoples, with certain scholars seeking to theorise this incipient law (Kingsbury 2002; a more recent example is Charters 2010). The concept of social movements was introduced into the international law literature as a way to understand the Third World's relationship with international institutions (Rajagopal 2003).

Discussions about the entitlement of non-state actors to direct input into the making of international law thrived in this period, when they chimed with domestic theorising of multiculturalism in liberal democratic states. In newer bodies of international law scholarship, these issues are more likely to be treated empirically or taken up obliquely. The emphasis is no longer on actors and who has the right to participate, but on law and how it works or what it is, international law in particular.

The turn to empiricism, mainly amongst North American international lawyers, tracks the emergence of a research interest shared with international relations scholars in how states behave. Much of this work is devoted to explaining, in Thomas Franck's words, why powerful nations obey powerless rules (Franck 1990, 3); why do states comply with international law in the absence of robust enforcement mechanisms? As such, it engages with the standard 'realist' paradigm of international relations, which takes the state as the relevant actor and treats state behaviour as rational and self-interested, viewing rules as instruments to attain its interests in power, wealth and so on. At first mainly non-instrumentalist in emphasis, the international law literature on compliance is increasingly diverse and now includes prominent instrumentalist accounts of state behaviour which reaffirm the realist paradigm. Amongst the various explanations are compliance as a function of the properties of legal rules (Franck 1990), notions of transnational legal process (Koh 1996), rational choice models (Goldsmith and Posner 2005) and socialisation theories (Goodman and Jinks 2004). Some strands of the scholarship look only at states (for example, Goldsmith and Posner 2005), while others pursue the supporting roles of international institutions, transnational actors, interest groups within the state and other actors (for example, Hathaway 2005). Some treat the state as a unitary actor, akin to an individual or a corporation, while others disaggregate it. Regardless of these differences, compliance remains framed as a question about states, and the effect, if not necessarily the intent, of all these explanatory pathways is to confirm the state as the touchstone in international law.

Much the same holds true insofar as this empirical work has extended from compliance to the creation of norms. For example, international lawyers have credited NGO action with *states'* adoption, or adoption in a particular form, of conventions ranging from the 1997 Convention on the Prohibition of the Use, Stockpiling, Production and Transfer of Antipersonnel Mines and of their Destruction (the 'Landmines Convention') to the 2001 UNIDROIT Convention on International Interests in Mobile Equipment (Boyle and Chinkin 2007, 62–77, 94).

The concern in this body of scholarship is not with subjecthood and entitlement to representation (contrast recent mainstream scholarship on NGOs canvassed in Charnovitz 2009). Non-state actors are taken as existing. Insofar as they are of interest, the question is how to theorise or test their impact on states when it comes to international law. The importance of their participation is rarely studied from such perspectives as democracy, legitimacy or expression. Some examine whether the influence of non-state actors furthers democracy or legitimacy, but this is not a prelude to a full-fledged justification in these terms or to a proposal for reform. The working definition of international law here is formal or, at least, state-made. Even when these authors recognise the informal norm-generating practices of non-state actors, they do not tend to dwell on these practices for their own sake.

At the other end of the spectrum, the legal pluralist scholarship on globalisation expands the range of law-making actors by expanding the definition of law. Legal pluralism emerged from the study of colonial and newly independent states and was originally concerned with problems stemming from the imposition of colonial law onto existing systems of customary and religious law. It was a reaction against legal positivism and its assumptions that the state has a monopoly on law, and that law and non-law must be strictly distinguished. To official law, legal pluralism added living law, positing that people's lives are regulated by a variety of legal orders. While these orders are related to one another, each is independent and valid on its own terms (see Merry 1988).

Legal pluralists argue that globalisation is de-centering the law-making process and creating multiple law-making processes in different sectors of international civil society, independently of states. The international business community, world-wide internet community and other transnational communities are analysed as having developed autonomous bodies of rules to regulate their interactions. From the 1960s onward, scholars and practitioners of international business law, private international law, commercial law and even contract law have debated whether *lex mercatoria*, arguably a modern successor to the medieval law merchant, is a-national law – 'global law without a state'. Some maintain, for instance, that the rules, institutions and procedures of international arbitration are sufficiently autonomous from the state and sufficiently legal in character to qualify as such a law. Others respond that *lex mercatoria* is scarce on the ground or, insofar as it does exist, is dependent on national laws and the freedom of contract they provide, and on the enforceability of arbitral awards by national courts. The take up of *lex mercatoria* in the 1990s by legal pluralist thinkers as the paradigmatic case of global law without a state has brought a new theoretical vigour to *lex mercatoria* (perhaps surpassing its reality) (see particularly Teubner's systems theory, Teubner 1997; see also Michaels 2008; Wai 2008). It has also precipitated criticisms related to the absence of the state – Third-World scholars, for example, have raised concerns about the lack of a 'public voice' (Chimni 2006, 13). In answer, some global legal pluralists assert that *lex mercatoria* is constitutionalising outside the state (see Michaels 2008, 451).

Although global legal pluralism is meant to correct for an over-emphasis on the state, some versions of global legal pluralism, in fact, re-entrench the centrality of the state by imagining non-state communities as mini-sovereigns. In comparison, others emphasise not only the growth of multiple legal orders but also their interlegality, meaning the superimposition, interpenetration and mixture of different legal spaces in both mind and action (Santos 2002, 437). Yet responses to the notion of interlegality remind us again about the state's value. With interlegality, an interrelationship of normative contestation is as much to be expected as is an interrelationship of harmonisation or unification, and hence states re-enter as important venues for contestation (Wai 2008, 109, 116–120).

A middle ground between the statist image of international law employed in much of the 'how international law really works' literature, as we might call it, and the non-state-centrism offered by legal pluralists is found in Anne-Marie Slaughter's influential theory of international law-making by governmental networks (Slaughter 2004). Slaughter describes the rise of governmental networks as a shift away from international treaties negotiated by generalist diplomats, to non-binding types of policy coordination amongst specialised national bureaucrats and their counterparts in other states through the exchange of information, best practices and other methods. In shifting attention from formal international legal instruments and institutions to informal ones, and from actors with international legal personality to functional nodes, Slaughter's approach shares a sensibility with the growing literature on global governance. Rather than proceeding from who has the right to make international law, that is, starting with issues of representation, these analyses tend to emanate from structures and procedures.

The resulting deformalisation of law is accompanied, it has been argued, by fragmentation and by empire. International law is increasingly made by networks of national technocrats who develop broadly formulated directives rather than formal law, who concentrate on effective problem-solving in environmental law, criminal law, human rights law or whatever their functionally defined regime happens to be, and who cooperate under legal and political conditions that privilege a single dominant actor (Koskenniemi 2007, 13).

Back to the state

In the context of this managerialism, the interest of many European international lawyers in the constitutionalisation of international law can be understood as a form of resistance to the marginalisation and instrumentalisation of the discipline. International or global constitutionalism has been defined as an 'agenda that identifies and advocates for the application of constitutionalist principles in the international legal sphere' (Peters 2009, 397; see also Klabbers, Peters and Ulfstein 2009). A straightforward example of such identification is the claim that the UN Charter is not only the document that constitutes the UN Organisation; it is *the* constitutional document of international law. On this version of constitutionalisation, the domestic state writ large is the way of thinking about the international system.

As we move away from this sort of concrete claim about correspondence toward analyses that combine the identification of emerging constitutional elements in international law with arguments in favour of their development, we move away from the domestic state as blueprint, yet return to it in another register. Taken as a blueprint for institutions or a set of legal rules, critics have argued, constitutionalisation is not the antidote. Neither institutions nor rules can provide determinate alternatives even if they could be shown to exist or be achieved. But constitutionalisation directs us to important normative questions such as participation, transparency and accountability, or rule of law and legality. One way to hold onto these questions is by understanding constitutionalism instead as a way of thinking or a style of argument. Martti Koskenniemi has proposed that constitutionalism's potential be understood as a mindset: the sort of vocabulary needed to articulate extreme inequality in the world 'as a scandal insofar as it violates the equal dignity and autonomy of human beings' (Koskenniemi 2007, 35). Jan Klabbers advocates 'constitutionalism lite' for international organisations as a style of politics that rejects instrumentalism (Klabbers 2004, 57–58). These lines of argument return us to the domestic state as 'the best-stocked normative reservoir' rather than as blueprint.

Models of how states behave, legal pluralism, governmental networks – each of the approaches introduced above has implications for who can act. Each also invites the kinds of concerns raised about public voice, contestation, constitutionalism, politics and legality. These concerns stem from traditions of political and legal thought about the state and from the historical experiences of actual states. The state thus reappears as the central organising idea in the international system: not as the basic unit (the state as individual) but as a repository of ideals for the international system that have been most fully theorised, critiqued and revised and have come closest to being realised in the context of domestic states (the international system analysed through key critical concepts developed mainly with reference to the domestic state).

The notion of 'publicness' is another major example of abstracting from the domestic state without mapping it directly onto the international system. For Benedict Kingsbury, an originator of the notion of global administrative law (GAL), the underlying concept of law includes a requirement of publicness. GAL refers to 'the legal mechanisms, principles, and practices, along with supporting social understandings, that promote or otherwise affect the accountability of global administrative bodies, in particular by ensuring these bodies meet adequate standards of transparency, consultation, participation, rationality, and legality, and by providing effective review of the rules and decisions these bodies make' (Kingsbury 2009b, 190).

The requirement of publicness may be seen as related to questions raised by some of GAL's interlocutors. Susan Marks questions, for example, whether GAL's focus on accountability can or should bracket issues of democracy. Similar to those who see constitutionalism as a critical concept, rather than instructions to be read off existing institutions and procedures, Marks argues for treating democracy as a set of particular evaluative principles, amongst them anti-paternalism, inclusion and equality (Marks 2005, 998–1001). David Dyzenhaus asks of GAL whether legal, as opposed to political, accountability requires the existence of a global state and concludes that the question is more aptly whether some form of global legal order is necessary (Dyzenhaus 2009). Like GAL's originators, Marks and Dyzenhaus are drawing on traditions of thought associated with the domestic state, but abstracting for a global context sometimes described as 'governance' as opposed to 'government'. In articulating the concept of law at work in GAL, Kingsbury endorses a Hartian 'social fact' conception of law and adds, crucially, that the Hartian rule of recognition also requires 'publicness', by which he means the claim that the law 'has been wrought by the whole society, by the public, and the connected claim that the law addresses matters of concern to the society as such' (Kingsbury 2009a, 31). The content of publicness is supplied by such general principles of public law as legality, rule of law and human rights. While this conception of law opens up questions of actors, it does not provide strong direction.

To deploy the domestic state as the best-stocked normative reservoir, be it for democracy, constitutionalism or legality is, of course, to invite the question 'what state?' As noted earlier, and elsewhere in this volume, international law itself testifies to the imposition of Western forms of the state onto the Rest. Even the Montevideo Convention's value-free test of effective control has been criticised as abstracting from the European state and hence being biased against other forms of sovereignty (see, for example, *Western Sahara*, Advisory Opinion, Separate Opinions of Vice-President Ammoun, Judge Forster and Judge Boni, ICJ Reports 1975, p. 12; Fadel 2009). What of the Rest? Are their experiences with the state a negative heritage, a range of 'alternative worlds' in the interstices of the Western forms that should be highlighted (see Tully 2008, 491; Young 2007, Ch. 1)? How ought they to be incorporated into counter-manoeuvres to managerialism? Is the European intellectual heritage with its tradition of secularism, echoed in international law, adequate to the task (compare, for example, Bhargava 2006)? And finally, we might add, is the international lawyer's reflex to return to 'the public' too quick? Does 'the private' provide its share of ideational resources for resisting what troubles her?

A common approach to the state in international law is to ask whether the state is on the wane as the discipline's main device for representing the world. This question is most often premised on a particular view of the state or a particular understanding of its centrality. This chapter has emphasised that international law varies in the representational work it demands of the state, and that international lawyers vary in how they make the state central, or not, to their analyses of the international order. The conclusion to be drawn need not be that the state is inescapable, but that its multiple significance as a structuring concept contributes to its sometimes obvious, sometimes subtle tenacity in international law.

Bibliography

Allott, P., 2001. *Eunomia: New Order for a New World*, 2nd edn., Oxford University Press

Anderson, B., 2006. *Imagined Communities: Reflections on the Origin and Spread of Nationalism*, London: Verso

Bell, C., 2009. 'Capitulations', in R. Wolfrum (ed.), *Max Planck Encyclopedia of Public International Law*, online

Berman, N., 1988. 'Sovereignty in Abeyance: Self-determination and International Law', *Wisconsin International Law Journal*, 7, 53–105

Bhargava, R., 2006. 'Indian Secularism: An Alternative Trans-cultural Ideal', in V. Mehta and T. Pantham (eds.), *Political Ideas in Modern India: Thematic Explorations*, New Delhi: Sage, 285–306

Boyle, A. and C. Chinkin, 2007. *The Making of International Law*, Oxford University Press

Cassese, A., 1995. *Self-Determination of Peoples: A Legal Reappraisal*, Cambridge University Press

Charlesworth, H., 2005. 'Not Waving but Drowning: Gender Mainstreaming and Human Rights at the United Nations', *Harvard Human Rights Journal*, 18, 1–18

Charnovitz, S., 2009. 'Recent Scholarship on NGOs', *American Journal of International Law*, 103, 777–784

Charters, C., 2010. 'A Self-Determination Approach to Justifying Indigenous Peoples' Participation in International Law and Policy-making', *International Journal on Minority and Group Rights*, 17, 215–240

Chimni, B. S., 2006. 'Third World Approaches to International Law: A Manifesto', *International Community Law Review*, 8, 3–27

Dyzenhaus, D., 2009. 'Accountability and the Concept of (Global) Administrative Law', *Acta Juridica*, 3–31

Fadel, M. 2009. 'International Law, Regional Developments: Islam', in R. Wolfrum (ed.), *Max Planck Encyclopedia of Public International Law*, online

Franck, T., 1990. *The Power of Legitimacy Among Nations*, Oxford University Press

Goldsmith, J. and E. Posner, 2005. *The Limits of International Law*, Oxford University Press

Goodman, R. and D. Jinks, 2004. 'How to Influence States: Socialization and International Human Rights Law', *Duke Law Journal*, 54, 621–703

Hathaway, O., 2005. 'Between Power and Principle: An Integrated Theory of International Law', *University of Chicago Law Review*, 72, 469–536

Held, D., 1995. '*Democracy and the Global Order: From the Modern State to Cosmopolitan Governance*', Cambridge: Polity Press

International Fund for Agricultural Development, 'Sending Money Home', www.ifad.org/remittances/maps/index.htm

Kingsbury, B., 2002. 'First Amendment Liberalism as Global Legal Architecture: Ascriptive Groups and the Problem of the Liberal NGO Model of International Civil Society', *Chicago Journal of International Law*, 3, 183–195

Kingsbury, B., 2009a. 'The Concept of "Law" in Global Administrative Law', *European Journal of International Law*, 20, 23–57

Kingsbury, B., 2009b. 'International Law as Inter-Public Law', in H. Richardson and M. Williams (eds.), *NOMOS XLIX: Moral Universalism and Pluralism*, New York University Press, 167–204

Klabbers, J., 2004. 'Constitutionalism Lite', *International Organisations Law Review*, 1, 31–58

Klabbers, J., A. Peters and G. Ulfstein, 2009. *The Constitutionalisation of International Law*, Oxford University Press

Koh, H., 1996. 'Transnational Legal Process', *Nebraska Law Review*, 75, 181–207

Koskenniemi, M., 1994. 'National Self-Determination Today: Problems of Legal Theory and Practice', *International and Comparative Law Quarterly*, 43, 241–269

Koskenniemi, M., 2007. 'Constitutionalism as Mindset: Reflections on Kantian Themes about International Law and Globalisation', *Theoretical Inquiries in Law*, 8, 9–36

Marks, S., 2005. 'Naming Global Administrative Law', *New York University Journal of International Law and Politics*, 27, 995–1001

Merry, S., 1988. 'Legal Pluralism', *Law and Society Review*, 22, 869–896

Michaels, R., 2008. 'The True Lex Mercatoria: Law Beyond the State', *Indiana Journal of Global Legal Studies*, 14, 447–468

Mutua, M., 1995. 'Why Redraw the Map of Africa: A Moral and Legal Inquiry', *Michigan Journal of International Law*, 16, 1113–1176

Pellet, A., 1991. 'Note sur la Commission d'arbitrage de la Conférence européenne pour la paix en Yougoslavie', *Annuaire français de droit international*, 37, 329–348

Peters, A., 2009. 'The Merits of Global Constitutionalism', *Indiana Journal of Global Legal Studies*, 16, 397–411

Rajagopal, B., 2003. *International Law From Below: Development, Social Movements, and Third World Resistance*, Cambridge University Press

Santos, B. de S., 2002. *Toward a New Legal Common Sense: Law, Globalization, Emancipation*, 2nd edn., London: Butterworths

Slaughter, A. -M., 2004. *A New World Order*, Princeton University Press

Spiro, P., 2006. 'Perfecting Political Diaspora', *New York University Law Review*, 81, 207–233

Teubner, G., 1997. '"Global Bukowina": Legal Pluralism in the World Society', in G. Teubner (ed.), *Global Law Without a State*, Aldershot: Dartmouth, 3–28

Touval, S., 1966. 'Treaties, Borders, and the Partition of Africa', *Journal of African History*, 7, 279–293

Tully, J., 2008. 'Modern Constitutional Democracy and Imperialism', *Osgoode Hall Law Journal*, 46, 461–493

Vitoria, F., 1991. *Political Writings*, A. Pagden and J. Lawrance (eds.), Cambridge University Press

Wai, R., 2008. 'The Interlegality of Transnational Private Law', *Law and Contemporary Problems*, 71, 107–127

Walker, N., 2001. 'The EU and the WTO: Constitutionalism in a New Key', in G. de Búrca and J. Scott (eds.), *The EU and the WTO: Legal and Constitutional Issues*, Oxford: Hart, 31–57

Whittington, S., 2000. 'The UN Transitional Administration in East Timor: Gender Affairs', *Development Bulletin*, 53, 74–80

Wilde, R., 2008. *International Territorial Administration: How Trusteeship and the Civilizing Mission Never Went Away*, Oxford University Press

Wood, N., 2001. 'Kosovo Leads Europe in Women Power', *BBC News*, 29 November

Young, I., 2007. *Global Challenges: War, Self-Determination and Responsibility for Justice*, Cambridge: Polity Press

5 Sovereignty as a legal value

James Crawford*

'Sovereignty' as a distinctive attribute of the state

Chapter 4 explored the question how it is that various peoples (the Lithuanians, the Thais . . .) have a state of their own; whereas others (the Kurds, the Tibetans . . .) do not. Despite the manifest historical contingencies involved, once statehood is generally recognised – evidenced most obviously by admission to the United Nations – then a new situation arises, a category divide is established, marked by the legal category of statehood. The new state *is* 'sovereign', *has* 'sovereignty'; and this is true, no matter how fragile its condition, how diminutive its resources. Vattel (1714–1767), who systematised the pre-1914 law of nations in his treatise of 1758, put it thus: sovereign states are to be considered as so many free persons living together in the state of nature, that is to say, without a common civil law or common institutions; in such a situation they are 'naturally equal', and inequality of power does not affect this equality; '[a] dwarf is as much a man as a giant; a small republic is no less a sovereign state than the most powerful kingdom' (Vattel 1758 [2008], Bk. I, Preliminaries, §18). And despite all that has changed since 1758, the basic concept remains: states are 'political entities equal in law, similar in form . . . , the direct subjects of international law' (*Reparation for Injuries suffered in the Service of the United Nations*, ICJ Reports 1949, p. 174, 177–178). As the Badinter Commission, established to advise on legal issues arising from the breakup of the former Yugoslavia, put it, 'such a state is characterised by sovereignty' (Opinion No. 1 (1991), 92 ILR 165).

In other words, the state is sovereign because it is a state; not one of a kind but one of a species, the species of states. The term 'sovereign state' is often used but one might as well say 'sovereign sovereign'. Yet the repetition can add a certain aura. For example, in dismissing a US argument about 'the militarisation of Nicaragua, which the United States deems excessive and

* Thanks to Surabhi Ranganathan, PhD candidate, Cambridge, for her assistance with this chapter.

such as to prove its aggressive intent', the International Court of Justice (ICJ) found it 'irrelevant and inappropriate ... to pass upon this allegation ... since in international law there are no rules other than such rules as may be accepted by the state concerned, by treaty or otherwise whereby the level of armaments of a sovereign state can be limited, and this principle is valid for all States without exception' (*Military and Paramilitary Activities in and against Nicaragua*, ICJ Reports 1986, p. 14, 135). The Court could not resist the pleonasm 'sovereign State' in a passage expressly applicable to all states. Apparently the sentence sounds more plausible than it would have done without the word 'sovereign': the two sentences have the same meaning, yet one seems less question-begging than the other.

The term 'sovereignty' has a variety of uses. In its origin it referred to supreme power within the state – an issue of constitutional rather than international law, and one which in many countries would be regarded as a non-issue. In accordance with the principle of separation of powers, there may be no single body within the state which has plenary authority; power is distributed, but the state remains 'sovereign'. International law leaves the distribution of authority internally to each state. It regards each state as sovereign, in the sense that it is presumed to have full authority to act not only internally but at the international level, to make (or not to make) treaties and other commitments, to relate (or not to relate) to other states in a wide variety of ways, to consent (or not to consent) to resolve international disputes (see Crawford 2006, 32–33, 40–44).

As sovereign the state's position contrasts with that of non-states (individuals, human groups, corporations, non-governmental organisations (NGOs), international governmental organisations (IGOs), etc). Non-states may have rights and obligations under international law. Individuals have rights under human rights treaties, and are potentially subject to criminal jurisdiction for a certain number of international crimes (see Chapter 12). IGOs can act 'on the international plane' vis-à-vis states, making treaties, bringing claims, litigating, even governing territory under specific mandates, e.g. Kosovo, East Timor (see Chapter 10). They have 'international legal personality' to the extent of their competence. In a given context they may have more extensive rights and immunities than do states. But despite the important role at least some IGOs play at the international level, they are not considered 'sovereign'; at most they may exercise state authority by processes such as delegation from member states. By a widespread understanding, 'sovereignty' is a quality inhering in each established state and in no other persons.

Moreover it is a quality which each such state has, irrespective of its size, structure, population, resources and other potential.

What is the difference between sovereigns and non-sovereigns, and how is this difference reflected in international legal reasoning? What are the consequences of sovereignty and what are the argumentative positions which, justifiably or not, rely on sovereignty? With the erosion of state prerogatives in many fields, does sovereignty matter any more? Or should we look to other, contingent, characteristics of some states – democratic institutions, actual control over the population – for an explanation of operative legal ideas?

These are highly contested questions, with implications going well beyond the field of international law. They are also questions on which international lawyers disagree – in contexts such as, for example, the so-called 'responsibility to protect'. Those who see the classical doctrine of sovereign equality of states as a fiction in the modern world tend to favour proposals for greater intervention in 'internal affairs', to privilege a sub-class of states seen as 'good' or at least tolerable, and to focus attention on the remainder as targets for aid or intervention. Those for whom the relative autonomy of territorial communities is a value in itself tend to stress respect for sovereignty; they note that proposals for intervention usually imply intervention in the affairs of *other* states.

The protection of sovereignty

When Vattel wrote, and for a long time afterwards, the sovereignty of states was only protected for as long as it lasted. States were considered as 'equal', but there was always the possibility of extinction of the state itself, or drastic loss of territory, through war or the treaty that followed a war. By 1945, the legal position had changed. Based on the experience of two world wars and many related conflicts, article 2(4) of the UN Charter provided that:

> All Members shall refrain in their international relations from the threat or use of force against the territorial integrity or political independence of any State, or in any other manner inconsistent with the Purposes of the United Nations.

Further, article 2(7) prohibited the United Nations from intervening in 'matters which are essentially within the domestic jurisdiction of any state' – though this did not apply to enforcement action by the Security Council under Chapter VII.

These provisions have been the subject of much debate and refinement in practice, and article 2(7) in particular provides only very limited protection. On the other hand, the ICJ has ignored all predictions of the desuetude or lapse of article 2(4), in a consistent jurisprudence from *Corfu Channel* (1949) to *Congo/Uganda* (2005). In *Oil Platforms*, it stated that 'the requirement of international law that measures taken avowedly in self-defence must have been necessary for that purpose is strict and objective, leaving no room for any "measure of discretion"' (ICJ Reports 2003, p. 161, para. 73). Statehood is now a protected status under international law, and to this extent sovereignty once achieved is entrenched.

Attempts have been made to build further guarantees upon this Charter base, for example through the notion of 'permanent sovereignty over natural resources' (see, e.g., Schrijver 1997). Proponents of the idea – in particular, Third-World governments – have sought thereby to increase their negotiating power vis-à-vis foreign corporations holding licences in the oil and mineral sectors. Capital exporting states responded with attempts at 'internationalising' licensing agreements, but more recently and more successfully with negotiating investment protection treaties giving investors standing at the international level to challenge host state action targeting investments (see, e.g., the ICSID Convention (1965) and the Energy Charter Treaty (1994)). Where available, the effect is to provide an international forum, at the instance of the investor, for scrutiny of host state action (see further Chapter 13).

Another element of legal protection of sovereignty is a presumption against loss of rights. It remains an open question whether or in what circumstances sovereignty can be lost by prescription (i.e. adverse possession of territory over time). In one case the ICJ held that the original sovereignty of the sultanate of Johor over islets off its coast had not been lost despite inaction by Johor (latterly Malaysia) for more than 100 years (*Malaysia/Singapore*, ICJ Reports 2008, p. 12, 98–101). Many disputes over territorial sovereignty involve issues of historical fact going back to the nineteenth century (e.g. the Falklands (Malvinas) dispute).

Sovereignty within the state and amongst states

In discussing sovereignty it has been usual to distinguish between governing authority within the state and sovereignty as between states. Within the state, sovereignty involves a monopoly of governing authority:

'Independence in regard to a portion of the globe is the right to exercise therein, to the exclusion of any other state, the functions of a state' (*Island of Palmas*, Award of 4 April 1928, 11 RIAA 831, 838). Except in special circumstances, only the government exercises authority within the state – 'government' understood in the broadest sense, to include organs and agencies of a legislative, executive and judicial kind. Apparently ignoring centuries of constitutional development, international law for most purposes aggregates these powers under the rubric of the state as a single, undivided entity. Its governmental authority extends to determining who may enter the territory, who belongs to the state as its nationals, what the law of the state shall be on any matter and how (or when) it is to be enforced, what taxes shall be paid and on what the proceeds shall be spent, what armaments the state shall have and how they will be deployed, and so on across the spectrum of possible matters for government. As a general matter, this authority is exclusive: normally, governmental activity carried out on the territory of another state is only lawful if performed there with the latter's consent, e.g. in the context of visiting forces, or overflight by civil or military aircraft.

By contrast, in inter-state relations, there are at least two and may be many states involved, and there is much less room for any one of them to assert a monopoly of authority. In international affairs, the claim to monopoly is to a collective monopoly, a monopoly of *process*; others (non-states) are allowed in only by invitation, and it may be only as observers. For example, despite the strong influence NGOs had in the debate leading up to the Rome Conference for an International Criminal Court, when it came to making the key decisions on the scope and structure of the Court, the NGO Coalition was excluded from the room.

Already two points will be clear. The first is that assertions in terms of sovereignty are not indefeasible; they are more in the character of presumptions than inflexible rules. For example the ICJ in the passage already cited from the *Nicaragua* case asserted that 'there are no rules *other than such rules as may be accepted by the state concerned, by treaty or otherwise* whereby the level of armaments of a sovereign state can be limited [emphasis added]', and a qualification along these lines is normal. Sovereignty does not mean uniformity.

The second point is that the apparently clear distinction between 'internal' and 'international' tends to break down, or to become a relative one, as new agreements are made or new areas of international concern opened up.

As the Permanent Court of International Justice (PCIJ) put it, it is 'an essentially relative question ... depend[ing] on the development of international relations' (*Nationality Decrees in Tunis and Morocco*, PCIJ (1923), Ser. B No. 4, p. 7, 23). The erosion of the domestic domain has been a notable result of the human rights movement (as to which see Chapter 12). But the sovereigntist would note that sovereignty is not exhausted by the concession or recognition of rights. Even when a state is found to be in breach of its human rights obligations, it retains the prerogative of implementing that adverse decision – the prerogative of responsibility – and thus the initiative in the matter; this carries with it the benefit of the 'margin of appreciation'. Most human rights treaties do not specify in any detail the state conduct they require. They are second order standards which can be satisfied in a variety of ways: it is for the state concerned to decide which. In other words, human rights standards qualify, but do not displace, the sovereignty of states. Indeed in subtle ways they reinforce it: the more we look to the state for human rights compliance, the more we may seem to concede to a state domain.

Sovereignty and obligation

Underlying both points is the premiss that sovereignty does not mean freedom from law but freedom within the law (including freedom to seek to change the law). This was made clear in the very first decision of the very first permanent international court – the Permanent Court of International Justice – in 1923. Germany objected that to interpret the freedom of transit provisions in the Treaty of Versailles so as to allow passage of armaments through the Kiel Canal would infringe its sovereignty: the armaments were destined for Poland in its war against Russia, a war in which Germany was a neutral. The PCIJ 'decline[d] to see in the conclusion of any Treaty by which a state undertakes to perform or refrain from performing a particular act an abandonment of its sovereignty. No doubt any convention creating an obligation of this kind places a restriction upon the exercise of the sovereign rights of the State, in the sense that it requires them to be exercised in a certain way. But the right of entering into international engagements is an attribute of state sovereignty' (*S.S. Wimbledon*, PCIJ (1923), Ser. A No. 1, p. 15, 25). Thus an argument from sovereignty is evaded by an appeal to sovereignty: if states could not enter into binding international obligations, they would lack an attribute of sovereignty. The problem shifts to the interpretation of the commitment actually made, which can then be treated as a more narrowly legal issue.

The Court went on to construe the relevant provisions of the Treaty of Versailles in accordance with their ordinary meaning, conceding that in case of doubt the more limited interpretation, i.e. the one least restrictive of sovereignty, would prevail. These days that concession would not be made: the language of treaties is not subject to any particular presumption but will be read so as to give effect to the object and purpose of the treaty in its context. Thus Costa Rica's right of perpetual freedom of commercial navigation on the San Juan river (a border river subject to Nicaraguan sovereignty) was to be read in a progressive way: 'where the parties have used generic terms in a treaty, the parties necessarily having been aware that the meaning of the terms was likely to evolve over time, and where the treaty has been entered into for a very long period or is "of continuing duration", the parties must be presumed, as a general rule, to have intended those terms to have an evolving meaning' (*Costa Rica/Nicaragua*, Judgment of 13 July 2009, para. 66; see also paras. 48–49).

A similar movement away from restrictive interpretation based on the principle of sovereignty occurred in the context of general (customary) international law. In *The S.S. Lotus*, the Permanent Court said:

> International law governs relations between independent states. The rules of law binding upon states therefore emanate from their own free will as expressed in conventions or by usages generally accepted as expressing principles of law and established in order to regulate the relations between these co-existing independent communities or with a view to the achievement of common aims. Restrictions upon the independence of states cannot therefore be presumed. (PCIJ (1927), Ser. A No. 10, p. 4, 18)

The Court used that presumption to deny the existence of any rule prohibiting Turkey from exercising jurisdiction over the captain of a French ship who was responsible for a collision with a Turkish ship at sea. The problem with such reasoning in inter-state relations is that one state's freedom is another's loss of freedom – assuming, as the Court assumed, that the rights and interests of the French captain were to be aggregated with those of France. These days an international tribunal would not start with any presumption. The criteria for demonstrating the existence of general international law rules look towards the general consensus of states supported by practice, and in that sense are protective of state freedom of action. But the dominant view is that a state cannot interpose its sovereignty to prevent the impact on it of a new rule articulated as law and widely supported by other states (see Chapter 8, and for the 'persistent objector' debate see Charney 1986). For example not even the United States could prevent the establishment of a 12-mile territorial sea; the most it could do was to seek to negotiate transitional access arrangements to coastal waters while forgoing for itself the advantages of the 12-mile limit. In the end that game was not worth the candle.

But sovereignty plays a central role in treaty-making. States are free to decide whether or not to become parties to treaties, and – unless the treaty otherwise provides – they also have considerable freedom to make reservations qualifying the terms of treaty acceptance. On the other hand, once they have entered into treaty relations, it may be more difficult to get out of them (unless the treaty specifically permits denunciation or withdrawal). state consent in such cases creates a new situation in which withdrawal of consent may be ineffective, temporarily or at all (for the durability of treaties notwithstanding change of circumstances see, e.g., *Gabčíkovo-Nagymaros Project*, ICJ Reports 1997, p. 7).

It is true that not all international law-making is treaty-making. Even governments frequently resort to 'soft law' mechanisms; and there is a substantial, partly subterranean practice of articulation of rules by private agencies, for example in the financial sector and in the field of corporate social responsibility (see, e.g., Peters, Koechlin, Förster and Zinkernagel 2009). It remains to be seen to what extent this will impinge on what has previously been a virtual state monopoly.

Sovereignty and enforcement

But it is one thing for a state to be under an obligation and another for the obligation to be effectively enforced. Inter-state disputes will normally be addressed through diplomatic means, with other processes very much a last resort (e.g. counter-measures, litigation). Moreover the jurisdiction of international courts and tribunals over states is dependent on consent, given in advance or at the time the case is instituted. At the international level, there is no 'inherent' jurisdiction over states, and this is true however serious the breach may be. All supranational jurisdiction depends on the consent of the states parties: '[t]here is a fundamental distinction between the acceptance by a state of the Court's jurisdiction and the compatibility of particular acts with international law . . . Whether or not States accept the jurisdiction of the Court, they remain in all cases responsible for acts attributable to them that violate the rights of other States' (*Fisheries Jurisdiction (Spain* v. *Canada)*, ICJ Reports 1998, p. 432, 456).

This might be thought to give counter-measures some considerable advantage as a form of enforcement (for the extent and limits on counter-measures see ILC Articles on State Responsibility (2001), articles 49–54). A vestige of older forms of reprisal or self-help, counter-measures do not depend on the consent of the target state; the right to take them is triggered by a breach of obligation on the part of that state. But in fact counter-measures, though in principle available, are only rarely taken in the field of general inter-state relations. (They are more common in trade disputes, where they are regulated in the context of the World Trade Organisation.)

In summary, international measures of enforcement through sanctions are unusual if not exceptional. It is true that the Security Council has extensive authority to act in matters of international peace and security and has been increasingly active in that role since 1989. But the Security Council is not a general enforcer of international obligations; it acts or not at discretion, but always subject to the veto of the five Permanent Members and under the rubric, admittedly expansive, of threats to or breaches of the peace (UN Charter, article 39).

Enforcement through domestic courts is sometimes put forward as an alternative mode of enforcement of international law – and against private persons it may well be. Whole areas of international law, e.g. in the field of commerce and communications, are enforced as part of national law by state courts. But for such courts to enforce international law against a foreign state is another matter and is still unusual. With few exceptions, foreign states may rely on sovereign immunity in respect of conduct in the exercise of sovereign authority (*iure imperii*); they also have a fairly extensive immunity from measures of execution or enforcement of judgments.

To summarise, the requirement of consent to jurisdiction applies in inter-state relations, independently of the merits of the claim and the significance of the obligation violated. The principle of sovereignty thus protects states which may be in breach of their obligations.

Implications of sovereignty for distribution of authority within the state

As noted, the origins of the idea of sovereignty are to be found not in the law of nations but in late medieval thinking about the location of ultimate authority within the state (see Hinsley 1986; Jackson 2007). Transplanted as an idea from the constitutional to the international level, sovereignty has often played in reverse, affecting the relations between central and regional or local governments.[1] For example, within federations it is normal for the conduct of international relations to be the prerogative on the federal government, with emphasis on the executive: internationally the heads of state and government and the minister of foreign affairs are considered to have full powers to represent the state. In consequence it is argued that the federal legislature must have legislative power to implement international commitments, irrespective of what would otherwise be the internal distribution of power over the subject matter in question. This argument – which is based on practicality, not on logical entailment – has prevailed, for example, in the United States and Australia (though not yet in Canada). Jurisdiction offshore has been largely federalised on the basis of the same argument.

In the European Union, issues of external relations are the subject of increasing contestation, the Commission arguing for a monopoly of external representation in EU-related matters, including mixed agreements, leaving implementation to be resolved as an internal matter between the European Union and member states. The aim, it has been said, is not a supranational sovereignty to rival the United States and China, but a new and different vision of inter-governmental cooperation. In the words of Konrad Schiemann:

> The EU offers the hope of transcending the sovereign State rather than simply replicating it in some new super-State, some new repository of absolute sovereignty. It creates new possibilities of imagining, and thus of subsequently realizing, political order on the basis of a pluralistic rather than a monolithic conception of the exercise of political power and legal authority. (Schiemann 2007, 487)

[1] See, e.g., the decisions of the International Court in *LaGrand*, ICJ Reports 2001, p. 466 and *Avena*, ICJ Reports 2004, p. 12 and 2009, p. 3; and the very reticent approach of the US Supreme Court in *Medellín* v. *Texas*, 128 SCR 1346 (2008).

The pathology of sovereignty

It is sometimes assumed that the weakness of international law and its absence of centralised sanctions (Chapter VII of the UN Charter apart) mean that the protections given to sovereignty by the law are of little account. But the fact is that since 1945 there have been a multitude of new states and hardly any extinctions (see Crawford 2006, 715–717). Even regionally powerful states (e.g. Indonesia in East Timor, Iraq in Kuwait) failed in annexation attempts, with international law playing a distinct, though quite different, role in the two cases. Rather the concern is that sovereignty has too much protection, and that human security and well-being suffer in consequence (see Hironaka 2005).

A term that has gained currency in this context is that of 'failed state' – essentially a debate about intervention couched in the language of sovereignty. The suggestion is that some or possibly many Third-World states amount to little more than damaging legal fictions (see, e.g., Jackson 1990, 202, who refers to the quasi-state 'under the one-dimensional negative sovereignty regime'). This vogue term has generated a substantial literature amongst authors from successful states. Its definition is not precise, but 'failed state' would seem to encompass various instances of governmental breakdown or prolonged institutional crisis in Africa and Asia. As part of the 'war against terror', the United States specifically included 'failed states' in its defence doctrine; it was suggested that 'state failure' may condition the application of treaty rights and even individual rights (see Greenberg and Dratel 2005, 38, 39).

The perils of the expression go back to a conceptual confusion. The situations of 'failed states' are, evidently, crises of government. None of the situations so described – Somalia, the Congo, Liberia, etc. – has involved the extinction of the state in question. No doubt in many cases the *regime* has failed – either in the narrow sense of the group controlling the Presidential palace or in the broader sense of the governmental system, civil service, army, opposition and all. But although there are many poor, even desperately poor, states, one must ask what they might otherwise be or have been – satellites of a neighbour, or equally poor or even poorer colonies? No doubt most Somalis, whose self-determination and security the governmental system of Somalia has conspicuously failed to protect, would prefer it were otherwise. But there is no indication that they wish to be – for example – Ethiopians. To talk of states as 'failed' sounds like blaming the victims.

A further problem lies in the assumption that 'state failure' arises from weakness and anarchy rather than overweening strength. The evils of the twentieth century were overwhelmingly due to strong regimes, and to their aftermath when eventually they collapsed. The Third Reich and Stalin's Russia, like the earlier Congo of King Leopold, were failures in any human or moral terms – but not in terms of the definitions of 'failed state' given in the literature.

This is not to deny the systematic problems that colonisation helped to produce and which decolonisation has revealed and in some cases exacerbated. When knowledgeable observers of Africa speak of 'the curse of the Nation-State' the situation has to be taken seriously (see Davidson 1992). But it is necessary to disaggregate the problem, which is for the most part not due to the qualified modern doctrine of sovereignty and would not be solved by abandoning that doctrine. A functioning International Criminal Court (ICC) (used as a last resort), a functioning Security Council, orderly regional initiatives (as with the Solomon Islands and Bougainville), a capacity to deliver humanitarian aid irrespective of non-recognition – these are potentially available now.

In short what is needed is not the abandonment of sovereignty (for some) but more effective measures. These may in the last resort involve military intervention, though the overall record of sustained, successful military intervention is unpromising. Above all a systematic set of measures not involving the use or threat of force, or the illusory (and inevitably temporary) 'relief' provided by an intervention force, is required – including freer access of Third-World countries to agricultural markets, appropriate arrangements for delivery of health care and medicine and so on. To this real debate about development and governance the language of state failure has added little but confusion.

The 'S' word

It is sometimes suggested that we stop using the 'S' word: 'the sovereignty of states in international relations is essentially a mistake, an illegitimate offspring' (Henkin 1999, 1). But in normal circumstances the state acts in international relations by virtue of its authority in internal relations, including its capacity to affect others, and the government does not cease to exercise that authority because the issue under discussion has ramifications beyond the state – as most issues do. If that capacity to act is normally referred to as 'sovereignty', there seems to be no reason to avoid the name.

A stronger challenge to sovereignty as a key organising concept of the international system is that with globalisation and privatisation, the idea of a sovereign state bears increasingly less resemblance to the real world – including such facts as the large-scale movement of persons and capital, of ideas and information, beyond the control even of militarily powerful states. Doubts are heightened when these developments are seen against a background of profound anti-formalism and rule scepticism (see, e.g., Kennedy 2008); from that perspective, sovereign equality, a formal rule if ever there was one, is an obvious target.

One response is to emphasise the disadvantages of any normative transformation, notably in light of the costly failures of military intervention in many cases:

> State sovereignty as a normative concept is increasingly challenged, especially by a functional view in which the state loses its normative priority and competes with supranational, private, and local actors in the optimal allocation of regulatory authority. But discarding sovereignty in favour of a functional approach will intensify inequality, weakening restraints on coercive intervention, diminishing critical roles of the state as a locus of identity and an autonomous zone of politics, and redividing the world into zones. (Kingsbury 1998, 599)

Another response is to stress the flexibility of the concept of sovereignty, which as has been seen carries only limited substantive consequences and which is consistent with a range of internal forms of government and with the evolution of international institutions. In that context it may be pointed out that international institutions may have the effect of expanding or reinforcing national sovereignty, as with the principle of complementarity in the Statute of the International Criminal Court (see, e.g., Cryer 2005, 985–986).

Despite repeated suggestions of the obsolescence or death of sovereignty as an idea, its normative basis remains. Indeed it may be doubted that entrenched ideas in the international system are likely to succumb, as distinct from being modified through practice and through the accretion of new institutions and values.

Whose state is it?

But there is a fundamental difficulty. Sovereignty operates in a system in which the constitution and composition of the government of the state is not (as a general matter) determined by international law. We are far from having a collective democratic guarantee. Article 25 of the International Covenant of Civil and Political Rights (ICCPR) of 1966 (dealing with certain democratic rights) is a pale shadow of such a guarantee. The principle of self-determination (article 1 of the same Covenant) applies to the people of the state and affirms their right to 'freely determine their political status', but outside the colonial context article 1 refers to no modalities whatever. In those circumstances the government of the state, effectively in control of its territory whether through electoral or other processes, has the exercise of sovereignty in its hands. The point is forcefully made by Roth:

> Those accredited to assert the right [of self-determination] in the name of its bearers earn their standard by achieving, not popular approval by democratic means, but popular acquiescence by whatever means (with the exception of interference from abroad). (Roth 2008, 130)

But what are the alternatives? The record of 'pro-democratic' intervention is slight and (as with Haiti) does not inspire confidence. It is not that the international system lacks the capacity to intervene: article 2(7) has no application to measures taken by the Security Council under Chapter VII of the UN Charter. It is rather that the experience of intervention has been an unhappy one, because the real factors at play locally leading to political instability have not been addressed, and have often been made worse. The principal alternative – the 'sovereignty-pooling' arrangement which underlies the European Union – is a work in progress; adaptations of the idea elsewhere (the Andean Union, the African Union) are embryonic or involve the mere re-labelling of international organisations.

According to the International Commission on Intervention and State Sovereignty (ICISS), state sovereignty should be re-characterised in terms of 'responsibility', with intervention as a potential consequence in case of grave failures of responsibility:

> 2.14 ... [T]he state itself, in signing the Charter, accepts the responsibilities of membership flowing from that signature. There is no transfer or dilution of state sovereignty. But there is a necessary re-characterisation involved: from *sovereignty as control* to *sovereignty as responsibility* in both internal functions and external duties.
>
> 2.15 Thinking of sovereignty as responsibility ... has a threefold significance. First, it implies that the state authorities are responsible for the functions of protecting the safety and lives of citizens and promotion of their welfare. Secondly, it suggests that

the national political authorities are responsible to the citizens internally and to the international community through the UN. And thirdly, it means that the agents of state are responsible for their actions; that is to say, they are accountable for their acts of commission and omission. (ICISS 2001, 13, emphasis in original)

The extent to which this materially develops the existing legal position is doubtful. As to the first and second points, it is not suggested that the state's own 'responsibility to protect' should have any particular legal incident, over and above existing obligations under human rights, humanitarian law and international criminal law. Accountability to the citizens of the state remains in principle an internal matter. Gross failures to protect human life – the ICISS' 'trigger' for intervention – are not matters of domestic jurisdiction in any event. As to the agents of state, they are already 'accountable' internationally for crimes under international law including torture, though subject to an immunity for serving senior officials (*Arrest Warrant* case, ICJ Reports 2002, p. 3, 22), and to many other constraints. Above all, the intervention which is envisaged depends on Security Council authorisation: at least, such was the conclusion of the debate triggered by the ICISS Report (see UN High-level Panel on Threats, Challenges and Change 2004, paras. 203, 207; UN Secretary-General 2005, 'In Larger Freedom: Towards Development, Security and Human Rights for all', paras. 125, 126; World Summit Outcome 2005, A/RES/60/1, paras. 138–139).

The policy underlying international law seems to be to encourage the development of stable indigenous institutions, while avoiding inter-state military conflict except under multilateral auspices. That policy served in the years leading up to the end of the Cold War, and it was powerfully reinforced by the Helsinki Declaration (1975), with its balance between human rights and non-intervention. Much – perhaps too much – was made of the turn to democracy at the end of the 1980s, but the policy can be said to have worked. There is some irony in the fact that the case for greater unilateralism was made at a time when the institutions for collective action, notably the Security Council, had shown some capacity to function as intended.

At any rate international law appears to say, simultaneously, that (a) sovereignty inheres in the state, considered as an autonomous territorial community across time; (b) sovereignty is the exclusive authority over territory, i.e. the capacity to exercise, to the exclusion of other states, state functions on or related to that territory, and includes the capacity to make binding commitments under international law; (c) such sovereignty is exercisable by the governmental institutions established within the state; (d) the government of the state depends on the fact of local control, not on democratic legitimacy. Those positions are no doubt in tension with each other but they are not in outright conflict. Arguably they reflect a balance between local autonomy and the need for international law to deal with facts on the ground. Sovereignty – qualified as sovereignty under the law – is the standard operating assumption of a decentralised international system. It is intervention that requires special justification, most notably by reference to Chapter VII of the UN Charter.

Conclusion

Two cheers, then, for sovereignty, understood as a defeasible but protected status in the international system, carrying with it the presumption of full governmental authority over a polity and territory. Reports of the death of sovereignty are much exaggerated: not only is the state free to exercise its sovereignty; the protection of its interests practically requires it. It can enter into a variety of political relations involving association with other states. It can decide to 'pool' sovereignty through regional institutions such as the European Union – assuming they are available to it. Or it can enter into specific substantive arrangements with other states and organisations. Short of full-scale integration in another state, its sovereignty survives such exercises of it, reflecting the continued identity of the territorial community to which its government should be (and sometimes is) accountable.

Bibliography

Charney, J., 1986. 'The Persistent Objector Rule and the Development of Customary International Law', *British Yearbook of International Law*, 56, 1–24

Crawford, J., 2006. *The Creation of States in International Law*, 2nd edn., Oxford: Clarendon

Cryer, R., 2005. 'International Criminal Law vs State Sovereignty: Another Round?', *European Journal of International Law*, 16, 979–1000

Davidson, B., 1992. *The Black Man's Burden: Africa and the Curse of the Nation-state*, Oxford: James Currey

Greenberg, K. and J. L. Dratel, 2005. *The Torture Papers: The Road to Abu Ghraib*, Cambridge University Press

Henkin, L., 1999. 'That "S" Word: Sovereignty, and Globalisation, and Human Rights, et cetera', *Fordham Law Review*, 68, 1–14

Hinsley, F. H., 1986. *Sovereignty*, 2nd edn., Cambridge University Press

Hironaka, A., 2005. *Neverending Wars: The International Community, Weak States, and the Perpetuation of Civil War*, Cambridge, MA: Harvard University Press

International Commission on Intervention and State Sovereignty (ICISS) 2001. *The Responsibility to* Protect, Ottawa: IDRC

Jackson, R., 1990. *Quasi-States: Sovereignty, International Relations and the Third World*, Cambridge University Press

Jackson, R., 2007. *Sovereignty: Evolution of an Idea*, Cambridge: Polity

Kennedy, D., 2008. 'The Mystery of Global Governance', *Ohio Northern University Law Review*, 34, 827–860

Kingsbury, B., 1998. 'Sovereignty and Inequality', *European Journal of International Law*, 9, 599–625

Peters, A., L. Koechlin, T. Förster and G. Zinkernagel (eds.), 2009. *Non-state Actors as Standard Setters*, Cambridge University Press

Roth, B., 2008. 'State Sovereignty, International Legality and Moral Disagreement', in T. Broude and Y. Shany (eds.), *The Shifting Allocation of Authority in International Law*, Oxford: Hart

Schiemann, K., 2007. 'Europe and the Loss of Sovereignty', *International and Comparative Law Quarterly*, 56, 475–489

Schrijver, N., 1997. *Sovereignty over Natural Resources*, Cambridge University Press

United Nations High-level Panel on Threats, Challenges and Change 2004. *A More Secure World: Our Shared Responsibility, Report*, A/59/565, 2 December

United Nations Secretary-General, 2005. *In Larger Freedom: Towards Development, Security and Human Rights For All, Report*, A/59/2005, 21 March

Vattel, E., 2008. *The Law of Nations or the Principles of Natural Law Applied to the Conduct and to the Affairs of Nations and of Sovereigns*, reprinted, Indianapolis: Liberty Fund

6 Exercise and limits of jurisdiction

Bruno Simma and Andreas Th. Müller

Introduction

For many, jurisdiction has the reputation of being a technical matter and thus of having a rather dry appeal, and not without cause. At the same time, the study of the rules assigning jurisdiction, limiting it and seeking to handle overlaps and tensions arising in this process of allocation is a fascinating lens through which to view the macro-structure of international law, since these very rules, in manifold ways, mirror the interplay, and conflict, of the governing principles of the international legal order.

The term 'jurisdiction' stems from the Latin *ius dicere*, which literally translates as 'speaking the law'. In its widest sense, jurisdiction therefore means an entity's entitlement to authoritatively say 'what the law is'. In the context of international law, two principal uses of the term must be distinguished.

In a first instance, in the domestic as well as the international realm, reference is had to the 'jurisdiction' of *institutional bodies*. This concerns the question under what conditions institutions, particularly those of a judicial or quasi-judicial character, may pronounce on what the law is. As there exists no single institution entitled to address all questions it deems fit, it is crucial to assess the reach of a body's jurisdiction and, correspondingly, to identify the limits of its jurisdiction. These limits typically manifest themselves on the temporal, spatial, personal and subject matter level. For instance, a judicial body, be it the Cambridge County Court or the International Court of Justice (ICJ), is only authorised to exercise its jurisdiction in regard to situations that have materialised (a) at certain times and (b) in certain places, which have been brought about (c) by certain classes of actors vis-à-vis certain other actors, and (d) whose subject matter is of the kind with which the body is set up to deal. As international law is an old-established discipline and jurisdiction one of its classical subjects, the Latin expressions of jurisdiction *ratione temporis*, *ratione loci*, *ratione personae* and *ratione materiae* are often employed in this regard. If a body exceeds the limits of the jurisdiction assigned to it, it is said to have acted *ultra vires* – that is, beyond its powers or off-limits. For lack of space, we have to leave the topic of jurisdiction of international courts and tribunals aside in the following, even though it is an increasingly significant subject of international law (for more on this, see Chapter 9).

The other common, and genuinely international, use of the concept is with regard to the entitlement of *states* (and, for that matter, intergovernmental organisations such as the United Nations or the European Union) to authoritatively declare what the law is in their domain and how it is to be enforced. States produce, apply and enforce legal norms in an extremely wide variety of fields and circumstances, in matters of criminal law, regarding elections, taxes, bankruptcy, families, environmental pollution and gambling, to name just a few. Yet, not only do courts have a delimited scope of action but, by virtue of international law, states too are not free to take up every set of facts and subject it to their normative action. What is to be noted here is that the regime of jurisdiction of states operates on a higher level of generality than the jurisdiction of courts and tribunals. It is on the basis, and within the limits, of the jurisdiction enjoyed by states that states, on their part, endow bodies on the domestic and the international level with authority to state the law. International law contains a number of principles and rules on how to organise jurisdiction of and amongst states, which together make up the 'international law of jurisdiction'.

The rationale for an international law of jurisdiction

Why does international law deal with the question of jurisdiction of states in the first place? The answer to this question is both obvious and telling of the very structure of international law. In spite of profound transformations in the international legal order, states remain its prime subjects. They stand with one another in a relation of *sovereign equality* (UN Charter, article 2(1); see also Chapter 5). This signifies that international law acknowledges in principle that states (a) constitute autonomous entities which decide for themselves on the legal, political, economic and social order to be established within their borders, and (b) that they are, as they all share this quality, perfectly on par with each other from the legal point of view, irrespective of huge factual asymmetries in terms of size and power.

The mere fact of a *plurality* of independent states poses a huge coordinative challenge to international law. It is not hard to imagine that if almost two hundred states were to devise rules according simply to their discretion, the risk of obstruction, paralysis and chaos would be immense and essential functions which international law is meant to fulfil would be severely jeopardised. The coordinative challenge appears in two steps: First, even though states are primary and sovereign subjects of international law, this does not imply that they have all-encompassing competences to address every set of facts materialising anywhere. Hence, international law has developed a normative framework according to which jurisdiction is allocated amongst states. This framework thus determines under what conditions a state can lawfully (i.e. with approval of the international legal order) say what the law is and what is to be done about some matter. Hence, international law provides criteria to assess when a state has acted beyond the proper reach of its jurisdiction and therefore *ultra vires*. This would clearly be the case, for instance, if New Zealand sought to establish speed limits in Mexico, or if Japan wanted to regulate access to Mount Kenya.

Secondly, even though a state acts within the confines of its jurisdiction, this does not exclude the entitlement of another state to deal with the same set of facts, in a different, but equally normative way. To be sure, international law strives to establish a relatively clear connection between a state of affairs and a state competent to regulate it, and for the bulk of matters this does not cause problems at all. It is pretty obvious that speed limits in Mexico fall into Mexican jurisdiction, while access to Mount Kenya is decided upon by the Kenyan authorities. However, the lawyer will be particularly interested in the frontiers, inconsistencies and tensions within a given legal order, particularly where the international law of jurisdiction creates overlaps, that is, instances of parallel or *concurrent* jurisdiction, which sometimes even lead to *conflicts* of jurisdiction. And in fact, who is in charge of speed limits for cars on the Oresund Bridge crossing the sea between Denmark and Sweden or on the premises of the UN headquarters in New York? And who may regulate access to Mount Everest which, while its peak is located in Nepal, is climbed from the Nepalese as well as from the Tibetan side or, for that matter, to Mont Blanc whose very summit lies on the French–Italian border? As long as there is agreement amongst the affected states, there will be no practical problems. However, in case of conflict, international law is expected to provide a solution. In light of this, it is necessary to identify the fundamental principles governing the allocation of jurisdiction to individual states.

Basic principles for the allocation of jurisdiction in international law

States aspire to build up comprehensive legal systems that regulate everything they deem pertinent to 'their' affairs. However, not every nexus a state may see between a set of facts and its sphere of interests and regulatory intent is accepted in international law as creating a legal entitlement to exercise jurisdiction. Amongst the multitude of existing relations, international law privileges some and qualifies them as 'substantial', 'sufficient' or 'genuine' links between a state's legal order and a given state of affairs. Let us reconsider the example of speed limits. While the fact that the roads for the use of which the limits shall be established are located in Mexico obviously suffices to produce a sufficient nexus to permit this state to exercise jurisdiction, Japan cannot demonstrate a comparable link. Even if Japan were to (presumably incorrectly) argue that most cars in Mexico are of Japanese origin and that this constitutes a special nexus to driving cars in Mexico, this would not be considered a valid argument to prove a genuine link. This is a straightforward case but, as we shall see, the test does not always produce such clear-cut results.

The question of what counts as a connecting factor, a genuine link, is decided by international law, and it should not come as any surprise that the relations privileged by it reflect fundamental normative choices underlying the international legal order itself. In other words, in the micro-discipline of jurisdiction the macro-principles of contemporary international law become manifest. It has been mentioned that states are, and remain, the building blocks of the international legal order. States, however, are also, first of all, territorial units exercising sovereignty over a certain portion of the planet's surface. At the same time, states are constituted by a number of human beings, a people whose members are linked to it by the special bond of nationality. Hence, the *territorial(ity)* and *personal(ity)* or *nationality* principles have advanced to the foremost bases of jurisdiction accepted by international law (see also Chapter 4).

The territoriality principle

The extent of territorial jurisdiction

As a rule, a state has jurisdiction over everything materialising in its territory. Accordingly, it can regulate all acts with regard to its land territory (including the subsoil), the territorial sea extending up to 12 nautical miles beyond its coasts as well as the air space above them. While in these areas, falling under a state's territorial sovereignty, it enjoys plenary jurisdiction, in other places international law will attribute more limited territorial jurisdiction. This is the case, for instance, for the contiguous zone that stretches 12 further miles beyond the territorial sea. There, the coastal state may exercise jurisdiction in customs, fiscal, sanitary and immigration matters. In the exclusive economic zone that extends 200 miles from the coast, a state may assert jurisdiction over the exploration for, and exploitation of, living (e.g. fish) and non-living (e.g. oil, gas) resources and over the establishment of artificial islands such as oil rigs (1982 UN Convention on the Law of the Sea (UNCLOS), articles 2, 33, 56, 60). Accordingly, territorial jurisdiction is gradually being reduced, fading out with increasing distance from land territory, which forms the core space of the territorial state. Ultimately, the high seas, outer space and Antarctica are beyond the territorial jurisdiction of any state. This does not imply that no jurisdiction can lawfully be exercised in these areas. International law has devised strategies to deal with this situation. After all, it is not only the scenario of overlapping and conflicting jurisdictions that is unsatisfactory; a lack or vacuum of jurisdiction poses considerable risks to the well functioning of the international legal order.

Strategies to compensate for the lack or absence of territorial jurisdiction

The most important instrument in this regard is the *flag state* principle. As human presence in areas free of territorial jurisdiction is normally closely linked to means of transportation such as ships, aircraft or spacecraft, it has become the rule to endow the state under whose flag a vehicle is registered and operates with full jurisdiction over persons and acts materialising thereupon. The flag principle is also of relevance in areas which are only partially subjected to territorial jurisdiction. For instance, apart from the competences specifically assigned to an adjacent territorial state over its sea zones, all matters relating to vessels finding themselves within these zones remain within the responsibility of the flag state (UNCLOS, articles 92, 94, 97). This is a striking example of the effort made by international law to reasonably distribute jurisdictional competences amongst states deemed to have a substantial link to events occurring in such spaces. This situation can give rise to concurrent jurisdiction that might lead to conflicts. It deserves mention here that there is controversy as to the precise nature of the flag state principle.

In the *Lotus* case, the Permanent Court of International Justice (PCIJ) ruled that a Turkish ship was 'a place assimilated to Turkish territory' (*S.S. Lotus*, Advisory Opinion, PCIJ (1927) Ser. A No. 10, p. 4, 23) and thus understood flag state jurisdiction as quasi-*territorial* jurisdiction. Others have argued that the flag reflects a link which is comparable to the bond of nationality and therefore treat it as quasi-*personal* jurisdiction (Lowe 2007, 175) with which we shall deal shortly. Without delving into this theoretical debate, there does not seem to be a need to opt for the one or other alternative since the flag state principle may adequately be understood as combining aspects of both concepts.

As an additional strategy, to the extent that states are permitted by international law to exercise jurisdiction over acts realised in another state's territory on the basis of the nationality and protective principles, they can also do so in zones of reduced territorial jurisdiction, and those characterised by the absence of territorial jurisdiction. One could even argue that, in view of international law's *horror vacui*, that is, its effort to avoid effectively jurisdiction-free, and in that sense 'anarchic', areas, there is even more reason to rely upon alternative grounds of jurisdiction.

This becomes manifest in particular with regard to a further device, namely the institution of the so-called *universality* principle or principle of *universal jurisdiction*. It permits a state to exercise criminal jurisdiction over acts of individuals without any specific link to the event in terms of the territoriality or nationality principles. Not surprisingly, the oldest instance of international law providing for the universality principle is piracy on the high seas, i.e. in sovereignty-free areas where no state has territorial jurisdiction.

Last but not least, the concept of the 'common heritage of mankind' also involves allocation of jurisdiction beyond classical territorial jurisdiction. By this vehicle, for instance, the so-called 'Area', that is the seabed and ocean floor and the subsoil thereof, is withdrawn from the jurisdiction of any single state. At the same time, the Area is subjected to a jurisdictional regime, designed for the benefit of the international community as a whole, whose administration is entrusted to the International Seabed Authority (UNCLOS articles 136 *et seq.*; see also Chapter 18).

Uncertainty with regard to the application of the territoriality principle

Even within the scope of undisputed spatial application of the territoriality principle, uncertainties remain. We have hitherto only spoken, in the abstract, of acts occurring in the territory of a state. But when precisely is this the case? Human acts can be very complex phenomena, with different aspects manifesting themselves in different states. In domestic law, for instance in the realm of criminal or tort law, the distinction between the *conduct* and *result* element of an act is a familiar one. Hence, for a murder to be committed, both the conduct of killing and the death of a person are necessary. These two can perfectly well materialise in the territories of two separate states (e.g. in case of a letter bomb sent from one state to another), let alone in case of the bombing of an aircraft, where the explosive device may be produced in one state with components supplied from a number of other states, and then loaded in a third state into the aircraft registered within a fourth state. If the device is brought to explosion in the airspace of a fifth state and the plane comes down on the territory of a sixth one, which of them has territorial jurisdiction over the crime(s) in question? This is not a far-fetched example, as the scenario described is quite similar to the terrorist bombing of a US passenger aircraft (PanAm Flight 103) at Lockerbie, Scotland on 21 December 1988. As a rule, the fact that either the conduct or its result is realised in a state's territory is considered a sufficient link to trigger that state's territorial jurisdiction. It is common to refer to these two constellations as the exercise of *subjective* and *objective* territorial jurisdiction, respectively (Brownlie 2008, 301).

The so-called *effects doctrine* is often considered a variation of objective territorial jurisdiction. This doctrine, first developed in US anti-trust law, claims that the sole fact of intentional production of economic effects (e.g. the extent and prices of imports and exports) in US territory permitted US authorities to regulate such acts (see the *Alcoa* case, *US* v. *Aluminum Co. of America*, 148 F 2d 416 (2nd Cir. 1945)). This assertion of jurisdiction was objected to by many states. However, more recently several European states have adopted a similar approach, and this has also been endorsed, to some extent, by the Court of Justice of the European Union (CJEU) (see the *Woodpulp* case, *Ahlström Osakeyhtiö and Others* v. *Commission*, [1998] ECR 5193, paras. 16-18 and in particular the Opinion of Advocate-General Darmon, paras. 7 et seq., notably paras. 57f.). To be sure, economic effects are certainly the result of human action, but it has been argued that there remains a difference in kind between physical constituents of an act realised in a state's territory and the mere economic consequences of the manipulation of market forces (Akehurst 1972–1973, 152, 195; Lowe and Staker 2010, 322). It could also be said that such effects are too remote from the initial acts; recognising them as the 'result' of these initial acts could bring almost everything within their ambit. An excessive effects doctrine would indeed bear the risk of creating a sort of jurisdictional 'butterfly effect', since, in the highly interconnected world economy, even inconspicuous and seemingly innocent acts can be traced back as being at the origin of all kinds of negative repercussions.

This does not disqualify, however, a reasonable application of the effects doctrine, and states do increasingly cite it as the basis for exercise of jurisdiction. The 'butterfly effect' argument also cuts in the other direction: the more complex and interlinked the world economy becomes and the more the liberal global economic order permits market-relevant activity to be performed from any place on the planet, the more it might prove necessary to adapt the concept of 'result' to the more complicated and interwoven reality of today's economy. Otherwise, it could at times become difficult to identify which state would have jurisdiction to deal, let alone to deal effectively, with certain kinds of transnational economic activity. This has been painfully underscored by the recent economic turbulence.

At the same time, the promotion of an effects doctrine can admittedly lead to a proliferation of jurisdiction, with several states adopting parallel, and even contradictory, legislation. To be sure, such collision of exercises of jurisdiction is a serious challenge to an international law aspiring to a reasonable and efficient allocation of jurisdiction amongst states. But as long as it is accepted that a state's susceptibility to economic effects brought about by conduct in another state is serious enough to constitute an interest that deserves international legal protection, there is no reason why it should not be recognised as a sufficient nexus for jurisdiction. This position is corroborated by commentators who see in the effects doctrine a subcategory of the protective principle permitting a state to protect itself against serious economic repercussions induced from abroad.

Whatever position one might take regarding the extension of territorial jurisdiction in this respect, the territoriality principle, far from being an obsolete model, constitutes the single most important basis for states to assert jurisdiction. It is striking in this regard that the other grounds of jurisdiction, even though gaining importance, are still collectively referred to as bases for the *extra-territorial* exercise of jurisdiction.

Personality or nationality principle

Custom has it that, when addressing the personality principle, homage is paid to the jurisdiction of sovereigns over 'their people' being older than over their territory, as personal jurisdiction dates back to the time before the emergence of the modern territorial state. Yet, this is first and foremost an indirect acknowledgement of today's precedence of the territoriality principle as immediate reflection of a world order founded on territorial states. The personality principle endowing a state with jurisdiction over its nationals, that is, persons linked to it by the bond of nationality, is nonetheless still of considerable significance. The idea underlying the principle is that nationality is accompanied by special allegiance on the part of the national vis-à-vis his or her state and a corresponding right or duty of protection of the state with regard to the national. This is generally held to satisfy the requirement of a substantial link so as to permit a state to exercise jurisdiction with regard to its nationals.

As a rule, it is up to each state to decide to whom to grant its nationality. Against this background, it might well be that a person has dual or multiple nationalities and thus falls within the ambit of personal jurisdiction of several states. This opens the possibility of concurring, and competing, jurisdictional claims, which might also raise human rights concerns. However, in international law, notably in the law of diplomatic protection, rules have been developed to specify conditions under which other international actors are bound to recognise the award of nationality by a State to an individual, be it a natural person (*Nottebohm* case *(Liechtenstein* v. *Guatemala)*, ICJ Reports 1955, p. 4) or a juridical person (*Barcelona Traction* case (*Belgium* v. *Spain*), ICJ Reports 1970, p. 3). The situation is somewhat different with regard to the special bond created for a vehicle on the sea, in the air or outer space by virtue of its registration in a state. It has been mentioned that some have tried to assimilate this relation to nationality, and there certainly are important parallels. However, a striking difference is that, as a matter of principle, ships and aircraft cannot have dual nationality, but are considered stateless if operating under two or more flags (UNCLOS, article 92).

In the context of the personality principle, normally a distinction is made between its active and passive strand. This notably relates to the application of the principle in criminal law which is not the only, but arguably the most prominent, area of law where it is used. Accordingly, the *active personality* principle entitles a state to assert jurisdiction over crimes committed by its nationals abroad and is relied upon by a great many national criminal codes. Compared to that, the *passive personality* principle, which is triggered when a state's national becomes the victim of a crime, is of lesser importance, and it is often doubted whether, and to what extent, it can count as a ground on which to found jurisdiction. The often-claimed asymmetry between the active and passive personality principles is further nourished, for example, by article 12 of the 1998 Rome Statute of the International Criminal Court (ICC Statute), which makes the exercise of the Court's jurisdiction dependent upon the consent of either the state where the crime was committed (territoriality principle) or that of the nationality of the perpetrator (active personality principle). This suggests that the passive personality principle was not considered of comparable weight as a ground of creating domestic criminal jurisdiction.

However, one should refrain from arriving at premature conclusions. There are areas where the principle is meanwhile well established: 'Passive personality jurisdiction, for so long regarded as controversial ... today meets with relatively little opposition, at least so far as a particular category of offences is concerned' (*Arrest Warrant* case (*Democratic Republic of the Congo* v. *Belgium*), Separate Opinion of Judges Higgins, Kooijmans and Buergenthal, ICJ Reports 2002, p. 3, para. 47). This notably holds true for a number of anti-terrorism conventions and instruments drawn upon for the protection of diplomats and other foreign dignitaries (for example the 1973 Convention on the Prevention and Punishment of Crimes Against Internationally Protected Persons). It should be noted that the closer the involvement of the victim in the exercise of state functions (which is also true with regard to victims of terrorist acts, since such acts are typically intended to prompt a state into certain behaviour), the higher is the chance that the international community will endorse the assertion of jurisdiction by the state of nationality and transform the somewhat doubtful credentials of the passive personality principle into impeccable references. The principle thus seems to be bolstered, as it were, by infiltration of the protective principle.

Protective principle

In addition to the principles of territoriality and personality, it has long been recognised that certain interests of states are so essential that acts directed against them qualify as sufficiently close to prompt those states' jurisdiction. This is the case with regard to counterfeiting of money or other state-issued documents or espionage, over which a state can assert jurisdiction irrespective of where or by whom such acts have been committed. Just as the territoriality and personality principles reflect two core elements of the very concept of the state, territory and people, one might well say that the protective principle reflects the third cardinal element, namely government power (see Chapter 4). Accordingly, acts that severely jeopardise a state's government functions are considered a sufficient basis for jurisdiction.

There has been a tendency in recent decades and years to expand jurisdiction based on the protective principle beyond traditionally accepted paradigmatic instances of its application and place acts such as trafficking in persons and narcotics or the violation of a state's customs and immigration laws under this label. While these instances, without doubt, concern legitimate and important state interests, it is questionable whether they are so vital for a state's existence as to justify reliance on the protective principle. In the post-2001 atmosphere where 'security' appears to have become to some a catch-all concept, a sweeping application of the protective principle may present itself as highly opportune, but this is far from being a commonly accepted position. The law seems to be in a state of flux here.

Universality principle (universal jurisdiction)

Finally, we have to turn to the so-called universality principle according to which a state may assert jurisdiction over a crime irrespective of the existence of any of the three previously mentioned connecting factors. This principle stands apart from the others since it has an ambiguous relationship with the substantial link doctrine. Some commentators have correctly observed that the universality principle combines two different strands (Lowe 2007, 348). On the one hand, and this is the standard reason given for its application, there are crimes such as genocide, crimes against humanity and serious war crimes that are 'of concern to the international community as a whole' (ICC Statute, preamble and article 5). Due to their characteristic traits, their heinousness and politically imbued character, they are considered to affect each and every state. This kind of reasoning seems to satisfy, by and in itself, the nexus requirement, without further calling for proof of a state's privileged connection to a given act. In this sense, the universality principle simultaneously confirms, and transcends, the substantial link doctrine.

On the other hand, in the long-recognised case of application of universal jurisdiction: piracy on the high seas (*In re Piracy Jure Gentium* [1934]

AC 568, 589 (per Viscount Sankey); UNCLOS, article 105), the rationale is different. While acts of piracy can be extremely brutal, they do not normally either in scope or character amount to the momentous crimes referred to above, but rather resemble serious crimes on the national level like armed robbery, taking of hostages and murder. The chief reason to provide for universal jurisdiction in the former, but not the latter case takes us back to the fact that there is no territorial jurisdiction on the high seas. In order to facilitate an effective response to piracy even beyond the reach of territorial jurisdiction of states, international law thus extends an invitation to all states to exercise jurisdiction over such acts. By extrapolation, states have been invited to exercise jurisdiction over acts of piracy off the coast of Somalia. However, even in the case of a failed State, international law remains reluctant to simply pass over the prerogatives of the nominal territorial sovereign. Accordingly, the pertinent Security Council Resolution 1851 (2008) not only bases itself on Chapter VII of the UN Charter but also expressly requires interested states to obtain the advance consent of the Transitional Federal Government of Somalia for the exercise of third-state jurisdiction in Somali territorial waters.

This difference also becomes manifest on another level. The first strand of the universality principle has been strongly inspired by post-1945 developments in the fields of international humanitarian law and international human rights law. Hence, it (or variations of it) was introduced into the 1949 Geneva Conventions, the 1979 International Convention Against the Taking of Hostages and the 1984 Convention Against Torture and Other Cruel, Inhuman or Degrading Treatment or Punishment. Inspired by the moral imperative that there must be no impunity for such crimes (see, e.g., ICC Statute, preambular para. 4), there has been a tendency to establish a *mandatory* universality regime and, if a presumed perpetrator is present in the territory of a state, to oblige that state to exercise its jurisdiction and prosecute such person or extradite him to another state prepared to prosecute (*aut dedere aut iudicare*). In contrast, the universality principle enshrined for piracy in UNCLOS is strictly *facultative*.

As with regard to the protective principle, this is a dynamic area with several states (e.g. Belgium, Spain, but also the United States under the Alien Tort Statute, 28 USC §1350) having asserted ambitious claims of universal jurisdiction in relation to gross human rights violations, and other states contesting such jurisdictional aspirations. Apart from the scope of crimes covered by the universality principle, a hotly disputed issue is whether the lawful exercise of universal jurisdiction requires as a minimum threshold the physical presence of the presumed perpetrator in the territory of the state asserting jurisdiction. The available case-law does not point in a clear direction (see *Arrest Warrant* case, Separate Opinion of Judges Higgins, Kooijmans and Buergenthal, para. 22 *et seq.*; 2001 Princeton Principles on Universal Jurisdiction). However, some clarification regarding the proper reach of the universality principle is to be expected from cases currently pending before the ICJ (e.g. *Questions relating to the Obligation to Prosecute or Extradite* (*Belgium* v. *Senegal*)). The increase in cases of European states relying on claims of universal jurisdiction vis-à-vis African states has led to concern and criticism on the part of African states (see, e.g., the creation and work of the African Union Commission on the Abuse of the Principles of Universal Jurisdiction).

Extra-territorial jurisdiction

While all cases of the application of the personality, protective and universality principles can be referred to as instances of *extra-territorial* exercise of jurisdiction, the extra-territorial application of international human rights treaties raises special problems. With the European Court of Human Rights' *Loizidou* (1995) and *Cyprus* v. *Turkey* (2001) judgments powerfully opening the door to the application of the European Convention on Human Rights (ECHR) to activities of a state beyond its borders, a series of further decisions of this and other human rights courts (see notably the ECtHR's *Assanidze* v. *Georgia* (2004), *Ilaşcu* v. *Moldova and Russia* (2004), *Öcalan* v. *Turkey* (2005), *Issa* v. *Turkey* (2004) cases) and, in particular, the ICJ decisions in the *Wall* (2004) and *Armed Activities* (2005) cases have contributed to consolidate this jurisprudence. Alas, the pertinent case-law has also generated more restrictive tendencies, in particular in the ECtHR's *Banković* case regarding the responsibility of NATO Member states for the bombardments of Yugoslavia in 1999. In its 2007 judgment in *R (Al-Skeini et al.)* v. *Secretary of State for Defence*, the House of Lords embraced this restrictive line of reasoning and applied it to acts of the United Kingdom in occupied Iraq. Arguments of a similar kind have been marshalled regarding the detainment by the United States of so-called unlawful enemy combatants in Guantánamo Bay, thus making manifest the ever-precarious nature of claims of extra-territorial application of human rights treaties.

Attempts at strict classification versus a flexible system of allocation of jurisdiction

Jurisdiction is not a monolithic or one-size-fits-all concept but appears in different forms. One of the most widespread and influential distinctions in the field is the one between so-called jurisdiction to *prescribe*, *adjudicate* and *enforce* (see, e.g., Restat. 3d of US Foreign Relations Law (1990), §401). While these different functions of jurisdiction can be exercised by all branches of the government of a state, the distinction is strongly informed by the division of state authority into the legislative, judicial and executive branches. Even though a useful tool in several contexts, this tripartite classification is not directly anchored in international law. Against this background, it has been proposed to collapse the first two types of jurisdiction into one and oppose them to enforcement jurisdiction (Lowe 2007, 339). The latter is commonly held to be governed by a straightforward territorial approach: acts of enforcement (e.g. detention, seizure, telephone surveillance) must not be carried out in another state's territory save with its consent.

It is this kind of distinction that the PCIJ had in mind when it famously stated in the *Lotus* (1927) case: 'Now the first and foremost restriction imposed by international law upon a State is that ... it may not exercise its power in any form in the territory in another State ... It does not, however, follow that international law prohibits a State from exercising jurisdiction in its own territory, in respect of acts which have taken place abroad ... Far from laying down a general prohibition to the effect that States may not extend the application of their laws and the jurisdiction of their courts to persons, property and acts outside their territory, it leaves them in this respect a wide measure of discretion' (*Lotus*, p. 18).

In fact, beyond attempts at strict categorisation and classification, the international law of jurisdiction also testifies to the malleability of international law. It endows the actors on the international plane with a considerable degree of discretion and generally abstains from providing bright-line rules and razor-sharp distinctions. Accordingly, the law of jurisdiction is better described as endorsing a flexible and differentiated approach, combining a series of factors such as the nature of the subject matter involved; the individual interests of affected states vis-à-vis the interest of the international community as whole; and the risks of under-allocating jurisdiction as well as over-extensive assignment of jurisdiction. In general, the situation most feared in the international legal context appears to be a *negative* conflict of jurisdiction (i.e. no state has jurisdiction or is prepared to exercise it). This becomes manifest in tendencies observable over recent decades to expand universal jurisdiction for gross human right violations as an alternative to relying upon other, often factually paralysed, bases for jurisdiction. In the decentralised and imperfect international legal order, the cardinal challenge is lack of exercise of jurisdiction, and international law might thus have a tendency to err on the side of caution and to 'over-jurisdictionalise'. This can in turn give rise to a *positive* conflict of jurisdiction.

However, in spite of serious limits and pitfalls in the process of allocation of jurisdiction, subject to the often conflicting and contradictory claims of interested states, in an overall perspective international law is fairly successful in assigning jurisdiction. In a number of fields this has led to the development of a well-established set of rules on jurisdiction that successfully balance different concerns. For instance, as a rule, international law gives states significant leeway in taking up criminal law matters as it acknowledges the considerable interest of the respective community in such matters. At the same time, there are specific risks related to simultaneous exercise of criminal jurisdiction by several states, ranging from chaos and tension resulting from jurisdictional conflict between states, to problematic consequences for the affected individuals (e.g. double jeopardy). Such risks are countered by the intricate interplay of jurisdiction-distributing principles.

A similar phenomenon may be observed in the law of the sea where there exists, as we have seen, a sophisticated regime of allocation of jurisdiction between the flag state and the adjacent territorial state, gradually shifting the exercise of jurisdiction from the latter to the former with increasing distance from the nucleus of territorial sovereignty: the land mass occupied by the state. However, there remain gray areas in this regard. Thus, there is controversy over the extent to which the territorial state has jurisdictional access to acts on board a ship anchoring in its ports, if these acts are claimed to have influence – evoking a variation of the effects doctrine – on nearby coastal communities (see the *Wildenhus'* case, 120 US 1 (1887); Akehurst 1972–1973, 164, 215; Oxman 2008). In other areas, such as in private law, states are relatively free to choose on the basis of what criteria to submit matters to their legislation (Akehurst 1972–1973, 170 *et seq.*). As the concurrent exercise of jurisdiction normally does not lead to problematic results similar to those encountered in criminal law, international law has contented itself with limited action in this regard. There are only few cogent rules excluding the reliance on certain bases of jurisdiction, and much is done on the basis of a long-grown development of accepted principles regarding typical connecting factors. However, this is a matter which pertains more to private international law and conflict of laws – to use the typical terms in the civil and common law traditions – and will not be further pursued here.

The international law of jurisdiction thus seems to perform a comprehensive evaluation and weighting of factors that add up to, or detract from, the extent of a state's affectedness that is needed for that state to lawfully claim jurisdiction. This constitutes the very essence of the 'substantial link' doctrine, and it should be clear against the backdrop of the foregoing that the establishment of such a link is not an abstract operation, but an assessment of the concrete interests involved. In addition, it should be noted that this assessment is not independent of whether there are competing jurisdictional claims of other states. In areas of reduced or lacking territorial jurisdiction, international law might, for instance, be prepared to allocate jurisdiction to a state on the basis of mere physical presence represented by a craft flying its flag (e.g. piracy). In a similar vein, in view of the lack in practice of a state realistically exercising jurisdiction, the mere physical presence of the presumed perpetrator in a state's territory may suffice to establish its jurisdiction for such crimes (see, e.g., the 1984 Torture Convention, article 7).

Against this background, there are two relevant thresholds to be considered in the process of allocation of jurisdiction. First, one will have to ask whether the ties of a matter to a state are strong and/or numerous enough to meet the 'substantial link' requirement. Once this threshold of *exercise of jurisdiction* is met, it will have to be further examined whether a state's relation to a set of facts is so close, and its interests involved in it so important, that international law recognises it as the state with by far the closest link and thus endows it with *exclusive* jurisdiction over the matter. This might explain some of the normative choices made by contemporary international law which provide, for example, for a state's exclusive jurisdiction as to the conditions of a grant of its nationality (the extent to which other states have to recognise it is a different question, discussed above) or over ships flying its flag or oil rigs (UNCLOS, articles 60, 92). While these cases are fairly different as to their nature, international law recognises in all of them overarching political and economic interests of one single state that supersede jurisdictional interests of other international actors. This, it is important to note, happens irrespective of whether the link is considered territorial or personal in character, or even based on the protective principle. What eventually counts is that the ties, in relation to potentially competing claims, add up to the critical mass that gives rise to exclusive jurisdiction. In a similar vein, in view of the above debate as to the territorial or personal basis of the flag state principle, it is submitted here that the two should be seen as mutually reinforcing and jointly contributing to establish the chief basis for exercise of jurisdiction on the sea.

Once this is kept in mind, even the otherwise often sidelined topic of jurisdiction to enforce appears to better blend into the general picture. On closer observation, its clear-cut master rule according to which enforcement acts may only be carried out by the territorial state, or with its permission, is nothing but the allocation of exclusive jurisdiction over enforcement to this very state. Should this come as a surprise in an international legal order founded on the territorially constituted sovereign equality of states (UN Charter, article 2(1))? Extra-territorial enforcement action stands in sharp tension with this conception so that international law reacts in a particularly allergic fashion when it comes to the carrying out of physical acts, possibly including the use of force, in foreign territory (UN Charter, article 2 (4)). In the absence of consent by the territorial state, such action is solely permitted by international law in narrowly defined circumstances (see UN Charter, articles 2(7) and 51).

Strategies of dealing with concurrent and conflicting jurisdiction

While assigning exclusive jurisdiction to a state is rather the exception than the rule, the lion's share of real-life cases have relevant ties only to one state so that it is *factually* the only one to exercise jurisdiction over it, for example, if a national of a state murders a compatriot on this state's territory. If there exists, however, a substantial link to more than one state, for example if the same murder happens in the territory of another state, we are confronted with a case of concurrent or parallel jurisdiction. This can easily turn into a conflict of jurisdiction, for instance, if the two affected states seek to exercise jurisdiction over the matter, by relying on the territorial and personality principles, respectively. This is far from being an unusual situation in international relations, and international law has devised a number of strategies in this regard which we shall discuss.

As a manifestation of the equality of states, international law does not establish a hierarchy of jurisdictional principles in such cases, nor does the *prior tempore potior iure* or first-come-first-served principle apply. Both states are perfectly on a par in taking up the matter in view of their respective grounds of jurisdiction, although the state with immediate access to the persons or objects in question has, as the *beatus possidens*, a certain practical advantage in the exercise of jurisdiction.

Immunities

One instrument provided by international law to tackle undesired conflicts of jurisdiction is *immunities*. Immunities are exceptions to a state's jurisdiction by virtue of which international law acknowledges the primordial interests of another state to deal with the matter in question. This makes them analogous to the above-described situation of exclusive jurisdiction, but the difference is that immunities do not do away with competing jurisdiction. Immunities only block the exercise of jurisdiction by the other state. If the state endowed with the right to immunity is prepared to *waive* it, the situation of concurrent jurisdiction is reactivated. With this proviso, immunities are one of the most prominent and effective means of limiting jurisdiction in international law. They come in several forms.

First, *state immunity* provides the legal person of the state as well as its property with immunity (according to the venerable principle of *par in parem non habet iurisdictionem*). However, the so-called *restrictive* or *relative* doctrine which limits immunity claims to acts of exercise of public authority (*acta iure imperii*) and permits bringing a state before the courts of another state if commercial transactions (*acta iure gestionis*) are involved, appears to be accepted by virtually all major states, with the notable exception of China (Fox 2010, 347; see however Sucharitkul 2005, 25 *et seq.*). However, far-reaching immunity is still granted with regard to measures of enforcement against state property, if it is not earmarked for commercial purposes (2004 UN Convention on Jurisdictional Immunities of States and Their Property, articles 5, 10, 18 and 19 (not yet in force); see also the, albeit poorly ratified, 1972 European Convention on State Immunity). Similarly, warships and ships solely used on government non-commercial service, on the high seas, enjoy complete immunity from the jurisdiction of any state other than the flag state (UNCLOS, articles 95, 96).

Secondly, two universally recognised legal instruments as well as customary law establish *diplomatic* and *consular* immunity for the premises of diplomatic and consular representations as well as for diplomatic and consular personnel (see the 1961 and 1963 Vienna Conventions on Diplomatic Relations and Consular Relations, respectively). This grant of immunity even outlives the end of diplomats' time in office, at least for official acts.

Thirdly, there also exists *personal* immunity for highest-level government officials such as Heads of States and Governments and (at least foreign) ministers. As incumbents, they enjoy absolute immunity (see the aforementioned *Arrest Warrant* case), and even afterwards immunity persists for their official acts. However, in recent cases, while the general principle of granting immunity to states and their high-ranking representatives is uncontroversial, there is an ongoing debate on the precise limits of such immunities, notably with respect to gross violations of human rights (see the House of Lords, *Pinochet No. 3* case [1999] 2 All ER 97, regarding Head of State immunity; the *Distomo* (2000) and *Kalavrita* (2007) affairs in the Greek courts and before the Court of Justice of the European Union regarding state immunity; and the case concerning *Jurisdictional Immunities of the State* (*Germany* v. *Italy*), currently before the ICJ).

In all these instances of immunity, however, it should be recalled that the state privileged by the right to immunity remains free to waive it. In addition, it merits mention that diplomatic and personal immunities cannot successfully hamper the exercise of jurisdiction of international criminal courts and tribunals (*Arrest Warrant* case, para. 61; *Prosecutor* v. *Charles Taylor*, Case number SCSL-2003-01-I, Decision on Immunity from Jurisdiction, 2004 (Special Court for Sierra Leone, Appeals Chamber); ICC Statute, article 27).

Battles of jurisdiction

Another traditional way for international law to deal with competing jurisdictional claims is to let the respective international actors carry out a jurisdictional battle. Thus, it occurs not infrequently that a state makes a sweeping claim by seeking to extend its authority to persons or objects at the very edge of its internationally recognised jurisdictional horizon. Often, it can only be said with the benefit of hindsight whether that state was merely exhausting the available potential of jurisdiction or transgressing it. The lines at the periphery tend to be blurred. Hence the precise reach of a state's jurisdiction is often only determined in the – conflictual – interplay of claim and counter-claim, with the other state(s) protesting against, but possibly at some point partly acquiescing in an arrogation of jurisdiction, thus leading, as the case may be, to a consolidation or reallocation of the jurisdictional prerogatives of the states involved.

So far as the acts carried out by states involved in jurisdictional conflicts contradict each other, affected individuals may be placed in a truly unenviable situation. One state may specifically oblige them to perform acts that the other explicitly forbids. For example, the US Congress prevented non-US companies based outside US territory from doing business with States like Cuba, Libya and Iran, if these companies also have business interests in the United States (Helms–Burton Act, 22 USC §6021–6091; D'Amato Act, 50 USC §1701). The (then) European Community considered this an excessive claim of jurisdiction and reacted with a so-called '*blocking statute*' (Council Regulation No. 2271/96; see also the 1982 Comments of the European Community regarding the so-called 'Pipeline dispute').

Jurisdictional battles between states are, from the point of view of international law, not unsettling *per se*. And while they are not particularly welcome either due to the legal insecurity and frictional losses they entail, they are not forbidden as long as the measures taken are in themselves lawful. Their often-serious effects and risks for affected individuals are mitigated to some extent at least by the principle that individuals must not be ordered to do something which would be criminalised in another state; they cannot be forced into criminal action (see 'foreign sovereign compulsion', Restat. 3d of US Foreign Relations Law (1990) §§441, 442; Lowe and Staker 2010, 333; see, however, Akehurst 1972–1973, 168, 208). Apart from that, actors engaged in different jurisdictions have to find their way through the inhospitable jungle of contradictory expectations of different legal orders.

Self-restraint and comity

Another strategy envisaged by international law in regard of competing jurisdictional claims which has been propagated particularly by common law courts is the exercise of judicial self-restraint, justified, amongst others, by doctrines such as non-justiciability, *forum non conveniens* or comity or relying on a 'balancing of interests' test or criteria of 'reasonableness' (as to the latter see *Timberlane Lumber Co.* v. *Bank of America* case, 549 F2d 597 (9th Cir. 1976)). Yet, this has often remained a rhetorical device, since the criteria applied, in many cases, led to the jurisdiction of the respective court's state being eventually confirmed. There are nonetheless interesting examples of tempered self-limitation with courts asserting jurisdiction but staying proceedings until the authorities of another state have dealt with the case at hand. A functional equivalent of this can be seen in the principles of primacy and complementarity which underlie the jurisdictional regimes of the International Criminal Tribunals for the Former Yugoslavia (ICTY) and Rwanda (ICTR) and the ICC, respectively (see ICTY Statute, article 9; ICTR Statute, article 8; ICC Statute, articles 1, 17).

Cooperation of states

This takes us to the most sophisticated and increasingly common form of handling situations of competing jurisdiction, namely cooperation between states. Consider the example of a state granting transfer of a person to a requesting state, thus abandoning its own jurisdictional claims. This may take the form of *ad hoc* cooperation through direct negotiations regarding that person, even if it has become rare to comply with such requests save on the basis of *institutionalised* cooperation within the framework of the dense global net of extradition treaties. The recent practice of unlawful 'renditions' in the so-called war on terrorism represents a disreputable exception in this regard. In general, cooperation on the basis of international treaties has become the paramount instrument in international law to deal with challenges arising from competing jurisdiction. It allows for the allocation of jurisdiction in a highly differentiated manner, depending on the multitude of subject matters affected, the interests of the states involved and the degree and forms of cooperation they seek or are prepared to concede. Presently there are literally hundreds and thousands of bilateral and multilateral treaties, often adopted under the auspices of or facilitated by intergovernmental organisations, which govern jurisdiction in one or the other form. While treaties are also used by states to clarify jurisdictional issues in single instances, the following types of treaty-based institutionalised cooperation can be distinguished.

First, there are treaties leaving the jurisdictional situation as it is, but approximating or harmonising the underlying substantive rules so as to alleviate the consequences of a parallel exercise of jurisdiction. Secondly, as a typical manifestation of jurisdictional treaties, they can seek to put an end to the lingering tension between the Scylla of lack of and the Charybdis of multiple jurisdiction by establishing a comprehensive legal regime allocating jurisdiction for a specific matter to one single state. This has been done, for instance, on the regional European level where judicial decision-making in civil, commercial and family law matters is assigned to the courts of one state with the other states having to recognise the legal outcome (see the so-called 'Brussels Regulation', EU Council Regulation (EC) No. 44/2001 of 22 December 2000; 1988 and 2007 Lugano Conventions on Jurisdiction and the Recognition and Enforcement of Judgments in Civil and Commercial matters. Efforts to this effect on the global level are much less advanced (see the 2005 Hague Convention on Choice of Court Agreements). Similar developments can be observed in the area of double taxation agreements, where two states agree on rules according to which they accept that a set of facts will fall within the jurisdiction of either of them or at least that they take into account the other's decision; with regard to international judicial assistance (see, the *Mutual Assistance* case (*Djibouti* v. *France*), ICJ Reports 2008, p. 177); and with respect to the so-called Status of Forces Agreements which typically provide for exclusive or at least primary jurisdiction of the sending state over its troops in another state's territory. Thirdly, in a wider sense, jurisdictional clauses in treaties referring the decision of a matter to the ICJ or international arbitration may also be considered forms of cooperation, by means of treaty, in clarifying an otherwise more entangled jurisdictional situation.

Finally, a further strategy is to dispose of national jurisdiction and to entrust certain matters to jurisdiction on the international plane, mostly to intergovernmental organisations or organs thereof. This manner of proceeding is far more frequent than it might appear at first. For instance, it is not only the power conferred upon the International Seabed Authority (UNCLOS, article 157) that falls in this category, but also the far-reaching powers to create legal norms entrusted to the European Union and other organisations of regional integration by their member states (even though these organisations normally do not have enforcement jurisdiction on their own). Whether one refers to this increasingly common phenomenon as 'pooling' of jurisdiction or otherwise, it constitutes a prime example of *re-allocation* of jurisdiction in view of the great many deficiencies and tensions produced by the first round of allocation of jurisdiction according to the general principles of international law.

Challenges for the international law of jurisdiction

As stated in the opening section of this chapter, the international law of jurisdiction mirrors the structure of the international legal order and its guiding principles. This also and particularly holds true for the dynamic evolvement of these principles.

Without contributing to the inflationary use of the concept of *globalisation*, it is correct to observe that on both the factual and legal levels the world has become more interconnected and complex. Transnational economic activity, transboundary environmental pollution, trans-frontier communication and not the least transstate crime (be it terrorism or cyber-crime) are phenomena that, by definition, fall into the jurisdiction of a number of states, if not the entirety of them. This reflects that they all have a substantial interest in such matters. Idiosyncratic approaches, however, risk jeopardising the efficacy of the international community's response. This poses more challenges than ever to a reasonable, efficient and effective allocation of jurisdiction on the horizontal (between states) and vertical levels (between states and intergovernmental organisations) and to the cooperation and coordination of these actors in the international arena.

Alas, this is still a fairly traditional way to look at jurisdiction. The world of international law has become more differentiated and colourful also in terms of its actors and beneficiaries. In particular, the development of *human rights* in the post-1945 world has left a characteristic imprint on contemporary international law. In this regard, it seems that the law of jurisdiction lags behind the evolution of general international law. To be sure, the prohibition of double jeopardy (*ne bis in idem*) has become a standard element in international human rights treaties and has also found its place in the realm of international criminal courts (1966 International Covenant on Civil and Political Rights, article 14(7); 1984 Protocol No. 7 to the (European) Convention for the Protection of Human Rights and Fundamental Freedoms, article 4; ICC Statute, article 20). While this prohibition seeks to prevent repercussions of concurrent criminal jurisdiction of states, in other areas jurisdictional battles between states may still have adverse consequences for individuals. We have referred to the development of the principle that concurrent jurisdiction must not force individuals into criminal action, but the law has not gone much further than that. A reflection of increasing sensitivity to human rights concerns is the extension of universal jurisdiction of states to avoid impunity for gross human rights violations on the horizontal level; and, on the vertical level, the endowment of international human rights courts and bodies with jurisdiction over violations of such rights.

As international law is, and will become, no monolithic construct, allocation of jurisdiction to and amongst its sub-units and settling conflicts arising from under- and over-allocation will remain a continuous challenge. This makes jurisdiction as topical a subject of international law as ever.

Bibliography

Akehurst, M., 1972–1973. 'Jurisdiction in International Law', *British Yearbook of International Law*, 46, 145–257

Brownlie, I., 2008. *Principles of Public International Law*, 7th edn., Oxford University Press

Fox, H., 2010. 'International Law and Restraints on the Exercise of Jurisdiction by National Courts of States', in M. Evans (ed.), *International Law*, Oxford University Press, 340–379

Lowe, V., 2007. *International Law*, Oxford University Press

Lowe, V. and C. Staker, 2010. 'Jurisdiction', in M. Evans, (ed.), *International Law*, Oxford University Press, 313–339

Oxman, B., 2008. 'Jurisdiction of States', in R. Wolfrum (ed.), *Max Planck Encyclopedia of Public International Law*, online

Sucharitkul, S., 2005. 'Jurisdictional Immunities in Contemporary International Law from Asian Perspectives', *Chinese Journal of International Law*, 4, 1–43

7 Lawfare and warfare

David Kennedy

Modern law and modern war: an introduction

Warfare has always been a central preoccupation and presented a kind of ultimate test for international law. It is hard to think of international law governing the relations amongst states without having something to say about war – when war is and is not an appropriate exercise of sovereign authority, how war can and cannot be conducted, which of war's outcomes will and will not become components of a post-war status quo, and so on. It is conventional to imagine that international law restrains war by making distinctions: this is war, and this is not; this is sovereignty, and this is not; this is legal warfare, and this is not. The terms with which these legal distinctions are drawn change over time. The vernacular may be more or less sodden with ethical considerations, more or less rooted in the specific treaty arrangements entered into by states. The distinctions may be drawn more or less sharply, may be matters of kind or degree. What goes on one or the other side of these distinctions may change, but the idea that law is about distinguishing war from peace, sovereign right from sovereign whim, legal from illegal conduct, on the battlefield and off, endures.

Discussions about international law and war usually unfold as if the participants were imagining an international law which would be able to substitute itself for sovereign power in a top-down fashion, first to distinguish legal from illegal violence and then, perhaps not today but eventually, or perhaps not directly but indirectly, to bring that distinction to bear in the life of sovereigns, extinguishing sovereign authority for war at the point it crosses a legal limit. The idea is that the articulation of right will discipline, limit and restrain sovereign power when it turns to violence. International law proposes to bring this about through a series of doctrines, definitions and arguments which *say* where war begins and ends, and then through an apparatus of institutions and relationships which are linked in one or another way to these doctrines and which are the locus for or the effect of these sayings.

Much work has been put into codifying the doctrines through which international law will be able to say what is and is not legal and to develop a canon of thought about how these doctrines are to be interpreted when making a distinction. On the institutional side, at the national level we have the apparatus of military justice, of courts martial and penalties, the institutions of political and strategic command, of media commentary and popular engagement, of international approval and condemnation, and so forth. At the international level, international lawyers have sought to empower the UN Security Council as the arbiter of war and to build an International Criminal Court (ICC) both to adjudicate past wars and, more importantly, to signal and deter future sovereign departures from what the Court determines is legal. Recognising the limits of such institutions, international lawyers have also re-conceptualised the international political process as a more interactive process through which norms are made real in a horizontal society of states – through the enforcement authority of hegemonic states acting in the name of law, by disaggregated citizen action de-legitimating sovereign activity, or simply by the increased military and political costs imposed on those who make war when, or in ways which are understood by others to be illegal.

This conventional framework has serious limitations. It overstates the distinctiveness of war and peace as well as the extent to which international law can be said to be on the 'side' of peace. It would be more accurate to say that the international law about war operates in two directions simultaneously. On the one hand, it offers a doctrinal and institutional terrain for a kind of combat over the effectiveness and limits of war which depends upon a professional practice of distinction and a series of institutional practices and sites for rendering these distinctions real in the operations of sovereign power. On the other hand, it offers a parallel doctrinal and institutional framework for transforming sovereign power and violence into right, continuing the projects of war by other means. By following these circuits between law and war in the operations of modern war, we may come to replace our image of a law outside war (and a sovereign power normally 'at peace') with an image of sovereign power and legal determination themselves bound up with war, having their origin in war and contributing through their routine practices in 'wartime' and 'peacetime' to the ongoing, if often silent, wars which are embedded in the structure of international life.

As a starting point, we should acknowledge that the doctrinal and institutional components of the international legal regime are in operation not only when they assert themselves against the exercise of military force or when they cabin violence within walls drawn by these doctrines. International law is equally – indeed, perhaps more routinely – the space within which war is conceived and validated and through which force is disciplined and rendered effective. It can be difficult to remember that the articulation and institutional enforcement of legal boundaries also expresses and continues projects of war. Yet sovereigns do routinely discipline and legitimate their military campaigns by pronouncing on the legality of bombing here or killing there. When this happens successfully, international law confirms the violent expression of sovereign power as right.

It is easy to understand the virtues of a powerful legal vocabulary, shared by elites around the world, which appears to distinguish legal from illegal war and wartime violence. It is exciting to see law become the mark of legitimacy as legitimacy has become the currency of power. It is more difficult to see the opportunities this opens for the military professional to harness law as a weapon, or for sovereigns to continue the exercise of power as right. Yet the humanist vocabulary of international law *is* routinely mobilised as a strategic asset in war, just as the vernacular of legal right is inseparable from the enforcement of sovereign power. We need to remember what it means when humanitarian international lawyers say that compliance with international law 'legitimates'. It means, of course, that killing, maiming, humiliating, wounding people is legally privileged, authorised, permitted and justified. The military has taken the hint.

The American military have coined a word for this: 'lawfare' – law as a weapon, law as a tactical ally, law as a strategic asset, an instrument of war. They observe that law can often accomplish what might once have been done with bombs and missiles: seize and secure territory, send messages about resolve and political seriousness, even break the will of a political opponent. When the military buys up commercial satellite capacity to deny it to an adversary – contract is their weapon. They could presumably have denied their adversary access to those pictures in many ways. When the United States and its allies use the Security Council to certify lists of terrorists and force seizure of assets abroad, they have weaponised the law. Those assets might also have been immobilised in other ways. It is not only the *use* of force that can do these things. Threats can sometimes work. And law often marks the line between what counts as the routine exercise of one's prerogative and a threat to cross that line and exact a penalty.

There is, in this sense, a kind of political continuity between international legal projects which seem to concern war and peace. When special courts are established by victors to adjudicate the criminality of opponents, it can be dressed up as the 'return' of law and peace – but it is hard to avoid thinking that law is also the continuation of war by other means. Something similar is at work when we empower the UN Security Council, itself established to institutionalise the outcome of the Second World War as a system of 'collective security', with the authority to determine the legality of wars today – when, for example, the 'legality' of the Iraq War hangs solely upon how France decides to vote. The legalisation of the last war's outcome presses itself on the legitimacy of future combat. The situation is similar when a hegemonic 'international community' sets up a court of general instance to try those who have, in their eyes, lost their 'legitimacy' as sovereigns. Whether or not anyone is prosecuted, a war has, in some sense, been lost. We might say that, through law, not all wars need to be fought to be lost decisively. These engagements of the international law about war with the ongoing relations of sovereign power enforced by war are emblematic of a more general relationship between modern war and modern law.

On the one hand, modern war has engaged the bureaucratic, commercial and cultural institutions we normally associate with peace. On the other, what I term 'modern law' has proliferated the doctrinal materials and interpretive methods which can be brought to bear in discussing the distinctiveness and legality of state violence. Lines are now harder to draw, both because the world of war has become more mixed up and because ambiguities, gaps and contradictions in the materials we use to draw the lines have become more pronounced. At the same time, however, there is a lot more line-drawing going on. There has been a vast dispersion of sites and institutions and procedures through which legal distinctions about war are made. This proliferation of legally framed activity has made war and sovereign power into legal institutions even as the experience of legal pluralism and fluidity has unhinged the idea of a law which, out there, somehow distinguishes. It would be more accurate today to speak about an international law which places legal distinction in strategic play as a part of war itself, further proliferating and fragmenting the sites of its doctrinal and institutional operation.

Moreover, in the retail operations of law about war, the experience of irresolvable debate, or of debate which can only be resolved by reference outside law to the political or ethical is ever more common. As is the experience, for soldiers and citizens alike, of vertigo amidst the shifting perspectives from which killing is evaluated. It is difficult to say just how this will come out.

New doctrinal tools may arise, old tools may regain their plausibility, institutional and doctrinal activity within the field may become less dispersed and more hegemonic. It may again become plausible to imagine an international law 'outside' and 'over' sovereign power, declaring and determining the limits of violence. In the meantime, however, international law about war offers us a window onto the political and ethical consequences of the fluid and strategic relations amongst sovereign power, force and law which characterise the experience of modern law in modern war – the experience of people who work with law and declare in its name.

Dispersion: modern war as a legal institution

In warfare today, the practice of distinction – central to both law and war – has been dispersed. The sites and technologies through which legal assertions about violence are translated back and forth into the vernacular of violence have proliferated. In this sense, law has infiltrated the war machine. Law now shapes the institutional, logistical and physical landscape of war and the battlespace has become as legally saturated as the rest of modern life. Law has become – for parties on all sides of even the most asymmetric confrontations – a vocabulary for marking legitimate power and justifiable death. It is not too much to say that war has become a legal institution – the continuation of law by other means.

The point here is not at all that everyone always follows the rules or even agrees on what the rules are and how they should be interpreted. Quite the contrary – people disagree about these matters all the time. The point, rather, is that the opportunities for law to make itself felt in the experience of those participating in modern war – at one or another distance from the battlefield itself – have multiplied dramatically.

The law which structures the macro and micro-operations of warfare is far broader than the 'law of force', the 'law of armed conflict' or 'international humanitarian law'. Law is certainly most visibly part of military life when it privileges the killing and destruction of battle. If you kill *this way*, and not that, *here* and not there, *these people* and not those – what you do is privileged. If not, it is criminal. And the war must itself be lawful. But this is hardly the entire story. Operating across dozens of jurisdictions, today's military must also comply with innumerable local, national and international rules regulating the use of territory, the mobilisation of men, the financing of arms and logistics and the deployment of force. War is waged across a terrain shaped by constitutional law, administrative law, private law and more. As warfare has evolved, law about the environment, social security, land-use, religious expression, finance and payments systems, government budgeting, privacy, as well as human rights, law of the sea, law of space, conflict of laws, law of nationality, jurisdiction are all implicated in the shape of warfare. Background doctrines of property and contract, of privacy and financial accountability, channel the legal mobilisation of violence, as do informal and customary laws of business practice, informal markets and clandestine flows of finance, information, goods and people. As a result, if we were to explore the role of law in war in a comprehensive fashion, we might not spend a great deal of time thinking about doctrines of international law which explicitly purport to deal with warfare.

At the same time, wars today are rarely fought between equivalent nations or coalitions of great industrial powers. They occur at the peripheries of the world system, amongst foes with wildly different institutional, economic and military capacities. Enemies are dispersed and decisive engagement is rare. Battle is at once intensely local and global in new ways. Soldiers train for tasks far from conventional combat: local diplomacy, intelligence gathering, humanitarian reconstruction, urban policing, or managing the routine tasks of local government. Violence follows patterns more familiar from epidemiology or cultural fashion than military strategy. Networks of fellow travellers exploit the infrastructures of the global economy to bring force to bear here and there. Satellite systems guide precision munitions from deep in Missouri to the outskirts of Kabul. And, of course, the whole thing happens in the glare of the modern media.

Moreover, if Clausewitz was right that war is the continuation of politics by other means, the politics continued by warfare today has itself been legalised. Today's sovereign stands atop a complex bureaucracy, exercising powers delegated by a constitution, and shared out with myriad agencies, bureaucracies and private actors, knit together in complex networks that spread across borders. Political leaders act in the shadow of a knowledgeable, demanding, engaged and institutionally entrenched local, national and global elite, which also has institutional forms and professional habits. Discourses of right have become the common vernacular of this dispersed elite, even as it argues about just what the law permits and forbids.

As a result, the sites at which official rules for war are given meaning and have institutional, political or personal purchase have become many. Ideas about what war is and is not, what uses of force are and are not legal, which wars are and are not legally legitimate, run through the political, institutional and social fabric of societies. The articulation of warfare has become everywhere bound up with questions of right, as much when we identify violations, isolate bad apples or denounce war criminals as when we interpret killing as compliance. In the first instance, this reflects the fact that war is a professional practice. Militaries today are linked to their nation's commercial life, integrated with civilian and peacetime governmental institutions, and covered by the same national and international media. Mobilising 'the military' means setting thousands of units forth in a coordinated way. Officers discipline their force and organise their operations with rules. Public and private actors must be enlisted in projects of death and destruction, which they must in turn explain to their families, their pastors, their comrades. Coalition partners must be brought on board. Delicate political arrangements and sensibilities must be translated into practical limits – and authorisations – for using force. Nor is the legal professionalisation of warfare an exclusively First-World practice. Indeed, it turns out the Taliban issues training materials outlining the rules of engagement designed to maximise the effect and legitimacy of their force in their own cultural time and place.

In each of the spaces in which war is made, the determination of what is and is not legal plays a role in constituting the entities who will act. Negotiations over participation in warfare are conducted as debates about the 'rules of engagement' – who could do what, when, to whom? For politicians who will take the heat, it is important to know just how trigger happy – or 'forward leaning' – the soldiers at the tip of the spear will be. Soldiers – and citizens – must be made in the image of these rules. At each of these sites, there are opportunities for adjusting, refining and making the distinction between legal and illegal – and it will often be these distinctions through which the political debates are resolved, the families are able to feel proud, the allies to establish a common front.

Modern law: rhetorical strategy

As the sites over which the regime of distinction has dispersed itself have proliferated, the doctrinal and conceptual materials used to distinguish war and peace or legal and illegal state violence have become surprisingly fluid.

No longer an affair of clear rules and sharp distinctions, international law rarely speaks clearly or with a single voice. That does not mean the making of distinctions is any less important. Whenever we call what we are doing *war*, we stress its discontinuity from the normal routines of peacetime and sharpen our collective identity against a common enemy. When the sword triumphs over the pen, our differences should be set aside – this is serious, important – a time of extraordinary powers and political deference. We are us – they are enemy. In war, different rules apply. To shoot a man – or a woman – on the battlefield is not murder. Distinction establishes the legal privilege to kill.

But just when does the privilege to kill replace the prohibition on murder? Where does war begin and end? What counts as 'perfidy', 'terror' or 'torture'? Which civilians *are* innocent? And when can civilians, innocent or not, be killed, their deaths 'collateral' to a legitimate military objective? As law has become an ever-more important yardstick for legitimacy, articulated and applied across a proliferating sea of institutional settings, the legal categories used to make those distinctions have become far too spongy to permit clear resolution – or become spongy enough to undergird the experience of self-confident outrage by parties on all sides of a conflict. As a result, we might say that modern law has become the instrument both for asserting the distinctiveness of warfare *and* for merging it with the routines of peace – and increasingly an instrument which can and is used strategically.

The law of armed conflict has become a confusing mix of principles and counter-principles, of firm rules and loose exceptions. In legal terms, 'war' itself has become a smorgasbord of finely differentiated activities: 'self-defence', 'hostilities', 'the use of force', 'resort to arms', 'police action', 'peace enforcement', 'peace-making', 'peace-keeping'. It becomes ever harder to keep it all straight. Meanwhile, warfare has itself come to comprise an ever-wider range of divergent activities. Troops in the same city are fighting and policing and building schools. Restoring water is part of winning the war. Private actors are everywhere – from insurgents who melt into the mosque to armed soldiers who turn out to work for private contractors, not to mention all the civilians providing moral and physical support to those who bomb and shoot, or who run the complex technology and logistical chains 'behind' modern warfare. In the confusion, military and humanitarian voices will often have a motive to insist on a bright line. For the military, defining the battlefield defines the privilege to kill. But aid agencies also want the guys digging the wells to be seen as humanitarians, not post-conflict combatants – privileged not to be killed. Defining the not-battlefield opens a 'space' for humanitarian action. Others will be moved to soften the distinctions, perhaps to permit military funds to be used for a police action, or to insist that human rights norms be applicable in combat. In a dispersed regime for articulating the legality of sovereign force, we can expect a constant push and pull, making and unmaking formal distinctions, in ways which reflect the calculations of actors pursuing very local strategies.

As it became a more plastic medium, international law offered an ever-wider range of instruments for making and unmaking the distinction between war and peace, allowing the boundaries of war to be managed strategically. Take the difficult question – when does war end? The answer is not to be found in law or fact – but in strategy. *Declaring* the end of hostilities might be a matter of election theatre or military assessment, just like announcing that there remains 'a long way to go', or that the 'insurgency is in its final throes'. We should understand these statements as *arguments*. As messages – but also as weapons. Law – legal categorisation – is a communication tool. And communicating the war is fighting the war. This is a war, this is an occupation, this is a police action, this is a security zone. These are insurgents, those are criminals, these are illegal combatants, and so on. All these are claims with audiences, made for a reason. Increasingly, defining the battlefield is not only a matter of deployed force – it is also a rhetorical and legal claim.

When people use the law strategically, moreover, they change it. The Red Cross changes it. Al Jazeera changes it. CNN changes it; the US Administration changes it. Humanitarians who seize on vivid images of civilian casualties to raise expectations about the accuracy of targeting are changing the legal fabric. When an Italian prosecutor decides to charge CIA operatives for their alleged participation in a black operation of kidnapping and rendition, the law of the battlefield has shifted. As US military forces in the Middle East have changed their military objectives and strategy over recent years, they have also adjusted their rules of engagement with respect to civilian death. In broad terms, what had seemed legally acceptable collateral damage in an invasion came to seem a threat to the success of an occupation – and what seemed acceptable to enforce an occupation came to seem counter-productive in 'counter-insurgency operations'. The rules were tightened and civilian death was meted out more parsimoniously. At the same time, however, observers (and civilian populations) altered their expectations about the civilian death which would occur and which had to be tolerated. They pushed back, tightening the reins on the US forces yet further until *any* dead civilian seemed to rebuke the legitimacy and prove the failure of the mission.

As a result, strange as it may seem, there is now more than one law of armed conflict. Different nations – even in the same coalition – will have signed different treaties. The same standards look different if you anticipate battle against a technologically superior foe – or live in a Palestinian refugee camp in Gaza. Although we might disagree with one or the other interpretation, we must recognise that the legal materials are elastic enough to permit diverse interpretations. Amnesty International called Israeli attacks on Hezbollah 'war crimes that give rise to individual criminal responsibility'. Israel rejected the charge that it 'acted outside international norms or international legality' and insisted that 'you are legally entitled to target infrastructure that your enemy is exploiting for its military campaign'.

There is no court of world public opinion on the international stage to adjudicate such claims. Speaking in such terms overstates the unity of the process by which these claims become real in the bodies of soldiers and citizens and in the institutions of civilian and military life. In the dispersed and multiple contexts through which law influences the conduct of warfare today, the process by which these diverse claims take institutional, political and professional form will vary. As a result, a lawyer advising about what the law of war means will need to make an rather precise assessment of the institutional, political, social and human context, before making a prediction about how people with the power to influence the client's interest will interpret and enact claims about the distinctiveness of what the client contemplates doing.

Some historical background to the modern rhetoric of distinction

The fluidity of the modern law about warfare is no accident. It is the result of two hundred years of professional struggle. At least twice over the last two hundred years, international law concerning war has dramatically transformed itself in an effort to provide a satisfying vernacular of distinction. Across the nineteenth century, the broad considerations of ethics and policy which had preoccupied the international law about war for centuries – when is war just, when is war wise, how ought the sovereign to treat his enemy, his ally, his subjects, and so forth – were gradually leeched out.

They were replaced by a series of sharp distinctions and clear rules which were either agreed between sovereigns (these weapons and not those) or deduced from the nature of war and sovereignty themselves (war and peace, civilians and combatants, belligerents and neutrals, law about going to war and law about conducting war). By the early twentieth century, the doctrinal materials had narrowed to focus on clear formal distinctions defined and agreed by sovereigns. War and peace were legally distinct, separated by a formal 'declaration of war'. A sharp distinction between public and private law made it seem reasonable to insist that private rights survived the violence of warfare which public powers did not. It was at this moment that the 'law of war' and the 'law in war' came to seem sharply distinct – separate ways of judging the legality of making war and then, irrespective of the legality of the war, of judging the legality of weaponry and tactics.

At the same time, the idea of law's own disciplinary function in relationship to war changed. At the start of the nineteenth century, international law offered a kind of handbook of advice and good sense to guide the action of statesmen. It focused on considerations affecting the right to make war and the sensible limits of warfare. It did not imagine the jurist and the statesmen or military commander as part of sharply distinct disciplines, but as part of a shared community of leaders struggling to make sense of natural law and national interest. By the end of the century, a more formal doctrinal law tracing its rules to state practice and consent – or simply to the nature of sovereign authority itself – offered itself as an external, autonomous and in some sense scientific judge of the legality of sovereign action in warfare. It treated the distinctions between legal and illegal war, weaponry or tactics as best able to be drawn by independent jurists ruminating on the nature of sovereignty and the meaning of agreed texts.

Over the course of the twentieth century, international law shifted again. From the First World War forward, many international lawyers thought the effort to restrain war by rules unrealistic. Some turned instead to diplomatic promises and institutional arrangements to provide for the 'collective security' and manage a process of 'peaceful change', primarily through the League of Nations. For those who continued to pursue the doctrinal route, considerations of justice and policy which had been exogenised found their way back in. Distinctions came to be drawn less sharply, often as matters of degree rather than kind.

Rumination on the nature of the international community, the obligations inherent in sovereignty and the potential for abuse of sovereign right joined meditation on the inherent powers and rights of sovereignty as foundations for international doctrines assessing the limits and legality of warfare. Agreed rules about weaponry were joined by broad principles – such as proportionality or military necessity – which expressed the limits of warfare in terms which seemed more pragmatic and could more readily be associated with reflections on justice. By the end of the Second World War, these doctrinal approaches were harnessed to the institutional framework of the United Nations, whose Charter shifted the focus from the rhetoric of legal declarations of war and distinctions between neutrals and belligerents to the institutional management of threats to the peace and the use of force. Over the years, as distinctions softened, it seemed reasonable to consider applying elements of what had been the law of peace – particularly the law of human rights – on the battlefield, and of blurring the boundaries between the legality of a war and the legality of weapons used and tactics chosen.

Across the twentieth century, this transformation was supported by both military specialists and humanitarians. Both came to doubt the viability and usefulness of sharp distinctions. For the military professional, bright lines can be helpful in the blur of combat, communicating a firewall between levels of combat to their own force, to allies and enemies alike. But they can also constrain in unpredictable ways. It will often be more useful to work with loose standards expressing broad principles, to weigh and balance the consequences of military action in light of its objectives. At the same time, ethical absolutes, let loose on matters of war and peace, can be dangerous, heightening enthusiasm for military campaigns beyond a sovereign's actual political capacity to follow through. They can focus attention in the wrong place and it may not be clear, in advance, which tactic or weapon will, in fact, cause the least harm. The rule against use of chemical weapons on the battlefield seems to preclude the use of tear gases routinely used in domestic policing – a line which led to the widespread use of flamethrowers to clear caves during combat in Afghanistan. Moreover, narrowly drawn rules permit a great deal – and legitimate what is permitted. From a humanitarian point of view, it seems wiser to assess things comparatively, contextually, in more pragmatic terms.

By the end of the twentieth century, international law's attitudes toward its own rules also changed. The authority of rules came less from their pedigree than from their effectiveness. International lawyers became less interested in whether a rule was valid – in the sense that it could be said to be rooted in consent, in sovereignty or in the nature of an inter-sovereign community – than in whether it worked. International law was what international law did. The observations of sociologists or political scientists about what functioned as a restraint or a reason became more important than the ruminations of jurists in determining what international law was and was not. As one might imagine, it became ever less possible to say in advance or with precision what rules would, in fact, be effective as law. To do so was to make a prediction about what would, in the end, be enforced. Acting under cover of law became a wager that the action's legality would be upheld in the unfolding of state practice. Moreover, it became clear that the effectiveness of rules depended less on something intrinsic to the rule than on aspects of society – how powerful was its proponent, how insistent its enforcement, how persuasive its reasons to the broad public who would determine its legitimacy. As a result, the discipline's image of itself was ever less one of autonomous juridical reason and ever more one of engaged social science and partner in statecraft or policy.

These shifts did not happen everywhere at the same time or to the same extent, nor did they happen in a vacuum. They were part of a widespread enthusiasm and then loss of faith in the formal distinctions of nineteenth-century legal thought – in the wisdom, as well as the plausibility, of separating law sharply from politics, or private right sharply from public power. Within that framework, much depended on the details of national legal cultures and upon the political strategies of leading jurists and others in particular locations. More importantly, these shifts were not decisive. Remnants of each discarded sensibility remain. As a result, people now speak about the legal distinctions of warfare in three different dialects, each reminiscent of a historical phase in the discipline's development.

At the start of the twenty-first century, international law, taken as a whole, speaks about warfare as a matter of justice and wise policy, recollecting the early nineteenth century; as an object for juristic assessment through rumination on first principles and elaboration of valid rules, in a way which recalls late nineteenth-century thinking; and as a very twentieth-century question of legitimacy determined by the persuasiveness of justification to international elites, whose granting or withholding of legitimation in turn validates or invalidates the distinctions and judgments which are made. Moreover, these dialects have been changed by their encounters with one another. They have become methodological options, rather than simply what law is all about. Focusing on questions of justice and policy, for example, may be picked up in a spirit of eclectic pragmatism, alongside the languages of juridical forms and sociological legitimacy, or as a matter of methodological – even ethical and political – commitment, responsive to what seem the limitations of both nineteenth- and twentieth-century ideas. Those who today give voice to legal distinctions – legal professionals, statesmen, media experts and law people – sometimes do so with passion about the mode of argument being made and sometimes with a kind of eclectic indifference to issues of method.

The transformation of historical modes of thought into styles of argument has arranged them in relation to one another as methodological positions on an imaginary continuum between political realism and ethical judgment. You are not speaking international law today if you seem to be expressing sovereign will or declaring what is just. Each analytic style offers a somewhat different way to declare what is and is not legal without sounding as if you are simply saying what you believe or desire. In each style, legal pronouncements are 'rooted' in sovereign consent, just as they are compatible with widely shared principles of justice. They have also pulled away from these roots, through a series of rituals and transformations which blend the two ambitions together. Those who speak about 'just war' in legal terms, for example, may feel confident that they are expressing more than an ethical preference because they have derived their definition of 'just war' by reference to the practice of sovereigns or the nature of an inter-sovereign society. Those who speak about the power of legitimacy feel they are doing more than restating political outcomes in legal terms because they have traced the attribution of legitimacy to rule-following, perhaps because, in social terms, rules exert a kind of pull toward compliance or because the psychology of statesmen can plausibly be reconstructed to suggest rules were followed even when states did not think doing so was in their best interest. As a result, in each of these three modes of distinction, law can be intertwined with sovereignty and with the violence of sovereign power while also being professionally practiced and articulated as if it were something altogether different.

Speaking in these ways, international law can echo with virtue and stand firmly on the side of peace while pursuing a proliferating institutional and professional engagement with the practice of war. Defending this doubled professional sensibility has itself become an important disciplinary project. The various rhetorical styles offer languages for tarring alternative modes of argument with the professional sins of either ethical or political subjectivism. In this sense, defence of an autonomous legal doctrinal and institutional determiner has been replaced by a professional practice of disciplining the boundaries of legal argument itself to exclude political whim and ethical preference. In such a profession, it is easy to mistake our ability to articulate law's autonomy – for which we have numerous discursive tools ready at hand – for an actual capability to restrain the power and violence of war.

At the same time, however, the proliferation of styles has allowed for the emergence of powerful antidotes to arguments that this or that death was legally compelled or justified. These antidotes – embedded in counter-styles of professional argument – often unravel the confidence with which people have asserted that this or that act of violence was legal or illegal. Indeed, it turns out that none of these vernaculars of distinction holds up very well to thoughtful criticism, which may help explain why there are three to begin with. An international law rooted in natural justice or wise policy seems unlikely to provide much of a solid foundation in a plural world. People will disagree about what justice means, which policy is wise – indeed, they may go to war over their disagreements – and it is hard to see how lawyers have any comparative advantage over sovereigns as auguries of justice or practical wisdom or, on the basis of their vision of wisdom and justice, any independent platform, expertise or mandate for distinguishing the legitimate from the illegitimate. That is partly why late nineteenth- and early twentieth-century international lawyers thought a narrower catalogue of rules rooted in sovereign power might offer a stronger perspective from which to judge state behaviour. It turned out, however, that an autonomous regime of valid rules was insufficiently robust to distinguish legal from illegal warfare with certainty. Agreed rules were too narrow, principles were ambiguous and ran in too many contradictory directions, and it seemed difficult for rumination on sovereignty to crowd out the actual exercise of sovereignty. That was partly why international jurists turned to more social and interactive conceptions of the relationship between international law and warfare. But here were also difficulties. The notion that law is what it does makes it terribly difficult to distinguish law from whatever happens in a convincing fashion. States did things for lots of reasons – just when had law been the dominant cause? The idea that statesmen are persuaded by law or that states act in the shadow of an international society which metes out legitimacy ultimately rests on a hypothesis about the existence of the community international law is intended to express and to construct.

In the end, there are good reasons to be sceptical of claims made in any of these modes that this act of war *is* legal and this is not, that this *is* war and this is peace, or that this *is* legitimate and this is not. That does not mean such claims are unimportant or that they never persuade. Speaking this way can be quite satisfying, and not only because it can be pleasurable to speak confidently about violence which is and is not legal. These performances also routinely take institutional form, disciplining and excusing soldiers, making or ruining careers, identifying targets, emboldening or disheartening allies, comforting or demoralising those who have killed or whose loved ones have died. This is knowledge which routinely becomes power, conjuring and shaping violence. But we will need to understand what it means for the vernacular of justification to have become both widely available for strategic use and subject to the experience of legal pluralism and a loss of certainty.

People pursuing projects: arguments about the legality of violence as strategy

We should think of international law as a set of arguments and counter-arguments, rhetorical performances and counter-performances, deployed by people pursuing projects of various kinds. To focus our attention on the practice of making and unmaking legal distinctions about war, it is useful to suspend the effort to determine who is right. To understand what happens to our ethics, to our politics, and to ourselves when we keep our noses to the grindstone of legal argument in the face of all the killing that people do in war, we will need to leave to one side the question of whether this or that war is legal, whether this or that doctrine is valid or persuasive or made legitimate through enforcement – or which mode of assertion offers the most robust, effective, or appropriate style for legal work. Worrying about these things, arguing about them, giving opinions about them, are all routine professional practices for international lawyers which one will surely want to master if one wants to work in the field.

We are also more likely to understand the strange alchemy of articulation and professional action if we suspend the effort to wring new legal norms from what we find, to look back at claims and counter-claims, panning for those which have been cashed out in the currency of behavioural change as a general proposition of law which will next time 'bind' sovereigns. At the moment, we lack the conceptual and social scientific tools to assess 'what happened' in a way which could disentangle the legal from everything else.

Moreover, the relationship between articulation and action is not one of back and forth – claim affecting practice, tempering claim, constraining action, strengthening norm, and so on. Things are more confusing, simultaneous, and un-decidable.

To orient ourselves as we follow the making of statements into the institutional arrangements and actual people whose relationships and practices are constituted through the making of claims, we should begin by imagining the terrain or stage upon which rhetorical claims about law and war might be made, the types of actors who may be involved, the kinds of interests they may bring to the effort to speak about the violence which is and is not legal. In the last few years, all sorts of people have performed legal arguments about war: military officers, human rights lawyers, Red Cross lawyers, demonstrators, ambassadors, presidents and prime ministers, media commentators and, of course, law professors. People from many countries and cultures have done so – Americans and Iranians, Europeans and Australians, members of Hamas, Israeli public officials and judges and citizens, UN officials and East Timorese citizens. We might begin by saying that the sum of their statements is what we mean by international law.

Doubtless, people spoke it more or less 'well' in a professional sense, more or less sincerely, with more or less passion and commitment. We may eventually want to throw out some statements which fail to meet some minimum standard of plausibility. Indeed, it is tempting to toss out arguments which no trained legal professional would treat as plausible international legal articulations, perhaps precisely because they seem to be exclusively ethical or political. There is a risk, however, that doing so will lead us to miss a whole range of institutions and practices set in motion by statements about the international legality of warfare which arise from the mobilisation of lay voices or those of adjacent professions, including politicians, soldiers, reporters, novelists, therapists or priests. To understand what law does in war we will not want to limit ourselves to what professionals in the discipline *say* that it does. After all, we know that the professional discourse is filled with statements that *other people's* claims about what is and is not legal are wrong because they are misusing the language or speaking about something else. To avoid adjudicating these claims, itself a routine professional practice, we ought to begin with a rather large tent.

This leaves us a large body of statements distinguishing violence into the legal and the illegal, the legitimate and the illegitimate, the just and the unjust. This is the material which might be arranged in a series of styles or dialects, loosely associated with historical periods, all of which remain in use. In each dialect there is a large vernacular of arguments and counter-arguments, at both the level of simple assertion about what is and is not legal, and at the level of method where claims and counter-claims are made about the appropriate way to identify and interpret international legal materials. Learning this body of material – and understanding the procedures and institutions through which it might be put to use – is, in the largest sense, what it means to become an international lawyer.

We ought then to consider the ways in which this material comes to be used, building a typology of projects and sites of articulation. Since we are speaking about warfare, we might think about it being used to pursue two types of projects. We might say that there are those who speak the language of law and war for the purpose of strengthening their military hand – by disciplining and directing their forces, legitimating their actions and justifying their means – and those who do so for the purpose of restraining or weakening a military force by un-disciplining and reorienting its forces or by de-legitimating its violence. Let us leave to one side, for a moment, those who speak it for another purpose – say to strengthen the language of law itself by embroidering it into an effort to justify or restrain a military action, whatever the consequences. In this basic picture, we have simply those who claim to strengthen and those who claim to weaken the hand of force. We might think of these rhetorical positions as those of friend and enemy or, perhaps more conventionally, of the national military and the international humanitarian. In every engagement, the one performs power as truth, the other speaks truth to power.

We can now begin to think about our model more dynamically. Where and how will modern law be brought to bear in modern war to further one or the other of these projects? Given the fluidity of modern law and the plasticity and dispersion of modern war, it will often be unclear precisely how a given statement might operate to strengthen or weaken the hand of force. Narrowing the rules of engagement, for example, may concentrate and discipline, or it may derail the effort, harnessing force to other objectives or demoralising and de-legitimating those who fight. A great deal will depend upon the larger regime through which statements are made, which offers an unending range of institutional manoeuvres from denouncing to commending, from sensationalising to routinising. Even here, much is in doubt. Prosecuting a soldier may be a way of locating responsibility or avoiding it, focusing or distracting attention, strengthening or weakening a campaign.

We might, following Clausewitz, postulate that if all this claiming has any effect at all in war, whatever strengthens one side weakens the other. As a starting point, we might say that it will be in the interests of one party to advance whenever it is in the interests of the other to rest or withdraw. Following his lead, we might begin with the hypothesis that whenever a claim for the legality of this war or this tactic would strengthen offence by allowing power to be exercised as right, we ought to expect the defence to think hard, not only about how to fight back so as to assert its own power as right, but also about how a claim of right might itself slow down the offence. The defence begins, then, by determining, if it can, that the attack is illegal, and speaking that truth to sovereign power. Of course, to be effective, this statement will need to pass through the institutions and regimes of law and politics and become a power which can, in fact, arrest the offence. In an opposite fashion, the offence must also make good its claim of right, through conquest, certainly, or more routinely through the capillaries of the world political regime through which such assertions succeed in strengthening one's hand in battle. Over time, where those who use the language have different – opposing – interests, it would be reasonable to expect that quite different performances will emerge which interpret rules or practices differently, stress different principles or precedents, shift amongst different dialects or frames of analysis, and which resonate with different audiences.

As on the terrain of battle itself, of course, this may not happen. Someone may win and the struggle may end. Either may acquiesce in the legal determination of their adversary. Perhaps they were not able to think of a legal way to claim what would be in their interest. Perhaps they carry on insincerely, if emphatically. Perhaps they become convinced that what *seemed* to be in their interest should be sacrificed to the argument of the other side – they may, in effect, switch sides. For Clausewitz, the tendency to pause in war – for neither side to attack or withdraw – could only be explained by bringing other factors and other players onto the stage – the friction of physical, technical and communication failures or the political calculations which emerge from mutual bargaining with third parties. Something parallel seems to be happening on the terrain of rhetorical engagement. Either or both party(ies) may play for the attention of third parties, in ways which temper their claims, although this will often simply intensify their opposing assertions. There may be friction of one or another sort, the technologies and sites for making their assertions may not be found, and so forth. They may simply lack the intellectual or communicative resources to develop the argumentative antidote and make it stick.

As we observe the struggle unfolding, we can explore the effect of participation on those involved at quite a micro-level of professional practice as well as the macro-level of national strategy and the deployment of political capital. We can be on the lookout for professional deformations and structural biases which enter the struggle through the making and unmaking of assertions. As a general matter, we could say that in this rhetorical war of manoeuvre amongst argumentative styles, the terrain is not symmetrical between those who assert their power as truth and those who claim to speak truth to power. When you believe you exercise power as right, it will be tempting to treat those who speak to you in the voice of a truth as enemies or traitors – or to dismiss them as dreamers who have not understood how effectively you have already restrained, disciplined and legitimated what you now perform. Of course, often those who aim to speak truth to your power will actually be your enemy or, if successful, will aid your enemy. As a result, it is easy to understand how important it will be for peace-makers to persuade those making war that knuckling under to the higher power of law will ultimately make them stronger, that those who speak truth to their power also share their realism, their pragmatism, their political savvy as well their commitment to the larger cause. They may be right in this – the party of war may have mistaken its interests, threatened to win the battle but lose the war, and so forth. But the effort to frame things in this way pulls those who seek to restrain the use of force by speaking truth into a strategic alliance with those whose power becomes truth.

At the same time, we must imagine that claims to make war in the name of right will rarely sound sincere or seem persuasive to those who believe the truth lies elsewhere – who oppose the war, are disgusted by the tactic, or simply expect themselves to be maimed or killed. They will be motivated to interpret those who would make legal assertions which discipline and strengthen the sword as perverse misuses of the rhetoric of peace to foul ends, conflating law with their own sovereign interest and ethics, uprooting it from a more general ethics, unravelling the careful process by which a more general and historical sovereignty had been codified as law. It will therefore be important for those who do seek to strengthen the military hand through law to make their assertions of right in a way which repositions them in alliance with the larger principles of law and peace. Their assertions may be correct – the party of peace may have mistaken its interests, sheathing precisely the sword which could have arrested a broader destruction.

Taking these two tendencies together, we should not be surprised, however, that those who exercise power as truth will be pulled toward ever more hyperbolic invocations of justice and law. The imbalance, then, lies in this: those who speak truth to power find themselves drawn into the collaborative exercise of violence, while those who exercise power as truth will tend to heighten the distance between what they do and what they say. Over time, justice will come to be articulated most robustly by those who make war, while war may well be made most effectively by those who began as masters of truth. This rather simple model suggests a hypothesis for exploration – that the back and forth of legal discourse about war tends towards a sharp differentiation of positions in which each is constantly motivated to align itself with or pose as the other. It is not surprising, in this light, that in law, enemies will sound like friends, and friends, enemies. Or that those who make war will speak as peace-makers, those who would restrain violence as strategic realists. We can expect a kind of endless dialogue, proliferating itself alongside warfare – very different from the image of law as the voice and hand of the universal, come to civilise swords into ploughshares. The action is less vertical – law to power, power to law – than horizontal, between claimants, amongst selves and positions. Rather than truth mud-wrestling with power, we find a far more human interaction of tit for tat, in which death and destruction unfold alongside a dialogue which seems to be terribly pertinent, but is nevertheless somehow about something else.

Pursuing the operations of law in war – and war in law – along these lines, we might see the practice of warfare and legal distinction, taken together, as part of a history of struggle, by humanitarians and military professionals, by friends and enemies, in times of 'peace' and 'war', over the relationship between international power and right. These struggles are normally not won and lost on the terrain of either rights or powers. They are not adjudicated by argument or force of arms – but through the variety of relatively small-scale technologies where assertion and action are blended together and their outcomes routinised into practices of governance and modes of global political or economic life. Over time, this practice may simultaneously become both power and right. In this sense, the law about war is not only an effective machinery for managing the military, for disciplining and legitimating recourse to arms, but also as part of the larger technology through which international power and right are made and known.

Modern law and modern war in action

Returning to the world in which modern law and war take place, we will not be surprised by the extent to which political leaders now routinely justify warfare in the language of human rights and international law, or by military commanders who frame strategic calculations in the language of law. They understand that violence one can articulate, disclose and proudly stand behind will be more effective, sustainable and legitimate. From a strategic point of view, we might imagine deploying a legal standard like 'military necessity' or 'proportionality' by calculating a kind of CNN effect, in which the additional opprobrium resulting from civilian deaths, discounted by the probability of it becoming known to relevant audiences, multiplied by the ability of that audience to hinder the continued prosecution of the war, will need to be added to the probable costs of the strike in calculating its proportionality and necessity – as well as its tactical value and strategic consequences. Claims about the legal distinctiveness of what one undertakes have become the currency in which cheques can be written against one's legitimacy balance, their persuasive power determining the price to be paid.

But calculations in that currency are terribly difficult to make and sustain, while the conflation of right and power at both the micro- and macro-level can lead people to lose critical distance on the violence of war. It is easy, for example, to substitute argument about the UN Charter for judgment about the ethical or political consequences of war. Yet it is difficult to think of a use of force that could not be legitimated in the language of the Charter. It is a rare statesman who launches a war simply to be aggressive. There is almost always something else to be said – the province is actually ours, our rights have been violated, our enemy is not, in fact, a state, we were invited to help, they were about to attack us, we are promoting the purposes and principles of the United Nations. Something.

We must recognise that neither humanitarian idealism nor military necessity provides a standpoint outside the ebbs and flows of political and strategic debate about how to achieve objectives on the battlefield. Conversing before the court of world public opinion, statesmen not only assert their prerogatives – they also test and establish those prerogatives through action. Political assertions come armed with little packets of legal legitimacy – just as legal assertions carry a small backpack of political corroboration. As lawyers must harness enforcement to their norms, states must defend their prerogatives to keep them – must back up their assertions with action to maintain their credibility. A great many military campaigns have been undertaken for just this kind of credibility – missiles become missives. In this environment, the experience can be one of self-confident assertion and pride in the strategic shrewdness of one's assertions – but also of uncertainty and unease when one remembers the experience of being defeased from certainty by the assertions and powers of others in a plural legal environment.

In war, moreover, the assertions of opposing forces on questions of legitimacy and legality will echo across a chasm of difference in perspective. The legal and pragmatic assessment of wartime violence can heighten each side's confidence while stigmatising their foe. For all sides, limiting civilian death has become a pragmatic commitment – no unnecessary damage, not one more civilian than necessary. The difficulty is determining what is necessary, necessary for what and for whom, and then making a claim to kill in a way that resonates. In today's asymmetric conflicts, it is all too easy to view tactics unavailable to one's own forces as perfidious, whether that means the shock and awe of bombing from a great height or hiding amongst civilians and placing one's weapons amongst the religious.

American Major General James Mattis, poised to invade Falluja in Iraq, concluded his demand that the insurgents stand down with these words: 'We will always be humanitarian in all our efforts. We will fight the enemy on our terms. May God help them when we're done with them' (CNN World, 10 April, 2004). His juxtaposition of humanitarian claims and blunt threats was as chilling as his self-confidence. In war, it is terribly hard to remember how this will sound to other ears, particularly when the law of armed conflict has so often been a vocabulary used by the rich to judge the poor. No one, after all, experiences the death of their husband or sister as humanitarian and proportional. And everyone who believes in the legitimacy of their struggle will applaud its pursuit – the more so if it seems to be pursued by the least violent means available against a perfidious foe. It was equally chilling to hear the Iraqi insurgents in Falluja respond to Mattis by threatening to decapitate civilian hostages if coalition forces did not withdraw. What could be more perfidious? Like Mattis, the insurgents were threatening innocent civilian death – less of it actually. We must remember that many will hear such a threat as a legitimate humanitarian effort to achieve a military objective with the least damage to civilian life and that is how they will record it in their calculus of legitimate power.

When things go well, modern international law can provide a framework for talking across cultures about the justice and efficacy of wartime violence. More often, the modern partnership of war and law leaves all parties feeling their cause is just and no one feeling responsible for the deaths and suffering of war. Good legal arguments can make people lose their moral compass and sense of responsibility for the violence of war while politics and ethics have successfully been held at bay. It is in this atmosphere that discipline has broken down in every asymmetric struggle, when neither clear rules nor broad standards of judgment seem adequate to moor one's ethical sense of responsibility and empowerment. All sides assess their adversaries by the strictest standards and prefer permissive rules of engagement. Everyone has a CNN camera on their shoulder – but who is watching – the enemy, the civilians, your family at home, your commanding officer, your buddies? In this context, soldiers, civilians, media commentators and politicians all begin to lose their ethical moorings.

There is no way to avoid decisions about whom to kill in warfare. The difficulty arises when humanitarian law transforms *decisions* about whom to kill into *judgments*. When it encourages us to think death results not from an exercise of human freedom, for which a moral being is responsible, but rather from the abstract operation of professional principles. What does it mean to pretend the decision to kill is a principled judgment? It can mean a loss of the experience of responsibility – command responsibility, ethical responsibility, political responsibility. Indeed, the greatest threat posed by the merger of law and war is loss of the human experience of moral jeopardy in the face of death, mutilation and all the other horrors of warfare.

Modern war and modern law are conjoined in this new situation. Indeed, it is a distinctively modern triumph to have transformed war into a legal institution while rendering law a flexible strategic instrument for military and humanitarian professionals alike. We modernised the law of war to hold those who use violence politically responsible. That is why we applaud law as a global vernacular of 'legitimacy'. Unfortunately, however, the experience of political responsibility for war has proved elusive. Law may do more to constitute and legitimate than restrain violence, impressing itself upon its subjects in myriad dispersed sites of discipline and aspiration. It may accelerate the vertigo of combat and contribute to the loss of ethical moorings for people on all sides of a conflict. Pressing beyond modern law and modern war would require that we feel the weight of the decision to kill or let live. Most professionals – and citizens – flee from this experience.

We all yearn for the reassurance of an external judgment – by political leaders, clergy, lawyers and others – that what we have gotten up to is, in fact, an ethically responsible politics. In the end, however, Clausewitz was right. War is the continuation of political intercourse in another language. For modern war, modern law has become that language.

War and law have teamed up to divorce our politics from ethical choice and responsibility while structuring and defending a global political or economic order of ongoing and unequal struggle. Power has become a mixed matter of identity, strategy, assertion and discipline, authority and violence. Law and war have become oddly reciprocal, communicating and killing along the boundaries of the world system, at once drenched in the certainty of ethics and detached from the responsibility of politics. Working in partnership, modern law and modern war have enforced and pacified the boundaries of today's global architecture, while erasing their complicity and partnership with power and evading both ethical and political responsibility.

Understanding the entanglement of law and force in international affairs suggests a reorientation in our thinking about international law more broadly. The international legal ambition to develop a distinctively legal mode of articulation and action, rooted in sovereign power and resonating with a common ethics, is simply too large a rock to be lifted. Nor is it as important – or altogether salutary – a project as we imagine. The spaces of law's engagement are not modelled easily as the application or enforcement of a norm, but constitute a more interactive practice suspended between authorisation and exercise.

We should come to see law implicated throughout the international political and economic system, not as the articulation of rights or restraints, but as a more subtle and dispersed practice through which people struggle with one another through articulation and action. Our question ought not to be whether law restrains or power enforces, but rather the modes and machinery of strategy and tactic, of the constitution of subjects and the fate of ethics and politics. In such an inquiry, we would attend carefully to the articulations made in law's name, focusing on their structure, and their translation into social practice and discussion, rather than their hegemony or veracity. The ambition would be to see law written into the ongoing struggles – let us call them wars – which structure the political economy and ethical vernacular of peacetime routines.

Although globalisation has fragmented economic and political power, it has neither de-legalised them nor legalised them in a coherent and comprehensible pattern of functions and policy directions. If we follow the articulation of international law about war into the capillaries of international social, political and economic life, rather than a battle between power and right, we find an ongoing struggle amongst assertions of each, carried forward by people defining their identities and jockeying for position. And we find a strange double consciousness, oscillating between sincerity and savvy, strategy and confession of faith. It is in spaces like this that those who support and oppose military violence in the language of law have been brought into such a strange and elegant partnership or duet. By tracing their strategy and struggle we may illuminate international law as a terrain for political and ethical engagement rather than as a substitute for political choice and ethical decision.

Part III

Techniques and arenas

8 Law-making and sources

Hilary Charlesworth

Introduction

International law is constantly under challenge as a *legal* system. Some scholars depict it as weak, mutable, unstable (Morgenthau 1948, 284), some as the mere product of states maximising their interests (Goldsmith and Posner 2005), some point to it as the framework of many mundane activities, for example as the basis of airline travel or international postal services (Henkin 1979, 29–30), while others explain its value as a 'placemarker for justice' or as a vehicle for the 'regulative ideal of the international community' (Koskenniemi 2007, 30). Perhaps because there is so much anxiety about whether international law can claim to be a branch of law, the topic of the making and sources of international law dominates most introductory works. It is as if pinning down the well-springs of international law will provide certainty and authority for the discipline.

Where does international law come from? The sources of international law are a complex tangle of ideas, commitments and aspirations. In national legal systems, law is typically regarded as the product of legislatures or court systems; it is relatively straightforward to identify the legal principle at stake in a dispute, even if there is debate about its application in a particular case. There are also institutions at the national level that enforce the law, such as police forces and civil authorities, reinforcing the significance of legal status. By contrast, modern international law is to some extent the product of the behaviour and agreement of states, and to some extent the product of abstract values such as 'humanity' (Peters 2009), 'fairness' (Franck 1998), or 'communitarian values' (Tasioulas 1996). Jurists debate the proper respective contributions of state consent and moral values to international law, although of course the two may sometimes coincide. However defined, this mixture is a volatile one, which, together with the less-certain enforcement of international law, makes it appear more negotiable and uncertain than domestic law.

The controversy about the invasion of Iraq in March 2003 is an example of recourse to and the contestability of the sources of international law. Proponents of the invasion identified various sources of justification, including UN Security Council resolutions, a rule of customary international law allowing pre-emptive self-defence and a moral principle that dictatorial regimes should be removed from office. For their part, critics of the invasion pointed to treaty commitments, particularly the terms of article 2(4) and Chapter VII of the UN Charter, to argue that the use of force was illegal. Inquiries into the Iraq invasion have shown that politicians contemplating action against Iraq felt constrained to make public arguments about its legality while regarding the rules of international law as vague and malleable, capable of endorsing almost any move. The talk of sources masked an array of political decisions, but it also allowed an assessment of the plausibility and weight of the proffered sources. In this context, then, sources doctrine was used as a formalist device 'to verify or validate the argumentative *materiel* that enables the legal profession to continue to carry out its legal job without having to transform itself into a legislative agency … or a priesthood of rights and wrong' (Koskenniemi 2000, xiii).

Sources of international law are inflected by the identities of those who have the power to designate them. For this reason they have attracted the attention of both Third-World and feminist scholars who have pointed to biases built into traditional accounts of sources and argued for extending the notion (and categories) of sources to support their projects. Some Third-World international lawyers, for example, have criticised the development of customary rules from the practices of colonial powers, while contending for the legal status of resolutions adopted by international institutions in which developing states hold large majorities, such as the UN General Assembly (Anghie and Chimni 2004). Feminist international lawyers have pointed to the lack of women involved in norm-generating institutions in the international community, as well as the narrowness of the categories of sources, effectively excluding the experiences and interests of women (Charlesworth and Chinkin 2000).

International lawyers traditionally start with the Statute of the International Court of Justice (ICJ) when considering sources of international law. Article 38(1) of the Statute lists the types of principles that the Court should apply in deciding cases before it. This catalogue was first endorsed in 1922 in the Statute of the Permanent Court of International Justice (PCIJ). Technically it is simply a direction to the Court to apply certain categories of rules, but article 38(1) has achieved an almost canonical status as a codification of the sources of international law. Why does this list exercise such sway? Part of the appeal of article 38(1) is that recourse to it allows international lawyers to sidestep complex debates about the function of international law and the relative legitimacies of state consent and claims of justice. It is a pithy mantra that offers a quasi-scientific formula for practitioners of international law, postponing (possibly indefinitely) discussion of the politics of the designated sources. The formal nature of article 38(1) obscures the fact that international law is generated by a multi-layered process of interactions, instruments, pressures and principles. Specialised fields of international law, such as trade law, human rights law, the law of armed conflict or environmental law, also differ in the priority that they accord to different sources and the approaches they take to them.

Article 38(1) records four separate categories of law: international treaties, international custom, general principles of law, and (together) judicial decisions and the work of scholars. The Statute also contains an intriguing provision (article 38(2)) allowing the Court to decide a case, if the parties agree, without reference to international law, *ex aequo et bono*. This Latin phrase means deciding a case on the basis of equity and justice, but the provision has never been used in the International Court.

The language of article 38 has been described as 'dated and increasingly misleading' (Boyle and Chinkin 2007, 211) and the considerable growth in significance of 'soft' international law has challenged the clarity of its neat typology of sources. The notion of soft law is famously slippery. It includes instruments that have legal implications but which do not have the imagined 'hardness' of binding international obligations: resolutions of international institutions, declarations of high-level meetings, statements of bodies that monitor treaties, voluntary codes of conduct and treaty provisions that do not contain commitments to action may all fit into this category.

Is there a hierarchy of sources in international law? Should one source be given preference over another? The ICJ Statute specifically designates judicial decisions and scholarly writings as 'subsidiary means for the determination of rules of law', but otherwise does not distinguish between the categories. The first three categories are all manifestations of state consent to particular principles. In practice, if there is a treaty relevant to a particular dispute, it is likely to be given priority because of the apparent certainty of the written word and the formal display of consent to the treaty terms by the states who are parties to it. By contrast, as we shall see, the existence of a principle of customary international law is more difficult to establish. It depends on intricate tracking of actions by states as well as evidence that the actions were considered required by law. So too, the category of general principles of law is more obscure in content than that of treaties. Although there may be a hierarchy of sources in terms of ease of identification, in theory treaties, custom and general principles are all equally capable of generating legal norms of comparable weight. Each source can have 'hard' and 'soft' manifestations and the legality of a particular principle will depend on context. This equality of sources reflects the range of international law-makers and the legally and morally pluralist nature of international society (Besson 2010, 181–182). By contrast, the category of peremptory norms (*jus cogens*) suggests a hierarchy of norms rather than sources.

Other chapters in this volume (e.g. Chapter 2) emphasise international law's uneasy mix of justifications for state behaviour on the one hand and commitment to apparently universal values such as justice and peace on the other. This is the tradition of apologetic and utopian thought entwined in international legal argument described by Martti Koskenniemi (2005). The sources of international law reflect this tension between the political reality that state consent is integral to the efficacy of the international legal system and the idealistic force of abstract principles such as justice and fairness. The increasing role of international institutions in law-making has, however, given values a boost and reduced the significance of individual state consent.

International conventions, whether general or particular, establishing rules expressly recognised by the contesting states

International conventions (i.e. treaties) are agreements between two or more states, which may contain binding or non-binding terms. It is possible for states to make formal agreements verbally through their officials, but this is rare. Treaty drafting, adoption and interpretation are governed by the rules set out in the Vienna Convention on the Law of Treaties of 1969 and I do not address these issues directly here. The binding nature of treaties rests on the maxim *pacta sunt servanda* (agreements must be observed) which is incorporated in the Vienna Convention (article 26). This principle is of course also the basis of contract law in many national legal systems. Treaties, then, may be sources of obligation, but how do they become sources of law?

Treaties come in all shapes and sizes. Bilateral treaties, between two states, may be quite specific and technical, for example free trade agreements. Such agreements constitute a source of law only in the limited sense that they bind the two parties and provide redress in case of a breach by one party. They do not have implications for the development of international law more generally. There are however limits on what can be included in a treaty: the Vienna Convention declares void treaty provisions that violate the *jus cogens*, principles of international law to which the international community allows no exception (article 53). The Convention presents such norms as those 'accepted and recognised by the international community of States as a whole as a norm from which no derogation is permitted and which can be modified only by a subsequent norm of general international law having the same character'. This text is based in the normative tradition of international law, assigning the 'international community' a central role in defining fundamental values that will limit the behaviour of individual states. The content of the *jus cogens* is contested, with various lists proffered (e.g. Restat. 3d of US Foreign Relations Law (1990), §102; Brownlie 2008, 511). There is wide support for the prohibitions of slavery, genocide and racial discrimination as part of the *jus cogens*. However, some jurists have challenged the very existence of a *jus cogens*, or what has been described as 'superlaw', arguing that it disrupts the unity of traditional international law which did not draw distinctions between types of legal principles (Weil 1983).

Multilateral treaties drafted by international institutions often have a more obviously legal character than bilateral treaties in the sense that they set out broad statements of principle to be applied in many different contexts. Some treaties codify customary rules of international law and thus have a status beyond mere contractual agreement. Examples include the Vienna Convention on Diplomatic Relations of 1961, and, indeed, the Vienna Convention on the Law of Treaties. Other treaties attain a special status by defining fundamental normative principles, such as human rights, and attracting significant participation by states. Thus the commitments in the UN human rights treaties constitute a legal obligation for all the states that have formally accepted their terms, but they can also have a legal effect on non-parties. Depending on its language, the moral force of the normative order that it prescribes and its global level of acceptance, a treaty provision may become legally binding generally, as custom, and govern the conduct even of states that have not formally accepted it. This is anathema to those who insist that state consent is the critical element of international law-making (e.g. Weil 1983, 439).

A feature of modern multilateral treaty-making is the tendency for treaty-makers in particular areas to develop specialised concepts and techniques. The International Law Commission (ILC) has described this as the 'fragmentation' of international law and considers such fragmentation problematic as it creates potential for conflict between treaty regimes. For example principles of international trade law may be in tension with environmental treaty rules and human rights treaty norms may be inconsistent with those contained in treaties dealing with the law of armed conflict. The ILC has recommended a principle of harmonisation to resolve these tensions which would encourage, as far as possible, interpretation of treaty obligations bearing on a particular subject to be compatible with each other.

Another modern feature in treaty-making is the growth of memoranda of understanding (MOUs) and other soft law arrangements not in themselves intended as treaties. But such instruments may produce legal effects. For example, it is possible for later agreements or understandings to affect the interpretation of a treaty; in this sense soft law can modify apparently hard law. It is often easier for drafters to adopt specific and precise terms in non-binding international agreements; such instruments also bypass the problems of national treaty-ratification processes (Boyle and Chinkin 2007, 214).

International custom as evidence of a general practice accepted as law

The category of 'international custom' as a source of international law has intrigued jurists. Customary international law is sometimes presented as similar to the 'common law' developed by judges in Anglo-American legal systems. The analogy is, however, imperfect, as customary international law is created primarily through evidence of state practice and state belief, rather than an apparent product of any legal or moral principle or of judicial law making case-by-case. So international custom in its traditional form gives priority to state consent as the source of the law over normative concepts.

Standard definitions of customary international law stipulate that it is comprised of two distinct elements: state practice and *opinio juris sive necessitatis.* The first element is established by actions of states. The relevant evidence can come from a wide range of sources, but it must indicate consistent and uniform state practice over time. Some scholars have argued that state practice should be limited to physical actions, such as the withdrawal of an ambassador, the monitoring of a border or a military strike (e.g. D'Amato 1971, Chapter 4). While such an approach has the advantage of ease of proof, a more widely held view is that state practice includes national laws, claims, correspondence, statements and other positions that can be attributed to a state (Brownlie 2008, 6). This broader analysis also includes omissions or failures to act. High levels of treaty participation can provide evidence of state practice of a particular rule, and it is even more significant if non-parties to the relevant treaty behave in accordance with its terms.

International courts and tribunals have taken widely divergent approaches in deeming state practice adequate for the formation of customary international law. For example in the *North Sea Continental Shelf* cases in 1969, the ICJ rejected evidence of the use by states of the equidistance principle in maritime boundary delimitations as numerically insignificant. Other relevant factors include the uniformity of the practice and its duration, with an inverse relationship between them: the shorter are the records of a particular practice the greater is the expectation of consistency; and vice versa. However in the *Nicaragua* case, discussed below, the International Court was prepared to identify a rule of custom on the basis of slender and equivocal state practice.

Opinio juris has been defined as the sense held by states that they are conforming to a legal obligation. This makes it more subtle and difficult to establish than state practice as it requires evidence that a particular action was undertaken by a state because it was considered legally required. How can we know what a particular state was thinking about a particular action? Hersch Lauterpacht suggested a presumption that all uniform conduct of governments evidenced *opinio juris* unless the contrary was proved (Lauterpacht 1958, 380, cited by Judge Sørensen, dissenting, *North Sea Continental Shelf*, ICJ Reports 1969, p. 242, 246–247). Other jurists have argued for an 'objective' test for *opinio juris* requiring the articulation of a claim of international legality in advance of, or concurrently with, the relevant state practice (e.g. D'Amato 1971, 74). More recent accounts of *opinio juris* present it as largely independent of individual state belief, depending rather on a diffuse consensus as to what is legally required (Henckaerts 2005).

To add to the confusion, the two elements of customary international law are often merged in particular cases. Take the *Nicaragua* case before the ICJ in 1986, for example (ICJ Reports 1986, p. 14). The Court had to consider whether there was a customary legal prohibition on the use of force, which would render illegal mining of Nicaraguan harbours by the United States. The Court accepted votes and statements made by states in the General Assembly of the United Nations condemning the use of force in international relations both as state practice and *opinio juris* supporting a customary rule precluding the use of force. Another such case is that of the *Texaco Arbitration* (1978) where the Arbitrator regarded the General Assembly's 1962 Declaration on Permanent Sovereignty over Natural Resources as evidence of customary international law (53 ILR 490). According to the Arbitrator, the legal character of a resolution depended on its type, form and the conditions under which it was adopted. Soft law can thus influence the development of customary principles. It has been suggested that this process is in fact typical of modern approaches to customary international law, which start with general statements of rules, in contrast to traditional approaches that focused on specific instances of state practice (Roberts 2001).

An apparent paradox is created by *opinio juris*, the psychological element of customary international law: it seems to require that states believe (mistakenly) that something is already law before it can become law, making the definition circular. But how should we understand state actions undertaken in a speculative way, without a sense of legal compulsion? John Tasioulas has proposed a resolution to the custom paradox, drawing on ethical reasoning. His argument distinguishes between cases where *opinio juris* relates to the creation or revision of customary international law on the one hand; and cases where *opinio juris* relates to the continuation of a principle that had earlier come into existence on the other hand. In the first case, according to Tasioulas, custom requires general state practice that can be ethically justified, and in fact receives ethical endorsement by states. In the second case, a custom retains legitimacy if it can be ethically justified. This resolution places much weight on the notion of the ethical, which Tasioulas defines broadly as 'the domain of reasons that bear on an agent that derive from proper regard for human interests, both his own and, especially, those of others' (Tasioulas 2007, 204). Tasioulas argues that his approach 'solves the problem of transparency [in the creation of international custom] without implausibly attributing overly complex attitudes to states'

(2007, 203); however the concept of 'proper regard for human interests' inserts a highly contestable element that may destabilise the solution.

Unlike a treaty, customary international law is understood to bind all states, new and old, whether or not they have participated in its generation. The International Court has acknowledged, however, the possibility of regional customary law, applicable in a limited geographic sphere. An example is the creation of rights of passage through another state's territory, built up over centuries of practice (*Rights of Passage over Indian Territory* (*Portugal* v. *India*), ICJ Reports 1960, p. 6).

The voluntary, or apologetic, nature of international law is emphasised in the notion of 'persistent objectors' to the formation of a rule of customary international law. Persistently objecting to a rule will not get you far in a national legal system, but international law has recognised the possibility of a state opting out of customary rules, while they are developing, through a process of public objections over a long period. Thus in the early 1950s Norway argued that it had resisted the development of certain rules to measure its territorial sea that would disadvantage it. The Norwegian persistent objection had occurred over the preceding century and took the form of decrees and refusal to participate in treaty regimes that precluded its claims (*Fisheries* (*United Kingdom* v *Norway*), ICJ Reports 1951, p. 116). Norway was able to defend successfully a claim by the United Kingdom to reduce Norway's sovereignty over the North Sea on this basis. Persistent objection is most powerful when other states do not themselves protest against the objection.

The effectiveness and coherence of the persistent objector principle have been challenged however and its dwindling status today reflects the vitality of the utopian tradition in international law (e.g. Charney 1993). In Chapter 5, James Crawford points out that, on an empirical level, persistent objection to a rule that is widely supported by the international community is very likely to fail. There have also been some attempts to articulate a 'subsequent objector' principle in the case of custom, both from Third-World jurists and from US scholars, but they have had as yet little impact.

The general principles of law recognised by civilised nations

The drafters of the PCIJ Statute regarded general principles of law as a type of safety net in the event that neither treaty nor custom provided the rules necessary to resolve a dispute. The wording of this category of international law sources was a compromise between two different approaches, one utopian in tendency and the other apologetic, on part of the Advisory Committee of Jurists which drafted the PCIJ Statute in 1920. The former approach was endorsed by the Belgian jurist, Baron Descamps, who supported a provision allowing the Court to apply 'the rules of international law as recognized by the legal conscience of civilized nations' as a supplement to consent-based sources such as treaties. This provision was strongly opposed by Elihu Root of the United States on the basis that it would promote 'subjective conceptions of the principles of justice'. He asked whether 'it was possible to compel nations to submit their disputes to a Court which would administer not merely law, but also what it deems to be the conscience of civilised peoples?' (quoted in van Hoof 1983, 137).

The final wording of article 38(1)(c) removed the idea of a legal conscience as the basis for international law and emphasised the role of states and their legal systems in identifying principles in this category. The reference to 'civilised nations' reflects the era, just after the adoption of the Covenant of the League of Nations. Proponents of the category had in mind principles found in many national legal systems such as good faith and *res judicata* (the finality of judgments). In this way, the category retained a consensual basis through the mechanism of acceptance of principles by states in their own legal systems.

Scholars have since debated whether general principles of law encompass a compilation of rules common to national legal systems or whether the term means a category of international rules to which all right-thinking states would subscribe. It is also unclear how many states would need to recognise a rule for it to qualify as a general principle. Despite (or perhaps because of) these debates, the category of general principles is seldom invoked explicitly in international legal argument.

Some jurists have recommended rehabilitation of general principles as a source of law to circumvent the technical difficulties of establishing customary international law. For example Oscar Schachter suggested that general principles of national law were ripe for recruitment into international law particularly in the area of individual rights, contractual remedies, liability for extra-hazardous activities and restraints on the use of common property (Schachter 1991). Bruno Simma and Philip Alston have encouraged the use of general principles as a 'modern' source of human rights law, derived particularly from consensus evidenced in resolutions of international organisations. They argue that this will retain the traditional consensual basis of international law, while avoiding the complexities of customary international law (Simma and Alston 1988). The development of a 'global administrative law' is an example of general principles of national legal systems being treated as absorbed into the international legal order. This renewed interest in general principles as a source of international law can be also understood as a way of finding a recognised legal umbrella for the vast array of soft law instruments.

Judicial decisions and the teachings of the most highly qualified publicists of the various nations

The last two sources referred to in the International Court's Statute are designated as subsidiary. The reference to judicial decisions is made subject to article 59 which provides that '[t]he decision of the Court has no binding force except between the parties and in respect of that particular case'. This accords a lower status to ICJ decisions than that given to the decisions of final courts in many legal systems. The drafting history of this provision indicates that its goal was to prevent international judges from regarding themselves as quasi-legislators. The ICJ, however, constantly refers to its previous decisions; indeed national and international judicial opinions are scrutinised and used in all international law-making fora to a much greater degree than suggested in article 38(1)(d). The weight given to judicial opinions is affected by factors such as the status and independence of the court, the availability of the written and oral pleadings and the quality and detail of the judicial reasoning (Boyle and Chinkin 2007, 302–310).

Writers such as Suárez and Grotius influenced, indeed defined, the early development of international law. Today scholarly writings are regularly cited in international legal argument, although the International Court itself has been wary about endorsing the views of particular jurists. This is perhaps because of the intensely political context of international disputes where the nationality of scholars may be assumed to colour their views. An English court noted another objection in 1905 in *West Rand Central Gold Mining Co.* v. *The King*:

> in many instances the ... pronouncements [of international legal scholars] must be regarded ... as the embodiments of their views as to what ought to be, from an

> ethical standpoint, the conduct of nations *inter se*, [rather] than the enunciation of a rule or practice so universally approved or assented to as to be fairly termed, even in the qualified sense in which the word can be understood in reference to the relations between independent political communities, 'law'. ([1905] 2 K.B. 391, 402)

The sources of soft law

Over the last twenty-five years, the phenomenon of soft law has attracted increasing attention. The traditional sources of international law were framed in 1922 in terms of the actions of individual states, while soft law, a creature of the UN Charter era, is a product of multilateral processes, institutions and even individuals operating in the international sphere. Exponents of soft law include the International Law Commission, treaty-interpretative bodies such as the Human Rights Committee, and Special Rapporteurs appointed by the Human Rights Council. The binding character of soft law principles may be debated, but they often address issues of almost universal agreement, such as sustainable development or human rights, and can provide powerful justifications for action. Soft law is not a *source* of law in the sense of article 38(1) of the ICJ Statute, but rather a category of principles, articulated through instruments or documents not binding as such, whose status is more contested and negotiable than those of hard legal norms. Principles of soft law may sometimes be regarded as 'probationary' candidates for eventual recognition as fully fledged law (Besson 2010, 170), although this will not always be the case. State consent remains significant in the case of soft law, but it is filtered though institutions and entities that do not necessarily echo the interests of particular states or groups of states. In essence, the sources of soft law do not differ from those of hard law although the idea of soft law stretches these familiar groupings and may ultimately collapse them. Indeed Samantha Besson argues that soft law instruments illustrate 'an increasing convergence in terms of law-making procedures and law-makers amongst the different sources of international law' (*ibid.*, 180).

One category of soft law often employed in legal argument is that of resolutions of international organisations. These differ in their legal effect. For example, article 25 of the UN Charter specifies that resolutions of the Security Council made under Chapter VII of the Charter are binding on all UN members. While resolutions of the General Assembly do not bind states as such, they may be legally significant as examples of state practice or evidence of *opinio juris*, or both, as noted above in the discussion of custom. The significance will depend on the nature of the resolution and the voting pattern associated with it. A resolution that attracted a polarised vote, or many abstentions, may not have any legal implications. Hersch Lauterpacht made a stern riposte to the claim that non-binding resolutions of international institutions may accrue legal authority in the case of the Universal Declaration of Human Rights, adopted by the UN General Assembly in 1948. He noted that almost all states had emphasised in debates preceding its adoption that the Declaration was not legally binding and he rejected arguments that it could have an indirect legal effect as incongruous and inconsistent with the wording of the Declaration (Lauterpacht 1950, 394–417).

Despite the development of soft law, modern international law-making continues to invoke the four categories set out in the ICJ Statute as the primary sources of law and understands the effect of soft law principles in relation to them, rather than as a distinct source of law. Soft law thus interacts with and blurs the boundaries of the traditional sources of international law, but it does not replace them. Indeed the tendency of courts and tribunals to recast asserted soft law principles in terms of the language of article 38(1) has led some scholars to dispute the logic or function of a category of 'soft law' (e.g. Klabbers 1996). Anthony D'Amato has attacked the concept as a vehicle used by impatient idealists to push international law far beyond the constraints of a consensual legal order into areas such as the protection of human rights and the environment. He laments the detachment of the sources of international law from state behaviour and has dismissed the value of soft law as 'a head without a body' (D'Amato 2009, 899). Others have been concerned with the implications of soft law for democracy at the national level: if law can be created softly and informally in the international sphere, it will bypass the usual national processes for acceptance. On the other hand, soft law can be read as a sign of the democratisation of international law-making processes in the sense that its development is more inclusive than hard law: it typically emerges not just from the interests of states but in multilateral fora with the engagement of international organisations, non-government organisations and individuals. This increases democratic markers such as equality and deliberation and brings the international law-making sphere closer to the national one (Boyle and Chinkin 2007, 214; Besson 2010).

Conclusion

The sources of international law seem disconcertingly negotiable to a domestic lawyer accustomed to a recognised hierarchy of legal sources. The legitimacy of domestic legal systems typically springs from the implicit consent of the governed as manifested through legislatures, although restrained in some cases through higher constitutional norms. In international law, the consent of the legal subject has been considerably more explicit. This has made international law appear unstable and manipulable compared to national legal orders. The contrast between international and domestic legal systems is, however, often exaggerated, ignoring the indeterminacy of principles of any legal order and the porosity of their implementation.

In any event, since the founding of the United Nations, the prominence of individual state consent in law-making has been reduced. International organisations, non-government groups and individuals now play a significant part in the law-making process, bringing the makers closer to the subjects of international law (Besson 2010, 163–164).

These developments have gone hand in hand with changing ideas of legitimacy. We have moved from an obsession with formal sources as the marker of legitimacy in international law to one with values. Prosper Weil's *cri de coeur* in the face of what he termed the 'relative normativity' of international law, generated by a retreat from the consent of states as the source of international law (Weil 1983), has now become a whisper. Indeed there have been calls for the recognition of ethical principles as an aspect of international law, or universal norms to prevent states from quarantining themselves from principles vital to human survival (e.g. Charney 1993). But most arguments about the content of international law still contain contradictory elements of both normative aspiration and assertions of state freedom of action and the priority of state consent.

A focus on sources of law comforts international lawyers that they are part of a truly legal system and that they are engaging in a technical, rather than political, craft. The international legal doctrines about sources, however, are selective and partial. They embody unease about whether international law should reflect the behaviour of states or a system of deeper human values.

Bibliography

Anghie A. and B. Chimni, 2004. 'Third World Approaches to International Law and Individual Responsibility in Internal Conflict', in S. Ratner and A.-M. Slaughter (eds.), *The Methods of International Law*, Washington, DC: The American Society of International Law, 185–210

Besson, S., 2010. 'Theorizing the Sources of International Law', in S. Besson and J. Tasioulas (eds.), *The Philosophy of International Law*, Oxford University Press, 163–186

Boyle, A. and C. Chinkin, 2007. *The Making of International Law*, Oxford University Press

Brownlie, I., 2008. *Principles of Public International Law*, 7th edn., Oxford University Press

Charlesworth, H. and C. Chinkin, 2000. *The Boundaries of International Law: A Feminist Analysis*, Manchester University Press

Charney, J., 1993. 'Universal International Law', *American Journal of International Law*, 87, 529–551

D'Amato, A., 1971. *The Concept of Custom in International Law*, Ithaca, NY: Cornell University Press

D'Amato, A., 2009. 'Softness in International Law: A Self-serving Quest for New Legal Materials. A Reply to Jean d'Aspremont', *European Journal of International Law*, 20, 897–910

Franck, T., 1998. *Fairness in International Law and Institutions*, Oxford University Press

Goldsmith, J. and E. Posner, 2005. *The Limits of International Law*, Oxford University Press

Henckaerts, J.-M., 2005. 'Study on Customary International Humanitarian Law: A Contribution to the Understanding and Respect for the Rule of Law in Armed Conflict', *International Review of the Red Cross*, 87, 175–212

Henkin, L., 1979. *How Nations Behave: Law and Foreign Policy*, New York: Columbia University Press

Koskenniemi, M., 2005. *From Apology to Utopia: The Structure of International Legal Argument. Reissue with a New Epilogue*, Cambridge University Press

Koskenniemi, M., 2007. 'The Fate of Public International Law: Between Technique and Politics', *Modern Law Review*, 70, 1–30

Koskenniemi, M., 2000. (ed.), *Sources of International Law*, Farnham: Ashgate

Klabbers, J., 1996. 'The Redundancy of Soft Law', *Nordic Journal of International Law*, 65, 167–182

Lauterpacht, H., 1950. *International Law and Human Rights*, London: Stevens & Sons

Lauterpacht, H., 1958. *The Development of International Law by the International Court*, New York: Praeger

Morgenthau, H., 1948. *Politics Among Nations: The Struggle for Power and Peace*, New York: Alfred A. Knopf

Peters, A., 2009. 'Humanity as the A and Ω of Sovereignty', *European Journal of International Law*, 20, 513–544

Roberts, A., 2001. 'Traditional and Modern Approaches to Customary International Law: A Reconciliation', *American Journal of International Law*, 95, 757–791

Schachter, O., 1991. *International Law in Theory and Practice*, The Hague: Martinus Nijhoff

Simma, B. and P. Alston, 1988. 'The Sources of Human Rights Law: Custom, Jus Cogens, and General Principles', *Australian Year Book of International Law*, 12, 82–108

Tasioulas, J., 1996. 'In Defence of Relative Normativity: Communitarian Values and the *Nicaragua* Case', *Oxford Journal of Legal Studies*, 16, 85–128

Tasioulas, J., 2007. '*Opinio Juris* and the Genesis of Custom: A Solution to the "Paradox"', *Australian Year Book of International Law*, 26, 199–206

van Hoof, G., 1983. *Rethinking the Sources of International Law*, Deventer: Kluwer

Weil, P., 1983. 'Towards Relative Normativity in International Law?', *American Journal of International Law*, 77, 413–442

International courts: uneven judicialisation in global order 9

Benedict Kingsbury

Introduction

'Law without courts' seemed to Hugo Grotius an entirely coherent approach to the juridification of international relations. The first edition of his *Law of War and Peace* (*De jure belli ac pacis*, 1625) reflects an intense commitment to framing claims and rules for conduct outside the state in terms of legal rights and duties, but not to judicialisation, even though arbitration between sovereigns was addressed in earlier works he had read, such as Alberico Gentili's *Law of War* (*De iure belli libri tres*, 1612 [1933]). Yet in modern times international judicialisation – the creation and use of international courts and tribunals – has been not only a significant component of liberal approaches to international order, but for some an indispensable concomitant of juridification.

The opening section of this chapter provides an overview of the formation of what are now ten basic types of international courts. The following section offers some balance to the tendencies (implicit in the approach taken in the first section) to acclaim each flourishing legal institution as an achievement and to study only what exists, by considering the marked unevenness in the issues and in the ranges of states currently subject to juridification through international courts and tribunals. The final section addresses the question whether the density and importance of the judicially focused juridification that now exists has implications for politics, law and justice that are qualitatively different from what has gone before. This is explored by examining some of the main roles and functions of international courts, considered not simply as a menu but as a complex aggregate.

International courts and tribunals are institutions, and are increasingly analysed as such. This includes basic institutional design, the specified functions and powers of the court, the degree of its embeddedness in related political institutions which may provide support or checks on it, the processes of appointment of the judges and their degree of independence and expertise as well as their socio-professional reference groups, the funding and work capacity of the institution in relation to demands on it and its efforts to expand its reach or scale, whether the institution has an enduring identity and whether its judges are part-time (as the World Trade Organisation (WTO) Appellate Body is, by design). Some studies focus principally on the institution, and the ways in which the court also acts not judicially but administratively e.g. supervising appointment of defence counsel, or a compensation fund for victims. Explaining why these institutional features are the way they are says much about a particular court: its judgments, its substantive motivations in different cases, and its legal methods. Tribunals develop their own hermeneutics connected with many of these institutional factors – thus the WTO Appellate Body purports to adhere closely to the underlying treaty texts, while the Court of Justice of the European Community (CJEU, formerly ECJ) is more expressly teleological in aiming to achieve the purposes of the EU treaties. It is something of an international law myth that there is one unified approach to interpretation that is embodied in the 1969 Vienna Convention on the Law of Treaties and shared amongst all tribunals. The sociology of those practising in particular courts, and the wider constituencies for those courts, are also important. These institutional questions cannot, however, be considered further in the confines of this chapter.

This chapter will not propose a tightly specified definition of 'international court'. 'Court' undoubtedly exerts some pull as a regulative idea, that is as an 'ideal type' which there is cognitive and sometimes political pressure for judicial-type institutions to approximate both in their design and in their operations. Mani (1980) put this in terms of rights to be heard, to a duly constituted tribunal free from corruption and fraud, to due deliberation, and to a reasoned judgment (which should more stringently be expressed as 'reasoned judgment in accordance with the applicable law'). But it is doubtful that a single sharply delimited concept of 'court' prevails in international law practice. The term 'international' is used here to indicate courts created by intergovernmental agreement (including agreements made within, or by, intergovernmental organisations), or by agreement between a national government and a foreign private entity, where the court is legally situated either fully or partly outside the national juridical and governmental system of any state.

Ten types of international courts: history and overview

This section provides a sketch of ten major types of international tribunals and courts. These are presented in a loosely chronological way reflecting the first significant appearance of each type in international practice. This typology is based on the form and function of the institutions, criteria chosen to provide an overview likely to be useful and accessible. Many other typologies are possible. International courts vary in the degree to which they rest on consent of (or delegation from) the affected states or legal persons, in the independence (or lack of it) of judicial appointments and judicial decisions from those actors, in their levels of independent agency as actors over time, in the extent of their impact on material outcomes or on political actors or on legal norms or on values such as individual or collective freedom or responsibility or self-determination, and in the reasons for their creation and for their sustained activity or inactivity.

The arbitrations of claims concerning losses to private individuals pursuant to the Britain–US Jay Treaty 1794, and of inter-state claims of the United States against Britain in the *Alabama* award of 1872, were by the late nineteenth century espoused as emblematic of the increasing possibilities of bilateral and multilateral arbitration. The 1899 Hague Peace Conference created the Permanent Court of Arbitration (PCA) which, despite its name, was and continues to be a structure enabling arbitration by *ad hoc* panels – after a flurry of cases in its first two–three decades, it was virtually unused from 1935 until a pronounced revival which began in the mid-1990s. By the beginning of the twentieth century there were thus established three basic structural patterns of international arbitration that continue to be significant.

1 **Inter-Governmental Claims Commissions** created by two governments on the Jay Treaty model, allowing private claims against the other state from a defined set of events to be presented (in the past this was done through the government, but increasingly it is done directly by the claimant's legal team or through special small-claims processes) for law-governed arbitral decision. The Iran–US Claims Tribunal (1981–, created under the 1981 Algiers Accords) and the Eritrea–Ethiopia Claims Commission (2001–2009, created under the 2000 Algiers Agreement) exemplify this form. Both operated during periods of difficult and sometimes hostile relations between the relevant states, which the tribunals themselves, based in The Hague, could do little to ameliorate beyond processing their dockets

of historic claims. Both also had jurisdiction over certain state–state claims – large claims by Iran against the United States relating to military equipment ordered and paid for by the Shah's government but not delivered by the United States to the post-revolution government were long left unresolved given the substantial political difficulties.

2 ***Ad hoc*** **inter-state arbitration** governed by law, on the *Alabama* model. Such tribunals have been created at a rate of about one per year since 1945. Territorial disputes and boundary delimitation (land or maritime), fishing, and some specific treaty disputes (e.g. US–France *Air Services*; New Zealand–France *Rainbow Warrior*) have comprised a large share of the arbitrated disputes.

3 **Inter-state arbitration embedded in pre-existing legal institutional structures,** with the PCA currently the dominant example (as in Ireland–UK *MOX Plant* 2008; Belgium–Netherlands *Iron Rhine* 2005). The PCA facilities, and some of its mechanisms, are now used also in arbitrations that are not simply state–state. Illustrative are the 2009 *Abyei* arbitration between the Government of Sudan and the SPLM/A, under the North–South peace agreement; the 2003 *Reineccius* awards against the Bank for International Settlements (BIS) in favour of private shareholders in the BIS with regard to the purchase price for buying out their shares; and the *Channel Tunnel* arbitration (2007) in which the commercial operator claimed against both France and the United Kingdom, while the two governments were themselves in disagreement over access to trains and the tunnel from a nearby French government-operated camp for political asylum seekers. The PCA also provides facilities in the competitive market for contract-based or treaty-based claims by individuals or corporations against foreign states, particularly under commercial arbitration rules such as those of the UN Commission on International Trade Law (UNCITRAL), which unlike the International Centre for Settlement of International Trade Disputes (ICSID) or the Stockholm Chamber of Commerce does not provide arbitral facilities even for cases under its rules.

Three further structures were formalised in the immediate aftermath of the First World War:

4 **Standing international courts:** Long-cherished hopes finally came to fruition in the decision of the Paris Peace Conference to create the Permanent Court of International Justice (PCIJ, established in 1922), which in its inter-state contentious jurisdiction was structured as a blend of arbitral-type bilateral dispute settlement and adjudication that communicated to a wider audience and took some account of systemic issues. Its separate jurisdiction to give legally grounded advisory opinions to the League of Nations brought intergovernmental organisations into the ambit of adjudicated international law – the PCIJ struggled

in its early opinions with the legal character and proper powers of these organisations before settling on a functional approach which allocated extensive powers to them provided these were needed to perform their treaty-specified functions. The PCIJ was replaced by the International Court of Justice (ICJ) in 1946, pursuant to the supersession of the League by the United Nations. The ICJ's Statute (a treaty annexed to the UN Charter), its jurisdiction, and its structure of fifteen permanent judges operating in plenary and augmented by *ad hoc* judges where states in a contentious case have no judge of their nationality on the court, are similar to those of the PCIJ, whose location at the Peace Palace in The Hague the ICJ also took over.

5 **International criminal courts**: A criminal trial of the German Kaiser for 'a supreme offence against international morality and the sanctity of treaties' (especially the violation of Belgium's neutrality) was envisaged in article 227 of the Treaty of Versailles (1919), although his flight to the Netherlands – which refused extradition – stalled the plan. Trials under Allied military authority of other German officers, contemplated in article 228, were abandoned in favour of lacklustre trials in German courts. More convincing precedents for multinational courts were set by the International Military Tribunal at Nuremberg, and the International Military Tribunal for the Far East in Tokyo, each of which were staffed with judges and prosecutors from a range of victor states. In the 1990s, the UN Security Council adopted binding resolutions establishing the International Criminal Tribunal for Former Yugoslavia (ICTY, 1993–) and the International Criminal Tribunal for Rwanda (ICTR, 1995–).[1] The Rome Statute of the International Criminal Court (ICC), a treaty adopted in 1998 which entered into force in 2000, created a standing criminal court empowered to try for specified categories of heinous offences persons whose country of nationality has ratified the treaty, or persons alleged to have committed these crimes in the territory of a state party, provided the states with jurisdiction are unable or unwilling to pursue prosecution. Situations may also be referred to the Court by states, the UN Security Council or the ICC itself. In contrast to the majority of non-criminal international courts, the consent of the defendant parties is not required for prosecutors to bring actions in these institutions.

6 **International administrative tribunals**: The dominant early model of an international administrative tribunal, established to address employment grievances of staff of international organisations, was that of the International Labour Organisation (ILOAT). This tribunal continues to be used by many other

[1] SC Res 1966 (2010) determined that the two *ad hoc* tribunals be wound up in 2012 and 2013, respectively and replaced by a 'International Residual Mechanism for Criminal Tribunals' for remaining cases.

organisations. After decades of lassitude, the United Nations reformed its internal justice system in 2009 to establish a two-tier structure with a UN Appeals Tribunal. Much reform of such tribunals has been precipitated by actual or threatened decisions of national courts to reject the immunity of the international organisation in employment-related cases if rights-respecting alternatives were not in place. Generally these tribunals do not have jurisdiction over claims by third parties (except staff dependents) against the organisation, leaving a substantial gap confronting victims of physical abuse or recklessness.

To these six structural forms that were put in place by the end of the 1920s, four further categories of tribunals may be added as post-1945 innovations (although each had some antecedents):

7 **Regional human rights courts**: The European Court of Human Rights (ECtHR, in Strasbourg, France) has jurisdiction over complaints against states parties by individuals claiming to be victims of violations of the 1950 European Convention on Human Rights (as well as jurisdiction in inter-state cases, utilised by Georgia against Russia in relation to the 2008 war). By 2010 the court had jurisdiction over all forty-seven Council of Europe states, with a total population of some 800 million. It was receiving some 60,000 applications per year and issuing some 1,500 substantive judgments annually, making it the international court with the largest caseload. The 1950 Convention also created a European Commission of Human Rights to screen and adjudicate individual claims, to promote 'friendly settlements' of cases, and in effect to filter cases reaching the court. It was eventually abolished in favour of direct access to a clearly judicial body. The Inter-American Commission on Human Rights (based in Washington, DC) was complemented by the establishment in 1979 in San José, Costa Rica, of the Inter-American Court of Human Rights, the jurisprudence of which has become increasingly important in national law and politics since 'third-wave' democratisation in Latin America. The African Commission of Human and People's Rights (based in Banjul, Gambia) was augmented by the creation in 2004 of the African Court of Human and People's Rights (in Arusha, Tanzania), which gave its first judgment in 2009. Comparable bodies do not exist in the greater Asia–Pacific area, nor is there any prospect of a World Court of Human Rights. Several supervisory bodies created by UN human rights treaties have powers to investigate and report on complaints by individuals against states accepting this jurisdiction, but these bodies generally do not hold hearings with the parties present, do not have powers to issue binding decisions and are at most quasi-judicial rather than functioning as courts. The UN Human Rights Committee is the leading example.

8 **Regional economic integration courts**: The European Court of Justice (ECJ, now CJEU), created under the 1957 Treaty of Rome and related European treaties, has been a driving force in legal integration of the twenty-seven-state European Union. The power of national courts to apply European law directly, and their acceptance of the authority of the CJEU as final judicial arbiter on such issues combined with their right (and in some circumstances their obligation) to seek preliminary rulings from the court, has brought national judicial institutions strongly into the European law project. A power of issuing preliminary rulings is also held by the Andean Court of Justice (mainly on intellectual property matters); The Caribbean Court of Justice and the proposed African Court of Justice are amongst other bodies that could interact closely with national courts on regional legal issues. But none of these is likely soon to come close to emulating the CJEU in reach and impact.

9 **The WTO dispute settlement system**: The General Agreement on Tariffs and Trade (GATT) of 1947, operated a system of panels to report on complaints by one state party against another. These reports could have legal effect if adopted by consensus by the plenary body of all states members of GATT. This system was transformed into a more formal and more judicial system with the creation of the World Trade Organisation (WTO) in 1994. Three-member *ad hoc* panels issue reports in the same way, but typically with much more legal reasoning; these can be appealed to a standing Appellate Body. Final panel reports or Appellate Body decisions become legally binding unless rejected by the member states by consensus (a rare occurrence). Legally reasoned rulings, in some cases with appeals processes, are also issued under other trade agreements such as Mercosur or Chapters 19 and 20 of the 1994 North American Free Trade Agreement (NAFTA).

10 **Investment arbitration tribunals**: Arbitration of claims by foreign investors against states was given a systematic structure in the World Bank's ICSID Convention of 1965 (albeit with other arbitration modalities often still available), accompanied by a lattice of what is now well over 2,500 bilateral investment treaties, a few comparable multilateral treaties such as the 1994 Energy Charter Treaty and Chapter 11 of the NAFTA, a structure of national laws for enforcement of commercial arbitral awards including under the 1958 New York Convention, and a raft of investor–state contracts.

Amongst other singular tribunals not fitting into these types are the International Tribunal for the Law of the Sea (ITLOS), established under the 1982 UN Convention on the Law of the Sea (UNCLOS) (its caseload has been small, apart from 'prompt release' proceedings concerning detained foreign-flag fishing boats, but the *Bangladesh–Myanmar* case may mark the beginning of an increase).

As this synoptic account indicates, much juridification occurred in the 1990s, often building on earlier precedents. The WTO, NAFTA and the Energy Charter Treaty were all adopted in 1994. ITLOS began to operate in Hamburg following a 1994 agreement that enabled entry into force with wide acceptance of the 1982 UNCLOS. Bilateral investment treaties (BITs) were adopted at a high rate, paving the way for the subsequent boom in investor–state arbitration. The ICTY, the ICTR and then the path-breaking ICC were created. The reach and impact of the European and Inter-American Courts of Human Rights grew, and other regional courts were mooted or established in partial emulation of existing bodies. The PCA and the ICJ both became much busier. From the late 1990s onward, many of these different tribunals began increasingly to refer to each other. 'Forum shopping', or multiple claims in different tribunals relating to the same basic factual situation, began to raise legitimacy issues, as when two investment arbitrations (*Lauder* and *CME*) against the Czech Republic produced opposing results on the same basic facts and law. Development of systemic principles such as *lis pendens* remained slow, but some comity and mutual accommodation was more readily achievable in inter-state contexts (as with a Law of the Sea arbitral tribunal giving priority to the ECJ on matters of EU law in the *Ireland* v. *UK MOX Plant* dispute). Case management strategies such as the NAFTA procedure for consolidation of multiple claims, or sampling of small claims in the UN Compensation Commission, began to develop. International courts began to be cited more by national courts, which became increasingly involved in international law and transnational governance (Benvenisti and Downs 2009). This involvement was symbolically epitomised by the 1999 *Pinochet* case in the English House of Lords (now the Supreme Court).

All of this has led to a new paradigm of routinised litigation and judicial governance being layered alongside the traditional paradigm of episodic international (inter-state) dispute settlement by tribunals. In some tribunals, on some kinds of issues, juridification is reaching the point where litigation is routine: while not quotidian, it is not rare, and is even habitual for some repeat players. The CJEU and the ECHR are the leading examples, but litigation is commonplace also in global bodies such as the WTO Dispute Settlement Body (DSB). The United States, the European Union and China between them were defendants in 11 of the 14 new cases initiated in the WTO in 2009, and the EU and the US file a third-party intervention in almost every case litigated in the WTO by any of the 153 members (there were over 400 cases in 1995–2009). International criminal trials and jurisprudence are also becoming more routinised: the ICTY had indicted 161 persons and had completed proceedings against 121 by early 2010 (local Bosnian courts, buttressed and influenced by such international regimes, had tried many more).

Unevenness in juridification through international courts and tribunals

This image of judicialisation and of a new paradigm can easily be exaggerated: international courts and tribunals are significant on some issues but not others, in some parts of the world much more than others.

The issues being adjudicated under this new paradigm are largely those of a global legal order dominated by liberal interests. The economy of freer trade, intellectual property, investor protection to increase flows of private funds and protect property rights, protection of basic civil and political rights (including for corporations and associations) and retrospective trials of perpetrators of certain carefully delimited kinds of atrocities, dominate. Environmental issues occupy a predictable position: they will receive a sympathetic hearing in many of these tribunals, but are not a central focus of the rules or causes of action or indeed of expertise. New global tribunals have almost all been created as parts of specialised regimes, rather than as courts of general jurisdiction which might reach too far beyond what the creating states wish to see investigated and adjudicated. It is notable that acceptance of the general jurisdiction of the ICJ under the Optional Clause has remained more or less constant (approximately 64 states out of 193 UN members), and newer treaties seldom include obligations to accept ICJ jurisdiction on treaty disputes. Indeed the ICJ's route into major security-related issues has in recent decades often been through oblique paths, such as the Genocide Convention (*Bosnia v. Serbia*, 2007), the Racial Discrimination Convention (*Georgia v. Russia*), or the advisory jurisdiction (the *Nuclear Weapons* case, 1996; the Israel *Wall* case, 2004; the *Kosovo* case, 2010). Specialist tribunals typically do not have mandates to adjudicate issues concerning the conduct of the global governance institutions of which they are part: thus the WTO Appellate Body does not rule on major actions or inactions of the WTO, only on what member states do. In NAFTA and the WTO, the contracting states retain the power to re-interpret a treaty if they disagree with a tribunal's interpretation, without needing to formally amend the treaty; the NAFTA Free Trade Commission used this power in 2001 in response to the first *Pope & Talbot* arbitral award.

Many kinds of issues are thus not densely judicialised in international courts, even if some may occasionally reach a tribunal. These include most military and intelligence issues including arms control, disarmament, nuclear weapons and nuclear energy governance; global financial governance; most anti-terrorism renditions and data-sharing; most religious issues; most issues concerning general migration policy; most issues concerned with taxation, education, social welfare, labour, local government, land, forests, water, air, urban policy and climate; corruption; social violence; political decision processes in almost every formal and informal global governance body; forms of pressure or encouragement by global bodies on specific governments and their policies; hazardous wastes; humanitarian assistance and disaster response; most support of tyranny; most participation in spoliation of natural resources; most forms of inequality and poverty, most issues affecting people's lives in poor countries. The relative absence of judicialisation of these subject areas is readily explicable and in many cases may be preferable, given the severe limits of what tribunals can manage or achieve. But this absence is an important part of the picture.

Which major states commit in advance to accept jurisdiction of international courts?

Uneven juridification is also reflected in the uneven rates of acceptance in advance of jurisdiction of international tribunals. One indication of such unevenness is a comparison of two different categories of major states: those with the largest populations (Table 9.1) and the largest economies (Table 9.2).

The world's most populous states tend not to accept in advance the jurisdiction of the ICJ, the ICC, human rights courts, or the UN Human Rights Committee. However, almost all are in the WTO, and in UNCLOS. The world's largest economies, which include more states committed to economic and political liberalism, are similarly engaged with the WTO and UNCLOS, but are much more likely to be in the ICC, and appreciably more likely to accept some international human rights tribunal. This may reflect the greater influence of these liberal states on the decisions to create these tribunals and on their specific design. This data also points to the possibility that with growing heterogeneity amongst major powers, as China, India, Brazil and others become major forces and potential veto

Table 9.1 Acceptance of jurisdiction of international courts and quasi-judicial international institutions (ten most populous states), 1 March 2010

	ICJ Compulsory Jurisdiction under 'optional clause'	UN Human Rights Committee First Optional Protocol Petitions by Individuals	Accepted 2008 Protocol to ICESC* Rights individual petitions	Accepted Regional Human Rights Courts (Including European Court of Human Rights and Inter-American Court of Human Rights)	Ratification of ICC Statute	WTO members	UNCLOS
China						X	X
India	X					X	X
USA						X	
Indonesia						X	X
Brazil		X		X	X	X	X
Pakistan	X					X	X
Russia		X		X			X
Bangladesh						X	X
Nigeria	X				X	X	X
Japan	X				X	X	X

* International Covenant on Economic, Social and Cultural Rights.

Table 9.2 Acceptance of jurisdiction of international courts and quasi-judicial international institutions (ten states with highest GDP), 1 March 2010

	ICJ Compulsory Jurisdiction under "optional clause"	UN Human Rights Committee First Optional Protocol Petitions by Individuals	Accepted 2008 Protocol to ICESC* Rights individual petitions	Accepted Regional Human Rights Courts (Including European Court of Human Rights and Inter-American Court of Human Rights)	Ratification of ICC Statute	WTO members	UNCLOS
USA						X	
Japan	X				X	X	X
Germany	X	X		X	X	X	X
China						X	X
UK	X			X	X	X	X
France		X		X	X	X	X
Italy		X		X	X	X	X
Canada	X	X			X	X	X
Spain	X	X	X	X	X	X	X
South Korea					X	X	X

*International Covenant on Economic, Social and Cultural Rights.

players in negotiations, creation of new international courts and indeed of new global treaty institutions may become less likely. If the ICJ did not already exist, it is far from clear that it could now be created. Even the WTO, which most states have been eager to join, might well not have been created in a comparable way at a later time, as the tortuous progress of the Doha Round of negotiations after 2001 illustrates. Liberal legalism continues to have substantial reach and influence, but further judicialisation through global treaty institutions may be unlikely in the near term, particularly outside the broad fields of trade, investment and property claims.

Divergent roles and functions of international courts

In keeping with the functionalist typology adopted in the first section, the creation, design, and practical juridical operations of these various international courts can be described in instrumental terms as the performance of different roles and functions. The headings below adopt this approach, although international courts can also be assessed in many other ways. The roles and functions any court actually plays are linked to the perceptions of participants and the expectations of their constituencies. These are thus connected to institutional culture and social relations with different audiences, which are often exchange relations or tied to status and values.

Courts as dispute settlers

Courts are a sub-set of third-party settlers of bilateral disputes. The acceptance by two parties of a role for a third, with a voice and involvement going beyond a mere post-box function, opens up the possibility of a triangular model of adjudication (Shapiro 1981). This model can often face relational instability. First, the two disputing parties may act jointly to bring the tribunal closer to their wishes (and away from some of its other constituencies or obligations). This is one way of understanding the problems posed for the ICJ when states asking it to create a five-member chamber sought to control which judges were then appointed, for example in the *Gulf of Maine* case (Canada/United States, 1984). Problems arise with sham litigation, where two parties collusively litigate against each other to obtain a court decision that helps them directly against third parties (as in some intellectual property cases) or indirectly by establishing a judicial precedent on the law that helps them elsewhere. Second, one party may withdraw its support if it believes or asserts that the third party (the adjudicator) has improperly aligned with the other party. Courts seek to avoid this through procedural rules such as those precluding *ex parte* communications between judges and one disputing party alone, and through structuring their decisions and reasoning to explicitly address the principal factual claims and legal arguments of each party. Many other techniques also used for these purposes are exemplified in the structure and practice of the ICJ, including judicious use of delay or timing. An example is the *Nicaragua* case, in which the ICJ made a substantive ruling on the merits in 1986, but forbore from issuing any ruling on the financial quantification of the United States' liability for long enough that a political understanding was reached between the governments and the case withdrawn.

Given that the jurisdiction of international courts over states depends on some act of consent by the state, why do states choose to submit any particular inter-state dispute to third-party legal settlement? Ordinary rational-choice analysis, in which the state is modelled as a unitary interest-maximising actor with ordinally ranked preferences, treats judicial settlement of bilateral disputes as a coordination game, in which both parties have more to gain from any plausible or reasonably likely judicial decision by a highly reputed and unbiased third party than they do from continuation of the dispute. These coordination problems have multiple possible equilibria, i.e. several possible solutions which would achieve the overall objective, but which would allocate the gains differently as between the two states (or which would produce different sets of winners and losers within the two states). Thus resort to a third-party legal institution rather than settling the dispute by bilateral negotiation is explained by desire of national politicians to avoid the audience costs they would face if they themselves negotiated and agreed to a solution that was less attractive for their constituents than other possible solutions. The *Gulf of Maine* case in the ICJ exemplifies this structure – the US Senate was unwilling to bear the political cost of endorsing the maritime boundary negotiated between the two countries' executive branches, while the US political elite accepted that the costs in fractious incidents and lost business opportunities resulting from not having a fixed boundary with a friendly neighbour were greater than the costs from any likely ICJ-set boundary. Estimates of the costs of unresolved boundary disputes have been attempted (Simmons 2002). The Argentina–Chile land boundary and territorial disputes that were resolved in 1995 were estimated to have reduced trade levels by about $9 billion over 1967–1994, an average of $326 million per year in lost trade (actual trade averaged $574 million per year, but without the boundary dispute its expected level was $900 million). Politicians who allow the state to be committed to binding international court proceedings do risk significant political costs themselves. Strong reaction in Nigeria to the ICJ's decision awarding the Bakassi Peninsula to Cameroon (*Cameroon* v. *Nigeria*, 2002) included intense criticism of the government's handling of the case, and delayed Nigerian implementation for several years. For maritime boundaries the political costs are often somewhat less, as many maritime areas have neither the symbolic significance and intense human histories nor long-time residents, and fewer vested economic interests (fishing and some oil wells excepted) because technological and legal bases for coastal state exploitation are recent or prospective. Uncertainty about many aspects of the law of maritime boundary delimitation makes it difficult for politicians to bargain accurately in the shadow of the law. For these reasons, reference to the ICJ or to binding inter-state arbitration of maritime boundary cases, and to a lesser extent terrestrial boundary and territorial cases, has been relatively common.

Courts as institutions to make commitments credible

The previous paragraphs considered why states might submit a specific dispute to third-party adjudication. A bigger puzzle is why states create international courts, or give advance acceptances of jurisdiction, in relation to unknown cases in which they may well be defendants.

Simple reciprocity provides a starting point, but a further element of the basic politics and bargaining which can lead to the creation and acceptance of jurisdiction of international courts is that these assist in making commitments credible. When states negotiate a treaty (e.g. a trade agreement) involving expensive changes in internal policies and administration as well as shifts in private economic patterns, the possibility of recourse to effective courts bolsters trust that reciprocal obligations will be fulfilled. Less powerful states in particular require assurances that the promises of powerful states are credible. The remedies available to them if they win a case may provide some bargaining leverage, but they rely much more on the prospect that the court process and eventual decision will help mobilise other major states to put pressure on the powerful state in order to maintain the rule-governed system and respect for its institutions. Furthermore, while an international court will seldom induce a very powerful state to do what its political elite and public are unified in refusing to do, on trade issues there are usually substantial domestic constituencies who benefit from compliance with the agreement in other cases, and who may suffer from remedial actions or from fraying of the bargain.

The credibility of commitments may also be essential if behaviour of private actors is to be motivated by the agreement, as in the argument that assurances of binding external arbitration are essential for some countries to attract foreign private investment.

Routinised adjudication as governance

Courts are created as part of the governance regime for particular issue areas, to enhance the success and effectiveness of the regime. Thus multilateral trade agreements, such as those of the WTO, establish courts with binding jurisdiction in inter-state cases, as well as political bodies with supervisory powers, to help ensure that the economic gains from the treaty commitments are in fact realised. Such courts may fill in terms on which agreement was not reached in the inter-state bargaining ('incomplete contracts'), and may operate to overcome or manage impasses in the ongoing political processes of the inter-state governance institutions to deal with new issues once these are operating. Thus the WTO Appellate Body commented that, since the inter-state trade and environment committee of the WTO had after lengthy negotiations not managed to produce normative materials, the Appellate Body would itself have to enunciate criteria for addressing certain environmentally based restrictions on trade.

A second kind of governance role for international courts is in enabling the influential articulation, and on occasion the legal vindication, of private commercial interests, non-commercial or public interests, and even governmental interests which are not adequately represented by the executive branch of the government. Acceptance of *amicus* briefs (which is now well established in the WTO, and in NAFTA and ICSID arbitral tribunals, but not in some other arbitral tribunals), and the *de facto* espousal by state litigators or third states of private interests in specific cases, may obliquely perform this role. But this governance role is more clearly central to institutions such as the European or Inter-American Court of Human

Rights, in which private individuals, religious entities and corporations (particularly in Europe), and indigenous groups or professional associations (particularly in Latin America) initiate and win cases against states. Investor–state arbitral tribunals, composed and conducted according to a pre-specified procedures and applying pre-specified bodies of law, operate in this way, although each particular tribunal is composed on an *ad hoc* basis, whereas standing courts exist in human rights.

Courts as producers of legal knowledge

The idea that juridification should as far as possible be accompanied by judicialisation – by the creation or empowerment of courts to adjudicate claims and render judgments – gathered momentum as a programmatic aspiration from the late nineteenth century. This was in part connected to the view that the existence and operations of courts should be part of the definition or at least the ideal of 'law', which has been seeping, particularly from Anglo-American legal thinking, into thought about international law since at least the late eighteenth century. As A.V. Dicey put it in *The Law of the Constitution*: 'A law may be defined as ... "any rule which will be enforced by the courts" ... [in contrast to] understandings, customs, or conventions which, not being enforced by the courts, are in no true sense of the word laws' (1960, 40, 469).

The rising quantum of judicial decisions, and the growth in materials (pleadings, commentaries, etc.) generated in the engagement of state institutions with them, has significant effects on international law as a field of practice and reflection. International law practitioners can and do specialise in branches of such litigation or advising about such possibilities, and both textbooks and judgments quote and cite judicial pronouncements as primary materials of first-order importance. The pronouncements of international courts and tribunals have added a layer to, and been one factor displacing heavy reliance on, the distillation of norms from masses of treaties found in Martens-style compilations or treaty series, or from other forms of 'state practice' found in national yearbooks. Judicialisation has thus become more than an aspiration for, and validation of, juridification. Courts that produce law and stimulate practice drive and shape juridification.

This can have important normative dimensions: many international lawyers see international courts as potentially building a legal order with its own core principles, and as influencing the norms and principles followed in international political behaviour, or in national law, with implications for basic political values such as commitments to equal concern and respect or to corrective justice (Bogdandy and Venzke 2011; Teitel and Howse 2009; Trinidade 2010).

As well as making statements about law, international courts are frequently required to elicit, marshal, re-package and formally authenticate and enunciate factual information. This function as manager of information confronts the basic problem that much of the key information is 'private information', that is, it is held by legal entities or individuals who do not make it readily available to the court. Other necessary information may be beyond anyone's capacity to obtain. Standard models of courts suggest that one level of appeal may be optimal in highly institutionalised systems to correct errors and elicit as much information and analysis as is reasonably attainable without driving up costs and delay excessively. The WTO and international criminal tribunals follow this pattern; ICSID does not. Indeed, the WTO excepted, arbitral and judicial tribunals dealing with inter-state cases are, for the most part, simultaneously first-instance and final-instance tribunals. As first-instance tribunals, they must ensure production of sufficient evidence, find facts and make legal rulings addressing the issues raised by these facts. Their powers to compel states to produce evidence are limited. While they can exert some leverage through threatening to make findings on a contested factual issue that are adverse to a party which holds but fails to produce key documents or other evidence, in some circumstances they will be reluctant even to use this power, as with the ICJ's unwillingness to try to force the Serbian Government to hand over unredacted cabinet minutes in the Genocide case brought by Bosnia (2007). Where some facts are sharply contested or obscure, these courts frequently try to rely on facts authoritatively established or admitted by organs of the state against whose interests such facts operate, as with the ICJ's use of US Congressional findings in *Nicaragua* (1986), or the ICJ's reliance on the Porter Commission established by the Uganda government in *DRC v. Uganda* (2005). They may also rely on findings by UN bodies (as in *DRC v. Uganda*), or by international criminal courts (the ICJ made some use of ICTY findings in *Bosnia v. Serbia*, 2007). Otherwise, they have little choice but to try to sidestep difficult factual issues and to structure their legal analyses accordingly.

Justice and rule of law

The relationship of international courts to political demands framed in terms of justice and substantive equality has been difficult. On such matters, international courts have been the frequent embodiments of hopes, episodically the objects of bitter controversy and rejection, and on occasion have engendered great disillusion. The ICJ's 1966 decision in the *South-West Africa* cases that it did not have a basis to adjudicate the claims of Ethiopia and Liberia against South Africa's introduction of apartheid into the Territory it had received to administer under a League of Nations Mandate caused much disillusion in developing countries. Japanese perceptions that the Yokohama *House Tax* arbitration award of 1905 reflected bias against Japan was a factor in Japan's reluctance to accept binding inter-state litigation until it joined the WTO and the Law of the Sea Convention in the 1990s (Japan's success in the 2000 *Southern Bluefin Tuna* arbitration in deflecting claims concerning overfishing brought by Australia and New Zealand, thus had further significance, unrelated to the merits of the issue). Thailand had a somewhat comparable experience with the *Temple of Preah Vihear* case in the ICJ (1962, reopened 2011).

Grotius argued that law reaching beyond a single state (*civitas*) should aspire to achieve corrective justice, but not distributive justice. This is, generally speaking, the pattern in modern tribunals adjudicating inter-state issues. In ICJ practice, money damages payments even for corrective purposes are very rarely awarded or quantified for injury to state (as opposed to private) interests (the *Corfu Channel* case, concerning Albania's responsibility for mining of British warships, was exceptional). Money claims by individuals before international tribunals are frequent, but are almost invariably decided on a corrective justice basis, apart from occasional small symbolic monetary awards.

Certain international tribunals play some marginal role in advancing other contemporary conceptions of justice. Cosmopolitan justice for individuals is at least symbolically associated with their *locus standi* in international cases. Deliberative conceptions of justice may be somewhat advanced by norms concerning participation, reason-giving and other features of voice, process and accountability, but international tribunals usually focus on these as duties of public authorities within states, and seldom apply them directly to global governance institutions. Republican ideas of non-dominance seem barely to figure in the jurisprudence of global governance, beyond basic principles of order that oppose forcible intervention and external imposition of public power. Overall there are large gulfs between contemporary political theorising about global justice and what actually is done in most international tribunals, although more is now being done to bring this theory into practice and this practice into theory.

Conclusion

This chapter cannot address three already important dimensions of judicialisation that may give the phenomenon a significantly different quality in the future.

First is the vital role of national courts, acting individually and in informal networks with each other and (in some situations) with international courts. Their jurisprudence on multilateral treaties and webs of bilateral treaties is much more important than the roles of international courts on many topics (for example, cross-border child abduction, or air and rail transport), and it is increasingly central on human rights, war crimes and other areas in which international courts are also active. National courts have strong interests in limiting executive branch activity or international institutions that would bypass national democratic controls. They are also much more likely to adjudicate issues concerning private (non-state) regulatory governance. One function of international courts can be to address negative externalities (external effects) of a particular state's law or actions, where the national courts and the national political system do not take adequate account of the interests adversely affected. Thus where the national courts do act, the role for international courts may decrease. The requirement that individuals adversely affected first exhaust reasonably available domestic remedies before resorting to international courts is an instantiation of this idea.

Second is the role in transnational governance of adjudication, arbitration or other dispute settlement not primarily involving, or dependent on, states. The Internet Corporation for Assigned Names and Numbers (ICANN) internet domain names dispute resolution, and the International Court of Arbitration for Sport (ICAS) rulings on doping allegations against athletes, are illustrative. These formally autonomous or self-regulatory structures are often closely connected to state and inter-state regulatory action.

Third is the role of bodies which are not judicial and not necessarily even quasi-judicial, but which make authoritative and reasoned rule-based determinations after some kind of hearing and extensive deliberation. The World Bank Inspection Panel, the UN Commission on the Limits of the Continental Shelf, and the Executive Board of the Clean Development Mechanism are amongst myriad examples. This kind of administrative–adjudicatory power is typically theorised quite separately from international courts, under rubrics such as global administrative law, but in functional and governance terms the lines of separation are much more indistinct.

From a normative perspective, the kinds of judicialisation addressed in this chapter do not *necessarily* produce better political outcomes, nor better socio-political processes, nor more justice, than would other means of governance. Fine-grained encompassing critiques are nowadays rarely articulated, but sophisticated specific critiques appear in debates on some international courts (concerns about structural bias, or procedural legitimation of what is substantively unjust, or non-litigability of important but juridically marginalised claims, or about distorting effects of de-localisation of trials of massive atrocities).

With the surge in the creation of international courts in the 1990s, and the rapid growth in cases in many existing and new international courts, the view that judicialisation might not always be a desirable objective seemed Procrustean – judicialisation was turned from a desideratum into an accomplishment, helping also to assuage Diceyan doubts about the law in international law. The more frequently senior national politicians in different countries make public comments on specific proceedings and decisions in international courts, whether critical or supportive, the more these courts seem salient to real controversies.

The wave of judicialisation in the 1990s resulted in the creation of several important international trade, investment, criminal and law of the sea courts and tribunals. Perceptible changes since then in the global distribution of power amongst major states, and shifts in dominant approaches to international order, have put in question both the prospects of governance through major new comprehensive global treaties, and the creation of new global courts under such treaties. However, the increase in caseloads and judicial output of major existing tribunals is likely to be sustained, and some regional projects for further judicialisation may well be pursued. A multi-polar global political order, especially one not dominated from the United States and Europe, would come into tension with these enduring structures of liberal–legalist juridical order that are particularly associated with open but regulated economic markets and information flows, basic liberal property and political rights setting limits on state powers, rule of law, and some hierarchical governance structures dominated by liberal polities and their corporate and civil society groupings. Debates about formalism versus anti-formalism, material versus non-material drivers of compliance, styles of legal method, etc., which have had a Euro-American internecine character, could thus rapidly be sidelined by struggles amongst quite different sets of ideas about what global governance is and how law and legal institutions can and should function.

Yet the very success of the judicialisation project – and its close ties to a liberal approach to international order which has become increasingly contested – have generated not only reformist criticisms, but some starker resistance and repudiation. The range extends from frustration with delays in high-volume international human rights courts and quasi-judicial bodies which reject selectivity and have not found other justice-respecting mechanisms to manage rising caseloads, to calls for improvements in processes of judicial appointment and in ethical norms for judges and lawyers, to attacks on the legitimacy of *ad hoc* investor–state arbitration tribunals reviewing public policy choices, and objections to the human and political costs or to more deep-seated inequality in certain indictments issued by the International Criminal Court. To these may be added more specific state policies: Russia's pushback in delaying reform of the European Convention on Human Rights (ECHR) for several years, then terminating its provisional application of the Energy Charter Treaty in 2009; continued opposition in the United States to multilateral treaties such as UNCLOS simply because of binding dispute settlement, and the refusal (in the *Medellín* case, 2008) of the US Supreme Court to assure compliance with the ICJ's *Avena* judgment; China's reluctance to accept international court jurisdiction over its activities outside the trade and investment sphere; the preference for non-treaty bodies such as the G20 or the Financial Action Task Force over formalised legal institutions in increasing swathes of global regulatory governance; several Latin American denunciations of the ICSID Convention. Despite all of this, neither juridification nor judicialisation has been the subject of strongly influential fundamental critique in contemporary international law and politics. Current global politics remain, in aggregate, reformist rather than rejectionist with regard to judicialisation. Whether that will change as world balances of power shift, is a question with high stakes; the answers are in the making, in a mixture of transnational dynamics and the national politics of many countries, which will determine the future of liberal-legalism as world order and transnational governance adjust to new realities of power and interdependence.

Bibliography

Benvenisti, E. and G. Downs, 2009. 'National Courts, Domestic Democracy, and the Evolution of International Law', *European Journal of International Law*, 20, 59–72

Bogdandy, A. and I. Venzke, 2011. 'Beyond Dispute: International Judicial Institutions as Lawmakers', *German Law Journal*, 12, 979–1004

Dicey, A. V., 1960. *The Law of the Constitution*, Chicago University Press

Gentili, A., 1933. *De iure belli libri tres*, 2 vols., J. C. Rolfe (trans.), Oxford: Clarendon

Grotius, H., 1625. *De jure belli ac pacis*

Mani, V. S., 1980. *International Adjudication: Procedural Aspects*, The Hague: Martinus Nijhoff

Shapiro, M., 1981. *Courts: A Comparative and Political Analysis*, University of Chicago Press

Simmons, B., 2002. 'Capacity, Commitment, and Compliance: International Institutions and Territorial Disputes', *Journal of Conflict Resolution*, 46, 829–56

Teitel R. and R. Howse, 2009. 'Cross-judging: Tribunalization in a Fragmented but Interconnected Global Order', *NYU Journal of International Law and Politics*, 41, 959–90

Trinidade, A. C., 2010. *International Law for Humankind: Towards a New Jus Gentium*, The Hague: Martinus Nijhoff

Cases

International Court of Justice

Accordance with International Law of the Unilateral Declaration of Independence in Respect of Kosovo, ICJ Gen. List 2010, No. 141

Application of the International Convention on the Elimination of All Forms of Racial Discrimination (Georgia v. *Russian Federation)*, ICJ Gen. List 2011, No. 140

Armed Activities on the Territory of the Congo (Democratic Republic of the Congo v. *Uganda)*, ICJ Reports 2005, p. 168

Avena and Other Mexican Nationals (Mexico v. *United States of America)*, ICJ Reports 2004, p. 12

Case Concerning the Application of the Convention on the Prevention and Punishment of the Crime of Genocide (Bosnia and Herzegovina v. *Serbia and Montenegro)*, ICJ Gen. List 2007, No. 91

Case Concerning the Land Boundary between Cameroon and Nigeria (Cameroon v. *Nigeria: Equatorial Guinea intervening)*, ICJ Reports 2002, p. 303

Case Concerning the Temple of Preah Vihear (Cambodia v. *Thailand)*, ICJ Reports, 1962, p. 6

Corfu Channel (UK v. *Albania)*, ICJ Reports 1949, p. 4

Delimitation of the Maritime Boundary in the Gulf of Maine Area (Canada/United States of America), ICJ Reports 1984, p. 246

Legal Consequences of the Construction of a Wall in the Occupied Palestinian Territory, ICJ Reports 2004, p. 136

Legality of the Threat or Use of Nuclear Weapons, ICJ Reports 1996, p. 226

Military and Paramilitary Activities in and against Nicaragua (Jurisdiction and Admissibility) (Nicaragua v. *United States of America)*, ICJ Reports 1984, p. 392

Military and Paramilitary Activities in and against Nicaragua (Merits) (Nicaragua v. *United States of America)*, ICJ Reports 1986, p. 14

South-West Africa (Second Phase) (Ethiopia v. *South Africa; Liberia* v. *South Africa)*, ICJ Reports 1966, p. 6

International Tribunal for the Law of the Sea

Dispute Concerning the Delimitation of the Maritime Boundary between Bangladesh and Myanmar in the Bay of Bengal, ITLOS Case No. 16 (pending)

Permanent Court of Arbitration

Abyei Arbitration (The Government of Sudan – The Sudan People's Liberation Movement/Army), Final Award of 22 July 2009

Arbitration Regarding the Iron Rhine ('IJzeren Rijn') Railway (Belgium–Netherlands), Award of 24 May 2005

Channel Tunnel Arbitration (*Channel Tunnel Group Ltd and France-Manche SA* v. *United Kingdom and France*), Partial Award of 30 January 2007

Japanese House Tax (Germany, France and Great Britain v. *Japan*), Award of 22 May 1905

MOX Plant (Ireland v. *UK)*, Order No. 6 of 6 June 2008 (terminating proceedings)

Reineccius v. *Bank for International Settlements*, Final Award of 19 September 2003

Other International Arbitrations

Alabama Claims Arbitration, United States of America–Great Britain, Award of 14 September 1872

Case Concerning the Air Services Agreement of 27 March 1946 between the United States of America and France, 54 ILR 304 (1979)

CME v. *Czech Republic (Partial Award of 13 September* 2001), 9 ICSID Reports 121; *(Final Award of 14 March 2003)*, 42 ILM 919 (2003)

Lauder v. *Czech Republic (Award of 3 September* 2001), 9 ICSID Reports 66

Pope & Talbot Inc. v. *Canada* (*Award on the Merits of Phase 2*), (2001) 7 ICSID Rep. 102

Rainbow Warrior (*New Zealand* v. *France*), 82 ILR 499 (1990)
Southern Bluefin Tuna (Australia and New Zealand v. *Japan)*, 39 ILM 1359 (2000)

National Court Decisions

R v. *Bow Street Magistrates; ex parte Pinochet Ugarte (No. 3)* (2000) 1 AC 147
Medellín v. *Texas*, 552 US 491 (2008)

10 International institutions

Jan Klabbers

Introduction

In politics and elsewhere, whenever people have banded into some form of organisation, be it a football club, a trade union or (why not?) a state, those entities tend to look for likeminded entities to cooperate with. Trade unions form federations of unions; football clubs form national associations that, in turn, form international associations; and states form international organisations.

States may do so for a variety of reasons. Often mentioned as a central element in the literature is the idea that international organisations may be of use when states have identified common purposes. Thus, so the argument runs, if states find that they need to organise the flow of mail across borders, they set up a Universal Postal Union. If they feel monetary stability needs to be guaranteed, they set up an International Monetary Fund. If they feel the need to cooperate more generally within their region, they may establish an African Union, or an Organisation of American States. And if they wish to form an ever-closer union, they may even set up something as ambitious as the European Union. This, at any rate, is the traditional, functionalist, story: states create organisations in order to achieve common goals and perform certain specified functions. However, as will be seen, this story leaves a few gaps.

States and their predecessors have established institutionalised forms of cooperation for many centuries. The ancient Greeks left the legacy of the so-called amphictyonic councils, sometimes held to be predecessors to today's international organisations, whereas some of the European city states organised themselves in Leagues such as the Hansa. Still, it is often suggested that today's international organisations owe much to developments during the late nineteenth and early twentieth century. Two such developments stand out. First, permanent institutions were created, from the mid nineteenth century onwards, to manage the maintenance and navigation of international rivers. River commissions were created for the management of such important international waterways as the Rhine and the Danube and, once these proved successful, similar (if more universal in terms of their proposed membership) institutions were set up to deal with other aspects of communication (postal traffic, telegraphic communication and railway traffic).

The second important development was the regular organisation of conferences to address pressing political issues, in particular perhaps the convocation, in 1899 and then in 1907, of the two Hague Peace Conferences. These were, and remained, incidental, isolated conferences, but were of great relevance in that they aspired to universal participation (including, amongst others, Latin American states) and introduced some formalities that proved to be of great use when, sometime later, the 'move to institutions' (Kennedy 1987) took off in earnest. In particular, the Hague Conferences introduced the notion of non-binding instruments that could be adopted by the conference (so-called '*voeux*'), giving a voice to the conference as a separate body and thereby paving the way for later institutionalisation. Such instruments, adopted by majority but considered non-binding, were later conceptualised as the way to reconcile state sovereignty with international organisation.

By the beginning of the twentieth century it had become commonplace to think of international organisations as possible frameworks for inter-state cooperation. These organisations would have the advantage of possessing a degree of permanence, and were predominantly thought useful for dealing with what seemed to be more or less technical, non-political issues, from communication to such things as agriculture or the harmonisation across boundaries of weights and measures. Early twentieth-century international lawyers worked hard to come to terms with these new creatures (Reinsch 1911), treating them first and foremost as treaty regimes without further institutional ramifications, but slowly coming to embrace the institutional element inherent in international organisations.

The story of the rise of international organisations and the development of international institutional law can be told in a number of different ways: as a historical progression from loose to more intense cooperation; as a narrative of progress in international cooperation; or as a move from politics to management in international life. Such narratives have the drawback, though, of doing an injustice to the topic, as the development never was linear to begin with: the formal character of international organisations, while following earlier informal cooperative devices (think for instance of the Holy Alliance), itself gave rise to calls for greater informality.

The story of international organisations can also be told as an enumeration of the birth and development of a number of specific organisations (but in that case, which to concentrate on?), or perhaps as the creation of a separate (sub-)discipline in which international lawyers engage (although treating the field as an independent discipline is implausible: see Klabbers, 2008). Still, I will tell the story in a different manner, focusing on the tension between stability and flexibility (formality and informality, if you will) and set against a background of globalisation, in which international organisations play a role in global governance. This predominantly pits two contending ideas against each other: the theory of functionalism in the law of international organisations, and the more overtly normative idea (theory being too grandiose a term) that the acts of organisations ought to be subject to some form of control – something functionalism is, as yet, ill equipped to address. It also informs the very design of international organisations, with some of them being kept outside the sphere of law altogether (ostensibly, at any rate), and others being given loose, almost non-institutional, structures: this will be further discussed below. The reason for taking this approach is to make clear that the standard story about international organisations (which this chapter started with) and indeed all writings about organisations are eventually coloured by the perspectives and biases of their authors and, more to the point perhaps, tend to hide the political character of international organisations and the legal doctrines that guide their functioning.

Functionalism and its limits

International organisations are most often discussed and analysed in terms of their functions; hence, many speak of functionalism as the leading approach to international organisations (Virally 1974). Even at this basic level though, the emphasis on functions has deceptive potential, for what exactly is the function of, for instance, the United Nations? Some might hold that the United Nations' main function is to guarantee international peace and security, and invoke the collective security mechanism embedded in the UN Charter in support. Others may claim that the United Nations' function is best seen as the transnational equivalent of the welfare state, providing for a more equitable distribution of wealth and aiming to guarantee development and sustainability, as demonstrated by the well-publicised adoption of the Millennium Development Goals (MDGs) in 2000.

What holds true for the United Nations holds true also for other organisations: their precise function is very much in the eye of the beholder. The World Bank's function can be seen as aiding development, but also as providing the framework for Western economic domination. The North Atlantic Treaty Organisation (NATO) can (or could perhaps, during the Cold War) be seen as a defensive alliance, but also as an ideological community of likeminded liberal states, spearheaded by the United States, aiming to roll back communism or, since the early 1990s, helping to spread the liberal ideology in places like Afghanistan. The International Labour Organisation (ILO), in turn, can be regarded as a venue where the labour movement is given pride of place, but also as the unique international site for corporatism. And sometimes the argument can be heard that organisations form the continuation of imperial designs by other means. While this may apply most obviously to organisations dedicated to cultural integration (the Organisation Internationale de la Francophonie, the Comunidade dos Paises de Lingua Portuguesa, possibly also the (British) Commonwealth), it has also been argued that the League of Nations and the United Nations are based on imperial blueprints (Mazower 2009).

Still, typically, institutional lawyers will interpret an institution's founding document in order to come to an interpretation of its main function, and then apply a set of doctrines – as the need arises – in order to do justice to this function. The more practically relevant of these doctrines include the doctrine that organisations can engage in all sorts of activities, even those left unmentioned in their foundational documents, as long as these activities can contribute to the organisation's functions (the doctrine of implied powers, as laid down in sweeping fashion by the International Court of Justice (ICJ) in *Reparation for Injuries*, ICJ Reports 1949, p. 174). This may have the result that the member states, who are responsible for writing the foundational document, may lose control over their creation: over time, the organisation may come to engage in all sorts of activities never envisaged by the drafting states but justified under reference to the functions of the organisation ('mission creep', in bureaucratic parlance). Some have gone even further and posited the existence of inherent powers (i.e. things that organisations can do simply because they are organisations, unless their own constituent documents do not allow the activity: see Seyersted 2008), but this has yet to meet with general acceptance.

Also of relevance is the doctrine of immunity: international organisations typically enjoy tax exemptions and also immunity from suit, on the theory that starting a lawsuit against an organisation would hinder its functioning, and would moreover allow the host state – the state where the organisation has its headquarters – to exercise undue political pressure. Surely, by threatening to sue the United Nations, the United States could gain a lot of leverage; surely, by threatening to sue the Paris-based Organisation for Economic Cooperation and Development (OECD), the French government could influence the OECD's policies. The drawback however is that this immunity from prosecution often also means that organisations are free from judicial intervention and control, even where their behaviour is unacceptable. There is no good reason why an international organisation should be allowed to engage in sexual harassment with impunity, or refuse to take fair trial concerns into consideration, or flaunt environmental standards (Singer 1995). Some organisations have set up their own administrative tribunals, and while these perform useful tasks in relations between the organisation and its staff members, their reach typically does not extend beyond those relations. Human rights courts, in turn, have so far been reluctant to intervene, but have at least come to accept that the acts of international organisations may have human rights ramifications (see, for instance, the judgment of the European Court of Human Rights (ECtHR) in *Waite* v. *Kennedy*, (1999) 118 ILR 121).

As all this suggests, the Achilles' heel of functionalism is control. Functionalism, as an academic theory about international organisations, has considerable explanatory force, but is eventually unhelpful when it comes to controlling organisations. Functionalism is able to help explain why states set up international organisations, why and how organisations are granted competences and why organisations are granted privileges and immunities. But the flipside is the issue of control: under functionalism, international organisations go through life as uncontrolled and, indeed, well-nigh uncontrollable entities. Their member states cannot control them because acts can often be justified on the basis of the implied powers doctrine and, moreover, if all member states agree to engage in an activity, then this common agreement is hard to ignore: the *ultra vires* doctrine, prohibiting entities from acting beyond their competences, is for all practical purposes overruled when all relevant actors agree that an act is within the entity's competences – and organisations themselves are considered best-placed to make this assessment (*Certain Expenses*, ICJ Reports 1962, p. 151).

The only control devices left then are blunt devices such as withholding contributions, or withdrawing from the organisation altogether, or trying to oust the organisation's leadership from office. The former was a big thorn in the relationship between the United States and the United Nations during much of the 1980s and 1990s, with US politicians suggesting that US contributions (which are compulsory under the UN Charter) be made conditional on all sorts of policy demands, many of these flagging a certain amount of dissatisfaction with some of the activities the United Nations was engaged in. By the same token, the United States withdrew from organisations such as the UN Economic, Social and Cultural Organisation (UNESCO) and the ILO when it found these were moving in directions that the United States was unhappy with, and the United States was instrumental in ousting José Bustani, in 2001, as the director-general of the Organisation for the Prohibition of Chemical Weapons (and, less overtly, in securing that Boutros Boutros-Ghali did not get a second term as Secretary-General of the United Nations).

By contrast, the more commonplace modalities of control are by and large absent. Few organisations are structured in such a way that some representative body can exercise political control before decisions are actually taken: the European Union, with its European Parliament, is very much the exception, and even then it is debated whether its powers measure up to the powers of domestic parliaments in established democracies. Likewise, organisations typically cannot be sued before domestic courts, and organisations typically are not subjected to the jurisdiction of international tribunals either (other than tribunals to decide staff cases). Indeed, it is plausible that precisely due to the overwhelming appeal of functionalism, the very idea that organisations could do wrong was for a long time anathema: the first studies published on the responsibility of international organisations, for example, refused to think of the organisation itself as wrongdoer, and quickly ended up discussing the responsibility of member states, rather than of the organisation itself (Eagleton 1950). As a result, it is not only the case that international tribunals are ill qualified to deal with international organisations but even that there are few, if any, rules dealing with wrongful behaviour of international organisations to begin with.

The bankruptcy of the International Tin Council, in the late 1980s, provided a turning point in the thinking about international organisations and signalled a move away from undiluted functionalism. The collapse of the Council made clear that organisations could actually come to hurt more or less innocent third parties. In this case, the collapse meant that many of the Council's creditors lost considerable sums of money, and aimed to retrieve these through the English courts. This opened the doors for discussions concerning the responsibility and accountability of international organisations and their member states, a task taken up with vigour by scholars as well as by learned bodies such as the Institut de Droit International and the International Law Association (ILA) and, a few years later, by the UN's International Law Commission (ILC). These various bodies have set themselves the task of finding or articulating sets of rules which would make it possible to hold international organisations (or, significantly, their member states) to account, on the basis of the idea that since they typically exercise public power, they should ideally (like all entities exercising public power) be accountable in one way or another.

Yet, this proves easier said than done, and two intellectual problems in particular have made any attempt to formulate a control regime so far less than fully satisfactory (and this says nothing at all about the practical possibilities of seizing tribunals). First, it is not always clear when exactly behaviour is to be attributed to an international organisation. Take, for example, the acts of peace-keepers, sent by a member state and commanded by that member state under UN authorisation. Should a peace-keeper in his (we may no doubt presume male activities here) spare time be engaged in organising prostitution, does this automatically mean that the United Nations is somehow implicated? The United Nations could claim, not without justification, that the peace-keeper was acting in a personal capacity and, moreover, was subject to the command structure of his own army rather than UN command; in such a case, so the United Nations could claim, there is fairly little it could have done to begin with – responsibility would rest with the individual peace-keeper and, perhaps, with his national state, but not with the United Nations.

The same argument is, indeed, structurally puzzling, in that organisations are always and by definition both the aggregate of their member states and, simultaneously, independent from their member states. A decision by the NATO Council to deploy troops can be seen as a decision by NATO (independent from its members), but can also be seen as a decision by NATO's member states acting together, for which each of them bears responsibility individually. The ICJ declined to shed light on the issue when confronted with a claim brought by Serbia against ten individual NATO member states for their involvement in the bombing of Belgrade, in the late 1990s (the *Legality of Use of Force* cases, ICJ Reports 2004, 279), largely for want of jurisdiction.

The second intellectual problem at stake resides in the circumstance that it is by no means self-evident which rules would apply to international organisations, and why. It is tempting to suggest that as subjects of international law, organisations are bound to respect the entire corpus of general international law and all treaties to which they are parties, as the ICJ held in an opinion on the location of the World Health Organisation's headquarters (*Interpretation of the Agreement of 25 March 1951 between WHO and Egypt*, ICJ Reports 1980, 73). But closer scrutiny reveals that this may not mean all that much: the body of general international law referred to by the ICJ presumably cannot include much more than the law of treaties and applicable rules on responsibility (largely elusive at any rate), whereas the treaty relations of organisations tend to be limited, and tend to be bilateral. It remains unclear why, for example, in the absence of a clear consensual link, the World Bank and the International Monetary Fund (IMF) would be legally bound to respect human rights, as is regularly claimed. One answer refers to customary international law (including human rights law), but this is only plausible if a double standard is accepted regarding the basis of obligation in international law (states would need to express consent, but organisations would be bound without their consent); this though is not all that easy to reconcile with the conception that organisations are independent actors in their own right, with a legal personality separate from that of their member states. Moreover, it would seem to presuppose that organisations can be held bound by the customs not of themselves, but rather those of states, which seems difficult to reconcile with the underlying rationale for accepting the possibility of customary law to begin with: giving legal effect to everyday practices within the relevant political community.

Institutional design

The tension between formality and informality also informs the very design of organisations and, again, it may be claimed that functionalism has come under fire. International organisations are typically regarded as formal creatures. According to the standard definition, organisations are set up, mostly, between states, on the basis of a treaty, with organs of their own and a will distinct from that of their member states (Schermers and Blokker 2003; Klabbers 2009). With the exception of the reference to the organisation's 'volonté distincte', these are rather formal requirements, and doubts arise when entities are set up which do not meet one or more of these criteria. In such circumstances, many would claim that the entity cannot be regarded as an international organisation or partake of the rights, privileges and obligations that organisations typically have.

A prominent example is the Organisation for Security and Co-operation in Europe (OSCE), set up, so it seems, on the basis of a non-legally binding document and thus, according to formal criteria, not really an international organisation. This then could have legal ramifications: if an entity is not properly an organisation, it might, for example, lack privileges and immunities; it might lack the power to conclude agreements with states or other entities, and, most curiously perhaps, it may seem to lack the capacity to engage in wrongful behaviour.

Other entities of doubtful status, created since the late 1980s, would include the permanent bodies set up under international environmental agreements, which often have a treaty basis and are set up by states, but with a limited institutional structure, limited mostly to a secretariat and a regular Meeting (or Conference) of the Parties (MOP or COP). There are also hybrid organisations, ranging from public–private partnerships (such the Swiss-based International Organisation for Standardisation) to joint ventures between several existing entities, with the Codex Alimentarius Commission a prominent example. Then there are informal networks, ranging on a high political level from the G20 (the rich states) to the Paris Club (creditor states), but also those encompassing industry representatives, such as the International Accounting Standards Board (Slaughter 2004).

Such 'soft organisations' are typically established in response to a perceived rigidity associated with formal organisation. The law, so the reasoning goes, is not very flexible, and does not allow for fine-tuning in light of ever-changing political configurations; instead, it might be more functional to provide an entity with a loose structure, or even to try and keep it out of the realm of law altogether. Here functionalism would help explain the rise of informal regimes, but at the expense of functionalism's own explanatory force: if functionalism can help explain both formal and informal organisation, its analytical sharpness would appear to be compromised.

Flexibility can take on various manifestations. Typically, such 'soft' bodies take their decisions in informal manner (no need for long and compulsory consultation processes), and those decisions, while influential, are often said to be devoid of legal force. Thus, technically, they are not considered binding, and as a result they can easily be amended, repealed, or replaced by more appropriate instruments. Indeed, with a loose set-up, the very entity itself can easily be repealed or reorganised – more easily, so the argument continues, than their more institutionalised counterparts.

This drive towards deformalisation would seem to have natural boundaries, in a variety of ways. For example, the more active an entity is, the more it will recognise the need for a certain amount of formalisation. Thus, the OSCE, the textbook example of an extra-legal organisation, itself started out as a mere Conference: being organised on a regular basis, the need arose to formalise the set-up, so as to avoid having to re-invent the wheel every two or three years. Other entities have gone through a similar process: starting out as mere conferences, at some point a secretariat is created; at some point, a plenary body with more or less well-defined powers is set up; at some point, decision-making processes are codified or streamlined and the expected effects of adopted instruments spelled out; and at some point, the organisation might become interested in acquiring privileges and immunities, if only to protect its staff on missions abroad, or in order to attract more qualified staff by being able to offer salaries free from taxation.

Moreover, it is easy to exaggerate the advantages of a flexible set-up. Even non-binding decisions (assuming this to be a meaningful category) may harden over time and create legal obligations through the formation of customary norms or through processes such as estoppel. If states execute non-binding decisions in good faith and incur expenses in doing so, they may resist attempts to change things overnight. Likewise, 'soft' organisations may 'harden' over time: a fine example is the highly flexible General Agreement on Tariffs and Trade (GATT) (originally created as a stop-gap solution when the more ambitious attempt to create an International Trade Organisation failed) which was slowly, over the years, given organs and an organisational structure, and eventually transformed into the very 'legal' World Trade Organisation (WTO). That process was difficult enough in its own right: the Uruguay Round of trade negotiations which culminated in the creation of the WTO, on the basis of the existing GATT framework, lasted eight years.

In the end, much of the thinking about the relevance of institutional design and of fitting the institution to its substantive needs is deceptive, in that it is difficult to escape from the workings of the international legal order, especially while attempting to reap its benefits. Still, one of the more tangible effects of deformalisation is the by-passing of any form of control. National parliaments may not need to be involved in the creation of institutions which are kept outside the realm of law (as parliamentary powers over foreign affairs typically extend only to the approval of international legally binding commitments), and with many of the decisions emanating from 'soft' entities not deemed to be legally binding either, control by courts is unlikely as well.

Towards accountability

If soft entities aim to escape from the formalities of law and accompanying structures of accountability, laudable attempts have been made in recent years to overcome the resulting accountability deficit, on the (not always articulated) basis that the governance of global affairs would benefit from increased legitimacy of international organisations. One way to increase legitimacy might be to hold international organisations accountable, which again signals a move away from functionalism.

Learned bodies such as the Institut de Droit International and the ILA have worked on the creation of responsibility regimes. The core of the Institut's position on the topic is that since international organisations are separate entities from their member states, those member states cannot be held responsible for wrongdoings by the organisation. The ILA, by contrast, focused on wrongs by the organisation itself, and adopted a broader accountability approach, positing Recommended Rules and Practices to guide organisational behaviour. Since 2000, moreover, the topic has been on the agenda of the ILC, whose special rapporteur, Giorgio Gaja, has been given the unenviable task of adapting the relatively well-established rules on state responsibility to wrongs committed by international organisations.

Perhaps the most notable attempt to establish accountability has been the attempt to posit the existence of a system of global administrative law (Kingsbury, Krisch and Stewart 2005). Based on the idea of actors taking decisions which have public effects, the existence of a global administrative space has been postulated where decisions, regardless of formalities, ought to be subjected to legal scrutiny. Thus, decisions of the OSCE, or of the Codex Alimentarius Commission, should – if and when appropriate – be subjected to the same sort of scrutiny as decisions of, say, the World Bank or UN High Commissioner for Refugees (UNHCR). The tools would be derived from an amalgam of administrative rules and principles borrowed from domestic administrative legal systems, and would focus more on procedure than on substance: what matters is whether decisions are taken in accordance with near-universal notions of transparency, whether the proper procedures have been followed, whether all stakeholders have been consulted, whether decisions are proportionate to their stated goals. In this way, so its proponents suggest, the exercise of public power on the global level can be curtailed without insisting on the need for universal (substantive) values.

The approach has its critics. In particular the question of the sources of those administrative law principles has been subject to critique, with some claiming that 'global administrative law' is too much based on Western principles and rules, and others suggesting that the focus on procedural requirements is deceptive: ultimately, one cannot dispense with building something based on universal values, yet this presupposes the sort of universal agreement that is out of reach to begin with.

Others have aspired further to refine global administrative law and provide it with a more systematic basis. In particular German scholars have taken up this challenge, inspired by Germany's rich administrative law tradition, even suggesting that non-deontic activities (i.e. exercises of authority which do not rely on standard-setting, but might cover the production of studies or rankings) should not be beyond control (Bogdandy *et al.* 2009).

Others have gone a step further, and have launched more ambitious ideas about at least some international organisations being subject to the demands of constitutionalism. For instance it has been claimed that the European Union, the United Nations or the WTO are subject to constitutionalisation, which can be taken to mean that they are subject to a set of standards with a quality akin to constitutional law, on the basis that only constitutional authority is legitimate authority. This would, like global administrative law, include procedural standards, but it would also cover more substantive standards, in particular human rights standards. On such a view, a constitutional organisation would only be legitimate if it respects a corpus of international constitutional norms and traditions. There is, to be sure, a profound ambivalence at work here: the argument about the constitutionalisation of the United Nations or the WTO often incorporates a claim not just that the organisation, *qua* organisation, is subject to a constitutional regime, but that the organisation concerned actually forms something like a constitution of the international community. Thus, those who write about the constitutionalisation of the WTO all too often envisage global governance and international law as revolving around the WTO, and much the same applies to the United Nations.

For its part, the European Union has been deemed to be in a process of constitutionalisation (largely driven by the European Court of Justice, ECJ, now CJEU) since the early 1970s (Stein 1981), and is often enough taken as the model for future developments. While attempts to adopt a formal EU Constitution have come to naught, there is widespread agreement that the European Union represents a constitutional legal order: its decisions are binding within its member states, have direct effect and are superior to domestic law. Moreover, the European Union now possesses a broad human rights catalogue, and its decision-making processes, in all their complexity, come with numerous guarantees relating to the involvement of all member states but also of representative bodies, in the form of the European Parliament and also representatives of industry, interest groups and civil society.

Less visibly, quite a few international organisations have started to think about control. While reluctant to accept being bound by external standards, some have drawn the conclusion that it would enhance their credibility if they were to be seen to respect at least their own internal standards, guidelines, decision-making procedures, etc. The best-known example of self-scrutiny is the World Bank Inspection Panel, established in 1994 following complaints about the impacts of some World Bank projects. The Panel is mandated to verify whether in its decision-making process the World Bank has paid sufficient respect to its own guidelines and procedures. It conclusions (though not binding) are taken very seriously.

Other organisations have adopted similar initiatives, for example through an Office of International Oversight or the appointment of a Compliance Officer. This applies most prominently to the financial institutions and international development banks, perhaps for the good reason that their work may have large-scale consequences. But it also applies elsewhere: the International Board of Auditors for NATO engages in performance audits in addition to the more regular financial audits, testing the efficiency and effectiveness of the operation of NATO bodies; the Food and Agricultural Organisation (FAO) has an Office of the Inspector-General; even the ostensibly extra-legal OSCE has an Office of Internal Oversight. The United Nations created the position of an ombudsperson to oversee its administration of Kosovo.

More active, less glamorous

This suggests that international organisations, after an over-long period when they were deemed to contribute diffusely to the 'salvation of mankind'

(Singh 1958), have come to be taken seriously as political actors. Their work, however mundane it may often seem, is informed by political considerations and has political effects. It should come as no surprise that they have slowly but surely come to be subjected to some form of scrutiny, all the more against the background of a general surge in controlling public power: organisations have entered 'the audit society' (Power 1997).

On no issue has this become more visible than the issue of sanctions ordained by the Security Council (see also Chapter 11). Faced with increased concerns about terrorism, the Security Council has started to employ sanctions against individuals and companies, and has created sanctions committees to oversee their implementation. In the process, it has been seen to act in conflict with recognised human rights law: financial sanctions may be considered as impeding the right to property, and the rather laconic procedure for imposing or lifting sanctions on individuals and companies is difficult to reconcile with the right to a fair trial and access to justice. It is sometimes even proposed, following the path-breaking initiative of the European Court of Justice in *Kadi* v. *Commission and Council* ([2008] 3 CMLR 41) that domestic courts should test the legality of UN sanctions against generally accepted human rights standards. In other words: judicial control of the acts of the Security Council should be put in place *somewhere*, if not centrally then in a decentralised manner. Thus organisations have moved from being unaccountable, almost literally above the law, to possibly being scrutinised by all possible courts – a remarkable turn of events, and indicative of a wider suspicion of public power.

The sanctions issue has given rise to heated debates about the possible law-making role of international organisations (Alvarez 2005). Although the Security Council comes dangerously close to assuming legislative powers, it was never created with this purpose in mind, and lacks any form of democratic legitimacy. In other organisations, law-making has come to be surrounded by certain guarantees; the WTO's emphasis on being member-driven, and the explicit injunction that its dispute settlement mechanism shall not add to existing rights or obligations, suggests that organisations are less trusted, by their own member states, than they once were.

Organisations, in other words, have clearly lost some of their glamour. This has become visible in the more restrained use of the implied powers doctrine and the introduction of notions such as subsidiarity, but also has come to affect other staples of international institutional law (Klabbers 2001). In many organisations, for instance, decision-making by consensus has become the norm, giving member states a virtual right of veto. Host states have come to assert themselves more strongly towards international organisations headquartered on their territories, sometimes aiming to unilaterally change existing arrangements, or suggesting that their local legislation has some applicability within the organisation's headquarters. Amendment of constitutional documents has traditionally been difficult (Zacklin 1968), and is now often done by informal means which, in turn, provokes arguments concerning accountability, legality and legitimacy. NATO's transformation from a Western defensive alliance to something approximating a global SWAT team is instructive, based as it is on the sequential adoption by NATO's member states of strategy documents, rather than on a formal amendment of NATO's constituent treaty.

By way of conclusion

One way of telling the story of the rise of international organisations and the development of international institutional law is by focusing on formality versus informality. It may even seem that there are distinct conceptions of organisation competing for attention, one favouring flexibility or informality, the other favouring stability or formality – and this helps to explain simultaneous complaints about the United Nations doing too much and too little, or about the WTO being too effective and ineffective at the same time (Klabbers 2005).

On the one hand, organisations are often cast, in the functionalist tradition, as 'can do' entities, set up to achieve particular purposes and given a range of instruments to achieve them. Here, the appropriate vocabulary includes terms such as technical expertise and management. The overwhelming concern is functional: the organisation is regarded as a place where experts manage common problems or aim to achieve common goals. On the other hand, organisations are also often held to be 'all talk and no action': fora for political discussion and debate, where statesmen and diplomats ventilate their frustrations, but without much practical impact.

Much of the appreciation for international organisations, and much of the law of international organisations, results from the interplay between these two concepts. Organisations cannot be regarded in complete independence from their member states, if only because member states retain their sovereignty and therewith the capacity to take action outside the organisation's framework: behind the organisational veil the member states continue to shine through (Brölmann 2007). Yet, like other political entities, international organisations are not just created to achieve tasks set by their member states – thinking in such terms does an injustice to the political role of secretariats, executive bodies and plenary bodies. As sensitive political scientists came to observe in the 1950s and 1960s, organisational leadership has its own role, relatively independent from the member states; lawyers have captured this in finding organisations to possess a '*volonté distincte*'.

Thus our understanding of international organisations and their activities may stand to gain by borrowing from sociology and public administration to explain the role of international bureaucracies; by concentrating on the role of experts and their works and artifacts or by zooming in on the ethics of organisational decision-makers. An increased understanding may translate into a more appropriate set of rules to control the activities of international organisations (Klabbers 2010).

International organisations have remained somewhat elusive creatures, difficult to capture, and it may well be that part of what makes them attractive is precisely their elusiveness. It is difficult to give an account of international law, or international affairs more generally, without regard to the role of international organisations and the rules and standards they produce and monitor. A history of the twentieth century which did not mention the League of Nations or the United Nations would be incomplete; international relations theories ignoring the role of international organisations border on the implausible; lawyers specialising in domestic affairs (say, transport lawyers, or refugee lawyers) ignore the work of international organisations at their peril. International law has come to a large extent to be developed and formulated under the auspices of international organisations: it has become *institutionalised* (Ruffert and Walter 2009).

Bibliography

Alvarez, J., 2005. *International Organisations as Law-makers*, Oxford University Press

Bogdandy, A., R. Wolfrum, J. Bernstorff and P. Dann (eds.), 2009. *The Exercise of Public Authority by International Institutions: Advancing International Institutional Law*, Berlin: Springer

Brölmann, C., 2007. *The Institutional Veil in Public International Law: International Organisations and the Law of Treaties*, Oxford: Hart

Eagleton, C., 1950. 'International Organisation and the Law of Responsibility', *Recueil des cours de l'Académie de droit international*, 76, 319–425

Kennedy, D., 1987. 'The Move to Institutions', *Cardozo Law Review*, 8, 841–988

Kingsbury, B., N. Krisch and R. Stewart, 2005. 'The Emergence of Global Administrative Law', *Law & Contemporary Problems*, 68, 15–61

Klabbers, J., 2001. 'The Changing Image of International Organisations', in J. Coicaud and V. Heiskanen (eds.), *The Legitimacy of International Organisations*, Tokyo: United Nations University Press, 221–255

Klabbers, J., 2005. 'Two Concepts of International Organisation', *International Organisations Law Review*, 2, 277–293

Klabbers, J., 2008. 'The Paradox of International Institutional Law', *International Organisations Law Review*, 5, 151–173

Klabbers, J., 2009. *An Introduction to International Institutional Law*, 2nd edn., Cambridge University Press

Klabbers, J., 2010. 'Constitutionalizing Virtue in International Institutional Law', in N. White and R. Collins (eds.), *International Organisations and the Idea of Autonomy*, London: Routledge

Mazower, M., 2009. *No Enchanted Palace: The End of Empire and the Ideological Origins of the United Nations*, Princeton University Press

Power, M., 1997. *The Audit Society: Rituals of Verification*, Oxford University Press

Reinsch, P., 1911. *Public International Unions, Their Work and Organisation: A Study in International Administrative Law*, Boston: Ginn & Co.

Ruffert, M. and C. Walter, 2009. *Institutionalisiertes Völkerrecht*, Munich: C.H. Beck

Schermers, H. and N. Blokker, 2003. *International Institutional Law: Unity within Diversity*, 4th edn., Leiden: Martinus Nijhoff

Seyersted, F., 2008. *Common Law of International Organisations*, Leiden: Martinus Nijhoff

Singer, M., 1995. 'Jurisdictional Immunity of International Organisations: Human Rights and Functional Necessity Concerns', *Virginia Journal of International Law*, 36, 53–165

Singh, N., 1958. *Termination of Membership of International Organisations*, London: Stevens & Sons

Slaughter, A. -M., 2004. *A New World Order*, Princeton University Press

Stein, E., 1981. 'Lawyers, Judges, and the Making of a Transnational Constitution', *American Journal of International Law*, 75, 1–27

Virally, M., 1974. 'La notion de fonction dans la théorie de l'organisation internationale', in S. Bastid *et al.* (eds.), *Mélanges offerts à Charles Rousseau: La communauté internationale*, Paris: Pédone, 277–300

Zacklin, R., 1968. *The Amendment of the Constitutive Instruments of the United Nations and Specialized Agencies*, Leiden: Sijthoff

11 International law and the relativities of enforcement

Dino Kritsiotis

Introduction

When the English philosopher John Austin delivered the six lectures he published as *The Province of Jurisprudence Determined* in 1832, he argued that there were laws properly so-called (commands that are 'armed with sanctions, and impose duties, in the proper acceptation of the terms' (Austin 1832 [1995], 119) and laws like international law that were laws improperly so-called, by virtue of an 'analogical extension' of terms such as 'law' and 'rule' (*ibid.*, 123). Austin considered enforcement, or at least enforceability, an essential ingredient for the existence of law. Since international law presented no obvious or readily identifiable machineries for its enforcement, it had taken the name of 'law' in vain and it could hold no claim to this status. To similar effect, a popular Japanese song of the 1880s had it that 'There is a Law of Nations, it is true,/but when the moment comes, remember,/the Strong Eat up the Weak' (Sansom 1965, 407). International law had, however, historically considered the matter of its existence as separate from its enforcement: the former spoke to the validation and authority of this law as law; the latter to questions of its effectiveness. And this stands to reason: a law can only be enforced once we have been assured of its promulgation.

Problematically, the Austinian conception of law had taken its cue from the universal paradigm for national law where enforcement was both an expected and emphasised commodity: 'the expression or intimation of a wish, with the power and purpose of enforcing it', Austin argued, 'are the constituent elements of a command' (Austin 1832 [1995], 30). Such a facile transposition of paradigms had little merit: for one thing, international law was principally interested in the actions of states and not those of individuals; moreover, the discipline had dissected its interests between 'war' and 'peace', making it a wholly distinct phenomenon from the paradigm of national law. Within this framework, international law had in fact turned its mind to 'the power and purpose' of its own enforcement. However, the dizzying range and diverse character of its rules meant that the modalities of enforcement, though often discrete, were individually tailored to the rules they were seeking to uphold. What might have proved relevant for the apprehension of pirates operating on the high seas – in *The Law of Nations or the Principles of Natural Law Applied to the Conduct and to the Affairs of Nations and of Sovereigns* (1758 [2008]), Emer de Vattel considered that pirates, as *hosti humani generis*, were to be 'sent to the gibbet by the first into whose hands they fall' – might not work for violations of treaties of peace:

> When the treaty of peace is violated by one of the contracting parties, the other has the option of either declaring the treaty null and void, or allow it still to subsist ... [I]f he chooses not to come to a rupture, the treaty remains valid and obligatory ... If the injured party be willing to let the treaty subsist, he may either pardon the infringement, – insist on an indemnification or adequate satisfaction, – or discharge himself, on his part, from those engagements corresponding with the violated article, – those promises he had made in consideration of a thing which has not been performed. But, if he determines on demanding a just indemnification, and the party in fault refuses it, then the treaty is necessarily broken, and the injured party has a very just cause for taking up arms again. (Bk. IV, Ch. V, §54)

Central to each of these claims was the fact that no agent or authority other than the state existed to execute the law and administer its varied requirements. In short, international law possessed nothing akin to the features of an 'external power' (Jennings and Watts 1992, 9), so that it invariably had to turn to the state to perform these crucial tasks. The state was to do so through the invocation of its existing infrastructure: Vattel wrote of the prosecution of pirates by the capturing state 'by a trial in due form of law' (Bk. I, Ch. XIX, §233). But this leverage came with limitations: it had been decided in *Underhill* v. *Hernandez* (1897) that, in deference to the principle of the sovereign equality of all states, '[e]very sovereign state is bound to respect the independence of every other sovereign state, and the court of one country will not sit in judgment on the acts of the government of another done within its own territory. Redress of grievances by reason of such acts must be obtained through the means open to be availed of by sovereign powers as between themselves.' And so it was that Vattel provided for the injured state of a violated treaty of peace to elect the appropriate means of redress. The state, then, as the injured state of a violated treaty of peace, was to assume the responsibilities of judge, jury and executioner in every particular.

To this state of affairs, international law appropriately awarded the term of 'self-help', expressing in doctrinal form the essence of the evocative metaphor of taking the law – including the enforcement of the law – into one's own hands (Brierly 1963, 398). In this decentralised system, states would prove the most viable option for actions of 'a remedial or repressive character in order to enforce legal rights' (Bowett 1958, 11), so that Hugo Grotius, in his celebrated *De jure belli ac pacis* (1625), envisaged that the 'justifiable causes generally assigned for war are three, defence, indemnity and punishment'. Such decentralisation affected not only how that law was made but how it would be realised and made relevant in the real world. Further to this, however, even Vattel admitted the need to conceive of the enforcement of international law other than by the entrenched structures of bilateral state relations, the simple and raw dynamics of the injured and the infractor state. He argued in respect of the 'common right' pertaining to the open sea that:

> a nation, which, without a legitimate claim, would arrogate to itself an exclusive right to the sea, and support its pretensions by force, does an injury to all nations; it infringes their common right; and they are justifiable in forming a general combination against it, in order to repress such an attempt. Nations have the greatest interest in causing the law of nations, which is the basis of their tranquillity, to be universally respected. If any one openly tramples it under foot, they all may and ought to rise up against him; and, by uniting their forces to chastise the common enemy, they will discharge their duty towards themselves, and towards human society, of which they are members. (Bk. I, Ch. XXIII, §283)

It is apparent that international law has traditionally relied greatly upon forms of violence, a situation that prevailed in theory until the transformative currents of the twentieth century made clear that '[w]ar, or other hostilities or acts of force, strictly settled nothing but the question of superior strength' (Fitzmaurice 1956, 3) – and in practice for much longer. In this chapter, we explore when and how these changes of commitment occurred, assessing how war, intervention, force and armed reprisals took their place alongside instruments such as (economic) counter-measures and retorsion – and how they still do. Pragmatically, Vattel advised against the 'taking up of arms' for each and every violation of the law of a given treaty of peace: 'there may, to the violation of each individual article [of these treaties] be annexed a penalty proportionate to its importance' (Bk. IV, Ch. IV, §49). This chapter therefore focuses on how schemes of enforcement are essentially relative to the rules they enjoin, detailing the evolution of arrangements within international organisations as well as the selected treaty practices of states.

The original burden of enforcement

Perhaps the most important achievement of the UN Charter was its prohibition of the threat or use of force by states in their international relations, overhauling centuries of practice. Article 2(4) was an acclaimed advance on previous efforts in this direction: the Kellogg–Briand Pact of June 1928 had prohibited 'war' but had not addressed lesser forms of violence; the Covenant of the League of Nations of April 1919 had not formally prohibited war at all but had, instead, established a series of procedural 'covenants' whereby disputes between its members should first be referred to arbitration, judicial settlement or to the League Council. The Hague Convention (II) Respecting the Limitation of the Employment of Force for the Recovery of Contract Debts of October 1907 prohibited recourse to armed force for the recovery of contract debts 'claimed from the Government of one country by the Government of another country as being due to its nationals', but this undertaking was inapplicable when the debtor state refused or neglected to reply to an offer of arbitration, or, after accepting the offer, prevented any settlement of the *compromis* or, after arbitration, failed to submit to the award (Finnemore 2003, 49).

The Charter's prohibition of force was not absolute, for the Charter assured all states their right of individual and collective self-defence, and it conferred so-called 'enforcement powers' upon the Security Council under Chapter VII, at least insofar as necessary to discharge its 'primary responsibility for the maintenance of international peace and security' contained in article 24. That meant, of course, that Austinian scepticism about the effectiveness of international law as a whole was destined to linger. But the achievement of article 2(4) and the Charter framework was quickly consolidated in the jurisprudence of the International Court of Justice (ICJ). In April 1949, the Court was called upon to assess the United Kingdom's minesweeping operation undertaken in the North Corfu Strait in November 1946; 'Operation Retail' was defended as a limited measure of self-help in order to secure evidence for the United Kingdom that Albania had been involved in the laying of mines causing damage to two destroyers with heavy loss of life. The Court left no doubt where it stood:

> The Court can only regard the alleged right of intervention as the manifestation of a policy of force, such as has in the past given rise to most serious abuses and such as cannot, whatever the present defects in international organisation, find a place in international law. Intervention is perhaps still less inadmissible in the particular form it would take here; for, from the nature of things, it would be reserved for the most powerful States, and might easily lead to perverting the administration of international justice itself. (*Corfu Channel*, ICJ Reports 1949, p. 35)

There followed many reaffirmations of these new principles in subsequent years – by the Court, by the General Assembly and by individual states.

The latitude for war, intervention and force has been dramatically reduced in the Charter order and can no longer be regarded as a general means for upholding international law. Armed reprisals, too, have not survived the prohibition of force of the Charter: the General Assembly concluded in its Friendly Relations Declaration that 'States have a duty to refrain from acts of reprisal involving the use of force' (UN General Assembly Resolution 2625 (1970)). Furthermore, in *Military and Paramilitary Activities in and against Nicaragua*, the ICJ observed in its scrutiny of potential legal justifications for activities undertaken by the United States against the Sandinista government of Nicaragua, that 'while the United States might form its own appraisal of the situation as to respect for human rights in Nicaragua, the use of force could not be the appropriate method to monitor or ensure such respect' (ICJ Reports 1986, p. 134).

In contrast to these changes, the right of self-defence is proclaimed as 'inherent' to all states under article 51; what exercised the Court in *Nicaragua* was the *scope* of the right of self-defence under the Charter. At the heart of the case was the right of collective self-defence, which the United States had invoked as the legal basis for its actions in Nicaragua, acting on behalf of (or so it said) Costa Rica, El Salvador and Honduras and in response to the 'armed attack' committed on each of these states by Nicaragua. To be sure, both forms of self-defence – individual and collective – are 'remedial' in character: they 'presuppose the breach of some duty' (Bowett 1974, 38). But does that mean that *any* state may invoke collective self-defence to rush to the rescue of any other state the victim of an armed attack? Is the enforcement of the prohibition of force in these circumstances to be a matter of the whim for any freelance (third) state? Judge Sir Robert Jennings did not think so in his eloquent dissent in that case; he argued against any interpretation of the right of collective self-defence as a 'vicarious defence by champions', for '[t]he assisting State is not an authorized champion, permitted under certain conditions to go to the aid of a favoured State [but] surely must, by going to the victim State's assistance, be also, and in addition to other requirements, be itself'. The idea was to prevent arbitrary enforcements of the law, lest these serve as pretexts for military action, undertaken at the say-so of the most powerful states. The Court was not inclined to this restrictive understanding of collective self-defence. Instead, it chose to respond to the concern about the potential abuse of this right by stipulating the requirement of an armed attack for both individual and collective self-defence, accompanied by additional procedural safeguards for collective self-defence: a victim state must have declared itself to be the subject of an armed attack and that it must have issued a request to the state or states who will act on its behalf. It was this conceptualisation of the right of collective self-defence that overwhelmingly informed the practice of states in the aftermath of the invasion of Kuwait by Iraq on 2 August 1990 (Greenwood 1992, 162–164).

The Court proceeded to take a narrow view of 'armed attack' in its *Nicaragua* judgment, which reduced the practical import of the right of self-defence and prompted the critical question of how states may lawfully respond to uses of force that fall short of an armed attack. For the Court:

> While an armed attack would give rise to an entitlement to collective self-defence, a use of force of a lesser degree of gravity cannot … produce any entitlement to take collective counter-measures involving the use of force. The acts of which Nicaragua is accused, even assuming them to have been established and imputable to that State, could only have justified proportionate counter-measures on the part of that State which had been the victim of these acts, namely El Salvador, Honduras or Costa Rica. They could not justify counter-measures taken by a third State, the United States, and particularly could not justify intervention involving the use of force. (Nicaragua, ICJ Reports 1986, p. 127)

The use of the language of *counter-measures* in this passage is unhelpful: the term had already acquired special resonance for referring to *unarmed* reprisals, especially of an economic kind. But in this *dictum*, the Court made use of the term to refer to *armed* counter-measures. It did so in order to consider the forcible techniques potentially open to the United States as a third state, i.e. 'collective armed counter-measures', as well as to El Salvador, Honduras and Costa Rica in *their* individual relations with Nicaragua, i.e. 'individual armed counter-measures'. It went on to find that, on its reading of the law as it then stood, collective armed counter-measures were impermissible as a matter of principle; individual armed counter-measures were acceptable, but only on condition of their proportionality.

That a distinction should be made between armed and unarmed responses available to states is evident from the General Assembly's rejection of reprisals involving the use of force, as if to suggest that reprisals conducted by means other than the use of force remain unaffected by the UN Charter. The International Law Commission (ILC) has endorsed this crucial distinction in its Articles on State Responsibility, where counter-measures (article 22) are treated separately from the right of self-defence (article 21), but where both are classified as circumstances precluding the wrongfulness of an otherwise internationally wrongful act. The ILC preferred the term to any mention of reprisals (i.e. 'economic reprisals') or 'sanctions' and used it to refer to the taking of non-forcible action by an injured state acting of its own accord against an unlawful act committed by another state. Ordinarily, that action by the responding state would itself be unlawful under international law – which is why we find the ILC mapping out the circumstances for precluding its wrongfulness – unlike an act of retorsion, which typically involves a lawful but unfriendly response by a State (e.g. the truncation of diplomatic relations) to either a prior unfriendly or unlawful act of another state.

As a practical matter it is difficult not to admit the limitations inherent in this approach to enforcement, including its assumptions as to the circumstances of the taking of counter-measures: what if the injured state is incapacitated by an internationally wrongful act to the point where it has lost the instruments of its own economic power and cannot freeze foreign assets or impose appropriate trade tariffs on the state it alleges of international wrongdoing? Such was the predicament of Kuwait following Iraq's occupation of its territory in August 1990. More generally, do counter-measures not rest on the premise that all states are equally able to initiate them in the first instance? Even supposing the ability to take some form of economic action, there is a policy concern that an injured state may in fact suffer twice where (for example) a trade obligation has been violated once from the restrictions that have been imposed on its product by other governments and, then, the 'retro-costs which may be considerable, that are borne by particular sectors of [its] national economy' (Reisman and Stevick 1998, 93). At the other end of the spectrum of the relationship 'between a strong and a weak Power' (Oppenheim 1952, 149), it could be that the counter-measures that are adopted assume the dimensions of economic coercion.

In general terms, the ILC's approach to counter-measures does not significantly depart from the bilateral mould of international legal relations. Once again, the state as injured state emerges as its own judge, jury and executioner in the cause of the greater good of enforcing international law (Zoller 1984, 70–75), although the ILC's articulation of conditions for the lawfulness of counter-measures, together with expanding judicial and arbitral possibilities, does suggest that states no longer have the last word on how breaches of international law are dealt with. In the *Gabčíkovo-Nagymaros* (1997) case, for example, the ICJ concluded that Slovakia's diversion of the Danube could not be regarded as a proportionate countermeasure to Hungary's prior violation of its commitments under a bilateral treaty. In *Air Services* (1978), the arbitral tribunal agreed that the United States had taken proportionate counter-measures in response to France's breach of a treaty.

To be sure, the ILC Articles also provide for the possibility that responsibility might be invoked by a state *other than an injured state*. This option will exist where '(a) the obligation breached is owed by a group of States including that State, and is established for the protection of the interest of the group; or (b) the obligation breached is owed to the international community as a whole' (article 48 (1)). For these *über*-norms, rules of a designated higher status within international law, the ILC has devised a privileged scheme of enforcement; the notion of 'international crimes' of states has been replaced by the concept of 'serious breach' by a state of an obligation arising under a peremptory norm, defined as involving 'a gross or systematic failure by the responsible State to fulfil' such an obligation' (article 40). The ILC has thus maintained the dichotomy of obligations evident in earlier formulations of its work without recourse to emotive terminologies. According to article 41, 'States shall cooperate to bring an end through lawful means any serious breach within the meaning of Article 40' and 'no State shall recognise as lawful a situation created by a serious breach within the meaning of Article 40, nor render aid or assistance in maintaining that situation' (see generally Crawford 2002).

The turn to sanctions

The threshold for the activation of the Security Council's 'enforcement powers' is identified in article 39 of the Charter as 'the existence of any threat to the peace, breach of the peace, or act of aggression'; it does not extend to breaches of international law *per se*. It is in this context that the vocabulary of 'sanctions' has taken a firm hold on the legal imagination (Kelsen 1946; Gowlland-Debbas 2002), as it had with the League Covenant, and even though neither document makes use of that term. Aspects of the law could now be enforced with an institutional imprimatur, not left solely to the serial vagaries of states:

> [i]f the Member States [of the United Nations] as well as the non-Member States are supposed to be under an obligation to refrain from conduct which the Security Council considers to be a threat to, or breach of, the peace, then an enforcement measure taken against a State guilty of a violation of that obligation is a true sanction because it is a reaction against an international delict, whether this measure is ordered or only recommended by the Council. (Kelsen 1951, 934)

Given this context, it is instructive to compare how the Covenant and the Charter chose to enforce the law: article 16 of the Covenant made plain that '[s]hould any Member of the League resort to war in disregard of its covenants under Articles 12, 13 or 15, it shall *ipso facto* be deemed to have committed an act of war against all other Members of the League, which hereby undertake immediately to subject it to the severance of all trade or financial restrictions, the prohibition of all intercourse between their nationals and the nationals of the covenant-breaking state, and the prevention of all financial, commercial or personal intercourse between the nationals of the covenant-breaking state and the nationals of any other state, whether a Member of the League or not' (article 16(1)). This formed the centrepiece of the 'higher law' of the Covenant (Lauterpacht 1936), even though the economic consequences for 'covenant-breaking' states were constructed in terms of a vicarious act of war committed against all other Members of the League. Furthermore the Council was obliged to recommend – but only to recommend – 'what effective military, naval or air force the Members of the League shall severally contribute to the armed forces to be used to protect the Covenant of the League' (article 16(2)).

In contrast to these arrangements, the Charter provides that once the Security Council makes the requisite determination under article 39, states are bound to implement the measures the Council decides to adopt (article 25). They include provisional measures under article 40 (calling for cease-fires or troop withdrawals) '[i]n order to prevent an aggravation of the situation', and other measures not involving the use of force under article 41 (complete or partial interruption of economic relations, means of communication and the severance of diplomatic relations). Should these measures be considered 'inadequate', under article 42 the Council may 'take such action by air, sea, or land forces as may be necessary to maintain or restore international peace and security', including demonstrations, blockades, and other operations. It can authorise military actions (Chapter VII), including by regional organisations (Chapter VIII), and it can enforce the directives contained in its own resolutions.

Although the Charter did not designate the Council as the overarching guarantor for the observance of international law as such, it was, curiously, during the period of the Cold War that the Council demonstrated how wide its discretion under Chapter VII could be. The Council condemned Southern Rhodesia's unilateral declaration of independence in November 1965 as an act by 'a racist minority' and called upon all states not to recognise or render assistance to the regime (Resolution 216 (1965)). In Resolution 217 (1965) the Council determined that 'the situation resulting from the proclamation of independence by the illegal authorities in Southern Rhodesia is extremely grave ... and that its continuance in time constitutes a threat to international peace and security', and characterised the declaration of independence 'as having no legal validity', calling upon all states 'not to recognise this illegal authority and not to entertain any diplomatic or other relations with it'. The episode highlighted the ease with which the Council's executive jurisdiction can be activated in order to respond to certain violations of international law. The Council followed the same approach to thwart South Africa's attempt to establish the *bantustan* states of Transkei (1976), Bophuthatswana (1977), Venda (1979) and Ciskei (1981). In Resolution 662 (1990), the Council considered Iraq's 'comprehensive and eternal merger' with Kuwait null and void and called upon all states, international organisations and specialised agencies 'not to recognise that annexation, and to refrain from any action or dealing that might be interpreted as an indirect recognition of the annexation'. In so doing, the Council demonstrated the value of non-recognition in its practices for maintaining 'the authority of international law' (Lauterpacht 1947, 430–431; Dugard 1987, 102–103).

The Council thus began to develop a record of imaginative measures under article 41, not confined to economic or diplomatic sanctions. For example, it demanded that Libya extradite to the United Kingdom or United States those suspected of bombing PanAm Flight 103 over Lockerbie in December 1988 (Resolution 748 (1992)); that Sudan take immediate action to extradite to Ethiopia those suspected of the attempted assassination of President Mubarak of Egypt in Addis Ababa in June 1995 (Resolution 1054

(1996)). With the consent of Lebanon, an international tribunal was established by the Council in Resolution 1757 (2007) to try those responsible for the 'terrorist crime' of assassinating former Lebanese Prime Minister Rafic al-Hariri in February 2005. In Resolution 1373 (2001), following the al-Qaeda attacks in the United States on 11 September 2001, the Council decided *inter alia* that all states must prevent and suppress the financing of terrorist acts and refrain from providing any form of support to entities or persons involved in terrorist acts. Under this resolution, states are required to take necessary steps to prevent the commission of terrorist acts including by providing early warning to other states – and deny safe haven to those who finance, plan, support, or commit terrorist attacks. A counter-terrorism committee was established for states to report on their implementation of the resolution. By virtue of Resolution 1540 (2004), all states must also refrain from providing any form of support to non-state actors that attempt to develop, acquire, or transfer nuclear, chemical, or biological weapons and report their implementation to the '1540 Committee'. See also SC Resolutions 1970 (2011) and 1973 (2011) on Libya.

The Security Council has also established international territorial administrations in Eastern Slavonia (Resolution 1037 (1996)), Kosovo (Resolution 1244 (1999)) and East Timor (Resolution 1272 (1999)), and created *ad hoc* international criminal tribunals for the former Yugoslavia (Resolution 808 (1993)) and Rwanda (Resolution 955 (1994)). These actions of expanding the enforcement process through mechanisms only known intermittently in the international sphere (e.g. the international military tribunals for Nuremberg (1946) and Tokyo (1948)) significantly contributed to the establishment of a *permanent* international criminal court in July 1998, designed on the principle enunciated in the Rome Statute of the International Criminal Court (ICC) 'that the most serious crimes of concern to the international community as a whole must not go unpunished and that their effective prosecution must be ensured by taking measures at the national level and by enhancing the principle of international co-operation'.

Where the Council has adopted economic sanctions, it has either done so on a comprehensive basis (as with Iraq: Resolution 661 (1990)) or through select measures, such as the arms embargoes imposed on South Africa (Resolution 418 (1977)), and Yugoslavia (Resolution 713 (1991)), and the 'smart sanctions' requiring the certificates-of-origin for trade in diamonds imposed on Angola (Resolutions 1173 (1998) and 1295 (2000)), Sierra Leone (Resolution 1306 (2000)) and Liberia (Resolution 1343 (2001)). The Council has also exercised its enforcement powers against entities other than states. It condemned Bosnian Serbs for their refusal to accept the proposed territorial settlement for the Republic of Bosnia and Herzegovina and demanded that they 'accept this settlement unconditionally and in full' (Resolution 942 (1994)). It condemned UNITA for its failure to abide by previous demands of the Council, imposed an arms and petroleum embargo upon it, and held its leadership 'responsible for not having taken the necessary measures to comply with the Council in its previous resolutions' (Resolution 864 (1993)), calling upon states 'to bring proceedings against persons and entities violating the measures imposed by this resolution and to impose appropriate penalties'.

In following through with these efforts, the Council has established sanctions committees as well as instituted humanitarian exceptions to some of its sanctions (e.g. the 'oil-for-food' programme in Iraq (Resolution 986 (1995)). Moreover, as the Security Council discovered in Southern Rhodesia, further measures may be necessary for enhancing the effectiveness of its sanctions. In Resolution 217 (1965), it called upon all states 'to refrain from any action which would assist and encourage the illegal régime and, in particular, to desist from providing it with arms, equipment and military material, and to do their utmost in order to break all economic relations with Southern Rhodesia, including an embargo on oil and petroleum products'. This formulation is interesting for the varied language it uses for different aspects of the sanctions: what is said in concrete terms for arms, equipment and military material is not said for oil and petroleum products, where states are simply exhorted to take action. Nevertheless, the Council firmed up this arrangement in Resolution 221 (1966), calling upon Portugal not to receive at the Mozambican port of Beira oil destined for Southern Rhodesia nor to permit oil to be pumped from there via the pipeline to Southern Rhodesia. Furthermore, the Council called upon the United Kingdom 'to prevent, by the use of force if necessary, the arrival at Beira of vessels reasonably believed to be carrying oil destined for Southern Rhodesia'. The Council was to relive this lesson much later in its history when, in order to enforce economic sanctions on Iraq, it authorised naval interdictions in the Persian Gulf (Resolution 665 (1990)).

These instances of controlled authorisation of force are now quite common in the practice of the Security Council. Resolution 794 (1992), in response to a humanitarian crisis due to the civil war in Somalia, approved 'all necessary means to establish as soon as possible a secure environment for humanitarian relief operations'; and following its establishment of the safe areas of Srebrenica (Resolution 819 (1993)) and Sarajevo, Tuzla, Zepa, Gorazde and Bihač (Resolution 824 (1993)), the Council decided to extend the mandate of the peace-keepers of the UN Protection Force 'in order to enable it ... to deter attacks against the safe areas', amongst other things (Resolution 836 (1993)). In Resolution 1816 (2008), the Council authorised states cooperating with the Transitional Federal Government of Somalia to enter Somali territorial waters 'for the purpose of repressing acts of piracy and armed robbery at sea'. One might question the significance of this authorisation given the actual and envisaged consent of Somalia in the resolution, but the purpose of this scheme was to supplement the established law of the high seas under which, as article 105 of the 1982 Law of the Sea Convention provides, 'every State may seize a pirate ship ... and arrest the persons and seize the property on board. The courts of the State which carried out the seizure may decide upon the penalties imposed.' The Security Council also called for increased coordination amongst states interested in the commercial maritime routes off the Somalian coast, and improved information-sharing and the provision of technical expertise to Somalia and related states.

Perhaps the most spectacular use of the Council's Chapter VII powers occurred in Resolution 678 (1990), authorising member states cooperating with Kuwait to use 'all necessary means' to uphold and implement Resolution 660 'and all subsequent relevant resolutions and to restore international peace and security in the area'. The Council thus relied on states for the action that became known as Operation Desert Storm. Operation Desert Storm occurred without any UN command, supervision or control (Greenwood 1992, 170). Such delegations of power have become a familiar feature of practice after the Cold War, where the Council has had to make do with the goodwill and the commitment of its members acting alone, in concert, or through regional organisations.

These are all testaments to the evolution of 'physical enforcement' within Chapter VII (Fitzmaurice 1956, 8). But article 42 also envisages certain typologies for armed action: 'demonstrations' and 'blockades' are mentioned, and we have seen how the Council used the concept of safe areas in Bosnia and Herzegovina. More successful was the Council's institution of a no-fly zone for military flights in the air space of Bosnia and Herzegovina as 'an essential element for the safety of the delivery of humanitarian assistance and a decisive step for the cessation of hostilities' (Resolution 781 (1992); Resolution 816 (1993); Gow 1997, 132–135). Related to this is the subliminal technique of the *threat* of military action that the Council has utilised from time to time (e.g. in Resolution 678 (1990) where the Council provided authorisation for force 'unless Iraq on or before 15 January 1991 fully implements . . . the foregoing resolutions').

This resurrects the old form of the ultimatum for modern purposes. Perhaps the example *par excellence* was Resolution 1441 (2002), in which the Council determined that Iraq was and remained in 'material breach' of its disarmament obligations arising under Resolution 687 (1991), and afforded Iraq 'a final opportunity' to comply with these obligations or 'face serious consequences as a result of its continued violation of its obligations'. These were clear indications that the Council would authorise military action against Iraq in the face of further recalcitrance: 'far from having abandoned or lost interest in the matter the Security Council was itself actively seized of the matter at all critical times' (Lowe 2003, 865–856). In the event, of course, the United States and the United Kingdom tabled a legal justification for Operation Iraqi Freedom based on the material breaches that Iraq had committed subsequent to Resolution 1441, arguing that these had rekindled the authorisation for force contained in Resolution 678 (1990). Intervening states thus presented themselves as 'organs' of international law, 'administering the law of nations' in a curious fashion (Lauterpacht 1947, 6), with their action accompanied by great controversy as to its conformity with the Charter.

The techniques of treaties

'Material breach' is a concept known to international law through the law of treaties. Article 60 of the Vienna Convention on the Law of Treaties provides that a 'material breach' of a bilateral treaty by one of its parties entitles the other party 'to invoke the breach as a ground for terminating the treaty or suspending its operation in whole or in part'. 'Material breach' is defined as '(a) a repudiation of the treaty not sanctioned by the present Convention; or (b) the violation of a provision essential to the accomplishment of the object or purpose of the treaty' (article 60(3)). Although this formulation introduces further questions regarding the meaning of 'a repudiation of the treaty' and of an 'essential' provision of the treaty (Sinclair 1984, 189–190), the matter of principle in regard to bilateral treaties is quite clear: everything depends upon the reaction of the injured treaty partner.

The situation is more complex for material beaches of multilateral treaties, for these give rise to entitlements belonging to certain defined constituencies as set out in article 60(2) of the 1969 Vienna Convention. Firstly, the other parties may 'by unanimous agreement' suspend or terminate the operation of the treaty in relations between themselves and the defaulting state or between all parties. Secondly, a party that is 'specially affected' by the breach is entitled to suspend or terminate the operation of the treaty in relations between itself and the defaulting state. Finally, any party other than the defaulting state may 'invoke the breach as a ground for suspending the operation of the treaty ... with respect to itself if the treaty is of such a character that a material breach of its provisions by one party radically changes the position of every party with respect to the further performance of its obligations under the treaty'. This last stipulation was intended for environmental and disarmament treaties where each treaty partner has an equal interest in the compliance of every other treaty partner; article 60(5) provides that this schema is inapplicable to 'provisions relating to the protection of the human person contained in treaties of a humanitarian character, in particular to provisions prohibiting any form of reprisals against persons protected by such treaties'.

The Convention's system for the enforcement of treaties thus amounts to an inventory of discretions regarding the suspension or termination of both bilateral and multilateral treaties, but, Vattel-like, it aligns its rules only to a certain *kind* of breach: these options for enforcement under the Convention are relative to certain, qualified treaty violations that might occur in practice and they are placed in the hands of states who are parties to any given treaty. Even then, the treaty partner(s) response must comport with the procedural particulars set forth in articles 65–68 of the Convention (which means, '[i]n effect', that 'the aggrieved party must continue compliance with a treaty which the other party is violating, while the protracted procedure of dispute settlement is in progress': Sinclair 1984, 188).

With its reference to 'provisions relating to the protection of the human person', and to reprisals against protected persons, the Vienna Convention adverts to the concept of belligerent reprisals which takes as its base 'any and every act of illegitimate warfare, whether [constituting] an international delinquency or not' (Oppenheim 1952, 562–563). Belligerent reprisals were to do for the laws of warfare what armed reprisals were designed to do for the laws of peace; Oppenheim was in no doubt that they '[could not] be dispensed with, for the effect of their use and of the fear of their being used cannot be denied' (Oppenheim 1952, 561–562). Similarly Julius Stone held that belligerent reprisals had a 'useful efficacy' on the battlefield (Stone 1954, 353). Yet traces of a different thinking can be found in the Geneva Convention Relative to the Treatment of Prisoners of War of July 1929 and in the four Geneva Conventions of August 1949. The condemnation of belligerent reprisals has strengthened since with, amongst other instruments, the 1977 First Additional Protocol to the Geneva Conventions. But the United Kingdom has entered a reservation to that Protocol: '[i]f an adverse party makes serious and deliberate attacks ... against the civilian population or against civilian objects ... the [United Kingdom] will regard itself as entitled to take measures otherwise prohibited by the [Protocol] to the extent that it considers such measures necessary for the sole purpose of compelling the adverse party to cease committing violations ... but only after formal warning ... requiring cessation of the violations has been disregarded and then only after a decision taken at the highest level of government'. This is the classic language of the *threat* of belligerent reprisals.

By contrast, the Geneva Conventions and the First Additional Protocol embody a much stronger commitment to the prosecution of war crimes with their provision of 'grave breaches' in international armed conflicts. A dual regime for enforcement is thus envisaged: whereas parties are 'under the obligation to search for persons alleged to have committed, or to have ordered to be committed, such grave breaches, and shall bring such persons, regardless of their nationality, before its own courts', they are only required to 'take measures necessary for the suppression of all acts contrary to the provisions of the present Convention other than grave breaches', including war crimes committed in non-international armed conflicts (the concern of common article 3 of the Conventions) (Plattner 1990). Looking at the plethora of rules in the Geneva Conventions – rules ranging from the prohibition of biological experimentation on civilian populations to the requirement of installing canteens in all prisoner-of-war camps – one can appreciate the need for such differentiation. But the limited implementation of these arrangements in practice (especially for non-international armed conflicts) has since been overtaken by the creation of international criminal tribunals, most notably the ICC, which has prosecutorial remit for war crimes committed in international and non-international armed conflicts, the crimes of aggression and genocide, and crimes against humanity.

The ICC possesses remarkable powers, including the ability to issue international arrest warrants against sitting heads of state such as President Al Bashir of Sudan; parties to the Statute of the Court are under a general obligation to co-operate (article 86) and to comply with requests for arrest and surrender (article 89). Thus far, the docket of the ICC has extended only to African situations (Uganda, Democratic Republic of Congo, Sudan, Central African Republic, Kenya, Côte d'Ivoire and Libya), leading to frequent claims of its inequitable decision processes and partiality. So-called hybrid courts have also flourished, such as the East Timor Special Panels for Serious Crimes (2000); the Special Court for Sierra Leone (2002); the Extraordinary Chambers of Cambodia (2003); the Iraqi High Tribunal (2003) and the Special Tribunal for Lebanon (2007). Collectively these should give us pause to reconsider continued assumptions of the absence of enforcement machineries within international law.

Admittedly, configuring systems for the enforcement of law in the thick of hostilities has proved more challenging than for the laws of peace; even if one could conceive of the possibility of a set of laws *for* hostilities, how could one ever ensure their effectiveness during the white heat of warfare? Or, as has been asked, '[s]hould there be battlefield wardens checking the weights of projectiles, like weights and measures inspectors in municipal halls?' (Lowe 2007, 264). No battlefield wardens made an appearance in the 1868 St Petersburg Declaration Renouncing the Use, in Times of War, of Explosive Projectiles under 400 Grammes in Weight, purporting to outlaw munitions that 'uselessly aggravate the sufferings of disabled men, or render their death inevitable'. In the case of the 1925 Geneva Protocol for the Prohibition of the Use in War of Asphyxiating, Poisonous or Other Gases, and of Bacteriological Methods of Warfare, many states followed the lead of France in subjecting its application to a 'first-use reservation' – that the Protocol 'shall *ipso facto* cease to be binding on the Government of the French Republic in regard to any enemy state whose armed forces or whose allies fail to respect the prohibitions laid down in the Protocol'. Strictly speaking, this did not involve any belligerent reprisal action, but it embedded the tactic of retaliatory action within the formal mechanics of the treaty – something that was not repeated in the Biological Weapons Conventions of 1972, whose various prohibitions are applicable 'in any circumstances'. Under article VI, parties who find any other party acting in breach of its obligations may lodge a complaint with the Security Council; all parties are obliged to cooperate with any investigation initiated by the

Council and to provide assistance upon request to any party if the Council has determined that that party has been exposed to danger as a result of a breach (article VII). Pursuant to article XII there is an annual reporting procedure of confidence-building measures, though efforts at securing a protocol for verification of compliance have so far been frustrated.

Contrast these arrangements with those of the Chemical Weapons Convention of 1993 which, in more robust terms than those of the Gas Protocol, admits no reservations. It established the Organisation for the Prohibition of Chemical Weapons (OPCW), based in The Hague, which is responsible for the implementation of the treaty. OPCW is given vital powers, including conducting routine on-site inspections as well as 'challenge inspections' on the request of any party 'of any facility or location under the jurisdiction or control of any other State party for the sole purpose of clarifying and resolving any questions concerning possible non-compliance' (article IX).

The Vienna Convention's reference to 'treaties of a humanitarian character' might also be taken to refer to human rights treaties, whether general (the 1966 UN Covenants on Civil and Political Rights and on Economic, Cultural and Social Rights) or thematic (the 1948 Genocide Convention; the 1965 Convention on the Elimination of All Forms of Racial Discrimination; the 1979 Convention on the Elimination of All Forms of Discrimination Against Women; the 1984 Convention against Torture and Other Cruel, Inhuman or Degrading Treatment or Punishment). For the most part, these treaty regimes operate by way of supervisory expert committees that receive reports from members, hear inter-state complaints and in some cases individual communications. They can make general suggestions, recommendations or comments, but cannot issue binding judgments. There is no equivalent of the regional human rights courts (as to which see Chapter 10). Even accounting for the provisions of the Genocide Convention, the question remains as to what is to be done in the actual event of aggravated or acute human rights abuses: the Security Council has regarded the repression of a civilian population as a threat to 'international peace and security in the region' (as in Iraq in Resolution 688 (1991)) or as an 'impending humanitarian catastrophe' (as with respect to Kosovo in Resolution 1199 (1998)). No action was authorised on either occasion, notwithstanding the fact that the Council had itself emphasised in Resolution 1199 'the need to prevent [the catastrophe] from happening'.

For Secretary-General Annan, this challenge ultimately concerned the 'enforcing' of international law in some general sense, and revolved around whether states had a 'right' of humanitarian intervention as they had claimed in Liberia (1990), northern Iraq (1991), southern Iraq (1992) and Kosovo (1999):

> To those for whom the greatest threat to the future of international order is the use of force in the absence of a Security Council mandate, one might say: leave Kosovo aside for a moment, and think about Rwanda. Imagine for one moment that, in those dark days and hours leading up to the genocide, there had been a coalition of states ready and willing to act in defence of the Tutsi population, but the Council had refused or delayed giving the green light. Should such a coalition then have stood idly by while the horror unfolded? To those for whom the Kosovo action heralded a new era when states and groups of states can take military action outside the established mechanisms for enforcing international law, one might equally ask: Is there not a danger of such interventions undermining the imperfect, yet resilient, security system created after the second world war, and of setting dangerous precedents for future interventions without a clear criterion to decide who might invoke these precedents and in what circumstances? Nothing in the UN Charter precludes a recognition that there are rights beyond borders. What the charter does say is that 'armed force shall not be used, save in the common interest'. But what is that common interest? Who shall define it? Who shall defend it? Under whose authority? And with what means of intervention?*

These age-old questions have returned rather forcefully in modern times. The paramount concern for action in urgent circumstances such as these has inspired the evolution of a 'responsibility to protect': see the International Commission on Intervention and State Sovereignty (2001); the UN High-Level Panel on Threats, Challenges and Change in *A More Secure World: Our Shared Responsibility* (2004); and the General Assembly in its World Summit Outcome (2005). According to *A More Secure World*, if a state fails to protect its own citizens, every state is to be engaged 'on assisting the cessation of violence through mediation and other tools and the protection of people through such measures as the dispatch of humanitarian, human rights and police missions. Force, if it needs to be used, should be deployed as a last resort' (para. 201). Cast in these terms, this appears to be more than a modern euphemism for the right of humanitarian intervention: its broader range of tools is envisaged within a specific framework of a 'responsibility' rather than

* Secretary-General Kofi A. Annan, Statement on Presentation of his Annual Report to the General Assembly, 20 September 1999, www.un.org/News/ossg/sg/stories/statments_search_full.asp?statID=28.

an entitlement to act. But what *kind* of responsibility is this to be? A responsibility that entails a legal obligation to act? Or a political and moral responsibility to test the consciousnesses of world leaders and global publics at any given time (Alvarez 2007, 11–12)? And what, if anything, does this proposition add to the debate on whether international law now permits humanitarian intervention independent of institutional authorisation or inaction? In their Kosovo intervention of March 1999, NATO members had to act extra-constitutionally in two respects – as regards the NATO Charter and the UN Charter – and, in consequence, had to make some sort of appeal to the right of humanitarian intervention. The Constitutive Act of the African Union of July 2000 has put on a treaty footing that Organisation's right to intervene in a member state pursuant to a decision of its Assembly in respect of grave circumstances, namely: war crimes, genocide and crimes against humanity (article 4(h)).

Of course treaty schemes are not immune to change. The General Agreement on Tariffs and Trade (GATT, 1947), which operated by consensus, transmuted into the World Trade Organisation (WTO, 1994) with its compulsory Understanding on Rules and Procedures Governing the Settlement of Disputes (DSU) and Dispute Settlement Body (DSB). The Law of the Sea Convention 1982 did something of the same by reference to the Geneva Conventions of 1958. The important factor here is the centrality of counter-measures common to both the GATT and the WTO, but also their different premises for the initiation of such measures. GATT relied on bilateral consultations, conciliation and panel reports to the GATT Council for adoption on consensus; failure to implement recommendations within a reasonable time could lead to the adoption of counter-measures once authorised by the Council. Under the WTO, bilateral consultations occur between disputing parties according to a rigorous timetable, followed by the possibility of good offices, conciliation or mediation. Failure of settlement could result in reference to the DSB that may establish a panel whose report is adopted *unless there is a consensus against adoption*; compliance with its recommendations must occur within a reasonable period, otherwise compensation must be agreed. If the dispute remains outstanding after this time, the DSB 'upon request, shall grant authorisation to suspend concessions or other obligations within 30 days of the expiry of the reasonable period of time unless the DSB decides by consensus to reject the request' (article 22(2) DSU).

The essentially automatic operation of counter-measures within the WTO might at first seem a mature method of securing effective and swift justice for world trade, at least when compared with the ICJ, which has no equivalent powers to compel compliance with its judgments (a matter for referral to the Security Council by affected states under article 94(2) of the Charter). However, the record of WTO practice suggests that this new system has been 'stranded against the wall of noncompliance', due in no small measure to 'an enforcement problem' (Pauwelyn 2000, 338), where counter-measures have become but one further prop on the field of power politics (e.g. as between the European Union and the United States). This should not come as a surprise, but it does suggest scope to expand the repertoire of remedies available within the WTO to include compensation for damage caused including loss of profits, and to make the application of 'counter-measures' more of a collective endeavour beyond the simple act of authorisation of the organisation. We have seen an alternative at work with article XII(3) of the Chemical Weapons Convention. Similarly article 33 of the Constitution of the International Labour Organisation (ILO) provides that if any member fails to carry out recommendations contained in the report of a commission of inquiry or in an ICJ decision, the governing body of the organisation 'may recommend to the conference such action as it may deem wise and expedient to secure compliance forthwith'. Such was the fate of Myanmar (Burma) when, in an unprecedented resolution of May 2000, the ILO recommended to its constituents (governments, employers and workers) 'that they review their relations with Myanmar and take appropriate measures to ensure that such relations do not perpetuate or extend the system of forced or compulsory labour in that country'. The Convention on International Trade in Endangered Species of Wild Fauna and Flora of March 1973 has also, in addition to a system of warnings and formal cautions for recalcitrant states, operated a system of recommending country-specific or species-specific suspensions of trade since 1985 (Reeve 2007, 150–151, 159).

Another technique with respect to treaties that should be mentioned is their potential application within domestic courts. In *LaGrand* (ICJ Reports 2001, p. 466), the ICJ noted that the 1963 Vienna Convention on Consular Relations 'admits of no doubt' in conferring rights upon individuals, and that these rights may be invoked before it by the national state of and on behalf of the detained person. Article 13 of the European Convention of Human Rights also makes provision for an 'effective remedy' for those bearing rights and freedoms under the Convention before relevant authorities of the contracting parties. The 1965 Convention on the Settlement of Investment Disputes Between States and Nationals of Other States, which created the International Centre for Settlement of Investment Disputes (ICSID) to administer *ad hoc* investment arbitrations between states and investors, provides that each contracting state shall recognise the awards of arbitration tribunals as binding 'and enforce the pecuniary obligations imposed by that award within its territories as if it were a final judgment of a court in that State' (article 54). The mechanism is now included in numerous bilateral investment treaties.

Conclusion

To conclude, international law had already developed a system of enforcement by the time of Austin's reflections in the nineteenth century – one that placed the burden squarely on the shoulders of states themselves. Austin took little or no notice of the varied instruments of state action in his celebrated dismissal of international law: to have done otherwise would have required some understanding of the actual dispositions of states, as reflected in the blunt instruments they had devised for themselves over time; indeed the prevailing attitude appears to have been the blunter the better. But as Thomas Franck argued (1990), 'powerless' rules of international law are in fact obeyed by powerful and less powerful states; so that international law can be said to exist apart from any arrangements for its enforcement.

This chapter has sought to chronicle the remnants of the Vattelian order, essentially the rights of individual and collective self-defence as well as (unarmed) counter-measures, which have accompanied the advent of the UN Charter. We have observed the momentous shift to 'sanctions' that occurred through international organisations in the twentieth century – now seen as integral to the workings of the legal order. These schemes of enforcement have come to co-exist with techniques developed in selected treaty relations: as the ICJ admitted in the *Nicaragua* case, 'it was never intended that the Charter should embody written confirmation of every essential principle of international law in force'. The details of enforcement have thus emerged from the specifics of the various treaties, which need to be read against the broader background of the evolution of permissible methods of enforcement in international law. Certainly these developments have been uneven and imperfect, but they can be interpreted as preludes to a more advanced normative system which commands the increased respect of states as well as other actors. Throughout, we have maintained how international law has produced a variegated system of enforcement that is defined and shaped by the particularities of norms themselves – its relativities essentially encoded in each of the laws that it provides for.

Bibliography

Alvarez, J. E., 2007. 'The Schizophrenias of R2P', *ASIL Newsletter*, 23, 1–12

Austin, J., 1995. *The Province of Jurisprudence Determined*, W. Rumble (ed.), Cambridge University Press

Bowett, D. W., 1958. *Self-Defence in International Law*, Manchester University Press

Bowett, D. W., 1974. 'The Interrelation of Theories of Intervention and Self-defence', in J. Moore (ed.), *Law and Civil War in the Modern World*, Baltimore, MD: Johns Hopkins University Press, 38–50

Brierly, J., 1963. *The Law of Nations: An Introduction to the International Law of Peace*, 6th edn., H. Waldock (ed.), Oxford: Clarendon Press

Crawford, J., 2002. *The International Law Commission's Articles on State Responsibility: Introduction, Text and Commentaries*, Cambridge University Press

Dugard, J., 1987. *Recognition and the United Nations*, Cambridge: Grotius Publications

Finnemore, M., 2003. *The Purpose of Intervention: Changing Beliefs About the Use of Force*, Ithaca, NY: Cornell University Press

Fitzmaurice, G., 1956. 'The Foundations of the Authority of International Law and the Problem of Enforcement', *Modern Law Review*, 19, 1–13

Franck, T., 1990. *The Power of Legitimacy Among Nations*, Oxford University Press

Gow, J., 1997. *Triumph of the Lack of Will: International Diplomacy and the Yugoslav War*, London: Hurst & Co.

Gowlland-Debbas, V. (ed.), 2002. *United Nations Sanctions and International Law*, The Hague, London and Boston: Kluwer Law International

Greenwood, C., 1992. 'New World Order or Old? The Invasion of Kuwait and the Rule of Law', *Modern Law Review*, 55, 153–178

Grotius, H., 1625. *De jure belli ac pacis*

Jennings, R. and A. Watts (eds.), 1992. *Oppenheim's International Law, Vol. 1: Peace*, 9th edn., London and New York: Longman

Kelsen, H., 1946. 'Sanctions in International Law under the Charter of the United Nations', *Iowa Law Review*, 31, 499–543

Kelsen, H., 1951. *The Law of the United Nations: A Critical Analysis of Its Fundamental Problems*, London: Stevens & Sons

Lauterpacht, H., 1936. 'The Covenant As "Higher Law"', *British Yearbook of International Law*, 17, 54–65

Lauterpacht, H., 1947. *Recognition in International Law*, Cambridge University Press

Lowe, V., 2003. 'The Iraq Crisis: What Now?', *International & Comparative Law Quarterly*, 52, 859–871

Lowe, V., 2007. *International Law*, Oxford University Press

Oppenheim, L., 1952. *International Law: A Treatise, Vol. II: Disputes, War and Neutrality*, 7th edn., London, New York and Toronto: Longmans, Green & Co.

Pauwelyn, J., 2000. 'Enforcement and Counter-measures in the WTO: Rules are Rules – Toward A More Collective Approach', *American Journal of International Law*, 94, 335–347

Plattner, D., 1990. 'The Penal Repression of Violations of International Humanitarian Law Applicable in Non-international Armed Conflict', *International Review of the Red Cross*, 30, 409–420

Reeve, R., 2007. 'The Convention on International Trade in Endangered Species of Wild Fauna and Flora (CITES)', in G. Ulfstein, T. Marauhn and A. Zimmermann (eds.), *Making Treaties Work: Human Rights, Environment and Arms Control*, Cambridge University Press, pp. 134–160

Riesman W. M., and D. L. Stevick, 1998. 'The Applicability of International Law Standards to United Nations Economic Sanctions Programmes', *European Journal of International Law*, 9, 86–141

Sansom, G., 1965. *The Western World and Japan*, New York: Alfred A. Knopf

Sinclair, I., 1984. *The Vienna Convention on the Law of Treaties*, 2nd edn., Manchester University Press

Stone, J., 1954. *Legal Controls of International Conflict: A Treatise on the Dynamics of Disputes- and War-Law*, London: Stevens & Sons

UN General Assembly, 2005. World Summit Outcome, A/RES/60/1

UN High-Level Panel on Threats, Challenges and Changes, 2004. *A More Secure World: Our Shared Responsibility, Report*, A/59/565, 2 December

Vattel, E., 2008. *The Law of Nations or the Principles of Natural Law Applied to the Conduct and to the Affairs of Nations and of Sovereigns*, reprinted, Indianapolis: Liberty Fund

Zoller, E., 1984. *Peacetime Unilateral Remedies: An Analysis of Counter-measures*, Dobbs Ferry, NY: Transnational Publishers

Part IV

Projects of international law

Constituting order 12

Anne Orford*

Introduction

The proper relation between law and order has long been a contested one. Attempting to determine the proper relation between *international* law and *international* order is an even more difficult task. Does international law exist to create and maintain international order? Should this be one of the functions of international law? If so, what kind of order is international law designed to secure and maintain? Does constituting order always take priority over all other goals, values or interests? Who decides? These are particularly difficult questions for international lawyers, because international law has predominantly been understood as a means of governing relations between sovereign states. In this view, states are the authors of law and the bearers of pluralism. International law only exists to the extent that sovereign states consent to be bound by specific obligations. International law, like private law, is thus portrayed as a system for governing relations between equals. In the case of international law, the equality of subjects plays an even more fundamental role than in domestic legal systems, where the idea that agreements must be honoured finds a guarantor in the state. Because international law is a system in which there is no higher guarantor, international jurisprudence is strongly shaped by the notion of consent and by the idea that law only exists to bind states to their commitments. According to this view, international lawyers fulfil their function when they find ways for these alienated entities to express their national interests or their instrumental objectives in the law they bring into being.

The idea that international law has a legitimate role to play in constituting international order or, even more ambitiously, representing an international order that is already constituted, remains controversial. Indeed, it has been an on-going challenge for international lawyers to explain how order could be created and maintained in such a system, either in terms of 'order' as a factual

* This chapter draws in part on Anne Orford, *International Authority and the Responsibility to Protect* (Cambridge University Press, 2011).

alternative to anarchy or in terms of 'order' as an authoritative regime that exists beyond the state. The assertion that international law has that kind of public law function has been made with greatest vigour during periods of revolution in the European state system: the bourgeois revolutions of the eighteenth century, the communist revolutions of the twentieth century and the revolution that is decolonisation. Those who believe that international law can and should play a part in constituting order have embraced it as a vehicle for wide-ranging public projects designed to reorder the world, from dividing up Africa at the end of the nineteenth century, to ending the scourge of war, managing decolonisation, humanising warfare and liberalising trade in the twentieth century. The strongest current advocates of a vision of an international order constituted by law are the cosmopolitan formalists of continental Europe, while the most vocal critics of that vision are the realists of the Anglo-American tradition. Each is defending a projection of power imagined in their own terms – one a form of power that depends upon the operation of international institutions envisaged as having moral authority, the other a form of power that depends upon the operation of largely bilateral relations premised upon economic or military domination. This chapter explores the oscillation between freedom and order, the part and the whole, that underpins these competing visions of international law.

The authority of the state and the priority of order

The question of how order might be secured in a world without universal values or shared traditions has been a central one for European thinkers since at least the sixteenth century. Martin Luther and John Calvin inaugurated a debate about the relation between the liberty of the Christian subject and the lawfulness of civil authority that has not yet ended. Protestant reformers proclaimed that the kingdom of God was still to come and there was thus no worldly power that could claim divine authority. The wars of religion that raged throughout Europe in the following centuries undermined appeals to a universal and shared set of values that might ground political and legal authority (Tuck 1987, 118). Competing religious beliefs and the post-sceptical spirit of the new sciences shook the foundations of established political orders. How worldly authority could be justified under such conditions became a pressing question. The state emerged as one solution to that Protestant problem of the relation between freedom and order.

Thomas Hobbes, for example, famously urged his compatriots to accept that the commonwealth represented the individual's best chance for self-preservation in a time of civil war. In his classic treatise *Leviathan*, Hobbes sought to explain why it was rational to submit to a political authority capable of containing warring religious factions and creating order out of the dangerous anarchy of the state of nature (Hobbes 1651 [1996]). Hobbes did not seek to justify authority by reference to tradition, inheritance, a shared set of moral values or some authentic relationship with God or the people. Rather, he argued that the creation of political order in conditions of civil war depended upon the establishment of a common power with the capacity to protect its subjects. An earthly power was needed to bring into being a condition in which the first and most fundamental principle of natural law – that men '*seek peace and follow it* ' – could be realised on earth (*ibid.*, 87). The problem in a situation of civil war was how to allow natural law to become reality. Order was not opposed to justice, but to war. According to Hobbes, men covenanted with each other as equals to bring into being a sovereign power for a particular end, 'the procuration of *the safety of the people*' (*ibid.*, 222). The lawful authority was the one who could achieve protection in the broad sense of bringing into being a condition in which order and the safety of the people could be achieved. The 'obligation of subjects' to obey the sovereign would 'last as long, and no longer, than the power lasteth, by which he is able to protect them' (*ibid.*, 147).

In appealing to *de facto* authority, Hobbes was seeking to challenge at least two other claimants to authority whose justification to rule was based on claims of right rather than fact, or justice rather than order. First, he was seeking to challenge the authority of the Pope and the Holy Roman Emperor. The idea that the papacy and the Emperor exercised dual forms of universal jurisdiction shaped medieval legal thought. The extent of papal and imperial jurisdiction, and the relation between jurisdiction and order, had important implications both within and beyond Europe. For example, questions about the extent of papal jurisdiction were at the heart of the dispute about the legitimacy of Alexander VI's bulls of donation through which the Spanish Crown claimed *dominium* over the New World. The papal bull *Inter caetera*, issued in 1493, granted to 'the illustrious sovereigns' King Ferdinand and Queen Isabella, and to their 'heirs and successors, kings of Castile and Leon', 'all islands and mainlands found and to be found, discovered and to be discovered' in the Atlantic world 'towards the west and south' of a line bisecting the Atlantic ocean (Alexander VI 1493 [1917]).

The Spanish crown interpreted *Inter caetera* and the other Bulls of Donation as grants that authorised Spanish *dominium* over the lands they 'discovered' in the New World. The Bulls continued to be invoked both by Spain and its imperial rivals in debates over the legal justifications for Spanish conquest of the New World until the late seventeenth century. For instance when Sir Francis Drake returned to England after his circumnavigation of the world in September 1580 with reports of having claimed land including Nova Albion and with commodities from the West Indies and South America, the Spanish Ambassador Mendoza lodged a formal complaint with Queen Elizabeth. Mendoza claimed 'that these territories belonged to the King of Spain by virtue of first discovery and the papal bull of donation' (MacMillan 2006, 75).

In return, most attacks on Spanish claims to sovereignty in the New World rejected the validity of the Bulls. Perhaps the most famous of these were the challenges to Spanish conquest of the New World posed by Francisco de Vitoria and his followers. Vitoria argued that 'the pope has no dominion (*dominium*) in the lands of the infidel' and those who think that he 'has temporal authority and jurisdiction over all princes in the world, are wrong' (Vitoria 1532 [1991], 84). According to Vitoria, '*the pope has no power, at least in the ordinary course of events, to judge the cases of princes, or the titles of jurisdictions or realms* . . .' (*ibid.*, 87). While Vitoria did accept that the Pope had authority 'to use temporal means' where necessary to fulfil a spiritual purpose, that did not give the Pope authority to allocate rights of *imperium* and *dominium* in the New World (*ibid.*, 92). The spiritual jurisdiction of the Pope did not extend to the temporal world.

In addition to debates over the extent of the spiritual jurisdiction exercised by the Pope, the extent of the Holy Roman Emperor's jurisdiction was also contested. The secular jurisdiction of the Holy Roman Emperor was conceived of as universal. The medieval jurist Bartolus of Sassoferrato made this clear in his defence of the claim that the Emperor was lord of the world despite the fact that there were numerous foreign peoples, cities and kings who did not obey him. Bartolus sought to show that the Emperor's universal jurisdiction could survive and co-exist with the new forms of territorial jurisdiction beginning to be exercised by princes and kings. The Emperor was lord of the world, not because he was lord of all the particular things, places, and people in the world, but rather because 'he alone had dominium over the world considered as a single whole' (Fasolt 2004, 192). Bartolus defended this claim by distinguishing between the universal jurisdiction of the Emperor and the particular jurisdictions of other rulers, such as the Kings of England and France. The two could co-exist because they were of a different nature. The universal jurisdiction of the Emperor involved jurisdiction over the world as a whole rather than as a collection of 'particular things', while the jurisdiction of Kings constituted jurisdiction over particular things (such as England or France). Jurisdiction was not an effect of power, but a form of power (Fasolt 2004, 192). The Emperor had universal jurisdiction over the world as a matter of right, not as a question of fact. However, when ambitious monarchs like Charles V or Ferdinand II succeeded to the title of Emperor, they sought to combine temporal authority with the universal rights to which they felt entitled as rulers of the Roman Empire. As a result, the reach of imperial authority became far worldlier and more threatening to peace in Europe.

The rulers of emerging states in Europe thus faced 'two universal antagonists outside their own realms' in the form of the Papacy and the Empire (Armitage 2000, 33). Both the Pope and the Emperor claimed universal jurisdiction, understood as the power to state what is lawful for the whole world. Those like Hobbes who championed state power sought to counter papal and imperial authority with detailed arguments showing why the claim to be *dominus mundi* or lord of the world was flawed. These statist arguments were premised on the claim that sovereignty, and thus jurisdiction, depended upon *de facto* control over territory. Worldly authority, to be legitimate, must be effective at maintaining order.

Second, by refusing to anchor the legitimacy of the state in its capacity to represent a romantic or historical collectivity of the people, Hobbes 'pulled the rug out' from under arguments based on the nation as a 'platform of resistance' to tyranny or misrule (Hont 2005, 130). The Norman Conquest had become a live political issue in seventeenth-century England – revolutionaries argued that the rule of the aristocracy, the King and indeed all property relations were invalidated by the Conquest. The disparaging of the 'Norman Yoke' was the language of the Levellers and others seeking to challenge the absolutism of James I and his advisors (Sharp 1998; Hill 1997). Hobbes was answering that historicist claim when he argued that it does not matter how a commonwealth was created, nor the form its government takes. After all, he comments, 'there is scarce a commonwealth in the world, whose beginnings can in conscience be justified' (Hobbes 1651 [1996], 479). His defence of power was based on its present efficacy rather than the validity of its origins. Hobbes argued that the continual debate about the legitimacy of the conditions under which authority was first constituted was radically destabilising and ultimately irresolvable. The authority of the state was simply grounded on its capacity in fact to ensure protection in accordance with the terms of the covenant.

The linkage of authority and order thus emerged alongside the modern state, as a way of distinguishing the state's *de facto* capacity to protect from *de jure* claims to authority made by revolutionaries, the Pope, the Holy Roman Emperor and rival claimants to territory in the New World (Orford 2009). Authority was not a matter of right, but a consequence of the fact of control. Yet this left open the question of how peace was to be guaranteed in a world consisting of alienated identities with no shared values. How could order be created in the ruins of Christian Europe? While this question was posed with new urgency in the aftermath of the wars of religion, the practice of encountering alien faiths and peoples was not completely novel for early modern Europeans. Italian states from at least the fourteenth century had been involved in commercial and diplomatic relations with the Ottoman Empire. Italian jurists, envoys and merchants, particularly the Genoese, Florentine and Venetian sojourners to the Ottoman Empire, had developed or borrowed protocols and techniques for encountering other laws, and these techniques shaped the practices of diplomacy and commerce that would be used to develop relations between European states (Goffman 2007). Drawing on that experience, norms and protocols governing the movement, immunity and privileges of diplomats would become one of the earliest forms of international law to develop in Europe (Mattingly 1955). The early development of ideas about the laws of war, trade and treaty-making also grew out of the experience of European commercial and political expansion into Asia and the Americas. For example, the problems addressed by the School of Salamanca were shaped by the problematic Spanish colonisation of the Americas. Their solutions in turn informed the approach taken by the young Hugo Grotius to the issues of commerce, war and alliance that arose while Grotius was an employee of the Dutch East India Company and a negotiator on behalf of the Dutch Republic at the Anglo-Dutch Colonial Conferences held in 1613 and 1615 (Borschberg 1999).

Thus by the seventeenth century European jurists, envoys and merchants had already developed a body of practices for encountering strangers in situations lacking any higher authority to guarantee the truth of one law rather than another. Norms and protocols dealing with diplomatic protection, the conduct of war, treaty-making and trade would inform the development of an international law that could govern relations between the newly sovereign states of Europe. Over time, that network of relations, treaties and practices would be relied upon as the basis for constituting new orders both within and beyond Europe.

Recognition and order in the age of revolution

With the gradual triumph of the modern state as the dominant political form in Europe and the demise of the Holy Roman Empire, debates over the divisibility of power ceased to be framed in terms of the competition between imperial and state jurisdiction. However, this is not to say that power was thought to have been unified in the form of the sovereign, as the mythologising of absolutist theorists of the state would seem to suggest. It was certainly no longer plausible to argue that the Pope or the Holy Roman Emperor had universal jurisdiction as lord of the world, while princes had rights to particular jurisdiction, and that both forms of jurisdiction could apply to the same territory. However, the idea that power might be divided, or that people, places and things might be subject to plural sources of law, did not disappear. Instead, it changed form. In particular, it persisted in a series of debates that inform contemporary international law.

The first debate concerns the effect of the recognition of a government or of a new state by external actors. Early modern state theorists such as Hobbes had proposed that the representative of lawful authority is recognisable as the one capable of guaranteeing protection, but this left open the question of who has the worldly responsibility to recognise the legitimacy of rulers. Who is responsible for bestowing recognition upon a government? Who decides whether an authority is functioning effectively? Who decides what security looks like, and whether achieving it is always more important than anything else? According to the declaratory theory, which was dominant until at least the late eighteenth century, the legal status of a ruler was understood to be determined internally. Within Europe, the law of nature and of nations had little to say about the basis of state legitimacy. The question of whether a duly appointed or elected ruler properly had authority over territory was not treated as a question for inter-state relations. When the people of a state elected a ruler, that election could not be challenged by other states. If the legitimacy of a government were understood to depend upon external recognition or championing by external powers, the uneasy peace that existed in the aftermath of the European wars of religion could quickly unravel.

Yet beginning in the early nineteenth century, the law of nations began to treat statehood as a question that was not perfected and determined internally. Jurists were confronted with frequent changes in the membership of the family of nations as a result of revolutions in Europe and the New World, and questions about the normative criteria of statehood began to appear in urgent need of resolution. International legal doctrine began to suggest that while internal sovereignty could be determined by the people of a state, external sovereignty required action on the part of other members of the community. States began to treat external recognition as the act that perfected sovereignty (Alexandrowicz 1958). In that sense, *de facto* control over territory was no longer sufficient to ground a claim to statehood.

Questions about whether fact or right should determine membership of the family of nations were also shaped by the experience of empire. The expansion and nature of the British Empire played a major role in shaping notions about membership of the family of nations during the nineteenth century. Though European states had long entered into commercial relations and treaties with Ottomans, British international lawyers were at the forefront of the nineteenth-century revisionist history that treated the Ottoman Empire as incapable of being included in the membership of the family of nations (Pitts 2007). By the end of the nineteenth century, the problem international lawyers had set themselves was how to create order 'amongst entities characterized as belonging to entirely different cultural systems' (Anghie 2005, 37). Their solutions included sociological projects such as that of the *Institut de droit international* aimed at determining as a matter of fact whether the beliefs and practices of Oriental peoples precluded them from admission to the community of nations (Koskenniemi 2001, 132), and developmental techniques for bridging the gap between Europe and its others or 'civilizing the uncivilized' (Anghie 2005, 37). The centuries-long history of European states entering into trade and diplomatic relations, treaties and alliances with rulers outside Europe was ignored or reinterpreted. That history would only be revisited again in the era of decolonisation, in the context of judicial findings that the eighteenth-century law of nations allowed for the recognition of the legal personality of an independent Asian state (*Right of Passage over Indian Territory*, ICJ Reports 1960, 35, 87) and in scholarship pointing to numerous treaties entered into by the Dutch, Portuguese, British and French prior to the nineteenth century recognising extra-European rulers as sovereign (Alexandrowicz 1961; Anand 1972).

A second debate about international ordering that would be taken up by jurists concerned the question of how to prevent any one state from becoming a new imperial power. This issue was of particular concern within Europe following the French revolution and the rise of Napoleon, and beyond Europe as mercantile powers sought to prevent any one state acquiring imperial dominance or control over trade in the New World. The idea that public order depended upon the creation of a balance of power between the independent sovereign states of Europe based upon treaty law emerged as a response to the challenge posed by the French revolution to Europe as a system of monarchies and by Napoleonic imperialism to Europe as a system of independent states (Keene 2002, 17–22). The notion that the foundations of European order had been established by a network of treaty obligations recognising the balance of power as a 'constituent principle' of international society would continue to shape thinking about international order into the twentieth century, particularly through the influence of Lassa Oppenheim on international law and the English School on international relations (Butterfield 1966; Wight 1966; Kingsbury 2002). Attempts to prevent any one state acquiring imperial dominance or control over trade in the New World also shaped the development of doctrines that treated freedom of trade, freedom of navigation and the appropriation of uncultivated waste lands as fundamental rights that could not be monopolised by any one European power (Grotius 1605 [2006]; Locke 1689 [1993]).

A third way in which the challenge to absolutist notions of state sovereignty persisted was in relation to the question of whether individuals within a state had fundamental rights that derived from a source other than the positive law of the state. While states were understood to have public authority over all people and things within their jurisdiction, from the seventeenth century onwards private individuals were also understood to have a form of subjective right to property in their persons, liberty, and estates that could co-exist with, and constrain, public authority. These inalienable property rights were argued to derive from a source other than social, political, or legal convention and to limit governmental power. The claim that the scope of such rights and freedoms were matters of truth that lay beyond the jurisdiction of the state strengthened those voluntary civil organisations that claimed to represent the moral authority of conscience (Koselleck 1988, 183), and fuelled both internal rebellion and external invasion.

From the nineteenth century onwards, the idea that the spheres of private life and civil society were subject to truths or laws that lay beyond the jurisdiction of the state also began to empower those who claimed knowledge of the higher truths that governed the economic realm and were beyond the sovereign's comprehension. The claim that sovereignty was divisible, and that private rights and economic freedoms might co-exist with and at times trump public authority, was used both to champion the rights of European individuals vis-à-vis European authority and to champion the rights of private European actors in their relations with non-European rulers. The notion of subjective rights thus supported the authority both of civil society and of private trading companies. The question of how best to ensure the protection of such rights and freedoms has ever since been understood as part of the project of international ordering.

Thus although by the end of the nineteenth century the state would appear to have emerged as the dominant political form in Europe, the state's claim to authority as the guarantor of order and the protector of freedom was not unchallenged. At periods of revolution and change, European jurists and philosophers had tended to stress the public and constitutive character of the task facing international law. Three significant limitations on the authority of the state – the idea that an external authority might exist that could determine the legitimacy of particular claimants to rule, the idea that the obligations of international society might override imperialist ambitions and the idea that state power was limited by an overriding responsibility to respect individual rights and market freedoms – converged with the turn to international institutions in the twentieth century. The creation of the United Nations, the World Bank and the International Monetary Fund (IMF) after the Second World War saw universal institutions once again begin to claim a significant role in determining the legitimacy of governments and the proper limits of state power.

Maintaining order and protecting life: international authority in the decolonised world

International law has long treated effective control over territory as an important criterion of statehood. In that sense, statehood is premised upon *de facto* authority. Yet the creation of the United Nations in 1945 saw the emergence of an international legal regime in which the principles of self-determination, sovereign equality and the prohibition against acquisition of territory through the use of force were also treated as central to determining the lawfulness of particular claimants to authority (Crawford 2006, 96). It was these principles that would shape the process of decolonisation and delegitimise imperial rule. The preamble of the UN Charter also expressed a determination 'to reaffirm faith in fundamental human rights' and 'the dignity and worth of the human person'. That faith would inform the body of international human rights law and international humanitarian law that developed over the course of the twentieth century as a constraint on state action. Under the UN Charter, the lawfulness of authority over a given territory was thus treated as a matter both of fact and of right.

That understanding of state authority informed the way that the UN Charter attempted to formulate the relationship between state and international jurisdiction. As the authority of sovereign states was understood to be an expression both of effective control over territory and of fundamental principles such as the right to self-determination, external intervention in the internal affairs of states was *prima facie* illegitimate. Yet because the legitimacy of state authority had become a matter for international law, as overseen by an organisation with supranational authority, intervention in the internal affairs of states must also, in some circumstances, be legitimate. As the earlier debates about the role of external actors in recognising elected monarchs or revolutionary states made clear, the treatment of authority as a matter for international law opened up new possibilities for destabilising external intervention and new threats to peace. It was the task of the UN Charter to articulate the jurisdictional grounds upon which the new organisation might exercise its authority to police and perfect the state, while at the same time establishing a commitment to fundamental principles of sovereign equality and self-determination.

The task initially envisaged for post-war institutions by international lawyers was the relatively modest one of harnessing the cooperative spirit required of allies during the war to rebuild a world order out of the ruins of depression, nationalist protectionism and total war (Woolsey 1942). Yet the powers needed to engage in that project of recreating world order were interpreted broadly. In an approach endorsed by the International Court of Justice (ICJ) early in the history of the organisation, the United Nations was 'deemed to have those powers, which, though not expressly provided in the Charter, are conferred on it by necessary implication as being essential to the performance of its duties' (*Reparation for Injuries suffered in the Service of the United Nations*, ICJ Reports 1949, 174, 182). With the successful UN interventions in Suez in 1956 and the Congo in 1960, the role envisaged for the United Nations as an agent of international executive rule began to expand. The Suez and Congo operations initiated a set of practices aimed at maintaining order and protecting life that grew rapidly during the era of decolonisation. Those practices were initiated during the early years of decolonisation by then UN Secretary-General Dag Hammarskjöld. Hammarskjöld argued forcefully that it was necessary to stop thinking of the United Nations merely as a forum for 'static conference diplomacy' and instead re-imagine it as a 'dynamic instrument' for 'executive action, undertaken on behalf of all members' (UN Secretary-General 1961, 1).

Although Hammarskjöld recognised that the UN Charter gave little attention to the development of the executive aspects of the organisation, he did not interpret this as a limitation on executive action. Instead, he argued that the United Nations' 'executive functions and their form' had 'been left largely to practice' (*ibid.*, 5). According to Hammarskjöld, it had become necessary to develop those inchoate executive functions in response to the twinned challenges posed by decolonisation and the Cold War. The United Nations had a responsibility to protect newly independent states from external interference. That responsibility could best be met by taking action to fill the 'power vacuums' that were arising as the colonial system was being 'liquidated' (*ibid.*, 7). By taking such action, the United Nations could occupy the position of guarantor of order and protector of life otherwise claimed in bad faith by powerful states seeking to control the choices made by the peoples of the decolonised world in general, and Africa in particular. That in turn would prevent the extension of the Cold War to those regions. The maintenance of peace and the protection of independent states were therefore linked.

For Oscar Schachter, reflecting a decade later upon the developments that had occurred during Hammarskjöld's tenure as Secretary-General, the expansion of 'executive action' was 'widely regarded as constituting a major feature' of Hammarskjöld's 'political legacy'. Although the forms of executive action developed by Hammarskjöld might 'not at first seem to be related to international law', Schachter argued that in fact they 'have an impact on the evolution of the standards of international behaviour, and the effective implementation of such standards'. Collective actions necessarily create 'new conceptions of permissible and impermissible interference' as well as new conceptions 'of the Charter obligations for mutual assistance and co-operation'. Such actions can therefore be 'regarded in a broader and more subtle sense' as giving 'a new dimension to the efforts to give rigor and efficacy to a normative structure based on the common interest of all peoples' (Schachter 1962, 8).

In the context of decolonisation, the need to engage in an active process of constituting international order had again become a task for international law, in the sense posited by the counter-revolutionary theorists of post-Napoleonic Europe. Grotius would become the intellectual forebear of choice for the complex twentieth-century project of discerning the ordering principles of a new international society from institutional charters or treaty relations, while attempting not to legitimise revolutionary natural law concepts of self-determination or fundamental rights in the process. Today doctrines like the responsibility to protect concept and the practice of including protection mandates in peace-keeping operations continue to strengthen the idea that the United Nations has the responsibility and the capacity to maintain order and protect life in the decolonised world. In claiming this authority, the United Nations has challenged other twentieth-century visions of world order, such as those projected by the British and the French at Suez or the Belgians in the Congo. Yet the United Nations has replaced those imperial visions of order with a new form of international executive rule (Orford 2011).

The project of creating and sustaining international order has also been central to the expanding role of other international institutions. For example, the establishment at Bretton Woods in 1944 of the World Bank and the IMF as institutions founded upon concepts of 'universality, equality and progressive liberalisation' was treated as the realisation of attempts to facilitate 'the future economic ordering of the world' (James 1996, 37, 58). In concert with the massive programme of American aid and the reconstruction of Western Europe implemented through the Marshall Plan, the creation of the Bretton Woods Institutions and the negotiation of the General Agreement on Tariffs and Trade (GATT) were central to establishing a set of relations and practices that projected American corporate capitalism into Europe and its former colonies.

Third World states have repeatedly challenged the division between public and private that this economic ordering produced, notably through the attempt in the 1970s to create a New International Economic Order (NIEO). The IMF, World Bank and the younger World Trade Organisation (WTO) have nonetheless proved to be extremely effective globalisers of a particular vision of economic order (Woods 2006). The IMF and the World Bank have had a significant effect on the policies of governments in those states seeking to make use of their resources through the imposition of conditions on access to credits and loans. Most people are familiar with the 'structural adjustment' conditions attached to the use of IMF and World Bank resources during the 1980s and 1990s. Those conditions generally required countries to adopt policies of foreign investment deregulation, privatisation, cuts to government spending, labour market deregulation, lowering of minimum wages, and a focus on production of goods for export rather than domestic consumption. Equally controversial were the so-called 'shock therapy' programmes implemented from the late 1980s throughout Eastern Europe. Membership of the WTO poses another source of constraint on the choices open to peoples and governments. The creation of the WTO at the completion of the Uruguay Round of GATT trade negotiations in 1995 saw a significant expansion in the range of activities brought within the scope of the international trade regime. The regulatory harmonisation required of WTO members extends to areas such as intellectual property protection, provision of services, foreign investment regulation, labelling, regulation of genetically modified foods and biotechnology, and public and animal health and safety laws (Orford 2003). Once a rule is agreed to as part of a trade negotiation it is very difficult to alter it, while the importance of the WTO for all its members means that the costs of withdrawal are enormous (Howse 2002, 107). The resulting irreversibility of obligations entered into under trade agreements has significant effects on the regulatory capacity of states.

The obligations overseen by these economic institutions have shifted the boundaries between collective welfare and private interest in the name of encouraging 'nation-states, and markets, not to stand in the way of increased general prosperity' (James 1996, 4). The judgments of international economic institutions have reduced the policy choices available to goverments, even where states are not directly subject to conditions imposed by such institutions or constrained by trade agreements. A particular representation of globalisation has played an important role in limiting the scope for political action in democratic countries that have adopted neoliberal economic policies. Many governments of industrialised states and their economic advisers argue that globalisation and the attendant need to attract newly mobile capital necessitates significant restructuring of political, social, and cultural life and institutions. The threat of 'unlimited options for capital exit' as a result of the deregulation of investment measures and financial markets acts as a constraint on economic, social, industrial, and cultural policy-making (Piven 1995, 109). Governments make use of an internationalist discourse about the need to adjust to a changing world economy in order to ensure that citizens endorse 'the modernizing actions taken by the state on their behalf' (Morris 1992, 76). The idea that there exists a global economic order in which states are subject to onerous legal and political constraints legitimises the development of a culture in which political decisions that would once have been at least theoretically within the realm of parliamentary decision-making, popular sovereignty or democratic government, are now made by experts in economics. The inability of many people to contest and challenge decisions about issues that shape their lives is presented as inevitable and natural – a consequence of the disciplines and requirements of international competitiveness and the shared vulnerabilities produced by globalisation (Orford 1997).

Instituting order: the work of law and politics

The logical end-point of a statist approach to international law would seem to be that any such new forms of expansive international jurisdiction must be the product of state consent. If a body other than a state has a particular form of jurisdiction, this can only have resulted from the decision of states to vest jurisdiction in that body. Yet the practice of the United Nations during the era of decolonisation reveals the persistence of an older European tradition for thinking about law, in which jurisdiction or the power of stating what is lawful do not derive simply from control over territory or the consent of sovereigns. In seventeenth-century Europe, the law of nations left it to the people of a state to decide whether a particular claimant to authority was in fact capable of guaranteeing their protection because it could still be assumed that Europeans were part of a shared culture. In the latter half of the twentieth century the 'rebirth of Asia and Africa' once again shattered 'the imagined calm of the closed world' upon which European international law was founded (Hammarskjöld 1959 [1962a]). The United Nations and its organs derived their jurisdiction to police the conduct of the newly independent states of the decolonised world not only from state consent, but also from their role as executive agents of a universal organisation that represents collective values of peace and justice

(Hammarskjöld 1961 [1962b]). Economic institutions in turn derive their jurisdiction from their claim to represent universal truths. For a growing number of cosmopolitan managerialists, the international community really does represent genuine universality, and individual states (and indeed individuals) obtain their freedom through their association as members of this international community.

Modern international law remained self-consciously functionalist in its attitude to international authority for much of the twentieth century. As international experiments in executive rule by universal institutions progressed, international lawyers insisted on the need to direct attention away from anachronistic concerns with juridical status and instead to focus on the functions of sovereignty. We might have expected pragmatic and no-nonsense proponents of functionalism to be more than usually free of the temptation to sanctify the new forms of international authority that were strengthened by this approach. Yet functionalism, as Felix Cohen once commented, is a Protestant movement (Cohen 1935, 822). Just as the sixteenth-century Protestant reformers rejected the sanctification of particular people, material objects and rituals, functionalism seeks to reject the sanctification of empty legal forms and ceremonies. Just as the secular project of Protestantism then 'discovered sanctification in the conduct of ordinary human relations' (Goldie 1987, 200), so modern functionalists have sanctified the everyday techniques of international managerial rule. Formal issues of self-determination, sovereignty or the status of territories administered by international agencies no longer matter. What is at issue is whether the system works effectively. The state is dealt with nonchalantly as if it were simply one of the many social groups or 'other associations in which men live' (Schmitt 1930 [1999]). The international order becomes comprehensible as a system in which 'functions' are vested in this or that social group or actor, in the way that a manager might vest a task in this or that organisational department. International lawyers now debate how best to realise 'the executive function of the international community' (Stahn 2008, 29). International law now exists to achieve 'systemic objectives' and 'to vindicate community interests' (*ibid.*, 34). While under international law the state has obligations to protect the welfare of its population and maintain order, it is 'only one contender amongst others' to fulfil these 'functions' (*ibid.*, 33). If it fails to do so, they are readily transferable to the international community (International Commission on Intervention and State Sovereignty 2001, 13).

International lawyers continue to move between understanding international law as a product of state consent that works to set rules for an ordered society of states, and understanding it as the constitution of an international community that champions freedom and in so doing transcends the interests of any particular member. International law, like much modern law, oscillates between emphasising individual consent and the collective good as the foundations of its legitimacy. International lawyers may at times see themselves as the representatives of a civilised conscience or shared sensibility that transcends worldly authority, yet they still rely upon worldly authorities as the vehicles through which this universal law is to find expression. To the extent that international law is fundamentally concerned with the relation between freedom and order, it can be understood as one site in which the Protestant project is today being worked through. In that sense, early modern debates about the proper relation between the part and the whole are not past and immutable, but rather represent a normative tradition that modern international law inherits and with which it remains actively engaged.

Bibliography

Alexander VI, 1917. 'The Bull Inter Caetera (1493)', reprinted in F. G. Davenport (ed.), *European Treaties bearing on the History of the United States and its Dependencies to 1648*, Washington, DC: Carnegie Institute of Washington, 71–78

Alexandrowicz, C. H., 1958. 'The Theory of Recognition *in Fieri*', *British Year Book of International Law*, 34, 176–198

Alexandrowicz, C. H., 1961. 'Doctrinal Aspects of the Universality of the Law of Nations', *British Year Book of International Law*, 37, 506–515

Anand, R. P., 1972. *New States and International Law*, Delhi: Vikas Publishing House

Anghie, A., 2005. *Imperialism, Sovereignty and the Making of International Law*, Cambridge University Press

Armitage, D., 2000. *The Ideological Origins of the British Empire*, Cambridge University Press

Borschberg, P., 1999. 'Hugo Grotius, East India Trade and the King of Johor', *Journal of Southeast Asian Studies*, 30, 225–248

Butterfield, H., 1966. 'The Balance of Power', in H. Butterfield and M. Wight (eds.), *Diplomatic Investigations: Essays in the Theory of International Politics*, London: Allen & Unwin, 132–148

Cohen, F., 1935. 'Transcendental Nonsense and the Functional Approach', *Columbia Law Review*, 35, 809–849

Crawford, J., 2006. *The Creation of States in International Law*, 2nd edn., Oxford University Press

Fasolt, C., 2004. *The Limits of History*, University of Chicago Press

Goffman, D., 2007. 'Negotiating with the Renaissance State: The Ottoman Empire and the New Diplomacy', in V. H. Aksan and D. Goffman (eds.), *The Early Modern Ottomans: Remapping the Empire*, Cambridge University Press, 61–74

Goldie, M., 1987. 'The Civil Religion of James Harrington', in A. Pagden (ed.), *The Languages of Political Theory in Early-Modern Europe*, Cambridge University Press, 197–224

Grotius, H., 2006. *Commentary on the Law of Prize and Booty*, M. J. Ittersum (ed.), Indianapolis: Liberty Fund

Hammarskjöld, D., 1962a. 'Asia, Africa and the West: Address before the Academic Association of the University of Lund, Lund, Sweden, 4 May 1959', in W. Foote (ed.), *The Servant of Peace: A Selection of the Speeches and Statements of Dag Hammarskjöld*, London: The Bodley Head, 212–219

Hammarskjöld, D., 1962b. 'The International Civil Servant in Law and in Fact: Lecture delivered to Congregation at Oxford University, 30 May 1961', in W. Foote (ed.), *The Servant of Peace: A Selection of the Speeches and Statements of Dag Hammarskjöld*, London: The Bodley Head, 329–353

Hill, C., 1997. *Puritanism and Revolution: Studies in Interpretation of the English Revolution of the 17th Century*, New York: St. Martin's Press

Hobbes, T., 1996. *Leviathan*, J. C. A. Gaskin (ed.), Oxford University Press

Hont, I., 2005. *Jealousy of Trade: International Competition and the Nation-state in Historical Perspective*, Cambridge, MA: Belknap Press

Howse, R., 2002. 'From Politics to Technocracy – and Back Again: The Fate of the Multilateral Trading Regime', *American Journal of International Law* 96, 94–117

International Commission on Intervention and State Sovereignty, 2001. *The Responsibility to Protect*, Ottawa: International Development Research Centre

James, H., 1996. *International Monetary Cooperation since Bretton Woods*, Washington, DC: International Monetary Fund and Oxford University Press

Keene, E., 2002. *Beyond the Anarchical Society: Grotius, Colonialism and Order in World Politics*, Cambridge University Press

Kingsbury, B., 2002. 'Legal Positivism as Normative Politics: International Society, Balance of Power and Lassa Oppenheim's Positive International Law', *European Journal of International Law* 13, 401–436

Koselleck, R., 1988. *Critique and Crisis: Enlightenment and the Pathogenesis of Modern Society*, Cambridge, MA: MIT Press

Koskenniemi, M., 2001. *The Gentle Civilizer of Nations: The Rise and Fall of International Law 1870–1960*, Cambridge University Press

Koskenniemi, M., 2007. 'The Fate of Public International Law: Between Technique and Politics', *Modern Law Review*, 70, 1–30

Locke, J., 1993. *Two Treatises of Government*, M. Goldie (ed.), London: Everyman

MacMillan, K., 2006. *Sovereignty and Possession in the English New World: The Legal Foundations of Empire, 1576–1640*, Cambridge University Press

Mattingly, G., 1955. *Renaissance Diplomacy*, Boston: Houghton Mifflin

Morris, M., 1992. *Ecstasy and Economics*, Sydney: EMPress

Orford, A., 1997. 'Locating the International: Military and Monetary Interventions after the Cold War', *Harvard International Law Journal*, 38, 443–485

Orford, A., 2003. *Reading Humanitarian Intervention: Human Rights and the Use of Force in International Law*, Cambridge University Press

Orford, A., 2009. 'Jurisdiction without Territory: From the Holy Roman Empire to the Responsibility to Protect', *Michigan Journal of International Law*, 30, 981–1015

Orford, A., 2011. *International Authority and the Responsibility to Protect*, Cambridge University Press

Pitts, J., 2007. 'Boundaries of Victorian International Law', in D. Bell (ed.), *Victorian Visions of Global Order: Empire and International Relations in Nineteenth-century Political Thought*, Cambridge University Press, 67–88

Piven, F. F., 1995. 'Is it Global Economics or Neo-Laissez-Faire?', *New Left Review*, I(213) September–October, 107–114

Schachter, O., 1962. 'Dag Hammarskjöld and the Relation of Law to Politics', *American Journal of International Law*, 56, 1–8

Schmitt, C., 1999. 'Ethic of State and Pluralistic State', D. Dyzenhaus (trans.), in C. Mouffe (ed.), *The Challenge of Carl Schmitt*, London: Verso, 196–208

Sharp, A. (ed.), 1998. *The English Levellers*, Cambridge University Press

Stahn, C., 2008. *The Law and Practice of International Territorial Administration: Versailles to Iraq and Beyond*, Cambridge University Press

Tuck, R., 1987. 'The "Modern" Theory of Natural Law', in A. Pagden (ed.), *The Languages of Political Theory in Early-Modern Europe*, Cambridge University Press, 99–119

UN Secretary-General, 1961. *Introduction to the Annual Report of the Secretary-General on the Work of the Organisation*, UN GAOR, 16th Sess., Su No. 1A, UN Doc. A/4800/Add.1

Vitoria, F., 1991. 'De potestate ecclesiae Prior', in *Political Writings*, A. Pagden and J. Lawrance (eds.), Cambridge University Press, 45–108

Wight, M., 1966. 'The Balance of Power', in H. Butterfield and M. Wight (eds.), *Diplomatic Investigations: Essays in the Theory of International Politics*, London: Allen & Unwin, 149–175

Woods, N., 2006. *The Globalizers: The IMF, the World Bank, and Their Borrowers*, Ithaca, NY: Cornell University Press

Woolsey, L. H., 1942. 'A Pattern of World Order', *American Journal of International Law*, 36, 621–628

13 Legitimating the international rule of law

B. S. Chimni

Introduction

Meaning of the 'rule of law'

The 'rule of law' signifies that all persons (natural or juridical), including organs of the state, should comply with laws adopted through prescribed constitutional procedures. Its essence is the prohibition of the exercise of arbitrary power. The scope of the rule of law includes the procedural guarantees of general laws and an 'impartial' due process (Neumann 1985, 265–267; Sypnowich 1990, 55). It has also come to be associated with the protection of core human rights. But despite a certain common understanding, the rule of law 'is an exceedingly elusive notion'; 'contrasting meanings are held' by reasonable people (Tamanaha 2004, 3). There are several reasons for this.

First, the differences can be traced to the use of a positivist as against a deliberative conception of law. The validity of a legal rule is usually traced to adherence to a prescribed procedure, most often laid down in a written constitution. But as Jürgen Habermas points out, rules based only on positive enactment may sometimes lack legitimacy for 'the belief in legality can produce legitimacy only if we already presuppose the legitimacy of the legal order that lays down what is legal. There is no way out of this circle' (Habermas 1987, 265). Legitimacy can be secured only if both particular laws and the legal order are justified by good arguments as opposed to drawing strength from compliance with formal processes or being the outcome of the mere exercise of power. Thus if the legal order is based on some originating violence, as it often is, the legitimacy of legal rules tends to be undermined (Derrida 1992, 6). This is of particular relevance when the relationship between colonialism and international law is explored. Habermas' understanding of the rule of law is however a regulative ideal. The extent to which it is complied with will bestow a greater or lesser degree of legitimacy on the legal order.

Second, differences arise because of the distinction between a formal and substantive conception of the rule of law. The former posits a weak relationship between the rule of law and principles of social justice, limiting it to a procedural morality that informs the administration of justice (e.g. the principle of due process). It is necessary here to distinguish between the general conception of the rule of law and the sum total of rules that constitute a legal system. The latter include rules that regulate different aspects of social, economic and political life. It is primarily the substance of these laws that are the subject of critique by those who subscribe to the substantive conception of the rule of law. In this view by limiting the meaning of the rule of law, the formal conception pre-empts a critique of the idea of the rule of law based on the impact substantive laws have on the lives of its final subjects, i.e. individuals. It thereby hinders the creation of a more egalitarian society.

Third, the differences as to the meaning of the rule of law are often a result of employing an a-cultural conception that does not admit of plurality of understandings. Such an a-cultural conception has its roots in the assumed superiority and universal applicability of the Western model. Werner Menski, for example, has drawn attention to 'the often unspoken but systematic denial that anything useful can be learnt from non-Western socio-legal traditions' and called for 'more explicit recognition of various Southern perspectives' (Menski 2006, 17, 30). Of course the mere fact of difference does not privilege any conception of the rule of law. But to ignore the enormous diversity of human experience is to have an unwarranted epistemological confidence that has its roots in hegemonic aspirations.

The different meanings assigned to the rule of law have given rise to divergent assessments of its place and role in democratic societies. But even critics of the positivist, formal and a-cultural conception of the rule of law concede its value. The Marxist historian E.P. Thompson has perhaps gone furthest, terming the idea and practices of the rule of law 'as an unqualified human good' and 'a cultural achievement of universal significance' (Thompson 1975, 265; Unger 1976, 56–57). The critics celebrate the rule of law partly because it represents the historical achievement of the struggles of the subaltern classes. Its prevalence also helps these groups, in particular through the protection of core human rights, to continue to fight for social justice by enabling them to organise and struggle for legitimate demands. A sanguine take on the rule of law is thus not in contradiction with the claim that law can legitimise a system of domination and exploitation. The duality simply captures a complex and dynamic relationship between the rule of law and principles of social justice. Any judgment as to the extent to which a legal order is successful in establishing the rule of law and meeting the goals of equality and justice can only be made with regard to the particularity of each legal order.

Meaning of the 'international rule of law'

Achieving the international rule of law has come to be accorded a high value. For example, the 1970 UN General Assembly Declaration on Principles of International law concerning Friendly Relations and Co-operation among States refers in its Preamble to the 'promotion of the rule of law amongst nations'. In the Millennium Declaration, UN member states resolved to 'strengthen respect for the rule of law in international as in national affairs'. But this is problematic: the idea of the rule of law was first formulated in relation to national legal systems with characteristics (a constitution, limited executive power, a judiciary with compulsory jurisdiction, some form of the separation of powers) which are not present or are only very imperfectly present at the international level. To institute 'respect for the rule of law in international ... affairs' would seem to involve a revolution away from the Westphalian system, or else a rather different conception of the term 'rule of law'.

We might start, however, with the idea that the international rule of law means, by analogy, that actors in the international system should abide by existing rules of international law. On this basis the international rule of law would be evolutionary rather than revolutionary, and would be framed by certain fundamental principles that regulate the conduct of international relations. The foundational international law principles are authoritatively stated in the Charter of the United Nations and the Declaration on Friendly Relations. These include the principle of sovereign equality of states, the principle of non-use of force, the principle of self-determination of peoples, the principle of non-intervention in the internal and external affairs of states, the principle of peaceful settlement of international disputes, the principle of cooperation between states, and the principle of fulfilling in good faith obligations assumed under international law.

What distinguishes the international rule of law from its internal counterpart is the decentralised character of international society. In the absence of a world state, international law is not made by an elected world legislature but by the principal subjects of the law, states themselves. The procedure for making international law is diffuse. The validity of international law rules is determined by reference to what are called 'sources' of international law, listed in article 38(1) of the Statute of the International Court of Justice – international treaties, international custom, general principles of law recognised by states, and (subsidiarily) judicial decisions and teachings of highly qualified subjects (see Chapter 8). Rules that are not validated through the specified sources of international law possess only persuasive value. Thus, a distinction is made in the literature of international law between hard law and soft law, the latter designating norms that are strictly speaking not binding on the subjects of international law (e.g. resolutions adopted by the General Assembly). The fact that the list of stated sources of international law cannot be expanded has had a bearing on the legitimacy of the international legal order in the eyes of Third-World governments wishing to bring about changes in the body of international law but unable to do so in the face of opposition from Western governments (Bedjaoui 1979).

A formal conception of the international rule of law suffers from the same problems as its internal analogue. It requires that the rules adopted through designated 'sources' be observed, but tells us nothing about the character of those rules. In the absence of a representative global legislature the legitimacy of rules adopted through established sources of international law carries less conviction. In keeping with the distinction between formal and substantive conceptions, this chapter will use the term 'the international rule of law' for the formal idea and 'international law' for the sum total of legal rules that constitute the international legal system. These regulate a wide variety of subject areas including asylum, environment, finance, intellectual property rights, oceans and trade.

Recent developments

The formal conception of the international rule of law is minimalist in its orientation as it tends to privilege the value of order over that of justice. However, there have emerged, or are in the process of emerging, international institutions that seek to expand the scope of international law beyond adherence to the foundational principles listed in the UN Charter and the Declaration on Friendly Relations. Reference may be made to four such developments.

First, a norm of democratic governance is said to have emerged that challenges the legitimacy of governments that have not been elected through free and fair elections (Franck 1992, 46). Second, a rapidly developing international human rights law has identified certain non-derogable human rights that must be respected by states even in situations of declared emergency. Third, the foundational principle of sovereignty is coming to be defined in terms of responsibility to protect citizens to bring it into accord with the norm of democratic governance and international human rights law. Fourth, a large number of tribunals have been established to interpret and implement international law, leading to the greater judicialisation of international law.

But even these developments fail to establish more than a feeble link between international law and international justice. It is true that the foundational principles and the emerging developments are helpful in protecting the interests of weaker states and subaltern peoples. For instance, the principles of sovereign equality of states and the non-use of force are dear to formerly colonised peoples. Likewise, the development of international human rights law is important for people struggling for a democratic polity in post-colonial states. Even so, substantive international law rules principally codify the interests of powerful states and social classes in the international system. What is more, many of the more recent developments help justify interventions of powerful Western states into the internal affairs of Third-World states.

In the following sections the idea of the international rule of law and its critique are further explored. The aim is to ascertain the limits of the idea in a world in which the principal actors have vastly different capabilities, resources and power. The next section reviews, in this context, different approaches – realist, liberal, critical, feminist and Third-World approaches. It will be argued that the mainstream realist and liberal approaches misread the relationship between power and international law and are therefore often blind to the fact that the principles, norms and practices that constitute international law can sustain and legitimise hegemony. The subsequent section seeks to evidence this by looking at the relationship of colonialism, imperialism and international law. The next section goes on to suggest that the use of an a-cultural conception of the international rule of law has meant that its understanding in non-Western civilisations has been neglected. It is argued that the idea and practices of international law can be enriched if the experiences of other civilisations are taken into account. A pluralist international law will in this view have much greater legitimacy. The final section contains some concluding reflections.

Some contemporary approaches to the international rule of law

The role and limits of the international rule of law are viewed differently by the proponents of different approaches to international law. Some of these differences are teased out in the following brief review.

The realist approach

The realist approach is primarily associated with the name of Hans Morgenthau whose classic work, *Politics among Nations*, continues to be influential in shaping attitudes towards international law (Morgenthau 1948). Relying on an essentialist and pessimistic view of human nature, the realist approach contends that the rule of law cannot prevail because international politics is all about the accumulation of power. Morgenthau went on to formulate as an 'iron law of politics' that 'legal obligations must yield to national interest' (Morgenthau 1981, 144). In this view international law is 'performing a labor of Sisyphus' in attempting to reign in the state in a decentralised international society (Meinecke 1984, 208). But Morgenthau does not conclude that there is no such thing as international law (Morgenthau 1948). In cases where critical national interests are not involved, mutual and complementary interests weigh in to sustain the rule of law, at least to some extent. Violations of international law are not a common occurrence also because rules that are likely to obstruct the course of power are often drafted in a manner that leaves sufficient room for maneouvre. But if the idea of an international rule of law is to be taken seriously it must also be effective in the relatively important cases of violation of international law. At present there are few effective enforcement mechanisms to deal with such cases, notably where major powers are involved. The invasions of Afghanistan and Iraq are cases in point. Hence, realism ultimately mounts a serious attack on the idea of an international rule of law.

The liberal approach

In contrast to the realist approach the liberal approach in its substantive variant contends that international law has the capacity to establish the international rule of law. It believes that developments such as the emergence of the norm of democratic governance and the rapid growth of human rights law have strengthened the project of establishing the international rule of law by linking it with the internal rule of law and modifying the principle of sovereignty in this light. Liberals also place faith in the instrument of international law to create conditions for the enhancement of the welfare of the international community.

First, liberals contend that the realist approach underplays the significance of law even in cases where crucial national interests are at stake. Even in such instances international law does not necessarily give way to national interests. Thus, for example, the United States and the European Union have by becoming members of the World Trade Organisation (WTO) agreed to submit their trade disputes, including those implicating core national interests, to the Dispute Settlement Body (DSB) of the WTO that hands down binding decisions. The decisions of the DSB have been, with rare exceptions, observed by the United States and European Union, despite the fact that these have hurt national interests.

Second, liberals claim that critics derive general conclusions about the effectiveness of central enforcement mechanisms such as the UN Security Council from their record in a particular phase of history of international relations with its unique features; the realist analysis thus draws its strength from the history of the Cold War. The critics disregard the fact that the post-Cold War period has seen a UN Security Council that is more active and effective.

Third, international rule of law sceptics also overlook the enhanced enforcement capacity of international law in recent years as national institutions have come to be deployed for the purpose. Thus, the application of 'universal jurisdiction' in the case of some types of international crimes extends the reach of national institutions to enforce international laws. The decision of the House of Lords in the *Pinochet* case (1999) 'showed that transnational prosecutions could be a viable alternative', and 'fired imaginations around the world' (Roht-Arriaza 2004, 375–389). This does not mean that enforcement gaps do not still remain. But liberals draw attention to the crucial role of international law rules in evaluating state behaviour, generating pressure for compliance. Since having law on one's side enhances the legitimacy of decisions, all states, including the sole superpower, seek to justify their actions in the vocabulary of international law.

Fourth, while liberals recognise that the element of determinacy, that is, the reliable understanding of 'what a rule permits and what it prohibits', goes to the heart of the legitimacy of a rule and that many rules of international law are open-ended and amenable to conflicting interpretations, they insist that this does not mean complete hermeneutic freedom, as claimed by realists and other critics. Most rules are in their view sufficiently determinate: the crucial elements of coherence, adherence and symbolic validation are nearly always present (Franck 2006, 93). The growth of international tribunals is also coming to contribute to the certainty and predictability of the law.

Finally, liberals note that international law retains its legitimacy less because of its directly constraining character and more because it is a dynamic instrument that helps the international community to meet new challenges through adopting appropriate rules and establishing desirable institutions. These may include challenges of democratic governance, sustainable development, gross violation of human rights, or the war against terrorism.

In sum, the liberal approach argues that international law not only plays a significant role in maintaining order in international society but also facilitates a cooperative response to key problems confronting the international community.

The critical approach

The critical approach[1] identifies a number of problems in the realist and liberal views.

First, the realist and liberal approaches treat international law as a neutral device that stands above power. This underplays the fact that power has the capability of inscribing its interests in international laws. It is this capability

[1] The term 'critical approach' is used here as a generic phrase for those approaches critical of the mainstream liberal approach to international law. It subsumes within it left-liberal scholars like Richard Falk and José Alvarez, critical legal studies scholars like David Kennedy and Martti Koskenniemi, feminist scholars such as Hilary Charlesworth and Christine Chinkin, and Third-World approaches to international law (TWAIL) articulated by, amongst others, Antony Anghie, B.S. Chimni, James Gathii, Obiora Okafor, Karin Mickelson and Vasuki Nesiah. The feminist and TWAIL critiques, in particular the latter, are elaborated separately.

that explains its infrequent violation and not the simple mutuality of interests or the commitment to an international rule of law. Since realist and liberal approaches adopt a positivist method to do international law, they overlook the many ways in which dominant states and social forces influence international law-making or the distributive consequences flowing from it.

Second, the liberal reliance on new developments such as the norm of democratic governance and growth of human rights law is exaggerated and simplistic. The norm of democratic governance, for instance, does not help reduce inequalities in society: rather it promotes low-intensity democracies. Susan Marks has rightly pointed to the potential of the norm of democratic governance 'to serve as an agent of neo-colonialism' for 'it is too easily turned against redistributive claims and towards hegemonic agendas' (Marks 2003, 140–141).

Third, the indeterminacies that characterise rules of international law can be and are used by powerful states to justify preferred courses of action. The critics point to two kinds of indeterminacy. The first is a function of the idea that the relations between legal texts and facts are amenable to multiple interpretations. In the circumstances (as the realists recognise) interpretations advanced by powerful states tend to prevail. A second kind of indeterminacy can be attributed to a process of justification that conveniently moves between feasible interpretations of concrete realities and competing abstract principles, including the foundational principles of international law. For every norm there is an exception, for every principle a counter-principle (Koskenniemi 2005). The prevalence of competing principles and exceptions allows powerful interests to contend that their actions are in compliance with international law.

Fourth, both the liberal and realist approach fail to appreciate the extent to which international institutions are complicit in the production of injustice in international society. The UN Security Council 'is not always used in a just manner' (UN Secretary-General, Address to the General Assembly, 21 September 2004). International financial institutions like the International Monetary Fund (IMF) and the World Bank take advantage of the ambiguities in their mandates, weighted voting and a system of conditionalities to compel Third-World countries to pursue policies that negatively impact the poor (Chimni 2004, Chimni 2010). At the same time, these institutions claim that they are not bound by international human rights law as their charters require that only economic criteria be taken into account in the decision to advance loans.

Feminist approaches

Feminists have incorporated many of the insights of the critical approach while challenging international law from a gender perspective. They argue that 'the reality of women's lives do not fit easily into the concepts and categories of international law ... international law is constructed upon particular male assumptions and experiences of life where "man" is taken to represent the "human"' (Charlesworth and Chinkin 2000, 17). International law like domestic law 'shows little concern for women, their interests and their special vulnerabilities' (*ibid.*, x). It has failed 'all groups of women' and 'legitimated the unequal position of women around the world' (*ibid.*, 1, 2). They have been 'almost completely excluded from international law-making arenas' (*ibid.*, 50). Any attempt to make strategic use of international law for the defense of women's claims and rights has led feminist critics 'to work with concepts that are problematic and inadequate' (*ibid.*, 95). Its vocabulary and institutions cannot be productively used to transform it from the inside. So the feminist critique is not, like the realist approach, a power critique *simpliciter* but more profound. A parallel critique can be made across class and race lines and has been advanced by Marxist and critical race approaches to international law (e.g. Chimni 2010, 57).

The Third-World approach

The Third-World approach to international law (TWAIL) has an affinity to the critical and feminist approaches. But it contends that the latter do not sufficiently appreciate the intimate relationship between capitalism, imperialism and international law. TWAIL demonstrates this relationship through undertaking a historical review of international law in the matrix of the different phases of imperialism – from the history of colonisation of Third-World peoples to newer forms of imperialism. This does not mean that TWAIL is dismissive of international law or the rule of law. While TWAIL does argue that international law sustains structures of domination and exploitation, it does not believe that it is simply a tool in the hands of powerful states. Its foundational principles possess a degree of autonomy from structures of power and influence. Furthermore, in an international system based on the principle of sovereign equality of states the making of international law is a complex and mediated process in which some amount of accommodation of the interests of weaker states becomes necessary. It is equally the case that once international law rules are adopted it is in the interest of even powerful countries to adhere to them if the legitimacy of international rule of law has to be sustained. These factors ensure that international law can sometimes be used by weaker states to embed their interests in the interstices of the ideology of liberalism and the economics of global capitalism. The idea of international rule of law can have certain beneficial consequences for Third-World states and peoples. But this has not always been the case.

Colonialism, imperialism and international law

In the TWAIL view the content and character of international law differs from era to era. In the colonial era the subjects of international law were an elite club of Western states. Excluded from the law's purview were subjugated peoples and states. This exclusion was deemed justified because, in the words of John Stuart Mill, 'nations which are still barbarous have not got beyond the period during which it is likely to be for their benefit that they should be conquered and held in subjection by foreigners' (Mill 1984, 118). But from the perspective of the colonised peoples it was a mockery of the international rule of law to frame things on the basis of an untenable civilised/uncivilised peoples' distinction (Anghie 1999, 1). The act of colonisation also revealed the absence of any firm link between the domestic observance of the rule of law and respect for it internationally.

It has been argued that a reason why Western liberal democracies tend to disrespect international law when it comes to the non-Western world is that while political liberalism need not necessarily be imperialistic, 'the urge is internal to it' (Mehta 1999, 20). This disposition is traced to the modern western conception of the political – evidenced by the Mill statement – that harbours 'a deep impulse to reform the world' (*ibid.*, 79). It explains 'the necessary tension [of the politics of empire] with other liberal notions such as tolerance, the right to representation, equality, and ... consent and sovereignty of the people' (*ibid.*, 80). One must hasten to add that the 'impulse to reform' is an integral part of the universalist thrust of 'entrenched modernity' that seeks to extend its univocal vision to all geographical spaces (for the idea of 'entrenched modernity' see Taylor 1979). It is therefore predisposed to reproduce the conceptual apparatus that was part of its armoury at the founding moments of modern international law.

The civilised/uncivilised distinction thus continues to find a presence in the post-colonial era, now assuming, amongst other things, the garb of a distinction between liberal/democratic and illiberal/undemocratic states. In this scheme of things 'democratic states can depart from the law and still be seen as acting legitimately, in the interests of cosmopolitan ideals, because they are democratic. Democratic states have these special privileges: they are not bound by international law, rather they make it' (Anghie 2006, 395). The mission is to bring democracy, the rule of law and good governance to others. Towards this end suitable international law concepts are adopted or adapted. Thus, the concept of humanitarian intervention, increasingly questioned by Third-World states and scholars in the wake of the unlawful armed interventions in Kosovo and Iraq, has today been reconfigured in the form of a new conception of sovereignty, sovereignty as responsibility to protect citizens. The new frame is interesting (and more disturbing) for what it does is to move away from the 'representation of intervention as an exceptional interference in the domestic affairs of states ... towards the representation of international presence as authorized, and indeed mandated, by international legal obligations' (Orford 2009, 999). It is not that under no circumstances should the international community intervene (e.g. to prevent genocide as in Rwanda), but the principle of 'responsibility to protect' facilitates the legitimation of the politics of imperialism.

Imperialism is however not simply the function of a certain conception of the political but equally of a certain kind of economics. Entrenched modernity has always been allied with capitalism driven by the logic of accumulation. Capital cannot rest till it has annihilated space. The exploitation of resources and peoples always accompanies the impulse to reform others. The currently dominant neo-liberal form of global capitalism seeks a borderless global economy that allows the free movement of capital, goods and services (to the exclusion of labour). It therefore calls for the principle of economic sovereignty to be given an interpretation that furthers the goal of creating a unified world market. It has meant an assemblage of international economic institutions to which economic sovereignty has been relocated (Chimni 2004). It has resulted in the loss of crucial policy space for Third-World states. The outcome is the exploitation of large segments of Third-World states and peoples. The north–south fracture is however coming to be overlaid by a global class divide. An emerging transnational capitalist class, constituted of the transnational fractions of the capitalist classes in the industrialised world and key Third-World powers such as Brazil, China and India, is today shaping international laws and institutions and is the key beneficiary of economic globalisation (Chimni 2010).

Different civilisations and the international rule of law

It is implicit in the TWAIL critique of the continuing presence of the civilised/uncivilised divide in international law that contemporary international law is not culturally neutral. The absence of cultural neutrality is reflected in the claim that international law is the exclusive product of European Christian civilisation. On the other hand, since "modern" international law is largely the creation of western civilisation, it 'has not helped itself sufficiently from the repositories of wisdom available to it in various cultures of the world. It is so far a monocultural construct' (Weeramantry 1997, 317). This has weakened the fabric of international law.

International rule of law discourse can integrate cultural differences in at least two ways to make it a multicultural and multi-civilisational construct. First, it must recognise the contribution of the non-West to the evolution and development of international law. A body of post-colonial scholarship has drawn attention to a well-defined corpus of inter-state rules of conduct in the pre-colonial era. Indeed, it has been demonstrated how key figures like Grotius were aware of these practices and used them to support particular doctrines (Alexandrowicz 1967). Second, there is a need to recover from the history of international law in the non-West cultural/civilisational concepts and practices that continue to influence the policy responses of non-Western states. The bulk of this section is devoted to the latter mode of taking cognisance of cultural/civilisational differences as it has received little attention in the existing literature of international law.

The international rule of law in the pre-colonial era: the concept of *dharma*

In pre-colonial non-West the idea of 'law' intermeshed with local social, cultural and religious traditions. A review of these practices can help distil ideas that go to strengthen the contemporary international rule of law by making its narrative more plural. The limited purpose of the ensuing discussion is to illustrate this possibility from the history of Indian civilisation. The point is not so much the accuracy of this account of history – and a degree of idealisation may be admitted – but rather the excavation of alternative perceptions and practices that inform the practice of international law. It may also be noted along with Sen that 'the origin of ideas is not the kind of thing to which "purity" happens easily' (Sen 2005, 132). But it would be mistaken to suggest that all ideas and practices have the same presence in all societies.

The idea of international law received a different meaning in different stages of pre-colonial history. For instance, in Ancient India it was interpreted in the matrix of Hindu cultural and religious traditions embodied in the concept of *dharma* (right conduct) which encompassed the phenomena of law and legal relations (see Menski 2006, 211). The duties to be observed by a ruler in the process of governance were termed *rajdharma*. Strictly speaking the ruler made no law but ensured, in later periods through legal processes, that an individual fulfilled his/her *dharma* and assured 'respect for people's customs' (*ibid.*, 226). The significant features of the idea of *dharma* – 'self-controlled ordering', plurality and a 'dialectical dynamism' – have allowed it to be adapted over the centuries to reflect changes in the social substratum (*ibid.*, 202). The supremacy of *dharma* 'was meant to regulate inter-state conduct as much as the internal governance of a state' (Chatterjee 1958, 6). Thus *dharma* also 'constituted the very essence of International Law in Ancient India' (*ibid.*, 6). Its ambit extended, amongst other things, to the conduct of diplomacy, laws of war and the grant of asylum.

It needs to be said that the concept of *dharma* came to be institutionalised in society in ways that allowed dominant social forces of the time, amongst other things, to sustain a hierarchical and oppressive caste system, with each caste having to conform to a particular code of conduct. Through this mechanism the lower castes in society were debarred from sharing power. Things have not substantially changed over the centuries, explaining why in recent years dalit organisations have taken the issue of caste oppression to international forums; the matter was debated at the Durban conference on the elimination of racial discrimination. The concept of *dharma* has also been used to institutionalise patriarchy. But some aspects of thinking about the rule of law as *dharma* can yet be elicited to facilitate a more plural and rich conception of international law.

First, its stress on duties can help strengthen the foundational principle of cooperation in international law.[2] Every state (like each individual) should be required to conduct itself in such a way as to produce, to use the words of Gandhi, 'a state of enlightened anarchy'. In so far as particular international legal regimes are concerned the language of duties is of obvious relevance to international human rights law. The emphasis on duties is an integral part of the discourse on rights in other civilisations as well. It may be noted that the African Charter of Human and Peoples' Rights of 1981 devotes a separate chapter to duties.

Second, the idea of *dharma*, as integrated later with the tenet of non-violence preached by Buddhism and Jainism, is of value in bringing about a peaceful world order.[3] The practice of non-violence is of course taught in other cultural traditions as well. What is of significance in the case of Indian civilisation is that there is historical evidence to show that in the first millennia elements of Sanskrit language and culture were spread in Asia unaccompanied by violence. Sanskrit culture was not spread through 'the actions of a conquest state' but 'by the circulation of traders, literati, religious professionals, and freelance adventurers' (Pollock 2000, 603). There was no sign of 'coercion, cooptation, juridical control, and even persuasion'. Rather 'those who participated in Sanskrit cosmopolitan culture chose to do so, and could choose to do so' (*ibid.*, 603). In the recent past what is unique about the Indian civilisation is the translation of the tenet of non-violence by Gandhi into an idiom of practical politics and a theory of resistance. Both these episodes of history show that the practice of non-violence is not a utopian ideal.

Third, the idea of *dharma* has been interpreted by more recent commentators to underline the significance of spiritualism to bring about true unity of humankind as opposed to the mechanical unity that is being brought about by the accelerated globalisation process. The contention is that a just world under law cannot be realised without inner change even if the requisite material conditions for 'enlightened anarchy' are in place (Sri Aurobindo, 1970). As Charles Taylor notes of entrenched modernity 'we tend in our culture to stifle the spirit' (Taylor 1992, 520).

[2] Indeed, Gandhi defined the very idea of civilisation in terms of duties: 'civilization is that mode of conduct which points out to man the path of duty' (Gandhi 1938, 55).

[3] Gandhi's concern with 'ahimsa', according to Thapar can be traced 'to the Jaina imprint on the culture of Kathiawar' where he grew up (Thapar 2003, 1042).

Medieval India and composite culture

Medieval India experienced the co-existence of Hindu and Islamic traditions, the latter brought by Muslim invaders and rulers, and later the interaction of the Sultanate of Delhi (established by Turkish invasion in the late twelfth and thirteenth centuries) and the Mughal Empire (sixteenth and seventeenth centuries) with the Christian West. This meant that 'states' with quite different understandings of international law interacted with each other (Singh 1973). In the initial phase this co-existence was marked by serious conflict and tensions. However, a degree of mutual toleration came to prevail with the establishment of the Mughal Empire. There was less insistence that the relations between different states, in particular the relations between religious communities, be conducted on the basis of one cultural or religious tradition. In the domestic legal sphere there emerged a 'pattern of strong legal pluralism' (Menski 2006, 237). The progressive thinking this represented for its time can be gauged from the fact that while Giordano Bruno was being burned at the stake in Rome for heresy in 1600, Akbar was preaching in Agra on toleration and the need for dialogue across 'the border of religions' (Sen 2005, 334, 36–39). The post-Akbar era saw a revival of religious persecution, but it did not erase the practices of toleration that had been embedded in the life-world of people. The consequent interpenetration of religious and cultural traditions gave rise to a *composite culture* that has been nurtured since the independence of India.

Global composite culture and international law

Bhiku Parekh writes that contemporary 'India offers one of the best examples of composite culture' (Parekh 2007, 14). Its essence is the idea of unity in diversity. A composite culture is a shared culture that is not 'unified or homogeneous' (*ibid.*, 9). It helps build bridges between oneself and the representative of other cultures or ways of life. In the case of India its composite culture unites Islamic influences with Hindu traditions whose impact can be seen in the social and political realm and in literature, music, painting and architecture (Sen 2005, 315). Great religious poets like Kabir 'were born Muslim but transcended sectional boundaries' (*ibid.*, 316). This composite culture has also been enriched by the teachings of Buddhism,

Christianity, Jainism and Sikhism. Thus, in the words of the doyen of Indian sociologists D.P. Mukerji, Indian culture is 'neither Hindu nor Islamic, neither a replica of the western modes of living and thought nor a purely Asiatic product' (Mukerji 1942, 1). At a time when there is endless talk of clash of civilisations, and multiculturalism is under stress in the Western world, it is important to retrieve traditions and practices from all civilisations that encourage tolerance and the peaceful co-existence of cultures and religions. The composite culture of India is today also strained, thanks to sections of the Hindu right wanting to privilege one version of Hindu culture over other religious traditions and cultures.

It is important that the process of cultural exchange not be conceived of as an accretion to entrenched modernity's understanding of international law but as an equal exchange between different cultures that are a product of alternative modernities (Kaviraj 2005). Until now other cultures have possessed, as Gramsci noted, 'a universal value only in so far as they have become constituent elements of European culture' and only if 'they have contributed to the process of European thought and been assimilated by it' (Gramsci 1971, 416). A global composite culture cannot evolve on the basis of assimilation. It can only emerge through a dialogue between equals.

In sum, there are multiple worlds of international law. While there are the stated sources of international law these tend to blend with social, cultural and religious sources to yield composite meaning and practices of the idea of the international rule of law. The debates in international human rights law are the most obvious example of this blending of legal, cultural and religious sources. These may at times yield unacceptable versions of cultural relativism. But their coming together also provides the basis for enhancing the observance of international human rights law.

Conclusion

The international rule of law means the proscription of arbitrary action by any actor in the international system. In recent years it has also come to stand for the protection of basic human rights. Despite its minimalism it would be short-sighted to reject the formal conception of the international rule of law. For the foundational principles of contemporary international law – sovereign equality of states, non-use of force, etc. – provide a shield for weak Third-World states and peoples against hegemonic powers. But it is equally important to remember that new forms of imperialism have found a home in current international law. The old colonial categories of civilised and uncivilised now assume other garbs. If the international rule of law is to possess greater legitimacy, it has to purge itself of hegemonic modes of thinking and accompanying practices. The legitimacy of an international rule of law is a function of its journey towards becoming a more plural construct, taking cognisance of cognate narratives in other cultures and civilisations.

Bibliography

Alexandrowicz, C. H., 1967. *International Law in the East Indies: Sixteenth, Seventeenth and Eighteenth Centuries*, Oxford: Clarendon

Anghie, A, 1999. 'Finding the Peripheries: Sovereignty and Colonialism in Nineteenth Century International Law', *Harvard International Law Journal*, 40, 1–80

Anghie, A., 2006. 'Of Critique and the Other', in A. Orford (ed.), *International Law and its Others*, Cambridge University Press, 389–401.

Bedjaoui, M. 1979. *Towards a New International Economic Order*, Paris: Holmes & Meir

Charlesworth, H. and C. Chinkin, 2000. *The Boundaries of International Law: A Feminist Analysis*, Manchester University Press

Chatterjee, H., 1958. *International Law and Inter-state Relations in Ancient India*, Calcutta: Mukhopadhyay

Chimni B. S., 2004. 'International Institutions Today: A Global Imperial state in the Making', *European Journal of International Law*, 15, 1–37

Chimni B. S., 2010. 'Prolegomenon to a Class approach to International Law', *European Journal of International Law*, 21, 57–82

Derrida, J., 1992. 'Force of Law: The "Mystical Foundation of Authority"', in D. Cornell, M. Rosenfeld and D. G. Carlson (eds.), *Deconstruction and the Possibility of Justice*, New York: Routledge, 3–67

Franck, T., 1992. 'The Emerging Right to Democratic Governance', *American Journal of International Law*, 86, 46–91

Franck, T., 2006. 'The Power of Legitimacy and the Legitimacy of Power: International Law in an Age of Disequilibrium', *American Journal of International Law*, 100, 88–106

Gandhi, M. K., 1938. *Hind Swaraj*, Ahmedabad: Navijivan Publishing House

Gramsci, A., 1971. *Selection from Prison Notebooks*, London: Lawrence & Wishart

Habermas, J., 1987. *Theory of Communicative Action*, Cambridge: Polity

Kaviraj, S., 2005. 'An Outline of a Revisionist Theory of Modernity', *Archives of European Sociology*, XLVI, 497–526

Koskenniemi, M., 2005. *From Apology to Utopia: The Structure of International Legal Argument. Reissue with a New Epilogue*, Cambridge University Press

Marks, S., 2003. *The Riddle of all Constitutions: International Law, Democracy, and the Critique of Ideology*, Oxford University Press

Mehta, U. S., 1999. *Liberalism and Empire: India in British Liberal Thought*, Oxford University Press

Meinecke, F., 1984. *Machiavellism: The Doctrine of Raison d'état and its Place in Modern History*, Boulder, CO: Westview Press

Menski, W., 2006. *Comparative Law in the Global Context: The Legal Systems of Asia and Africa*, Cambridge University Press

Mill, J. S., 1984. 'A Few Words on Non-intervention', in *Essays on Equality, Law and Education*, University of Toronto Press, 111–124

Morgenthau, H. J., 1948. *Politics among Nations*, New York: Alfred A. Knopf

Morgenthau, H. J., 1981. *In Defense of the National Interest*, New York: Alfred A. Knopf

Mukerji, D. P., 1942. *Sociology of Indian Culture*, Jaipur: Rawat

Neumann, F., 1985. *The Rule of Law: Political Theory and the Legal System in Modern Society*, Leamington Spa: Berg

Orford, A., 2009. 'Jurisdiction without Territory: From the Holy Roman Empire to the Responsibility to Protect', *Michigan Journal of International Law*, 30, 984–1014

Parekh, B., 2007. 'Composite Culture and Multicultural Society', in B. Chandra and S. Mahajan, (eds.), *Composite Culture in a Multinational Society*, Delhi: National Book Trust, 3–17

Pollock, S., 2000. 'Cosmopolitan and Vernacular in History', *Public Culture*, 12, 591–625

Roht-Arriaza, N., 2004. 'Universal Jurisdiction: Steps Forward, Steps Back', *Leiden Journal of International Law*, 17, 375–389

Sen, A., 2005. *The Argumentative Indian*, London: Allen Lane

Singh, N., 1973. *India and International Law: Ancient and Mediaeval*, vol. I, New Delhi: S. Chand

Sri Aurobindo, 1970. *The Ideal of Human Unity*, Pondicherry: Sri Aurobindo Ashram

Sypnowich, C., 1990. *The Concept of Socialist Law*, Oxford: Clarendon Press

Tamanaha, B., 2004. *On the Rule of Law: History, Politics, Theory*, Cambridge University Press

Taylor, C., 1979. *Hegel and Modern Society*, Cambridge University Press

Taylor, C., 1992. *Sources of the Self: The Making of Modern Identity*, Cambridge, MA: Harvard University Press

Thapar, R., 2003. *Cultural Pasts: Essays in Early Indian History*, Oxford University Press

Thompson, E. P., 1975. *Whigs and Hunters: The Origins of the Black Act*, New York: Pantheon

Unger, R. M., 1976. *Law in Modern Society*, New York: Free Press

Weeramantry, C. G., 1997. 'The Function of the International Court of Justice in the Development of International Law', *Leiden Journal of International Law*, 10, 309–340

Human rights in disastrous times 14

Susan Marks

C.L.R. James's book *The Black Jacobins* tells the story of the Haitian revolution of 1791–1803, the only slave revolt in history that brought permanent emancipation and a new independent state (James 1963). Central to the story is the magnificent figure of Toussaint L'Ouverture. A former slave, he became the pre-eminent leader of the revolt, but lost the chance to lead it to its conclusion when, in 1802, he was arrested and taken to France. Imprisoned in the mountains of the Jura with deficient heating and reduced rations, he died nine months after arriving there.

James's book was originally published in 1938, and then revised and reissued in 1963. In a recent work, David Scott calls attention to an intriguing feature of the revisions that James made for the book's second edition, namely that he shifted the register of his story from romance to tragedy (Scott 2004). Whereas in the original version James told a romantic tale of revolutionary triumph, in the revised edition there was a new emphasis on Toussaint's tragic predicament, and on the dilemmas, disappointments, ironies and uncertainties of enlightenment and liberation.

The aspect of international law which is the subject of this chapter is human rights, and I shall be showing how, in that very different context, something similar can be observed. If the story of the international protection of human rights has been conventionally told as a romance, there is, at present, a significant body of opinion that invites us to re-imagine it in the register of tragedy. Of course, the words 'tragedy' and 'romance' are used in a wide variety of ways. In everyday language tragedy is what we call events that are deeply sad or calamitous, while romance is about affairs of the heart. Here, however, as explained further below, I follow Scott (and many others) in treating these as modes of emplotment that involve, above all, different perspectives on the possibilities and nature of ethical, political and epistemic progress.

The chapter begins with the main lines of the romantic account of human rights, the story of the establishment and consolidation of the international human rights regime. Turning next to recent critical literature, we shall review some of the respects in which that regime's progressive character has been put in question. In a final section, we shall return to (present-day) Haiti. When in January 2010 the capital and surrounding areas were devastated by an earthquake, the United Nations Human Rights Council met in a special session to discuss the Haitian recovery process from the perspective of a 'human rights approach'. Delegates spoke of the need not to forget human rights, even at such a time of 'immense tragedy'. How does that tragedy relate to the others we shall be encountering in this chapter, and can the answer help us to get the measure of international human rights law today?

International Protection of Human Rights

While recognising that the protection of human rights has deep roots and important antecedents, most accounts of the history of international human rights law begin in the mid-20th century. It was then, in the aftermath of World War II, that the institutional and textual foundations were laid for the contemporary human rights 'system'. A common starting-point is the establishment of the United Nations in 1945, with reference in the organisation's Charter to a shared '[determination to] reaffirm faith in fundamental human rights [and] in the dignity and worth of the human person'. The Charter indeed declared as one of the *purposes* of the UN the promotion and encouragement of 'respect for human rights and for fundamental freedoms for all', but it said nothing more specific about what those rights and freedoms were.

That was left to the Universal Declaration of Human Rights, adopted as a resolution of the UN General Assembly in 1948. Alluding to President Roosevelt's 'four freedoms' – freedom of speech and belief, and freedom from fear and want – the Declaration set out a broad catalogue of rights which it pronounced the 'equal and inalienable rights of all members of the human family'. This included, among other rights, the right to life and the right not to be subjected to torture or inhuman or degrading treatment, the right to adequate food, housing and medical care, the right to education and work and to just and favourable conditions of work, the right to personal liberty and security and to a fair trial, the right to privacy and to freedom of thought, conscience and religion, and the right to freedoms of expression, information, assembly and association. The implementation of these rights was proclaimed a 'common standard of achievement for all peoples and all nations'.

A common standard of achievement is one thing; legally binding obligations, with institutional oversight, are another, and the focus of subsequent activity was the negotiation of treaties. The first general human rights treaty was the European Convention on Human Rights, adopted within the framework of the Council of Europe in 1950. Further Council of Europe treaties followed, along with treaties elaborated by the Organisation of American States, the Organisation for African Unity (now replaced by the African Union), and other regional organisations. Under the auspices of the UN too, negotiations were initiated for the adoption of a treaty that would impose on participating states legal obligations to uphold human rights. When those negotiations finally came to a close in 1966, the outcome was in fact two treaties, the International Covenant on Civil and Political Rights and the International Covenant on Economic, Social and Cultural Rights. The bifurcated approach is usually explained in terms of the West-East rivalry of the Cold War era; with the antagonism between liberal states and state socialism came a separation of civil and political rights from social, economic and cultural rights.

It is a feature of all these treaties that they provided for compliance to be internationally monitored. In the case of the regional treaties, there are 'courts' and in some cases also 'commissions'. In the case of the two International Covenants, there are 'committees' – the Human Rights Committee and the (more recently established) Committee on Economic, Social and Cultural Rights. Monitoring procedures vary from treaty to treaty, but they generally include the possibility of rendering opinions in certain circumstances on claims by individuals that their rights have been violated. (Where the Committee on Economic, Social and Cultural Rights is concerned, this procedure is based on an Optional Protocol adopted only in 2009 and not yet in force.) Evidence is mostly in the form of written testimony, but investigative visits to the country concerned are sometimes made. Under the two International Covenants and also under some regional arrangements, states parties are obligated to make regular reports on the extent to which national law and practice comply with the obligations undertaken, and the examination of these reports, aided often by 'alternative reports' submitted by civil society organisations, is seen as a key element of the monitoring process.

In the years that followed the adoption of the International Covenants, new international treaties were concluded which laid down more detailed commitments concerning specific forms of abuse and specific categories of people. A core set of treaties – on racial discrimination, discrimination against women, torture, the rights of the child, the rights of migrant workers, the rights of persons with disabilities, and enforced disappearance – set up monitoring institutions ('treaty bodies' like the Human Rights Committee and Economic, Social and Cultural Rights Committee); oversight again involves the examination of state reports and in some cases also the competence to render opinions on specific complaints. At the same time, within the framework of the UN and under the authority of the Charter, arrangements were put in place to promote and protect human rights throughout the world. Modified over the years, these arrangements revolve currently around the Office of the High Commissioner for Human Rights, the intergovernmental Human Rights Council, and a large array of 'special procedures', some linked to country-specific mandates, others to mandates cast in thematic terms. Long-standing thematic mandates include disappearances and extrajudicial execution; more recent ones include trafficking in persons and access to safe water and sanitation.

The emergence of so many texts, institutions and procedures in a relatively short space of time unsurprisingly prompted concerns about the efficacy and coherence of the system as a whole. Are not the rights – and especially some of them – vitiatingly vague? Is not the scheme of enforcement too weak to be effective? Does not the proliferation of procedures simply widen the scope for confusion, inefficiency, and empire-building? Such concerns have been at least partly allayed by two developments. On the one hand, through the operation of the various supervisory processes, the content of internationally protected human rights and of the obligations correlative with them has been considerably clarified. A vast and constantly expanding literature now exists glossing the texts of international human rights law. On the other hand, high priority has for some years been attached to improving the system's efficiency and assessing its effectiveness. This has resulted in enhanced coordination and an emphasis on indicators and benchmarks, along with ongoing processes of adjustment and review. Whatever their remaining shortfalls, human rights procedures can undeniably be credited with helping to catalyse important changes to law and practice in many countries.

But the system's efficacy and coherence have not been the only issues. Alongside 'internal' preoccupations of that sort, there has also been discussion of 'external' phenomena that affect international human rights law. Thus, towards the end of the 1990s, an important debate was initiated on the relationship between trade (and more generally globalisation) and human rights. After 9/11 attention turned to the problem of how counter-terrorism impinges on the protection of human rights. An emergent topic today is the relevance of human rights for approaches to climate change and its management. There are also long-standing controversies about the relationship between human rights and culture, about the ethical claims associated with human rights and how those claims may be explained philosophically, and about the place within human rights procedures of global civil society. In some of these arenas, the focus is on the changing context in which human rights norms are interpreted and applied. In other arenas, the central issues have to do with the justification for internationally protected human rights, and with the practical measures needed to redress legitimacy deficits.

If at one level these and other challenges point to strains in the system of human rights, at another level they are, of course, tokens of the extraordinary prominence which human rights have now attained – and not just within legal landscapes. The discussion today is not simply of the organised promotion and protection of human rights; it is also of the specification and implementation of a 'human rights approach' to global policy-making. Applied to international development, poverty reduction and refugee assistance, but also to a huge array of other problems from prison administration to (as we shall see) disaster relief, this is seen to bring with it an orientation towards dignity and rights. Under a human rights approach, charity and benevolence are replaced by the recognition that there exist universal and inalienable entitlements which impose legal obligations on states and others; that those obligations must be implemented on a non-discriminatory basis, and with particular regard for the most vulnerable social groups; that human rights are interdependent, so that programmes must be framed in a manner which ensures that no right is downgraded or impaired; and that underpinning all this are human dignity and the moral demand to respect, uphold and protect it.

Yet the penetration of human rights into global public policy still captures only a small part of what makes human rights so prominent in the world today. According to the contemporary cliché, human rights have become a secular religion: an object of faith, a basis for hope and a code of morality we can all accept, whatever other systems of belief we may cherish or reject. At the least, it is hard to escape the impression that human rights have become an ethical shibboleth or test of right, indeed of righteousness. One aspect of this is their function as an all-purpose, all-pervasive language of responsibility and claim – that is to say, a language used to assert or avow responsibility, and to express and validate claims, in a wide and seemingly limitless variety of contexts. In this sense, human rights represent one of the more striking successes of globalisation. And that accomplishment, in turn, represents one of the more striking recent successes of international law. For if we live today in an 'Age of Human Rights', this is in significant part because of the international legal context with reference to which human rights are today defined, invoked, contested, promoted, explicated and debated.

There is a great deal more to the story of the establishment and consolidation of the international human rights regime than can be conveyed in a few pages. But I have perhaps related enough of it to be able to pause now and take stock of the general register in which the story unfolds. I suggested earlier that it bears the hallmarks of a romance, and referred to David Scott's analysis of C.L.R. James's *The Black Jacobins*. Before going further with our discussion of human rights, let us briefly step aside to consider that book.

The basic facts with which James was concerned have to do with European colonisation in the Caribbean. Specifically, they have to do with the French colony of Saint-Domingue on the island of Hispaniola, the regime of plantation slavery that was established there, the overthrow of that regime by the slaves themselves under the leadership of Toussaint L'Ouverture, Toussaint's enforced removal to France and his death there shortly afterwards, and the subsequent founding of Haiti as the first – and for a long time only – independent black republic outside Africa. Clearly, however, these facts can provide material for a variety of narratives, involving plot structures, forms of characterisation, and recourse to particular tropes that belong with a variety of registers. So what was it, according to Scott, that made James's initial telling of the Haitian revolution – the account that appeared in his first edition of 1938 – a romance?

It was the way James put Toussaint at the centre of his story, and lionised him as a hero with vision, courage, and an undaunted belief in – his own and others' – humanity, who paid to end injustice with his life. It was also the way James described in terrible detail the suffering from which so many longed to be delivered, and evoked the sweet deliverance that would one day be theirs. It was the way he included in his story the many vicissitudes associated with this deliverance – the obstacles, challenges and setbacks that were faced on its path. It was the way he narrated the events as an epic struggle for freedom against oppression (self-government against despotism, integrity against corruption, respect against abuse, and so on). It was the way he wrote of great deeds and noble sentiments, and of the eventual redress of wrongs, the overcoming of adversity and the vindication of those whose dignity had been traduced. As Scott describes it, what made James's initial version a romance was, above all, the distinctive direction, rhythm and 'moral' of his story – the sense that successive events were moving towards some definite horizon; that momentum was gathering, and achievements were being racked up; and that there was inspiration to be gained here, for in this tale of a particular time and place was an allegory of universal significance.

If we return now to human rights, it is not difficult to see the parallels. There too is an inspiring story of great deeds and noble sentiments. Developed through that story are the same themes of suffering and longing, freedom and oppression, vindication and deliverance. Humanity and dignity are again the key values, reasserted through a collective enterprise that calls on courage, determination, sacrifice (albeit usually non-mortal), and leadership. Though it would have unduly prolonged my earlier account to go into them, heroes likewise populate that story; to name just two who are associated with the Universal Declaration of Human Rights: the 'indomitable' Eleanor Roosevelt, first chairperson of the UN commission that negotiated the Declaration, and (more of 'backroom' hero) John Humphrey, the UN official who was principally responsible for drafting the document. The human rights story also proceeds by the same progressive rhythm and with the same clear direction and 'moral'. There are achievements and successes, along with obstacles, challenges and setbacks. Sometimes the successes are themselves challenges, as with the concerns about efficacy and coherence that have attended the proliferation of human rights texts, institutions and procedures. Throughout, however, one senses the unyielding momentum of consolidation, correction, refinement, and reform. Equally, and in consequence, one senses the accumulating results of universalisation or, perhaps better, inclusion within the human rights system of that which was previously missing or left out – inclusion most obviously of more law and more organisation, but also of more states, more victims, more experts, more issues, more perspectives, more stakeholders, and more influence and prestige.

Human Rights in Critical Perspective

What I call inclusion, someone else may call inflation. Indeed, James Griffin is the latest of a long line of scholars to remark on the conceptual inflation of human rights. He writes of the 'tendency to ... uncritical generosity' in the Universal Declaration of Human Rights that brought us, among other rights, the human right to paid holidays (see article 24), and got 'worse in later rights documents' (Griffin 2008, 186). I think it is fair to say that the internationally protected right to paid holidays would have many defenders, who would insist on its indispensability in ensuring the conditions for a decent life, but let us put that aside and stay where we are. The issue for now is: does Griffin's complaint place him at odds with the romantic conventions of human rights commentary just described? No. As we have seen, those conventions are progressive, but not, in fact, uncritical. Griffin's call for a parsimonious approach to human rights (if that is what it is) is advanced in the spirit of correction. He believes that we need criteria to determine when the concept of 'human rights' is being correctly used and when it is being overextended, and he offers help in supplying those criteria, which in his view must depend ultimately on philosophy, not law. So he has a plan to remedy the defects he identifies; he means to provide the rudder without which he considers human rights have drifted badly off-course.

To observe that Griffin's stern criticism still belongs within the romantic conventions of writing about human rights is not, however, to say that all criticism of human rights does so. In what follows we shall review critical arguments of a different sort. They can be found in a relatively recent literature (for a selection of works, see the end of this book), though one that draws on traditions of thought which go back decades and in some cases centuries. These arguments are advanced not so much in the spirit of correction as in the spirit of interrogation. What animates them is not a concern that human rights have drifted off-course, but that questions need to be asked about what it means for them to sail on-course. The focus is, accordingly, on structural features of the human rights system – presuppositions, tendencies and effects that are unremarkable, or at any rate generally unremarked, within the romantic story of human rights. One consequence is that, if that story (at least as I related it above) reads like a history, the story I am about to outline may read more like theory. But part of its point is to offer elements towards an alternative historical narrative of the international protection of human rights, and also to show how the romantic narrative itself embeds theoretical propositions that need to be brought out and challenged. So, if that is right, there is history and theory in both.

What then are these structural features? To get the discussion of them started, let us consider a short text by Chidi Odinkalu entitled 'Why More Africans Don't Use Human Rights Language' (Odinkalu 1999). According to Odinkalu, Africa presents us with a case of both 'a human rights crisis and a crisis for human rights'. The human rights crisis is well known, and has to do with the chasm that separates rights from realities for the vast majority of people on the continent. The crisis for human rights is less well known, or anyway less often mentioned. It is reflected in the fact that most Africans 'do not describe their problems in human rights terms'. As he explains the situation, 'people are acutely aware of the injustices inflicted upon them'; for that knowledge, they don't need the Universal Declaration of Human Rights and the treaties and other instruments that make up international human rights law. What they do need is 'a movement that channels these frustrations into articulate demands that evoke responses from the political process'. Yet the insistence of human rights institutions and organisations on being 'neutral', 'impartial' and 'non-political' means that that is the one thing which the international human rights system cannot provide. Thus alienated from those they are meant to protect, human rights become increasingly the specialised idiom of a select group of professionals – less a 'badge of honour' than a 'certificate of privilege'.

Put forward here, quite plainly, is an account of human rights in which our appreciation of their successes is tempered by an awareness of their significant failures and limitations. Odinkalu's analysis is useful because he touches on a number of the matters that are similarly highlighted and called into question by other authors. To begin with, there is the depoliticisation of which he writes. The effort to keep the international protection of human rights as 'non-political' as possible belongs, of course, with the much broader ideal in liberal thought of separating law from politics. As has long been observed, however, law fundamentally depends on politics, even as politics is itself shaped by the concepts and categories of the law. There are many aspects to this, but one, emphasised by Odinkalu, is that legal rights do not of themselves translate into social realities; to realise rights it is necessary to act on political processes. And just as political processes determine what can be made of legal rights, so too they determine what constitute those legal rights in the first place; in theoretical language, rights are not 'pre-political'. So, for example, the nature and scope of human rights in any given situation will be conditioned by the particular treaties that have been ratified by the state or states involved, the extent to which reservations have been made and monitoring procedures accepted with respect to those treaties, and the way relevant norms of the law of treaties are understood and applied by state authorities.

Alongside depoliticisation, Odinkalu directs attention to the related phenomenon of professionalisation. Although human rights have had, and still at times retain, an important role in mobilising, consolidating and fortifying popular struggles against oppression, the context for this role is today a countervailing prioritisation of expertise. Thus, Odinkalu highlights the emergence of human rights as an object of specialised knowledge, and of the human rights movement as a privileged domain with limited participation by, and even less accountability to, the constituencies it is supposed to protect. Insofar as human rights organisations act on behalf of groups to whom they do not answer, there creeps in a potential for arrogance or, at the least, loss of solidarity; the focus is instead on the donor agencies and 'partner' organisations to which ties are stronger. This points to another notable dimension of the professionalisation of human rights: bureaucratisation. As human rights institutions and procedures have proliferated, so also have the people and practices required to run them, and to do so, as observed above, efficiently and effectively. Of course, efficiency and effectiveness are laudable and appropriate goals, but the point here is that bureaucratic indicators can be misleading. Through them a vision of the world is fostered in which we too hastily assume that more meetings, more reports, more monitoring mechanisms, and more treaty ratifications equate to better social conditions.

Depoliticisation and professionalisation are the key issues evoked in Odinkalu's text, but implicit in his analysis are some further concerns. One has to do with the production of victims. By this is not meant the production of what occasions victimhood (though, as we shall see, that too may be at stake); the reference is instead to the production of victims as a particular category, identity or form of 'subjectivity'. For human rights do not simply ascribe rights to people already constituted as subjects; part of what they do is to constitute those subjects. So, for instance, although the Universal Declaration of Human Rights and the other texts of international human rights law are written as though the 'human being' or 'member of the human family' who is the subject of human rights were their basis, it needs rather to be understood as their effect. More than that, it needs to be understood as an effect with distinctive characteristics, for rights produce the particular sort of right-holders who fit them. The question then becomes: what sort of right-holders are they? What specificities are concealed inside this person-in-general, this neutrality which is the 'human being', and what social hierarchies and forms of power and privilege are thereby naturalised and reinforced? Within that line of enquiry, it is significant that the victim of human rights is a largely passive identity, defined by suffering, and waiting for vindication through the heroic agency of the international human rights system.

The victim of human rights is an identity that also has the characteristic of privileging abuses in the domain of public life. This leads to another concern, inasmuch as that is helpful to those seeking redress in connection with misconduct by state officials, but not so helpful in dealing with violence, exploitation and oppression in the 'private' sphere of economic, associational and intimate relations. To be sure, important steps have been taken in recent decades to extend the scope of state responsibility. We speak today not just of the (negative) obligations of states to refrain from interfering with human rights, but also of their 'positive' obligations to prevent and punish interferences by 'non-state actors'. So too we speak of the obligations of states not just to 'respect' human rights, but also to 'protect' and 'ensure' them, again through regulation of 'non-state' conduct. But the responsibility remains that of the state, and this reflects a notable state-centricity that, as discussed elsewhere in this book, pervades international law in general. To place the state at the centre of all liberatory possibilities is not just to marginalise 'non-state actors' – the very phrase already underscores the primordiality of states. It is also to gloss over the constraints imposed on state action by socio-economic forces and relations, both within national boundaries and across the world. According to a familiar analysis, state-centricity is offset in the case of human rights by a focus on individuals (or collectivities) and their rights. This idea of human rights as 'incursions into' state sovereignty presupposes that power gained by individuals is power lost by states. Yet we know that, in reality, things are not so simple; rights empower right-holders, but they also empower states to order and control the social environment in which right-holding arises and becomes consequential.

This double empowerment has another dimension, which brings us to perhaps the most telling structural feature of the international human rights system. If human rights are a language of responsibility and claim, they are also a language of exoneration and justification. That is so for at least three reasons. One is the simple fact of conceptual boundaries: what is not in is out. To prohibit abuse is to authorise whatever does not constitute abuse. Regulatory activity is always at once repressive and permissive. A second reason is that it is also invariably the case that the relation between repression and permission gets mediated in a multiplicity of ways. With rights come rationales for setting them aside, whether in the shape of in-built exceptions and qualifications, overriding principles of exoneration or excuse, general norms to do with the making or application of international law, or indeed other, equally compelling but potentially incompatible human rights. And a third reason is that all this calls for interpretation. Human rights do not themselves speak; they are made to speak in the service of particular people and particular purposes. The question is always which people and purposes. What arguments does the international human rights system make available, to whom, and under what conditions? To point to the justificatory aspect of human rights is to invite attention to their legitimating function in many different contexts. But one context in which the legitimating function of human rights has attracted particular attention in recent years is war. The centrality of human rights in virtually all justificatory arguments today for war, whether through the doctrine of humanitarian intervention, the more recent principle of the responsibility to protect, or the rules of international human rights law (and the related bodies of international humanitarian law and international criminal law) themselves, is at one level a measure of the rise of human rights; at another, a measure of their fall; and at yet another, a measure of their abiding contradictions.

As with the story of the establishment and consolidation of the human rights regime, there is much more to this 'counter-narrative' than can be captured in a few pages. But rather than pressing further, let us return now to the question of register, and to *The Black Jacobins* that is serving as our reference-point in that regard. The key aspect, you will recall, is the shift observed by David Scott from romance to tragedy. We have seen the main elements that can be said to have made C.L.R. James's original edition of 1938 a romance. How did he revise it for his second edition of 1963 so as to re-code the story as a tragedy, and what parallels may again connect the history of this book with our investigation into the international protection of human rights?James made a number of changes for the work's second edition, but for Scott the most significant is the insertion of a new passage in which James reflects on his hero's 'tragic alternatives' (James 1963, 236). Either Toussaint could ensure the permanent emancipation of slaves in Saint-Domingue, or he could maintain colonial ties with France. He could not do both, for the French authorities were determined to restore slavery in the colony; the bourgeoisie profited from it too much to let it go. Yet he had to do both, for true emancipation depended on ties with modern, enlightened France – or so Toussaint believed, as a modern, enlightened child of the French revolution himself.

Scott calls this kind of dilemma, about which many have written in recent decades, the 'tragedy of colonial enlightenment', and he shows how, in emphasising the tragedy of colonial enlightenment, James interrupts the romantic narrative of progress. Instead of a progressive movement in the direction of some definite horizon, we are left with the sense that we do not know where the future may lead. Instead of an epic struggle between starkly opposed phenomena (freedom and oppression, self-government and despotism, and so on), we are presented with a much more interconnected set of problems. Instead of the eventual redress of wrongs, we are confronted with the possibility of an outcome that is contradictory, ambiguous and unresolved. And instead of an inspiring story in which the universal is disclosed within the local, we are thrown back on the contingency of events we should neither sentimentalise nor judge. Scott suggests that the altered register of James's second edition may reflect the impact on James of the nationalist struggles in Africa then reaching fruition. But whatever prompted the change, Scott's main point – the point he wants us to take from his book (as distinct from James's) – is that the tragedy of colonial enlightenment is a more compelling story today than the romance of anti-colonial nationalism, inasmuch as the latter simply is not now helpful.

And this, surely, is the principal message too of the arguments we have just reviewed. The romantic narrative of human rights is not wrong, but it is inadequate. Its well-meaning tale of vindication and deliverance needs interruption. For if the international human rights system can serve as an instrument of the powerless, it can also serve as an agent of the powerful. If it can be used for resistance, it can also be deployed for hegemony. If it can impugn violence, it can also justify violence. And if it can help to challenge prevailing power relations, it can also help efforts to keep things as they are. We have seen some of the factors that contribute to this ambiguity: depoliticisation, professionalisation, the production of victims, state-centricity and the justificatory capacity of human rights. In each case, the forward march of progress is unsettled by a more complex and uncertain rhythm. The international protection of human rights may well be moving in the direction of consolidation, correction, refinement, and reform, but if so, that is not the only direction in which it is moving. We need to consider the other directions too, and scrutinise them with equal vigour. In this context, Toussaint's dilemma stands as a permanent reminder that the gates of modernity are guarded with two faces. What enables emancipatory struggle may also enable the brutality of a global order in which the secular religion is not (or not only) human rights, but, of course, capitalism.

Haiti and the Human Rights Approach

The Black Jacobins deals with Haitian history from colonisation to independence. Fast-forward a little over two hundred years. On 12 January 2010 a catastrophic earthquake hit southern Haiti, with its epicentre near the capital, Port-au-Prince. Hundreds of thousands of people were killed, many more injured, and more still left without homes. Two weeks later the UN Human Rights Council held an emergency meeting (or 'special session') to discuss the situation. The theme was 'a human rights approach to the recovery process in Haiti'. In a statement to the session, UN High Commissioner for Human Rights Navanethem Pillay paid tribute to the 'bravery, resilience and mutual solidarity that had been displayed in the face of immense adversity'. This was the 'worst tragedy' experienced in the Western hemisphere for many decades. Its effects had been 'exacerbated by pre-existing inhuman conditions of poverty, instability and feeble institutions', and if these were to be overcome, initiatives had to be 'anchored in human rights'. 'A human rights approach helps ensure that the root causes of vulnerabilities, in this case poverty and discrimination, are addressed.' Government and civil society delegates likewise spoke of the tragedy that had befallen Haiti, and of the need not to let human rights be eclipsed by the immediate demands of humanitarian aid. For it was crucial to be aware that 'natural disasters and the way in which international organizations responded to them [have] clear human rights implications'.

Was this, however, a 'natural' disaster? At the same time as that discussion was unfolding in the Human Rights Council, another debate was underway on the historical context in which 'poverty and discrimination' had caused so many people to be killed, injured and made homeless. Writing in the *New Statesman*, Peter Hallward recalled the course of Haitian history since the overthrow of colonial slavery and the establishment of the new state in 1803 (Hallward 2010; see also Hallward 2007). Beginning with a punishing blockade and the imposition by France of massive 'reparations' for the loss of slaves and other colonial property, it is a litany of interventionary episodes in support of foreign commercial interests and the tiny local elite, the successors to the colonial plantation owners. The viciousness of Duvalier *père et fils*, the US-backed despots who ruled Haiti from the 1950s to the 1980s, is well known, and it was during the younger Duvalier's reign of terror that economic 'modernisation' came to Haiti. Hallward reports that Haitians referred to the scheme of privatisation, fiscal austerity, and de-agrarianisation as the 'death plan'. Several more monetary and military interventions later, that has certainly been, and in January 2010 remained, its significance for many. When the earthquake struck, huge numbers of people were living in and around Port-au-Prince, in flimsy slum dwellings pushed to the precarious edge of deforested and eroding ravines.

The message here is clear. If nature brought the earthquake to Haiti, the catastrophe it caused was decidedly man-made. The Human Rights Council was plainly aware of this. In speech after speech, poverty and discrimination were held up as the root causes of what had happened. But what caused poverty and discrimination?As Seamus Milne writes in commentary about the public reaction to the earthquake in the United Kingdom, these realities of the Haitian situation were treated as 'baffling quirks of history or culture' (Milne 2010). To be sure, Pillay referred at one stage to the 'Duvalier regime which forced people from rural areas and farmers from rice fields to the capital to provide cheap labour for Haiti's elite'. But she did not – indeed, she could not – mention the relation of that regime to the United States, and nor did she say anything about the role of the international financial institutions and later also the UN itself in carrying the policies forward through 'structural adjustment'. There is an important general point here. The concept of 'root causes' is today a conspicuous feature of the international human rights system. Root causes, as we see, are part of what a 'human rights approach' is supposed to address. But in the manner in which this discourse has developed, it risks concealing more than it reveals. We are left to think of the misery of Haiti's poor not as an outcome of determinate forces and relations, including forces and relations that stretch across the

world, but as a local dysfunction and accident of history. We seem confronted with the work of a cruel dictatorship that simply arrived one fearful day and wreaked havoc, almost as though it were ... an earthquake.

This opens up a fascinating question. Could it be that to call something a violation (or 'root cause' of a violation) of human rights is *always* to treat it is a baffling quirk of history or culture, that is to say, as a disaster which, if man-made, may just as well be natural? Could it be, in other words, that 'natural disaster' is the model on which in this context *everything* is imaginatively constructed? If so, then the Human Rights Council exposes here, however unwittingly, a truth about the international protection of human rights that goes well beyond the question of a human rights approach to the post-earthquake recovery process in Haiti. That is, in fact, a truth to which many have alluded in diverse ways. Naomi Klein, for example, has evoked the case of torture and disappearance in Chile and Argentina during the 1970s and 80s (Klein 2007, 118 *et seq.*). The human rights movement never raised the question as to whether there was a connection between these atrocities and the extreme form of neo-liberal economic restructuring then being imposed on the societies concerned. Klein maintains that this was because the movement committed itself during this formative period to the style of anti-political politics on which Odinkalu also comments in the text discussed above. While there were reasons for that, the effect was to occlude any awareness that the abuses were a form of 'planned misery' (this is Rodolfo Walsh's phrase. See Klein 2007, 95). They could only be grasped as 'random, free-floating bad events, drifting in the political ether, to be condemned by all people of conscience but impossible to understand' (Klein 2007, 120).

Conclusion

Let us briefly retrace our steps before concluding. Taking our cue from David Scott's analysis of C.L.R. James's *The Black Jacobins*, we have considered the international protection of human rights with reference to two distinct narrative modes. A romantic account describes the establishment and consolidation of the international human rights regime. It is a story of proliferating texts, institutions and procedures, and of the patient labour of interpretation, co-ordination and reform. There are setbacks and strains, but also incontrovertible achievements. All states of the world are today parties to at least one human rights treaty, and most are parties to more than one. Monitoring mechanisms created under these treaties, and within the UN, have catalysed countless changes of great legal and practical significance.

A tragic account reminds us that more treaty adherences do not necessarily correlate to improved social circumstances, even if sometimes they do. Bureaucratic indicators can be misleading, just as the professionalisation of human rights can be corrosive. Emancipatory struggles are not a matter of rescue by heroic professionals, but of people altering the conditions of their lives. This means acting on political processes that include, but also extend beyond, the state. International human rights law creates avenues for redress in connection with misconduct or neglect by state officials. But it also offers justification for state policies. And it provides few direct remedies against private actors, indeed strengthening the latter's hand insofar as it treats economy, society and culture as the given background against which rights may be claimed.

Interwoven with that story of two narratives about human rights has also been another story, about Haiti from revolutionary times to the present day. This is a story of three tragedies. The first is the tragedy related by the UN High Commissioner for Human Rights and the delegates to the Human Rights Council's special session of January 2010. That story tells of tragedy in the sense of fate, chance, destiny or malign nature; the accent is on the ineluctability of events and the nobility of suffering. The second is the tragedy that preoccupies James (in his second edition) and Scott. That story tells of tragedy in the different sense of contradiction, indeterminacy and dilemma – the tragedy of colonial enlightenment. And the third is the tragedy to which Hallward, Milne and Klein direct our attention. Questioning both the ineluctability of events and their historical indeterminacy, that final story tells of tragedy in the different sense again of planned misery or 'necessary suffering' (see Asad 1996).

In elaborating the idea of 'necessary suffering', Talal Asad quotes Lord Cromer, British Consul-General to Egypt from 1883 to 1907 (and later leading anti-suffragette). If cruelties were imposed in the course of colonial administration, then – Cromer matter-of-factly observed – this was because 'civilisation must, unfortunately, have its victims'. Necessary suffering, like planned misery, invites consideration of the organisation of imperial power, and of the persistence, and changing forms, of exploitation in the modern world. This third form of tragedy is vivid in writing about Haiti. But, with few exceptions, it has had relatively little impact on writing about the international protection of human rights. Perhaps, though, the moment has come for another shift in register, a new human rights narrative for our disastrous times.

BIBLIOGRAPHY

Asad, T., 1996. 'On Torture, or Cruel, Inhuman, and Degrading Treatment', *Social Research*, 63, 1081–1109

Griffin, J., 2008. *On Human Rights*, Oxford University Press

Hallward, P., 2007. *Damming the Flood: Haiti, Aristide and the Politics of Containment*, London: Verso

Hallward, P., 2010. 'The land that wouldn't lie', *New Statesman*, 28 January

James, C. L. R., 1963. *The Black Jacobins*, London: Penguin

Klein, N., 2007. *The Shock Doctrine*, London: Penguin

Milne, S., 2010. 'Haiti's suffering is a result of calculated impoverishment', *The Guardian*, 20 January

Odinkalu, C., 1999. 'Why more Africans don't use human rights language', *Human Rights Dialogue*, 2.1, Winter

Scott, D., 2004. *Conscripts of Modernity: The Tragedy of Colonial Enlightenment*, Duke University Press

15 Justifying justice

Sarah M. H. Nouwen

Until lions have their own historians, tales of the hunt shall always glorify the hunter.
(Ibo proverb)

Sudan, December 2008

In a camp for displaced persons in Darfur, children have tied a cord around a hedgehog's neck. 'This is President Bashir and we are taking him to the International Criminal Court.' Awaiting the BBC and CNN, spokespersons for the displaced chant: 'We need NATO, the EU and the ICC.' Tribal leaders, asked why they no longer use traditional justice mechanisms, explain: 'This is genocide and only the International Criminal Court can address genocide.' New-born boys have been named 'Ocambo', after the Court's Prosecutor. Bolstered by 'brother' Ocampo's request for an arrest warrant for the Sudanese President on charges of genocide, crimes against humanity and war crimes, one of the rebel movements has launched an attack on the Sudanese capital and another has refused to participate in peace talks, arguing that one should not negotiate with 'war criminals'. The Sudanese government, in turn, publicly denounces the International Criminal Court (ICC). Driving from the airport into Khartoum one is greeted by enormous billboards showing a strong President and reading: 'Ocampo's Plot: A Malicious Move in the Siege', 'Protect the International Law from Ocampo's Illusions' and 'No for the Oppression of Peoples under the Name of International Law!'[1]

[1] Unless otherwise provided, the quotes and stories from Uganda and Sudan provided in this chapter can be found in Nouwen (2012) (in press).

The attraction of international criminal justice

For an international criminal lawyer it is gratifying to write a chapter on her specialisation: her field is attractive.[2]

First, the field's accepted history is one of success. The judges at the Nuremberg tribunal planted the seeds of a new sub-discipline of international law by declaring that '[c]rimes against international law are committed by men, not by abstract entities, and only by punishing individuals who commit such crimes can the provisions of international law be enforced' (Nuremberg Judgment 1947, 221). For some time, the Cold War froze the development of international criminal tribunals. However, with the emergence of a 'new world order', the UN Security Council could agree on the establishment of international criminal tribunals for the former Yugoslavia and Rwanda. The creation of the two *ad hoc* tribunals with limited territorial jurisdiction gave momentum, and a different direction, to the project of a permanent court with a potentially world-wide jurisdiction. The year 2002 saw the entry into force of the Rome Statute, creating a permanent International Criminal Court with 'jurisdiction over persons for the most serious crimes of international concern' (article 1), namely genocide, crimes against humanity, war crimes, and – once defined – aggression. Meanwhile, in places such as Sierra Leone and Cambodia, a new category of international criminal tribunals emerged: so-called 'hybrid' or 'internationalised' courts. These courts apply international as well as national law or/and their bench and prosecution teams are composed of both nationals and foreigners. In sum, in a few 'generations' (Romano, Nollkaemper and Kleffner 2004, x), international(ised) criminal courts have spread around the world, 'from Nuremberg to The Hague' (Sands 2003), via Tokyo, Arusha, Dili, Phnom Penh and Freetown, prosecuting crimes committed in the Balkans, Rwanda, Cambodia, East Timor, Sierra Leone, Beirut, Uganda, Darfur, the Democratic Republic of the Congo, the Central African Republic, Kenya, Côte d'Ivoire and Libya. Meanwhile, the ICC Prosecutor closely monitors Colombia, Georgia, Afghanistan, Guinea and Palestine. International criminal law has grown not only institutionally but also in substantive terms.

[2] By equating international criminal law with international criminal tribunals, the story fails to mention the more established field of international criminal law concerning inter-state cooperation in addressing domestic crimes. It also omits the important role that domestic courts play in the enforcement of international criminal law.

The tribunals' case-law has, for instance, determined the legal threshold for armed conflict (international and non-international); established that violations of international humanitarian law during non-international armed conflicts are also crimes; found that rape may constitute an act of genocide, a crime against humanity and a war crime; and set out the modalities of individual criminal responsibility. In addition, the tribunals have developed previously non-existent international criminal procedural law. International criminal law has become a voluminous body of international law.

The seeming strength of international criminal law, particularly when compared with some other fields of international law, is a second attractive feature of the field. International lawyers are constantly challenged that their law is not 'real' law because its enforcement is so decentralised. While international criminal tribunals, too, are sometimes aptly described as giants without limbs (Cassese 1998, 13), their enforcement handicap is overcome once the accused is in the dock. The record suggests that even powerful leaders can be subjected to international law.

International criminal law is also one of international law's most sensational fields. As a theatre of human drama, the criminal court-room, domestic or international, attracts attention. Public interest may be lost in procedural labyrinths and legal detail, but is awakened by indictments, arrests and scandals. A court-room confrontation between a top model and a war lord, revealing the beast in the beauty, puts international criminal justice on the front page (SCSL-2003-01-T 2010, 4561–5489).

A fourth facet is the modernity of international criminal law: it fits with *die Zeitgeist*. In dominant globalisation discourse, states are out and non-state actors in, sovereignty and immunity mere shields for human rights violations, global institutions the solution, and individuals either heroic forces of progress or despicable sources of misery. International criminal courts, at least in name, are global institutions that pierce state sovereignty and assign responsibility to individuals.

But perhaps the most attractive element of international criminal law is that it offers the idealist lawyer a profession in which she can express her humanitarian interest and fulfil her part of the 'global responsibility to protect'. In doing so, she follows in the footsteps of giants, the lawyers who convinced the Allies of the importance of a legal response to the major crimes of the Second World War; the heroic lawyer-activists – some themselves victims of the crimes that international criminal law proscribes – whose prolific writing and legal drafting kept the idea of a permanent International Criminal Court alive when the *esprit du temps* was against it; the diplomats negotiating the Rome Statute, at least as committed to the project of international criminal justice as to their national briefs; the legal scholars who nourished the field with concepts, structured it with detailed commentaries and enthused their students; the dedicated lawyers at international tribunals, attempting to overcome politics with law; and the many national and international non-governmental organisations (NGOs) that have been the beating heart of the international criminal justice movement.

In the spirit of John Donne ('any man's death diminishes me, because I am involved in Mankind'), the international criminal justice movement advocates for humanity by accusing, condemning and punishing in its name. Or at least, it protects the *idea* of a common humanity: 'If the international community cannot prevent, at least it must not condone' (Orentlicher 1991, 2615). International criminal justice inspires hope (see Tallgren 2002, 593). The project of international criminal justice assuages the moral hunger for a response to visible and yet unimaginable human suffering, reassures the idealist of her own identity ('I am a good person who responds to bad things', Koller 2008, 1034) and nurtures a sense of belonging to an 'international community'.

Darfur, December 2008

'Why do Darfurians need the ICC?', asks the interviewer to the person who stated 'We need NATO, the EU and the ICC'.

For justice.
What is 'justice'*?*
Justice is the end of the war.
How is the ICC going to end the war?
By arresting President Bashir and his party.
And then?
Once there is peace in Darfur, the *ajaweed* [respected elders] will do real justice.
What is real *justice?*
Real justice is done through *judiya* [a mix of mediation and arbitration between groups, resulting in compensation and arrangements for future co-existence].[3]

[3] Author's interview, Nyala, December 2008.

Justice as an instrument for peace

The Darfurians' expectation that justice leads to peace reflects the most ambitious and yet dominant justification of international criminal justice. The protagonists seldom spell out the causal pathway, but underlying their statements is the theory that international criminal justice prevents crimes by combating impunity, and by preventing crime promotes peace. In the words of former ICC President Kirsch:

> The International Criminal Court was created to break this vicious cycle of crimes, impunity and conflict. It was set up to contribute to justice and the prevention of crimes, and thereby to peace and security. (Kirsch 2007, 3)

The ICC's Office of the Prosecutor (OTP), in turn, has identified 'maximi[sing] the impact of the activities of the office' with a view to prevention of crimes as one of its 'guiding principles' (OTP 2010, para. 23). 'This [preventive] effect is not limited to the situation under investigation but extends to all states Parties and reverberates worldwide' (*ibid.*).

One way in which international criminal justice could contribute to the prevention of crimes is through deterrence. However, lawyers have had to acknowledge that the deterrent effect of criminal law, whether across the globe or in the particular situation where an international tribunal investigates crimes, is at best questionable (Koller 2008, 1027–1029; see also Koskenniemi 2002, 7–8; Tallgren 2002, 575–576).

A more concrete way in which international criminal justice could contribute to prevention is through incapacitation of alleged criminals. This argument is heavily relied on by the ICC Prosecutor. For instance, with respect to Ahmed Harun, a Sudanese official for whom the Court has issued an arrest warrant, he has argued:

> In Darfur today, there can be no political solution, no security solution, and no humanitarian solution as long as Harun remains free in Sudan. Harun exemplifies the need to end impunity in order to create lasting peace. In the 1990s, he was active in Southern Sudan . . . . He was allegedly called 'The Butcher of the Nuba'; yet, his crimes were forgotten after a peace agreement was reached. He started committing atrocities again in 2002–03 and continues to commit crimes now. It is time to stop him. Arresting him will break the system and change the behaviours. (Moreno-Ocampo 2007–2008, 223)

Against this background, the Prosecutor predicts:

Arresting and removing Harun today will contribute to breaking the criminal system established in Darfur [and] will help peace, the political process and the deployment of peacekeepers. (Moreno-Ocampo 2008a, 8)

It is worthwhile to reflect on the meaning given in these statements to the rich concepts 'peace' and 'justice'. As the rallying cry of the Coalition for the International Criminal Court (CICC) reflects ('Together for Justice: Civil society ... advocating for a fair, effective and independent ICC'), the field arrogates the term 'justice', which could include dimensions such as economic and social justice, to the project of international criminal law; and then reduces the entire field of international criminal law to the ICC. The resulting equation reads: Justice = the ICC. Peace, in turn, could refer to a situation in which the causes of violence have been addressed, in other words 'positive peace'. But in the statements above, the Prosecutor uses peace in the narrower meaning of 'negative peace': that is, the absence of violence. (The Prosecutor must be taken to argue that criminal justice leads to negative peace only; for even by turning Ahmed Harun into a demon, one cannot maintain that by arresting this one person the causes of violence in Darfur, which include political and economic grievances, will have been addressed.)

With respect to Uganda, too, the Prosecutor has invoked the peace-by-incapacitation theory. In December 2003 the Ugandan Government referred the 'situation concerning the Lord's Resistance Army' (LRA) to the ICC, citing its own inability to arrest the leadership of the rebel movement that is notorious for murders, mutilations and abductions. According to the ICC Prosecutor, who brought charges against LRA leader Joseph Kony and four other LRA commanders, the ICC offers a straightforward solution:

There is no tension between Peace and Justice in Uganda: arrest the sought criminals today, and you will have Peace and Justice tomorrow. (Moreno-Ocampo 2007, 3)

Northern Uganda, September 2008

'The International Criminal Court leads to death.' Elaborating on his view, the Ugandan bishop who is being interviewed juxtaposes the system of criminal courts with Acholi traditional justice:

The court system is justice through punishment after truth. We don't do it like that. Once the truth has been revealed we look for a healing process. We have restorative justice. *Mato oput* [an Acholi justice mechanism] is pro life and holistic. The court system is justice through punishment. The offender and offended are put aside. This leads to polarisation which will lead to death.[4]

The bishop begins by challenging the 'justice' justification of international criminal law. He and other northern Ugandans argue that court proceedings, whether in Uganda or elsewhere, do not result in justice in the restorative sense. As one traditional leader observes, '[t]here is a balance in the community that cannot be found in the briefcase of the white man' (quoted in Allen 2006, 87). International criminal justice, unlike traditional justice, does not aim for reconciliation between the offender and the spirits of the offended persons. As a result, *cen*, the vengeance of the spirit world, will manifest itself in the form of nightmares, sickness or death, and will haunt the entire clan of the wrongdoer, if not in this generation then in the next. Only Acholi elders, not ICC judges, are believed to be close enough to the spiritual world to be able to appease bad omens (Liu Institute *et al.* 2005; Gulu District NGO Forum *et al.* 2007; Ochola II 2009).

Other traditional leaders argue that the ICC fails to do justice because it does not do distributive justice. By portraying the conflict in northern Uganda as one between a legitimate government and a criminal organisation, the ICC ignores the political and economic grievances of the Acholi, the traditional leaders contend. In their view, 'political solutions have never been found in a court room'.

Almost all northern Ugandans interviewed point out that selective justice is injustice. They argue that the ICC Prosecutor should have equally investigated crimes allegedly committed by state actors. Or they criticise the fact that international law apparently does not consider the conduct of the Ugandan government as 'criminal'. They mention the government's forcing the Acholi off their land to 'protected camps' thereby undermining their economic base and culture without providing security in return; the camps have become 'pick-up centres' for LRA abduction raids. One bishop explains his view of selective justice as injustice through a metaphor:

Suppose the Government of Uganda were a parent of children trapped in a burning house (Northern Uganda), which was set on fire by an arsonist (the LRA): what justice is there for the children abandoned in the burning house while their 'parent' is single-mindedly focused on chasing the 'arsonist' (the LRA) for over [the] last twenty years?

[4] Author's interview, Kitgum, September 2008.

> And what justice is served when the children's 'parent' decides to invite the ICC to join the chase of the arsonist (LRA) three to four years after his twenty or so years' chase? (Ochola II 2009, 20–21)

Some interviewees even challenge the claim that the ICC achieves punitive justice. One elder states:

> If [the leaders of the LRA] are taken to The Hague, they will be locked up with air conditioning and will live the lifestyle of Ugandan ministers. But they [should] come here and make up with the community. Let them live with the people whose ears they have chopped off. Let them see for the rest of their lives what suffering they have caused. That is punishment. In our view, ICC punishment is very light. Let them morally come and confess.

Finally, northern Ugandans challenge the 'peace' justification of international criminal justice. The bishop whose interview was cited above argues that the character of retributive justice is to polarise, which leads to death. In another interview, elders of the Acholi community argue in more literal terms that the ICC leads to death. The Acholi were stunned, the elders recount, to discover that the ICC has no more capacity than the Ugandan government (and indeed depends on the Ugandan government), when it comes to arresting the LRA leaders. In the elders' view:

> If you want to issue arrest warrants, then make sure that Kony is within your reach. If you cannot arrest Kony, then it is the local people that will suffer. This is what [the government's] *Operation Iron Fist* has shown. Arms were cut off, because they had responded to the [government's] call to take up weapons against Kony. Ears were cut off because they had been used for picking up LRA messages for the government. Lips were cut off because they had been used for talking about the LRA to the government.[5]

Interviewed Acholi argue that the intervention of an outside international court paints the LRA leadership into a corner, and serves as a disincentive to sign a peace agreement since the ICC has indicated that even signature of a peace agreement would not cause it to lift its warrants.

Justice as an instrument for peace: in practice

The ICC's OTP, however, has taken pride in the claim that it has *promoted* peace in northern Uganda. It cites 'the positive effect that [its] warrants have

[5] Author's interview, Gulu, September 2008.

had in motivating the LRA to attend peace talks' (OTP 2006, 3). The Juba peace talks began a few months after the ICC had unsealed arrest warrants against the LRA leadership and resulted in the most comprehensive set of agreements yet reached between the Ugandan government and an LRA delegation. Moreover, the Prosecutor says he is 'very glad that the situation in Northern Uganda has changed so drastically since the Court's arrest warrants forced Joseph Kony to leave his safe haven in the Sudan and move to the DRC' (Moreno-Ocampo 2010b, 4).

There are, however, two unfortunate 'details' not mentioned in this account. First, Joseph Kony has refused to sign the agreement that consolidates the agreements reached in Juba. While his precise motivation is unknown, it is clear that, owing to the ICC's involvement, there was limited scope for the talks to produce an outcome he would find acceptable. From the outset, the LRA delegation had insisted that the ICC arrest warrants be 'withdrawn' (Wierda and Otim 2008, 23), but the Rome Statute does not provide for simple withdrawal of the arrest warrants. Article 16 of the Statute provides for the Security Council's deferral of proceedings, but only for twelve months at a time. Article 53(2)(c) allows the Prosecutor to decide not to prosecute on the ground that prosecution would not serve 'the interests of justice'. However, the Prosecutor has stated that '[t]he "interests of justice" must of course not be confused with the interests of peace and security, which falls within the mandate of other institutions, such as the UN Security Council' (Moreno-Ocampo 2010a, 6).

The only avenue open to Uganda for terminating the ICC's case against the LRA leadership would be to challenge the admissibility of the case on the ground of the Rome Statute's principle of complementarity (articles 17 and 20(3)). Pursuant to this principle, the ICC's case against the LRA leaders would be inadmissible if Uganda itself conducted genuine criminal proceedings against them. It is for this reason that the Juba Agreements envisage Ugandan proceedings. Kony, however, referring to Charles Taylor's fate (the former Liberian president who was transferred to the Special Court for Sierra Leone despite a promise of asylum), has demanded guarantees for his security and will not sign 'if the ICC indictments are not dropped' (Nyakairu 2008).

The second omitted detail is that while Kony has moved away from northern Uganda, he has taken the insecurity with him. Since the end of the Juba peace talks, the LRA has made hundreds of victims in southern Sudan, the Democratic Republic of the Congo and the Central African Republic.

The ICC arrest warrants have thus served as a double-edged sword,[6] being on one side an incentive for talks but on the sharper side an apparently insurmountable obstacle to the conclusion of an agreement. As de Waal and Flint have observed, 'pressure works if the party under pressure can agree with the end point. If that is life imprisonment, pressure only generates counter-pressure' (de Waal and Flint 2009). Having blocked the avenue of agreement, international criminal justice can lead to peace only by way of total victory. International criminal justice does its part in the war for a total victory by delegitimising one side of the conflict and seemingly legitimising the other (see Nouwen and Werner, 2011). Theoretically, the ICC's OTP could investigate both sides equally. However, because it is 'endowed with no more powers than any tourist in a foreign state' (Swart and Sluiter 1999, 115), it depends on state cooperation for almost all of its operations, ranging from issuing visas for its investigators to the execution of arrest warrants. It thus considers it in its institutional interest either to avoid antagonising the government or to portray the government as *hostis humani generis*, thereby legitimising the opposition.

The ICC's promise of incapacitation intensifies conflict by fuelling the hopes of the one party (and the fears of the other) that it may be possible to achieve peace on that party's terms through a total victory, rather than a negotiated peace through compromise and accommodation (Nouwen and Werner, 2011).

Sudan, 4 March 2009

Fifteen minutes after the ICC's decision to issue an arrest warrant against President Bashir is released, the Sudanese authorities expel international humanitarian NGOs from Darfur. Sudanese human rights organisations are closed down. A few months ago the Sudanese National Intelligence and Security Services began torturing human rights defenders. The NGOs and human rights defenders are alleged to have cooperated with the ICC. In anticipation of the warrant, one of the rebel movements has promised that if the ICC judges were to issue the warrant against the President, it would 'work hard to bring him down', adding that if the President 'doesn't cooperate with the ICC, the war will intensify' (*Sudan Tribune* 2009).

[6] A term suggested in this context by Anton Baaré.

The tragedy of international criminal justice activists

The discrepancy between the universal ideals that drive her and the actual consequences of the work to which she is contributing, reveals to the international criminal justice activist the tragedy of her field. As de Waal has observed with respect to the humanitarians' tragedy, '[r]ather than a litany of woe, tragedy is properly seen as a clash between rights, determined by a world in which human ideals fail to match the realities of the human condition' (de Waal 2010, 130). The tragedy 'arises from a mismatch between a universal idealism and a reality of horrific constraint' (de Waal 2009, 1; see also Chapter 14). The international criminal justice activists' tragedy stems from a commitment to the idea of an ideal type independent court that functions in accordance with the ideal type *trias politica*, whereas international criminal justice in fact operates in the fog of war and is heavily dependent on actors with various (legitimate) interests other than the enforcement of international criminal law. The ensuing tragedy is that 'the impulse to ameliorate suffering leads [the activist] into the unwelcome situation of acting cruelly' (de Waal 2010, 130).

Several of the cruelties that de Waal identifies as consequences of the humanitarians' tragedy also confront international criminal justice activists. For the cruelty of 'feeding dreams of an alternative but unattainable reality', we only have to consider the expectation amongst the displaced persons in Darfur that the ICC will end the war. Another cruelty is 'compromising clearly held principles'; for international criminal justice activists this is the acceptance that justice is done only selectively, the selection being based on where cooperation could be forthcoming. The cruel outcome of this reality is that the ICC, *de jure* independent but *de facto* constrained by the interests of powerful states, 'not only mak[es] justice conform unapologetically to power, but also mak[es] justice an unaccountable tool of further violence and injustice' (Branch 2010). Finally, the cruelty of '[i]nsisting on a normative standard that cannot in practice be realized' (de Waal 2009, 10) arises when the international criminal justice activist (rightfully) insists that criminals must be arrested instead of appeased (Moreno-Ocampo 2010b, 5) but in practice the quest for a perfect peace and 'for justice for yesterday's victims ... [is] pursued in such a manner that makes today's living the dead of tomorrow' (Anon. 1996, 258).

Coping mechanisms

How does the international criminal justice activist, who has committed her life, or at least career, in all genuineness to standing up for victims, to combating 'evil' and to doing 'justice', respond to the dissenting voices of people in whose interests she thought to act, who scream that justice is something else than criminal law and that criminal justice itself can be evil? How does she grapple with the fact that good intentions can have disastrous consequences? How does she deal with 'the clash between the values that constitute an individual's sense of self and the actions carried out'? In other words, how does she cope with 'cognitive dissonance'? (de Waal 2010, 132 (citing Milgram and Cooper))

Amongst her colleagues, the prevailing coping strategy is that of argumentative defence. Rational arguments are put forward to reason the observed dissonance away. One such argument decouples justice from peace. It holds that while peace may be a welcome derivative of ICC-style justice, only the latter is the objective. Thus, justice must be done irrespective of its consequences and should never be sacrificed in negotiations. On this account it is in fact praiseworthy if the ICC's involvement precludes a peace agreement that would have resulted in impunity.

The strength of this defence is its deontological character: it cannot be rebutted by empirical arguments. But this is also its weakness. By dismissing empirical arguments, this defence relies exclusively on morality, whereas even on moral grounds retribution has since long been discredited as justification of criminal law (see Koller 2008, 1025; Tallgren 2002, 591).

In view of the limited persuasiveness of deontology, advocates of ICC-style justice turn to consequentialist arguments. They argue, for example, that irrespective of the consequences in the situation concerned, the ICC, by not giving in on justice in that situation, has positive consequences for peace across the world.

A second consequentialist argument is that negative consequences in fact prove the Prosecutor's assertions about the need for ICC-style justice. In this line of argument there is no peace because the ICC's arrest warrants have not been executed. In this vein the ICC Prosecutor has tried to convince the Security Council to arrest Ahmed Harun when arguing:

> Impunity is not an abstract notion ... [Ahmed Harun] was sent to Abyei to manage the conflict. And Abyei was burned down, 50000 citizens displaced. (Moreno-Ocampo 2008b, 3)

The Prosecutor's message is *a contrario*: had Harun been arrested, the violence in Abyei would not have occurred.

A third argument is that it is good if the ICC's involvement obstructs a peace agreement that – in seeking acceptance from both parties – would anyway lack accountability and therefore would not last. This argument is encapsulated in the mantra 'no peace without justice'. Note how in this argument, in contrast to the peace-by-incapacitation justification, the term 'peace' is read as 'positive peace' (see also Mégret 2001, 202). A lack of accountability is presumed to be one of the causes of the violence. The assumption is that without addressing this cause, negative peace will never turn into positive peace.

A final consequentialist argument is one which presents an alternative causal account: the negative consequences, for instance the absence of a peace agreement, do not stem from the ICC's involvement but from other factors. Along these lines, the ICC Prosecutor commented on the Juba talks:

> Kony will never make peace ... When he is weak, he goes for peace negotiation. Then he gets money, he gets food, he buys weapons and he attacks again. How many times will he cheat? (New Vision 2009)

Similarly, the Deputy Prosecutor commented with respect to Darfur:

> [I]t is worth recalling that in 2008, before the Prosecutor's application for an arrest warrant, there was no peace process ... The ICC gave new life to the negotiations ... President Al Bashir was cornered and needed to sound reasonable ... His efforts to sound constructive led to renewed negotiations with the rebels. (Bensouda 2010, 6)

These consequentialist arguments presume too much. Does any prosecutor have sufficient insight into a conflict to understand the causal processes at work? For instance, officials working on the ground have argued that Harun has been a check on, rather than a cause of, violence in Abyei. Many Sudan watchers will also take issue with the Deputy Prosecutor's statement that there was no Darfur peace process before the Prosecutor's application for an arrest warrant for President Bashir, or that it was the ICC that gave new life to the negotiations. The no-peace-without-justice argument, too, is contestable on empirical grounds: history is full of examples of lasting peace without criminal justice. Historically, one could argue that where criminal justice and peace have gone together, it has been peace that has made criminal justice possible, not vice versa. 'Justice does not lead; it follows' (Snyder and Vinjamuri 2003–2004, 6).

If tracing past causal relations is difficult, it is even more unrealistic to expect that an international prosecutor can predict correctly the consequences of judicial interventions in complex conflict dynamics. As Eric Blumenson has written, the consequentialist approach presents the Prosecutor with the 'unavoidable but extraordinarily difficult task ... to make decisions that invoke such magnificent hopes and terrible costs with so little predictive information' (Blumenson 2005–2006, 829).

Consequentialist arguments also present a question of accountability. Even if the Prosecutor were to have sufficient information, he would have to weigh the consequences of his own decisions for others: the short-term versus the long-term, the local versus the universal, consequences for identified victims versus those for abstract future victims. To whom is the ICC Prosecutor accountable when he decides that short-term negative peace should be forfeited in the interest of long-term positive peace or in the interest of deterring crimes elsewhere in the world? Legally, the Prosecutor is accountable only to the Assembly of States Parties, and only for his professional conduct (Rome Statute, article 46(2)(b)).

Rhetorically, however, 'the victims' have become the overriding justification of the Prosecutor's decisions, of the Court and of the international criminal justice movement. 'We are their Court', stated the Prosecutor, 'all of them are contributing to the prosecution of perpetrators ... and to the legitimacy of the system' (Moreno-Ocampo 2010a, 12). A national prosecutor acts on behalf of the state; the international criminal justice movement has elevated 'the victims' to the level of its sovereign. This sovereign is easy to please and provides an inexhaustible justification: in the event that specific victims, those who participate in the proceedings, those who have been victimised by a particular accused or those who bear the consequences of ICC intervention, disagree with the justice conducted in their name, there are always other victims who can be invoked to 'contribut[e] to ... the legitimacy of the system'. Victims silenced by death or future victims make ready candidates. Cabined into one monolithic category, 'the victims' that are the alpha and omega of the international criminal justice movement are not concrete persons of flesh, blood and water, with individual names and individual opinions, but a deity-like abstraction that is disembodied, depersonified, and most of all, depoliticised (see Clarke 2007 and 2009).

Finally, when deontological and consequentialist arguments fail to convince, there is the institutional defence. According to this bureaucratic argument, the ICC's sole responsibility is to do ICC-style justice simply because this is the mandate of this institution; other institutions should be responsible for the consequences. This 'no-agency' defence is implied in the ICC Prosecutor's above-cited statement that 'the "interests of justice" must of course not be confused with the interests of peace and security, which falls within the mandate of other institutions'.

The institutional defence successfully absolves the ICC of responsibility for the consequences of its actions, but it is difficult to maintain in the present international order. It is based on an analogy with ideal type domestic systems, in which institutions other than courts are responsible for maintaining law and order, and for adapting the law in view of court decisions' adverse consequences. The international system, however, is not checked and balanced. With the ICC, an international (criminal) justice bulwark has been created, absent an equally strong world legislature or executive. If the ICC's justice threatens security, there are few institutional safeguards to correct any imbalance. Even the Security Council can only defer ICC proceedings for one year at a time.

The imbalance is exacerbated by the international criminal justice regime's (natural) struggle for hegemony (see Koskenniemi 2004). Arguing that the ICC is responsible for ICC-style justice only, and that other actors are responsible for peace, international criminal justice advocates maintain at the same time that other 'actors have to adjust to the law' (Moreno-Ocampo 2010a, 6). In this view, there is a division of labour but the ICC is the supervisor, like courts in an ideal type domestic justice system. In the words of the ICC's OTP:

> With the entry into force of the Rome Statute, a new legal framework has emerged and this framework necessarily impacts on conflict management efforts. The issue is no longer about whether we agree or disagree with the pursuit of justice in moral or practical terms: it is the law. Any political or security initiative must be compatible with the new legal framework insofar as it involves parties bound by the Rome Statute. (OTP 2007, 4)

The hegemonic move is that the 'new legal framework' as interpreted by the OTP goes far beyond the obligations on states as provided for in the Rome Statute. Apparently acting within this framework, the OTP has criticised those who supported peace talks that concerned – but did not involve – persons sought by the ICC (e.g. Moreno-Ocampo 2008a, 5–6), even though the Statute does not include 'a crime to talk' (Afako 2006). The OTP has engaged in 'dialogue with peace mediators ... to ensure ... that peace and political agreements exclude amnesties for Rome Statute crimes' (OTP 2010, para. 49), even though the Rome Statute does not prohibit states to use amnesties. The Prosecutor has advised mediators how not to conduct their work, for instance sequencing peace and justice (e.g. Moreno-Ocampo 2009, 10); he has told diplomats what to do instead (e.g. Moreno-Ocampo 2010b, 5) and he has given the Security Council a lesson in world history and Sudanese politics, via an op-ed in the *Guardian*:

> The world once claimed ignorance of the Nazi atrocities. Fifty years later, the world refused to recognise an unfolding genocide in Rwanda. On Darfur, the world is now officially on notice. Bashir will not provide the solution. He ... makes peace agreements that result in new attacks. At the same time, he ... is ... laying the groundwork for new crimes against Darfuris and against the south of Sudan. ... The council, which extensively reviewed its failure to act in Rwanda, should grab this opportunity. (Moreno-Ocampo 2010c)

The 'civil society' that backs the ICC has encouraged this hegemony of international criminal justice. For instance, when a joint communiqué of a UN high-level meeting on Sudan made no mention of a need for international accountability, the Coalition for the International Court issued a statement – preceded by the standard rider that 'the CICC will not take a position on potential and current situations before the Court or situations under analysis' – in which it

> note[d] that the pursuit of justice and the fight against impunity in Darfur are inextricably linked to the achievement of sustainable peace in Sudan and deplore[d] the lack of any reference in the meeting's outcome communiqué to the ongoing investigation by the ... ICC ... into crimes committed in Darfur, and the need for justice for victims. (CICC 2010)

The deontological, consequentialist and institutional arguments all have their strengths and weaknesses, but none is convincing. The way to sustain the defence is therefore constantly to jump from one kind of argument to the other. When peace appears possible without criminal justice, the mantra that there can be 'no peace without justice' is transformed into the safe tautology that there can be 'no *true* peace without justice'. Or when ICC-style justice is in fact obstructing peace, the causal idea of 'there *can be* no peace without (ICC-style) justice' is read as 'there *shall be* no peace without (ICC-style) justice'. While the project is promoted on account of promised consequences, it is defended when the consequences turn out differently by transforming the project into a matter of principle rather than consequence. It is thus made immune to the challenge of contrary empirical evidence. As Benjamin Ferencz, in the avant-garde of the international criminal justice movement since he was a Prosecutor in Nuremberg, has advocated: '[T]he law is an act of faith. But we have to believe in the deterrent effect of the law' (quoted in Cryer 2010, 205).

This reveals another strategy to cope with cognitive dissonance: if rational arguments fail to convince, religion, the human way to accept life as an inevitable defeat (Leszek Kolakowski, quoted in Otten 1999, 15) can bridge the gap between real and ideal. International criminal law, cloaked in rationality, has become a secular faith. In line with Engels' description of the juridical worldview as a 'secularisation of the theological' in which human law replaces the divine and the state the church (1887, 492), international criminal courts, in which prosecutors 'reckon' with evil[7] as if they were gods,[8] help believers to make sense of the past, trust the future and provide comfort for the present. For the Security Council, international criminal tribunals are instruments of therapeutic governance, providing an acceptable compromise between despicable apathy and authorisation of military interventions that UN members are unwilling or unable to carry out: if not peace, then justice (see also Anderson 2009, 333–337; Mégret 2001, 209). In the temples of justice, legal rituals seem victorious over the chaos of war. Complex conflicts with intractable structural causes are distilled to individual agency (see also Koskenniemi 2002). Those who are not convicted, for instance those who stood by or benefited, are absolved by the law's silence.

One of the comforting articles of faith is that 'passing sentence' equals 'doing justice' (Mulisch 2006, 11). This illusion is created by appropriating the rich concept 'international justice' for the narrow project of the application and enforcement of international criminal law, and focusing on a few emotive crimes that can be captured by image-based and minute-timed news coverage. Monopolising the definition of injustice, the international criminal justice movement quells advocacy to address less visible but more structural wrongs that have not been criminalised, for instance humiliating

[7] See the 'documentary' *The Reckoning: The Battle for the International Criminal Court* (Yates, de Onis and Kinoy 2009).

[8] In the documentary *War Don Don* the Prosecutor of the Special Court for Sierra Leone recounts that prosecuting 'was almost a religious experience', commenting on the accused 'they have no soul' and referring to an 'army of evil' (Richman-Cohen 2010).

poverty and extreme inequality, the causes of which are located in the structure of the same international community in whose name 'international justice' is performed (see also Allott 2002, 62–69; Branch 2010; Tallgren 2002, 594–595). Even when confronted with these non-criminalised injustices, 'faith' can provide comfort, responding, with the eternal perspective that it shares with other faiths, that the injustice is only temporal.

Koller has defended international criminal justice as a faith, arguing:

> That the commitment to international criminal law is a matter of faith more than reason should not necessarily be taken as grounds for criticism. The recourse to faith is something the field of international criminal law shares with all other attempts to address important moral questions through law. In the absence of empirical answers to such questions, one can either act on the basis of faith or refuse to act until these questions can be answered ... In due course, empirical analysis will, ideally, bring us close to answers to the fundamental questions of whether and how we should pursue international criminal law. Until then, faith will continue to play a critical role in motivating human action in response to genocide, crimes against humanity, and war crimes. (2008, 1021–1022)

This argument leaves three fundamental questions. First, considering the lack of solid empirical evidence and the inapplicability of natural laws of causality, who bears the burden of proof with respect to establishing the positive or negative consequences of international criminal justice? In the procedural framework of the Rome Statute, the Prosecutor does not have to prove any positive impact, while those who suffer adverse consequences have no procedural avenue to rebut the assumption that international criminal justice is a force only for good. Secondly, what does this faith believe international criminal law to do? If, as Koller argues, '[t]he ultimate value of international criminal law may rest ... in its role in identity construction, in particular in constructing a cosmopolitan community identity embracing all of humankind' (*ibid.*, 1060), the faith in international criminal law is more important than the consequences of international criminal law; it is the shared faith, more than the actual consequences of the law, that constructs identity and a sense of belonging. Once the faith has become more important than the object of faith, proselytising is prioritised over realising the underlying aims (see also Kennedy 2004, 23, 116). Finally, of what relevance is empirical analysis once international criminal law has been adopted as a faith? When confronted with contrary empirical evidence, true believers continue to believe and doubters are advised to believe harder.

For an international criminal justice apostate, convinced neither by rational defences nor by faith, few mechanisms remain to cope with cognitive dissonance. One option is to deny the tragedy and to make it a taboo. Another is to blame those who point out the tragedy, for instance by portraying them as deniers or apologists of crimes, or by questioning their level of education. Final exit, less coping mechanism than sign of not coping: drug habits, or madness.

Darfur, May 2010

Sudanese human rights lawyers who were interviewed two years ago are not to be found. One is still in Darfur, but hiding; the others have fled abroad, fearing for the government's reading of their work as support for the ICC. Darfuri elders are beginning to revive *judiya* in order to regain some agency in the situation. Leaders of the militarily strong armed movements, not living in Darfur, still refuse to engage in peace talks, sticking to the principle that one cannot negotiate with 'war criminals'. To them, the ICC is part of the 'global responsibility to protect' arsenal that can be exploited to topple the government. The displaced are what they were, displaced, but their spokespersons have relegated the ICC to the list of international organisations that promised peace but failed to bring it: 'African Union, United Nations, International Criminal Court.'

Kampala, Munyonyo Commonwealth Resort, Friday 4 June 2010[9]

Alongside the Olympic-size swimming-pool, in the five-star restaurant, and on the terrace of the resort that offers 'the ultimate in luxury leisure and conference facilities in East Africa',[10] memories are recited ('Remember that last night in Rome? Yes, already twelve years ago! Haven't we grown ...'), the prodigal sons belittled ('Luis should never have gone into the Sudan business') and personal triumphs celebrated. The latecomer who has just

[9] This section is based on the author's participant observation from 4 to 7 June 2010 at the ICC Review Conference. It has been strongly influenced by Tallgren (1999).

[10] www.munyonyocommonwealth.com.

obtained her badge to the 'International Criminal Court Review Conference' enters a reunion of her 4,600-person professional family.

Two types of review are on the agenda. The review of the Statute, in particular the question of how the crime of aggression should come under the Court's jurisdiction, has been reserved for next week. Last week was dedicated to a review that transcends the Rome Statute: 'stocktaking of international criminal justice', including of the area of 'peace and justice'. This item provided an occasion for a rational, empirical assessment of the successes and failures of international criminal justice, for instance in Uganda and Sudan, in the light of the aims ascribed to it.

Interested in evaluations of the first week, the latecomer sits down on the resort's terrace overlooking Lake Victoria. Sipping away at cocktails and cappuccinos, her colleagues are positive: 'It is *so* good we have come to Africa.' Another recalls the War Victim Day Football Match, featuring FC Dignity versus FC Justice, which had been captained, for six minutes, by the Ugandan President and the UN Secretary-General. Others speculate on the outcome of the negotiations on the crime of aggression.

The official accounts of the stocktaking reveal that the exercise took stock of successes only. A press release of the Secretariat of the Assembly of States Parties announced it as an occasion 'during which the overall success and impact of the Rome Statute will be considered' (ICC–ASP 2010). In the same vein, the UN Secretary-General's opening address referred to it as 'a chance … to take stock of our progress'.

The Secretary-General acknowledged that there can be a tension between peace and justice, but explicitly chose to forfeit (negative) peace if unaccompanied by accountability:

> Perhaps the most contentious challenge you face is the balance between peace and justice. Yet frankly, I see it as a false choice … Armies or militias rape, maim, kill and devastate towns, villages, crops, cattle and water sources, all as a strategy of war … Any victim would understandably yearn to stop such horrors, even at the cost of granting immunity to those who have wronged them. But this is a false peace. This is a truce at gunpoint, without dignity, justice or hope for a better future. Yes, it may be true: demanding criminal accountability, at the wrong time, can discourage warring parties from sitting down at the negotiating table. Yes, it may even perpetuate bloodshed. Even so, one thing is clear: the time has passed when we might speak of peace versus justice, or think of them as somehow opposed to each other. (Ban Ki-Moon 2010, 4)

The Secretary-General set the tone for the debate on peace and justice: even if 'demanding criminal accountability ... may ... perpetuate bloodshed', it is 'clear' that 'the time has passed when we might speak of peace versus justice, or think of them as somehow opposed to each other'. The peace versus justice debate is *passé*, indeed, taboo.

The actual stocktaking of 'peace and justice' was conducted by a panel of both human rights activists and peace negotiators. According to his own report,[11] the moderator began with 'some preliminary lessons learned' (without indicating where or by whom they had been learned). These lessons left little scope for acknowledging potential tensions between insisting on criminal justice and achieving peace. The introduction notwithstanding, the peace negotiators on the panel tried to bring to the fore obstacles that they had encountered. One 'expressed doubts as to what extent the idea of a new era of international justice had penetrated the minds of potential perpetrators and the public in general, beyond the international justice community'. The other opened by stating that 'there was an undeniable dilemma between peace and justice, which would persist for as long as there would be ongoing conflicts'. On the basis of his experience at the Juba peace talks, the lawyer–negotiator observed that

> [t]he international community, through the Rome Statute, had chosen a legal regime that required prosecutions for the most serious crimes and this could complicate peace negotiations. The Ugandan people and the international community would have to live with the consequences of that decision.

'Summarizing the discussion', the moderator, however, concluded that 'there was now a positive relation between peace and justice'. The problem was redefined as one of a lack of education on the side of the victims:

> As for victims, experience showed that their views shifted over time, with an immediate goal for peace followed by a quest for justice. Questions arose as to how to educate victims about the option of pursuing justice, without unduly raising their expectations.

The moderator ...

> called upon states and other stakeholders to stand up to those defiant of the Court. Justice, he concluded, is never going to be without enemies.

[11] RC/ST/PJ/1/Rev.1 2010 (the source of the quotes from the debate that follow).

On the basis of this 'debate', the Kampala Declaration concluded the stocktaking as the Secretary-General had opened it – on a positive note:

We, high-level representatives of States Parties to the Rome Statute of the International Criminal Court, gathered in Kampala, Uganda, at the first Review Conference under this Statute, ...

Recalling the aims and purposes of the Rome Statute and *recognizing* the noble mission and the role of the International Criminal Court in a multilateral system that aims to end impunity, establish the rule of law, promote and encourage respect for human rights and achieve sustainable peace ...,

Convinced that there can be no lasting peace without justice and that peace and justice are thus complementary requirements, ...

Together solemnly:

1 *Reaffirm* our commitment to the Rome Statute of the International Criminal Court and its full implementation, as well as to its universality and integrity;
2 *Reiterate* our determination to put an end to impunity for perpetrators of the most serious crimes of international concern ... and thus to *contribute* to the prevention of such crimes that threaten the peace, security and well-being of the world;
3 *Emphasize* that justice is a fundamental building block of sustainable peace; ... (RC-4-ENG-04062010 2010)

With the stocktaking exercise done and dusted, the crowd on the terrace turns to the dilemmas of the immediate future:

What are you going to do this weekend? Rafting on the Nile or the Gorilla Tour?

Staying at the pool.

Don't forget your sun-block.

Bibliography

Afako, B., 2006. 'Not a Crime to Talk: Legal Aspects of Dialogue with the Lord's Resistance Army', 25 June, unpublished paper, on file with author

Allen, T., 2006. *Trial Justice: The International Criminal Court and the Lord's Resistance Army*, London and New York: Zed Books

Allott, P., 2002. *The Health of Nations: Society and Law beyond the State*, Cambridge University Press

Anderson, K., 2009. 'The Rise of International Criminal Law: Intended and Unintended Consequences', *European Journal of International Law*, 20, 331–358

Anon., 1996. 'Human Rights in Peace Negotiations', *Human Rights Quarterly*, 18, 249–258

Ban Ki-Moon, 2010. 'An Age of Accountability', Address to the Review Conference on the International Criminal Court, Kampala, 31 May

Bensouda, F., 2010. 'Keynote Address: Peace and Justice, Friends or Foes?', *De Iure Humanitatis, Peace, Justice and International Law*, 74th Conference of the International Law Association, The Hague, 17 August

Blumenson, E., 2005–2006. 'The Challenge of a Global Standard of Justice: Peace, Pluralism, and Punishment at the International Criminal Court', *Columbia Journal of Transnational Law*, 33, 801–874

Branch, A., 2010. 'What the ICC Review Conference Can't Fix', http://africanarguments.org/2010/03/what-the-icc-review-conference-can't-fix

Cassese, A., 1998. 'On the Current Trends Towards Criminal Prosecution and Punishment of Breaches of International Humanitarian Law', *European Journal of International Law*, 1, 2–17

CICC, 2010. 'UN Fails to Affirm Support for Justice for Darfur Victims', 24 September

Clarke, K. M., 2007. 'Global Justice, Local Controversies: The International Criminal Court and the Sovereignty of Victims', in T. Keller and M.-B. Dembour (eds.), *Paths to International Justice: Social and Legal Perspectives*, Cambridge University Press, 134–160

Clarke, K. M., 2009. *Fictions of Justice: The ICC and the Challenge of Legal Pluralism in Sub-Saharan Africa*, Cambridge University Press

Cryer, R., 2010. 'Book Review: H. Verrijn Stuart and M. Simons (eds.), The Prosecutor and the Judge: Benjamin Ferencz and Antonio Cassese: Interviews and Writings', *Journal of Conflict & Security Law*, 15, 203–207

de Waal, A., 2009. 'The Humanitarians' Tragedy: On the Escapable and Inescapable Cruelties in the Humanitarian Predicament', Keynote Address to World Conference on Humanitarian Studies, Groningen, The Netherlands, 4 February

de Waal, A., 2010. 'The Humanitarians' Tragedy: Escapable and Inescapable Cruelties', *Disasters*, 34, 130–137

de Waal, A. and J. Flint, 2009. 'To Put Justice before Peace Spells Disaster for Sudan', *Guardian*, 6 March

Engels, F., 1887. 'Juristen-Sozialismus', Die Neue Zeit, Heft 2, www.mlwerke.de/me/me21/me21_491.htm

Gulu District NGO Forum and Liu Institute for Global Issues, 2007. 'The Cooling of Hearts: Community Truth-telling in Acholi-Land', Justice and Reconciliation Project, July

ICC–ASP, 2010, 'Opening of the Review Conference of the Rome Statute in Kampala', Press Release, 26 May

Kennedy, D., 2004. *The Dark Sides of Virtue: Reassessing International Humanitarianism*, Princeton University Press

Kirsch, P., 2007. 'Address to the United Nations General Assembly', 1 November

Koller, D. S., 2008. 'The Faith of the International Criminal Lawyer', *New York University Journal of International Law and Politics*, 40, 1019–1069

Koskenniemi, M., 2002. 'Between Impunity and Show Trials', *Max Planck Yearbook of United Nations Law*, 6, 1–35

Koskenniemi, M., 2004. 'International Law and Hegemony: A Reconfiguration', *Cambridge Review of International Affairs*, 17, 197–218

Liu Institute for Global Issues and Gulu District NGO Forum, 2005. 'Roco Wat I Acoli, Restoring Relations in Acholi-Land: Traditional Approaches to Reintegration and Justice', September

Mégret, F., 2001. 'Three Dangers for the International Criminal Court: A Critical Look at a Consensual Project', *Finnish Yearbook of International Law*, XII, 193–247

Moreno-Ocampo, L., 2007. 'Statement at the Eleventh Diplomatic Briefing of the International Criminal Court', The Hague, 10 October

Moreno-Ocampo, L., 2007–2008. 'The International Criminal Court: Seeking Global Justice', *Case Western Reserve Journal of International Law*, 40, 215–225

Moreno-Ocampo, L., 2008a. 'Remarks by the Prosecutor of the International Criminal Court', Chicago, 9 April

Moreno-Ocampo, L., 2008b. 'Statement of the Prosecutor of the International Criminal Court to the United Nations Security Council pursuant to UNSCR 1593 (2005)', 5 June

Moreno-Ocampo, L., 2009. 'Keynote Address', New Haven, 6 February 2009

Moreno-Ocampo, L., 2010a. 'Keynote Address', Council on Foreign Relations, Washington, DC, 4 February

Moreno-Ocampo, L., 2010b. 'Statement', Review Conference – General Debate, Kampala, 31 May

Moreno-Ocampo, L., 2010c. 'Now End This Darfur Denial: We Have Laid Charges for Genocide. The UN Must Seize the Moment to Act for the Victims of Sudan', *Guardian*, 15 July

Mulisch, H., 2006. *De Zaak 40/61: Een Reportage*, Amsterdam: De Bezige Bij

New Vision, 2009. 'Joseph Kony Will Never Make Peace – ICC', 14 July

Nouwen, S., 2012. *Complementarity in the Line of Fire: The Catalysing Effect of the International Criminal Court in Uganda and Sudan*, Cambridge University Press (in press)

Nouwen, S. and W. Werner, 2011, 'Doing Justice to the Political: The International Criminal Court in Uganda and Sudan', *European Journal of International Law*, 21, 941–965

Nuremberg Judgment 1947, International Military Tribunal (Nuremberg), Judgment and Sentences, reproduced in *American Journal of International Law*, 41, 172–333

Nyakairu, F., 2008. 'Juba Talks Close as LRA Tables Fresh Demands', *The Monitor*, 2 March

Ochola II, M. B., 2009. 'Spirituality of Reconciliation: A Case Study of *Mato Oput* within the Context of the Cultural and Traditional Justice System of the Nilotic Acholi/Central Luo People of Northern Uganda', October

Orentlicher, D., 1991. 'Settling Accounts: The Duty to Prosecute Human Rights Violations of a Prior Regime', *Yale Law Journal*, 100, 2537–2615

OTP, 2006. *Prosecutor* v. *Joseph Kony, Vincent Otti, Raska Lukwiya, Okot Odhiambo and Dominic Ongwen, Submission of Information on the Status of the Warrants of Arrest in Uganda*, ICC-02/04-01/05-116, 6 October

OTP, 2007. 'Policy Paper on the Interests of Justice', 17 September

OTP, 2010. 'Prosecutorial Strategy, 2009–2012', 1 February

Otten, W.-J., 1999. 'Het Raadsel van het Verklaarbare Kwaad', in C. Van der Ven (ed.), *Het Kwaad: Visies en Verhalen*, Breda: De Geus, 7–18

RC-4-ENG-04062010, 2010. 'Kampala Declaration'

RC/ST/PJ/1/Rev.1, 2010. Review Conference of the Rome Statute, Stocktaking of International Criminal Justice, Peace and Justice, Moderator's Summary, 7 June

Richman-Cohen, R., 2010. *War Don Don*, Racing Horse Productions/Naked Edge Films

Romano, C., A. Nollkaemper and J. Kleffner, 2004. *Internationalized Criminal Courts and Tribunals: Sierra Leone, East Timor, Kosovo and Cambodia*, Oxford University Press

Sands, P., 2003. (ed.), *From Nuremberg to The Hague: The Future of International Criminal Justice*, Cambridge University Press

SCSL-2003-01-T, 2010. *The Prosecutor of the Special Court* v. *Charles Ghankay Taylor*, transcripts of 5, 9 and 10 August (testimony of Naomi Campbell, Mia Farrow and Carole White)

Snyder, J. and L. Vinjamuri, 2003–2004. 'Trials and Errors: Principle and Pragmatism in Strategies of International Justice', *International Security*, 24, 5–44

Sudan Tribune, 2009. 'Darfur Rebels Vow Full ICC Cooperation Ahead of Ruling on Bashir Case', 2 March

Swart, B. and G. Sluiter, 1999. 'The International Criminal Court and International Criminal Co-operation', in H. A. M. von Hebel, J. G. Lammers and J. Schukking (eds.), *Reflections on the International Criminal Court*, The Hague: T. M. C. Asser Press, 91–127

Tallgren, I., 1999. 'We Did It? The Vertigo of Law and Everyday Life at the Diplomatic Conference on the Establishment of an International Criminal Court', *Leiden Journal of International Law*, 12, 683–707

Tallgren, I., 2002. 'The Sensibility and Sense of International Criminal Law', *European Journal of International Law*, 13, 561–595

Wierda, M. and M. Otim, 2008. 'Justice at Juba: International Obligations and Local Demands in Northern Uganda', in N. Waddell and P. Clark (eds.), *Courting Conflict? Justice, Peace and the ICC in Africa*, London: Royal African Society, 21–28

Yates, P., P. de Onis and P. Kinoy, 2009. *The Reckoning: The Battle for the International Criminal Court*, Skylight Pictures

16 Regulating trade, investment and money

Hélène Ruiz Fabri

A fragmenting arena

Analysis of regulation in trade, investment and money must take account of the specific characteristics of each field. The following discussion will be macroeconomic, leaving aside the legal dimension pertaining to economic actors' individual behaviours and transactions. The field of the investigation is complex, whether approached from a normative angle (how are trade, investment and finance regulated?) or an organic angle (who regulates trade, investment and finance?). The complexity increases when both endogenous and exogenous perspectives are taken into account. From the endogenous perspective, the traditional fragmentation allowing for the cohabitation of the distinct fields of trade, investment and monetary regulation is called into question by their increasing interdependence. From the exogenous perspective, complexity arises from the progressive penetration of international economic regulation into other fields of regulation, such as the environment, health and human rights. Tensions are often created by the way an economic approach is imposed on fields alien to economics. The various interconnections and more or less confrontational frictions thus reveal a distinct need for linkage.

Though this need – and the search for consistency – has been intellectually identified for a long time, its expression in the practice of law and politics is relatively recent and, overall, little has been achieved in terms of concrete results. Two remarks can, however, be made at this point.

First, the situation is surprising. Indeed, more clearly than in other areas, the development of international economic law is related to the development of interdependence, because it is tied to that of exchanges and communication. The interests that logically govern rule-making are particularly visible. If they are not always perfectly univocal, it is nonetheless true that each country seeks to negotiate advantages or obtain concessions to maximise its riches (illustrating the well-known idea that since the economy is the primary concern in peacetime, this is where advantages must be gained).

This univocal teleology is supported by the idea that this is a game in which everyone can win (prosperity) and where therefore consensus should reign (the Washington consensus, for example). This supposed consensus is obviously not enough to purge it of its ideological dimension, a vision led by faith in the virtues of the free market, the free flow, deregulation and privatisation. However, the teleology is incorporated into the theory of comparative advantage (according to which each country would reap gains from specialising in what it is best at producing and trading with other nations: the theory is usually attributed to Ricardo, who explained it in his book *On the Principles of Political Economy and Taxation* (1817)). In this theory, which purports to manage competition amongst interests, reciprocity is supposed to play an essential role. It is easy to see, at least in the abstract, the value of common rules that promote the openness which brings enrichment. In short, the goal is to ensure the free movement of production factors. In this sense, trade, investment and money may seem indissociable. But even though flexibility and pragmatism have been promoted as attributes of high-quality economic law, this law did not develop similarly with respect to techniques or coherently with respect to contents, and its needs are far from having been satisfied. On the contrary, this is an area where the diversity of both norms and actors is remarkable.

The second remark is that the importance now of linkage issues also marks the return to the foreground of politics – politics that one might think were swept away when liberalism triumphed. The myth of the separation of economics from politics is formally illustrated by the prohibition on international economic organisations engaging in political activities and, therefore, from making anything other than economic considerations the criteria of their action (see for example, International Bank for Reconstruction and Development (IBRD) Articles of Agreement, article 4(10)). Supposedly an aspect of non-interference in internal affairs or respect for the *domaine réservé*, this prohibition tends to make us forget how much these organisations' normative and operational activities, and the development of international economic law in general, has a modelling and thus political effect on states, and the international world at large.

More broadly, this opened the door to managerialism (application of managerial techniques of business to the running of other fields), which fits very well with the claims of flexibility and pragmatism. The desire is still strong to seek managerial solutions to linkage issues, but it is now supplemented by increasing calls to 'moralise' international economic law or introducing an ethical dimension into it. The latter claims are expressed in the omnipresent concepts of security, predictability and transparency, but also in the idea of shared responsibilities. This is of course a way of emphasising that states are not the only normative bodies, but it also represents a rejection of certain partitions or categorisations. This undoubtedly leads back to the very idea of interdependence, but in a more comprehensive way, by giving room to issues of common interest to the human community. In a way, the issue of linkages and tensions is part of the controversies concerning the direction of globalisation.

A short history: one ideological trend, three historical movements, many legal steps

Although there are earlier traces, the history of international economic law begins with the Second World War, at least if the regulatory ambition is given primary consideration. However, one should not forget how much the 1929 crisis served as a bogeyman (and thus a standard) for, during and after the war, deriving economic principles and conceiving the rules designed to lay the foundations for what was supposed to be a genuine international economic order. An 'order' is indeed the terms in which it was claimed to be conceived, even if the original idea was incomplete and the legal instruments and realisations did not exactly follow.

The original plan was rooted in the UN Charter, which confers on the organisation the task of developing international economic cooperation, resting on three pillars: monetary, financial and commercial, without explicitly targeting investment. The order thus conceived consisted in conventional regimes administered by international organisations with the status of specialised institutions within the UN system, and gravitating around the UN General Assembly and the Economic and Social Council. The 1944 Bretton Woods conference indeed created two organisations, the International Monetary Fund (IMF) and the International Bank for Reconstruction and Development. These are specialised institutions with complementary objectives (assisting states with economic or structural difficulties). The International Trade Organisation (ITO), which was intended to complete the structure and whose Charter was concluded at Havana in 1948, was never established, however, except in the truncated version of the General Agreement on Tariffs and Trade (GATT). The GATT was devoted to trade in goods and initially considered as a merely temporary body, anticipating entry into force of the ITO Charter. In the end the GATT institution lasted close to half a century before the World Trade Organisation (WTO) incorporated it in 1995.

These initial tribulations may be better understood if one recalls that two systemic views of the order to be instituted challenged each other at the time: the liberal view and the Keynesian view (which assumes that private sector decisions sometimes lead to inefficient macroeconomic outcomes and therefore advocates active policy responses by the government to stabilise the economic output), with the former progressively supplanting the latter until it triumphed in the 1970s. The GATT had, in a way, anticipated this tendency: it was the liberal part of the ITO Charter; the interventionist part, which notably mentioned full employment as well as trade in commodities, was abandoned. The ideological triumph of economic liberalism became patent in the 1980s. After having subverted the claim by the developing world for a 'New International Economic Order' (NIEO), liberalism was complemented and consecrated in the 1990s by the triumph of capitalism and the market economy over alternative types of economic organisation, particularly managed economies. Liberalism became practically the sole mode of thought in the international economic field. This dynamic was not, however, accompanied by a linear and coherent development of trade, investment or monetary regulation. On the contrary, these three areas evolved in a disparate and fragmented way during the three major phases of the post-Second World War era (reconstruction, decolonisation, globalisation), due in significant part to the various crises that punctuated these phases. Though greatly varied, there are traces of these three phases in each of the bodies of rules, on trade, investment and monetary regulation.

International trade

International trade law undoubtedly evolved in the most linear fashion, perhaps because it began on a minor scale. It consisted of a brief Agreement whose purpose (the negotiation and reduction of tariffs which, at an average level of 40 per cent at the end of the war, constituted a serious obstacle to trade development) and the number of participating countries was limited. The GATT met with resistance in the late 1950s from developing countries who found that it failed to consider their specific problems. They preferred the newly created UN Conference on Trade and Development

(UNCTAD) as a forum in which to express their regulatory objectives. The GATT responded to this essentially rhetorical competition by adding, in 1964, a Part IV specifically addressing such countries. But this only included a preferential system for exports from developing countries. The granting of those preferences, however, depended on the developed countries' good will. At the same time, the GATT was also the framework for negotiating an agreement of regulated protectionism in textiles that, while guaranteeing certain quotas (and therefore certain outlets) to developing countries, channelled the competition they represented for developed countries in an industrial sector highly dependent on manual labour. This did not dissuade developing countries from acceding in great numbers to a system over which they ultimately had little influence. This was not only because the negotiating techniques clearly gave priority to those who held the largest shares of global trade, but also because granting the developing countries differential treatment in the newly negotiated agreements, beginning in the late 1980s, deprived them of any real control over the content of numerous new rules that had to be adopted. Textiles were reincorporated into the framework of the general disciplines (a term used to designate the rules in WTO law, notably the most favoured nation clause and the national treatment clause), but this was a concession obtained in exchange for the strict constraints introduced in the area of intellectual property under pressure from the developed countries. Intellectual property was one of the new areas incorporated into the field of trade law which, in adapting to the spectacular development of international trade in services, was extended through a framework agreement (GATS) conceived on the GATT model.

The normative corpus that entered into force in 1995 resulted from eight years of negotiations between some 120 states. It included provisions on trade-related investment and reincorporated agriculture (which had escaped the general disciplines since the 1950s), in particular addressing subsidies and sanitary and phytosanitary norms to quell the protectionist tendencies otherwise manifest here. Although the various issues were the subject of distinct agreements, they were included in an ensemble that was now integrated from a legal point of view. This was highlighted by the adoption of the 'single-undertaking' principle that required acceptance of the whole package while prohibiting 'forum shopping'. From an institutional point of view, the integration of the agreements was manifested by placing them under the responsibility of a new international organisation, the WTO. The ensemble thus instituted bore the traces of the main concern: to extend the multilateral disciplines to the greatest number of areas possible in order to facilitate liberalisation. But since the previous period had shown there could be more disadvantages than advantages to a flexible law, a number of regulatory mechanisms were adopted and the dispute resolution mechanism was reinforced. This gave birth to a judicialisation of the international trade order. As a consequence, trade disputes increased in unprecedented numbers.

The 'big players' (mainly the United States and the European Union) thought they could almost simultaneously launch a new round of negotiations to increase liberalisation in the field of services. But the atmosphere in the late 1990s turned into one of increasing challenge to a liberal globalisation, perceived as sacrificing people in order to promote competition and growth. Moreover, some developing countries gained increased power in the so-called 'emerging markets'. The negotiations re-launched with difficulty in 2001 were symbolically dedicated to a development agenda, but this was not enough. If their failure is generally explained by recurring problems such as agricultural subsidies, the more fundamental issue seems to be the cost of liberalisation on a multilateral scale (or the lack of sufficient prospective gains). The multitude and diversity of interests which need to be accommodated have so far proven overwhelming. The warning signs have been visible since the mid-1990s. The WTO had begun to worry about the proliferation of free trade agreements (FTAs), a phenomenon which gained speed in the following decade. States seemed to be seeking trade liberalisation through bilateral, regional or even inter-regional agreements which seemed out of reach at the multilateral level. But do FTAs really threaten or rather complement multilateralism? The situation still remains unclear and is difficult to evaluate. On the one hand, the turn to bilateral and regional instruments could be interpreted as a form of division of labour which places liberalisation at the level where it is easiest to achieve, for whatever reason (geographical proximity, power relations, etc.), while maintaining regulation at the global level (such a suggestion can be deduced from the fact that many FTAs claim to duplicate or refer to WTO law). But this optimistic vision runs counter to the idea that in the absence of any development (in particular regulatory) by the WTO, there is a risk that the various agreements create discrepancies and that the multilateral law will become marginalised, while systemic issues such as environment, health, etc. will not be adequately addressed at the regional or bilateral levels. Moreover, numerous FTAs have a broad scope, creating a link between trade and investment, which raises the question of the missing link(s) at the multilateral level.

Investment law

Unlike the position in the trade and monetary sectors, there has been no multilateral or institutional basis for investment law which could provide this legal area with 'constitutional' foundations. International investments were conventionally dealt with in treaties combining trade and investment. It was only after the Second World War that the two areas began to dissociate, with treaties exclusively devoted to investment juxtaposed to the essentially customary provisions that had governed this area until then. This reveals the two tendencies entangled but not subsumed in investment law, and can help explain the swings in its development.

On the one hand investment law has historically been underpinned by the law relating to the treatment of aliens. The legal standards in this field protect both the persons and the property of aliens, and now generally require fair and equitable treatment ensuring investor security. This standard, which implies compensation for investors who were denied the fruits of their investment, and which has historically been asserted in the case law, was called into question during the period of decolonisation and of the demand for a new international economic order. The newly independent states challenged the consequences of a customary law in whose formation they did not participate and which prevented them from purging the past, as they wished, through nationalisations which enabled them to recover control (under the rubric of 'permanent sovereignty over natural resources'). Their claims were supported by resolutions adopted by the UN General Assembly (Resolutions 1803 (1962), 'Permanent Sovereignty over Natural Resources' and 3281 (1974), 'Charter of Economic Rights and Duties of States'). They also sought to revivify the Calvo doctrine, under which investors renounced the right to diplomatic protection of their home state. This contestation of established customary law by means of soft law texts created a zone of turbulence and uncertainty.

The issue proved to be all the more sensitive because, on the other hand, the opening up of economic exchanges rapidly increased interest in foreign investment. There was a call not only to protect foreign investments but also to facilitate them. The accompanying search for guarantees must be understood in the long-term perspective that underlies investments and throws a particular light on the concepts of risk and reliance; it explains in part the tension between the desire to internationalise the guarantees of investors and their issuing states, and the desire of host states to remain in control through their domestic law. However, even though multilateral drafts were elaborated from the late 1950s (within the framework of the Organisation for Economic Cooperation and Development, OECD), lack of consensus prevented progress beyond proposals for model treaties. The only multilateral convention adopted during this period is the 1965 Washington Convention creating the International Centre for Settlement of Investment Disputes (ICSID). This is a dispute settlement mechanism whose very creation was an important symbol. It gives investors a direct means of international action that enables them to avoid relying on diplomatic protection, which is random in both its triggering and its outcome. Nevertheless, ICSID lay dormant until the 1990s. At that point the movement towards bilateral investment treaties (BITs), reputed purveyors of legal certainty, really took off. No doubt legal stability is but one factor amongst many in investment decisions in which economic considerations play the leading role. But the incitement to conclude BITs was strong and became more so as they proliferated; 'investment treaties [being] today seen as admission tickets to international investment markets' (Dolzer and Schreuer 2008, 9). It was all about creating an investment-friendly climate (see the Preamble of the World Bank's Guidelines on the Treatment of Foreign Direct Investment). The so-called 'Hull Rule' (requirement of 'prompt, adequate and effective' compensation for expropriation) became a standard element of BITs as well as of plurilateral treaties such as the Energy Charter Treaty and the North American Free Trade Agreement (NAFTA). The treaties also included state–investor dispute settlement clauses providing for mixed arbitration at the international level, mostly under the ICSID system. The number of BITs quintupled between 1990 and 2005, when there were roughly 2,500, while the number of cases submitted to arbitration also increased greatly during the same period.

Putting this global project into context requires paying attention to two related facts. The first is that the rules regarding foreign investment are highly intrusive. Once investment is accepted, the rules affect numerous sectors of domestic law (property, environmental and labour law) as well as the judicial structure, and limit host states' regulatory margin, and therefore their range of political choices. No doubt states remain free not to accept incoming investment. But what is true from a formal legal perspective is not so true from an economic one. Many states really have little choice. The second notable fact is the promotion, since the 1980s, of the concept of good governance. This has taken firm root: no one would dispute that a well-functioning state (and institutions) is best also from the perspective of creating a stable investment atmosphere. Moreover, international institutions promoting this concept deftly refer to the rule of law, democratic principles, human rights, etc. as essential elements of development and poverty-reduction policies. But one cannot disregard that these are the same institutions that promoted the Washington consensus that encourages, amongst other things, states to privatise their economies, to deregulate their markets, and to liberalise foreign investments.

The collapse of several developing countries – which put them more than ever at the mercy of international aid – ensured the triumph of these principles. The fact that developing countries have, over the last twenty years, begun to negotiate BITs amongst themselves that do not substantially deviate from those resulting from the models promoted by developed countries has been seen as a sign that there is in truth a substantive balance, which is expressed in the mutual interests of host and issuing states in creating a favourable (stable and foreseeable) environment.

However, this widely held view does not resolve the issue of the balance of rights and obligations. Despite their supposed reciprocity, BITs are built on a logic which creates obligations mainly for the host state. Similarly, the structure of arbitration always puts the host state in the defendant's position. One might argue that such biases are desirable and accepted, but they nonetheless raise two types of issues:

The first concerns the evolution of international arbitration. Cases are generally brought by major companies, small investors having neither the time nor the means for such procedures. The economic stakes of arbitration itself have become very heavy, with the risk that the machine begins to feed itself. In addition, arbitration lacks transparency (due to the confidentiality of the procedures) although it deals with matters of public interest; it also tends to produce contradictory outcomes (to the extent that they are known). Above all, the extension of protection given to investors through sometimes very broad interpretations of notions such as 'investment', 'indirect expropriation' and 'reliance' has led to an imbalance against to host states (see Waibel *et al.*, 2010). The latter find their regulatory capacity more limited by the BIT regime than they had anticipated. Significantly, since developed countries became not only sending but also host states, they have tended to modify their model BITs to give greater consideration to the general interest. Events such as the Argentine financial crisis, which led to some forty arbitrations, have placed the system under heavy stress. This is not only due to contradictory awards but also to assessments of damages whose economic weight may be impossible to bear. One might tentatively conclude that the balance that had swung far in favour of investors, is starting to swing back. This may be because there now is distinct awareness that states' regulatory capacity must regain legitimacy as an instrument for managing or organising competing interests, and for promoting the general interest.

This leads fairly naturally to issues regarding investors' obligations. The concern is not entirely new, as illustrated by controversies over the role of multinational firms, for example during work on the Draft UN Code of Conduct for Transnational Corporations in the 1970s and 1980s. The OECD declaration and decisions on international investment and multinational enterprises exist only as soft law (though one must not underestimate their effect). Originally adopted in 1976 and revised in 1979, 1982, 1984, 1991 and 2000, the OECD Guidelines for Multinational Enterprises are annexed to the 2000 OECD Declaration on International Investment and Multinational Enterprises. The guidelines are recommendations providing voluntary principles and standards for responsible business conduct (covering business ethics on employment, human rights, environment, information disclosure, combating bribery, consumer interests, science and technology, competition, taxation) for multinational corporations operating in, or from, countries adhering to the Declaration. More recently, the UN Secretary-General's (non-binding) Global Compact initiative promoted the idea that companies are not only economic actors, but must also take their share of social responsibility. Officially launched in 2000, the UN Global Compact encourages businesses world-wide to adopt sustainable and socially responsible policies, and to report on their implementation. Inasmuch as it contains no mechanisms to sanction member companies for non-compliance with the principles, the Compact has been criticised for being, at the end of the day, meaningless. However, the entire discussion of corporate social responsibility indicates, amongst other things, a desire to encourage companies to respect and promote human rights (see, for example, the work of the UN Special Representative on Business and Human Rights). For the time being, this leads mainly to private actors' self-regulation, essentially through codes of conduct that resemble publicity stunts more than genuine regulation.

Monetary regulation

The same can undoubtedly be said for the profound imbalance and harmful effects resulting from states not exercising their regulatory capacity. The problem appears particularly important in the field of money market regulation. For too long, the need to develop public supervision of such markets was expressed at an essentially rhetorical level, in part because of deep scepticism as to the role of law in this field. It is true that the desire for international regulation has eroded the traditional principle of monetary sovereignty. But state regulation has been too weak to deal with emerging problems.

The foundations for the international monetary system were laid simultaneously with those of the IMF. The approach was a public, inter-state one; the objective to prevent monetary crises and remedy any that occurred. The IMF's Articles of Agreement set out a code of good monetary conduct oriented towards maintaining orderly exchange rates, with gold as the common denominator of currencies; convertibility of currencies; and progressive elimination of exchange restrictions. The IMF was given broad supervisory powers and could provide assistance in the form of loans to member states suffering temporary difficulties. However, the mechanism did not cover capital movements, which left the system without a financial component that could have given it overall consistency. There were also gaps with respect to states' monetary reserves, the status of central banks, interest rates and domestic economic policy, even though it is well known that a currency's stability depends on the domestic economic balance.

The monetary code of conduct progressively materialised during the 1950s, such that the currencies of the main industrialised countries were freely usable in international trade as of the early 1960s. The world seemed to be moving toward liberalism and multilateralism in its international monetary relations, while the IMF perfected its methods of providing assistance, to the extent that it even conceived the first international currency, Special Drawing Rights, a convention-based currency, in 1969. What seemed to be an apotheosis, however, concealed how close the crises were that would eventually bring this system down.

The underlying causes were related to the system's orientation towards a gold exchange standard that was based on the dollar, making it the international currency of reference. The increasing need for international liquidity was satisfied by the deficit of the US balance of payments, which eventually rendered the dollar's convertibility to gold merely theoretical. The United States was therefore not encouraged to exercise monetary discipline, and in fact took advantage of the situation to finance the Vietnam War with inflation, while other IMF members were reluctant to make the monetary adjustments necessary to their economic situation. The crisis that began in 1971 with the US decision to suspend the dollar's convertibility to gold and allow it to float was followed by a second crisis that resulted in abandoning the currency parity regime and allowing all currencies to float. The system instituted after the war thus lost its central pillar. In a context of economic crisis linked, amongst other things, to the quintupling of oil prices, the reform that produced the second amendment of the IMF Articles of Agreement in 1978 fell short of restoring an international monetary order and, instead, seemed to bring about a generalised floating of currencies. Subsequent attempts at reform did not produce better results. Most of the IMF's activity has since then been limited to assisting members in difficulty, for the most part developing countries. This has taken place notwithstanding the fact that economic underdevelopment had not been specifically mentioned in the IMF Articles of Agreement.

Although it is supposed to provide only short-term loans (long-term loans are the province of the World Bank), the IMF has diversified its financial assistance so much that the two institutions are now in a situation of unhealthy competition. This is one consequence of the reorientation of the IMF's activities towards developing countries. Another is the impact on their economies. Its classical role of supporting members in difficulty declined due to the decrease in the relative value of the IMF's resources; moreover since the 1970s the IMF found itself competing with private banks able to loan significantly greater amounts. It nonetheless continued to have influence in crisis situations of excessive debt, with contradictory results. Its involvement was a sign of confidence that almost became a prerequisite to private banks' lending money, with the perverse effect that this quasi-insurance of public intervention as a last resort partially exculpated states and private banks with respect to their debt policies. However, IMF support was not unconditional. Quite the contrary, it set demanding and intrusive conditions on aid to the developing countries that became its regular customers in the late 1970s (through conditionalities in return for new loans from the IMF or World Bank, or for obtaining lower interest rates on existing loans). Structural Adjustment

Programs generally implemented 'free market' programmes and policy, including internal changes, notably privatisation and deregulation, and external ones, especially the reduction of trade barriers. In effect beneficiary countries had no choice but to comply. Substantively, these conditions corresponded to the Washington consensus, turning plans for structural adjustment into a very bitter pill for the countries concerned. Beginning in the mid 1990s, the combination of these factors caused a legitimacy crisis for a system that privatised profits and publicised risks. This crisis extended to the issue of under-representation of emerging markets in decision-making structures. In the end, it was the financial crisis that began in 2007 which allowed the IMF to gain new impetus. Its ability to intervene has been considerably strengthened.

This, however, raises two issues. First, past experience has caused a certain amount of distrust regarding the IMF's neo-liberal orientation. Above all its neglect of the social costs of following budgetary orthodoxy has been the object of fierce criticism. The other is the institution's actual decision-making power, which is related to the issue of its resources. In the 1980s, the policy of borrowing from members, which existed since the early 1960s, was accelerated and supplemented. The lending countries then began to establish themselves as a sort of executive board. This began with the Group of Ten (G10, periodic meetings of the finance ministers of states parties to general loan agreements) progressively establishing itself at the centre of decision-making at the IMF. The G10's influence faded only to make room for other 'Gs' (the G7, then the G8, more recently the G20). Such groups, established by the major economic powers and progressively enlarged so as to respond to legitimacy concerns, have become the driving forces in the IMF. This was particularly clear during the financial crisis that began in 2007. This was a systemic crisis calling for strong action and effective norms, including coordinated public regulatory intervention, and infinitely closer supervision of the private banking and finance system's activity. Such norms have yet to emerge.

A wide-angle perspective on norms

In describing the normative landscape, one cannot ignore domestic laws as producers of unilateral acts capable of having – and even being designed to have – international effects. This is classically true for setting currency exchange rates, as illustrated by the long-lasting controversy between the United States and China with respect to setting the yuan's parity; China, the only state which does not let its currency float, is at the receiving end of accusations that the yuan is unfairly undervalued.

Even so, most regulation of trade, investment and monetary policy today has an international origin, which has a strong modelling effect on domestic laws. To understand the characteristics – and the reality – of such regulation, one must examine an entire set of criteria: the role of conventional law as compared to other sources of law, the role of multilateralism, and the role of dispute settlement.

Placing things in a comparative perspective reveals three configurations. The first is that of a multilateral, public, conventional trade law, where dispute settlement – inter-state and unified – plays an important role. The second configuration is that of an investment law dominated by bilateral treaties, corrected by conventional modelling, and making room for the customary and soft law produced by international organisations as well as for mixed dispute settlement, which is open to private actors but has no unifying core. The third configuration is that of a monetary law with strong conventional, institutional, public inter-state origins, but without any dispute settlement component. Today, monetary regulation is almost entirely marginalised by what is optimistically called private regulation. The public aspect now seems limited to concerted declarations by more or less formal groups of states (the 'Gs'), which no doubt have the power to speak but not necessarily the will to produce effective consequences.

International trade

International trade law has undoubtedly remained the most classic in its method of elaboration, normative structures and means of implementation, especially taking into account the significant role of its case law. It was initially rooted in the GATT, avatar of the ITO. But the GATT was able to transform itself, through the magic of practice, from a temporary agreement into an international organisation without a constitutive charter. The WTO, albeit perfectly conventional, has not completely cleared itself of this heritage, which survives through the persistent myth of the member-driven organisation. The fact remains that international trade law remained limited for almost fifty years to trade in goods. But it was not static, considering that the periodic negotiation rounds allowed not only for enlarging the scope of liberalisation (more and more types of merchandise, greater and greater tariff reductions) but also for developing the regulatory dimension through complementary agreements.

The normative apparatus of this law is *a priori* fairly simple in its conception. The opening up of markets negotiated within the organisation rests on the principle of non-discrimination. This principle, the backbone of the multilateral system, includes the prohibitions on discriminating amongst foreign products to which the domestic market is open (most favoured nation clause), and on granting foreign products less favourable treatment than similar or competing domestic products receive (national treatment clause). This principle has several regulatory corollaries that have been refined over time, especially since progressively eliminating tariff barriers revealed (or was compensated by) non-tariff barriers, which are more difficult to dismantle. This difficulty stems less from their nature (non-tariff) than from the fact that they result from regulations which are generally necessary (technical norms, sanitary norms, etc.) but which may be misused by states to protect production or a domestic market that they have agreed to open. The issue is thus to provide a framework for such regulatory mechanisms, with the implicit goal of harmonisation. This goal was initially not expressly mentioned out of respect for state sovereignty – but it emerged more and more clearly once the WTO was established. Meanwhile, various agreements have been added to the GATT system in the 1960s (such as the anti-dumping code produced during the Kennedy Round) and the late 1970s (Tokyo Round codes on technical norms and anti-dumping, for example). But this ensemble was never fully integrated, and because the ratification of the additional agreements was optional, GATT members ended up having differing obligations while the normative apparatus retained its original defects. A 'club mentality' allowed states to release each other from obligations through informal agreements. GATT law did of course acquire a dispute settlement mechanism that was much more developed and consolidated than articles XXII and XXIII of the Agreement seemed to provide for. However, although the mechanism acquired judicial characteristics over time, the effects of its decisions depended on members' endorsement and thus suffered from the consensus mode of decision-making: unanimity was excluded as soon as relations were strained.

From a legal standpoint, several decisive changes were made to the trade system during the negotiations that gave birth to the WTO. The new organisation's charter may be seen as a sort of complex codification of GATT law, to which entire sections of progressive development have been added. The whole is bound together by the principle of the 'single undertaking' which is expected to guarantee that all members are held to the same obligations, even if each makes its own commitments in terms of opening its markets. Overall, there has been a tightening of regulatory constraints, not only in terms of substantive obligations, but also – and this is an important aspect – in terms of procedure, which imposes a certain amount of transparency on member states. It is possible to speak so clearly about tightening regulatory constraints because of the prominent case law resulting from heavy use of the dispute settlement mechanism. This involves a two-tiered jurisdiction with a permanent Appellate Body able to promote a unified interpretation of WTO law. This case-law plays an important role not only within WTO law, clarifying its contents and the relationship between its components, but also beyond the WTO, in order to relate WTO law to the rest of international law.

Investment law

Investment law has a different normative aspect. The practice of BITs began in Europe in the 1950s and became generalised a quarter-century later. The increase in conventions did not, however, eliminate customary law. BITs are partially fed by customary law and contribute to it in two main ways. The first is related to conventional repetition, which is in part the effect of conventional modelling, but goes further. In fact, the BITs concluded in increasing numbers today between developing countries are not substantially different from those concluded with developed countries. The second is related to the development of dispute settlement, which focuses attention on interpreting BITs and, more broadly, the applicable rules, which fosters references to customary law. It is nonetheless increasingly difficult to claim that investment law is unified. It seems to be awaiting multilateralisation without managing to cross the threshold, and its dispersed condition is only accentuated by dispute settlement. There have been many multilateral attempts, but since they remained unsuccessful they were transformed into unilateral acts of the organisations in which they took place and became soft law, such as the World Bank Guidelines on the Treatment of Foreign Direct Investment adopted in the 1990s, or the OECD Declaration and Decisions of 21 June 1976 on international investment and multinational enterprises.

Another multilateral attempt launched by the OECD in 1995 to draft a Multilateral Agreement on Investment failed. The WTO put this issue on its agenda in 1996, but suspended consideration of it after the failure of the Cancún ministerial conference. It is therefore still open, it being understood that regional agreements have been added in the interim, such as the Energy Charter and NAFTA, but also a certain number of free trade agreements (FTAs) that broadened their scope to include investment, marking a return to an old practice in a new context.

In the absence of a multilateral treaty (except for the Seoul Convention of 1985 that created the Multilateral Investment Guarantee Agency), unity could have come from case-law. But although disputes have proliferated, several factors act as barriers. The problem comes less from the increase in arbitration fora than from certain characteristics of arbitration. The fact that the procedures rely on multilateral structures, such as the ICSID, and that arbitration has been institutionalised, does not eliminate characteristics such as confidentiality not only of the procedure but very frequently of the decision itself. This constitutes a barrier to constructing a coherent case-law, since the meaning of notions as basic as 'investment' are still not entirely clear. The proliferation of arbitration proceedings increases contradictions, as illustrated by the abundant disputes arising from the Argentine crisis. This situation raises questions about the degree to which the imperative of legal certainty advanced to justify BITs has been satisfied.

Monetary regulation

Reliance is also at issue in regulating the monetary and financial system, since it is first and foremost designed to avoid, or at least remedy, crises. To achieve such a goal, one would expect strong public – and international – regulation. It has been clear for a long time that only coordinated regulatory activity by states can produce an effective frame. The 2008 financial crisis was an opportunity to hear this claim being reaffirmed numerous times, which at the same time delivers a normative diagnosis. In addition to a public monetary system that lost its regulatory ability in the early 1970s when floating currencies were accepted, there is no public international regulation of financial markets, although they have become more and more integrated.

There is of course some slight coordination, such as the activities of the Bank for International Settlements (BIS) in the area of prudential supervision. But this is soft law, which may or may not be incorporated into domestic laws, thus distorting competition for private actors who are subject to varying constraints depending on their country of origin. With domestic laws as the primary source of regulation, the obvious consequence is a dispersion of supervision amongst national entities, which are not all equally rigorous, nor sufficiently coordinated despite the development of networks. This is so in large part because even the most developed and richest states have not overcome the contradiction between the need to produce a coordinated regulatory framework and their own interest in allowing the free development of financial markets which are capable of providing them with the needed credit. Because they have had to and still do benefit from being borrowers, states are more likely to endorse the practices created by private actors than to regulate them. Beyond a few attempts to clean up certain financial practices (such as drug money laundering and bribery) which led to the adoption of international conventions, most 'rules' are produced by private self-regulation. But it probably takes some optimism to believe that these indicate a move towards genuine regulation. Despite the systemic crisis of 2009, the vigorous cooperation that has been recognised as necessary is far off and the monetary and financial area shows (if demonstration is necessary) that there is a panoply of actors who are not naturally cooperative, and a multitude of interests which are difficult to reconcile. And yet, the first decade of the 2000s has given evidence of the increasing urgency of connecting the different legal fields.

A focus on linkages/connections

Globalisation has made 'linkages' a major problem of government policy. Linkages are the logical consequence of interdependence, and they extend from relations between the various fields of economic law to relationships between economic law and other normative fields (human rights, environment and development, for example).

With respect to relations between fields of economic law, it has by now become clear that trade and investment cannot remain completely dissociated. The liberalisation of trade in services, especially when it implies establishment, has direct consequences for the investment regime. Similarly, the commitments states make in the WTO in the area of financial services have a direct effect on their ability to regulate market activities, the uncontrolled development of which played a major role in the current financial crisis. And yet, there is no coordination mechanism anywhere in sight, other than the informal impetuses that might possibly come from groups such as the G20. Without real coordination between international organisations – something provided for in their statutes – only these informal groups seem able to establish the necessary connections. But an action plan needs to be prepared that is expressed in binding norms going beyond responses to emergency. The issue is not to undo in one field what has been achieved in another.

This is not something that only concerns relations between the different branches of economic law, but the regulation of globalisation in its entirety. The increase in commercial exchanges reveals their 'dark' side, such as pollution or delinquency, and these problems cannot be considered separately. Moreover, the problem of climate change is global and calls for global solutions. How can one ignore that the recipes for producing economic development have not stopped the spread of poverty, even of extreme poverty (see Pogge, Chapter 17)? Awareness of these problems was raised more than three decades ago with the realisation that the environment is more than just an inexhaustible resources tank. Along with this awareness emerged concepts such as sustainable development, its syncretism clearly indicating that the problems are indissociable. Development cannot be considered exclusively in economic terms; its environmental and social aspects much also be recognised. This is what the Millennium Development Goals (MDGs) sought to reflect, incidentally raising the fundamental question about whether, and for whom, ever-more growth, riches and prosperity should be produced. But the mere setting out of such goals, something that has become an imperative of political correctness, does not itself produce operative results. Merely stating that it is essential to reconcile various goals, and specifying that this must be done proportionately, does not provide the terms of any such reconciliation. One might think these are essentially political decisions, because taking responsibility for choices with short-term costs (such as protecting the environment or promoting social norms) in the name of middle- and long-term gains (such as the welfare of future generations) is difficult. In practice such choices are postponed to the moment when the rules are implemented, with at least two types of consequences. On the one hand, there is no guarantee that some of the goals emphasised will not be set aside or subordinated, given the margin of interpretation left to the actors. On the other hand, in those cases where judicial review is accessible, the judges will have the last word, at least momentarily, with the risk that they are accused of being activists making what are in effect political choices. To add to the problems, the dispersion of international judicial fora does not guarantee consistent approaches.

In such conditions, it is significant that the linkage questions are increasingly raised before the WTO Dispute Settlement Body (DSB) and, to a lesser extent, in investment disputes. This calls for two remarks. First, whether one likes this or not, this puts tribunals in the position of making political decisions, a position for which they feel more or less able to take responsibility. Trade-related case law indicates that the Appellate Body has a relatively clear judicial policy in favour of recognising the legitimacy of measures that protect the environment or health but are detrimental to trade commitments. The reference to sustainable development in the preamble of the WTO Charter has provided justification for the interpretation of WTO law in light of developments in international environmental law. However, one should not be overoptimistic. The temptation has been to bring the treatment of so-called 'trade and ...' issues before the Appellate Body owing to the relative effectiveness of its decisions. This tendency, however, has its limits due to the fact that the applicable law is above all WTO law and that it is through the interpretation of this law that the judge can take on board non-trade concerns. Legal asymmetries are, at best, reduced. Investment dispute settlement is similarly and increasingly confronted with issues such as combining the protection of investors stated by the BITs with the increasing necessity for states to exert their regulatory competence as a consequence of commitments in other fields. This is evidence of the fact that states may over time have to assume obligations they had not initially foreseen such as environment protection and its associated costs, while the extensive interpretation of investors' protection has, at the same time, put their regulatory autonomy under heavy constraints. Nevertheless, investment arbitrators find it difficult to avoid the temptation of focusing on investment issues, without any appreciation of the broader perspective.

In this game, where the rules are not fixed and team spirit must be learned, courts have become fora where matters of common or public interest are debated. This makes non-governmental organisations (NGOs) participate through *amicus* briefs. NGOs appear indeed as representatives of public opinion – or civil society – that has trouble finding ways of expressing itself as a whole, although it may have interests that would not otherwise be taken into account. This is just one of the facets of the importance of the role of private actors. The desire to turn multinational enterprises into citizen actors is another facet, entailing a recognition of their power and of the key role they play. Involving them in decision-making is also a way of promoting the idea of shared responsibility as regards matters of common interest.

International law is sometimes described as a set of interconnected islands. Improving the connections between norms and actors is a challenge, at a time when it is necessary to find the path to new modes of development. This has been expressed through concepts such as sustainable development that promotes the idea that development must rest on three pillars of equal importance: economic, environmental and social. The tribulations that affect regulation in trade, investment and money could be a sign that although sustainable development is too often considered merely a buzzword, what it implies is nevertheless slowly maturing – the idea of growth more temperate as regards natural resources and more oriented towards social and individual welfare.

Bibliography

Dolzer, R. and C. Schreuer, 2008. *Principles of International Investment Law*, Oxford University Press

Ricardo, D., 1817. *On the Principles of Political Economy and Taxation*, London: John Murray

Waibel, M., A. Kaushal, K-H. Chung and C. Balchin (eds.), 2010. *The Backlash against Investment Arbitration*, Alphen aan den Rijn: Wolters Kluwer

Divided against itself: aspiration and reality of international law 17

Thomas Pogge

Introduction

Various human rights are widely recognised in codified and customary international law. These human rights promise all human beings protection against specific severe harms that might be inflicted on them domestically or by foreigners. Yet, international law also establishes and maintains institutional structures that greatly contribute to violations of these same human rights: central components of international law systematically obstruct the aspirations of poor populations for democratic self-government, civil rights, and minimal economic sufficiency. And central international organisations, like the World Trade Organisation (WTO), the International Monetary Fund (IMF) and the World Bank, are designed in ways that systematically contribute to the persistence of severe poverty.

We know, or certainly should know, that even today about a third of all human deaths – some 18 million annually – are due to poverty-related causes such as malnutrition, perinatal and maternal conditions, measles, diarrhoea, pneumonia, tuberculosis, or malaria (WHO 2008, 54–59, Table A1). Most of this annual death toll and the much larger poverty problem it epitomises are avoidable through minor modifications in supranational institutional arrangements that would entail only slight reductions in the incomes of the affluent. Such reforms have been blocked by the governments of the affluent countries that, advancing their own interests and those of their corporations and citizens, are designing and imposing a global institutional order that, continually and foreseeably, produces vast excesses of severe poverty and premature poverty-related deaths.

There are three main strategies for denying this charge. One can deny that variations in the design of the global order have any significant impact on the evolution of severe poverty world-wide. Failing this, one can claim that the present global order is close to optimal in terms of poverty avoidance. Should this strategy fail as well, one can still contend that the present global order is not *causing* severe poverty but merely failing to alleviate such poverty as much as it might. In the first three sections, I discuss these three strategies in order, to show that each is unsuccessful. I also discuss the direct and indirect ways in which the global order perpetuates poverty. It does so through asymmetrical rules that unfairly disfavour poor populations. It also favours oppressive and corrupt governments in poor countries: by facilitating bribery of corrupt officials, by allowing embezzled money to be secreted into foreign banks, and by conferring *resource* and *borrowing privileges* even on wholly illegitimate *de facto* rulers who enrich and entrench themselves by selling off the natural resources of the countries they oppress and by imposing onerous debt obligations upon these countries' populations.

If the imposition of the current global order constitutes a massive human rights violation, then what should we citizens of more powerful states do about it? In the fourth section, I argue that attempts to compensate for the harm through voluntary donations and aid programmes cannot alone end the catastrophe of world poverty. We should collaborate toward achieving institutional reforms that can eradicate severe poverty for good. Even small changes in the rules governing international trade, lending, investment, resource use, or intellectual property can have a large and durable impact on the global incidence of life-threatening poverty.

In the fourth section, I also deal with some important objections to the argument for privileging institutional reform. These arise out of the scepticism regarding the efficacy of rules and institutions in achieving moral and political goals. In recent years, international lawyers have raised two points that are particularly relevant to the international context. First, problems in the international context tend to be 'fact-intensive', so that it is difficult to apply any universal criteria as would be demanded by international rules. For this reason, international lawyers have been unable to agree on effective rules to address terrorism or humanitarian intervention, and one worries that poverty eradication may present a similar challenge. Second, the 'fragmentation' of international law prevents the use of logrolling tactics by the less powerful to achieve equitable reforms and allows the more powerful the opportunity to engage in 'forum shopping' for the most advantageous rules. I will reflect on some reasons why meaningful global institutional reform may nonetheless be possible. Moreover, as I argue throughout the final sections of the chapter, structural reforms are easier to achieve and much easier to sustain than equally significant unilateral improvements in the conduct of individual and collective agents.

I The purely domestic poverty thesis

Those who wish to deny that variations in the design of the global institutional order have a significant impact on the evolution of severe poverty explain such poverty by reference to national or local factors alone. John Rawls is a prominent example. He claims that when societies fail to thrive, 'the problem is commonly the nature of the public political culture and the religious and philosophical traditions that underlie its institutions. The great social evils in poorer societies are likely to be oppressive government and corrupt elites' (Rawls 1993, 77). He adds that:

> the causes of the wealth of a people and the forms it takes lie in their political culture and in the religious, philosophical and moral traditions that support the basic structure of their political and social institutions, as well as in the industriousness and cooperative talents of its members, all supported by their political virtues ... the political culture of a burdened society is all-important ... Crucial also is the country's population policy. (Rawls 1999, 108)

Accordingly, Rawls holds that our moral responsibility with regard to severe poverty abroad can be fully described as a 'duty of assistance' (*ibid.*, 37–38, 106–120). In response, one might detail the continuing legacies of colonialism, slavery, and genocide which have shaped the political culture of many presently poor societies. Leaving these aside, let me focus on the empirical view that, in the post-colonial era, the causes of the *persistence* of severe poverty, and hence the key to its eradication, lie within the poor countries themselves. Many find this view compelling in light of the great variation in how the former colonies have evolved over the last fifty years. Some of them have achieved solid growth and poverty reduction while others exhibit worsening poverty and declining *per capita* incomes. Is it not obvious that such strongly divergent national trajectories must be due to differing *domestic* causal factors in the countries concerned? And is it not clear, then, that the persistence of severe poverty is due to local causes?

However oft repeated and well received, this reasoning is fallacious. When national economic trajectories diverge, then there must indeed be local (country-specific) factors at work that explain the divergence. But it does not follow that global factors play no role. We can see this by considering an analogous case. There may be great variations in the performance of students in one class. These must be due to student-specific factors. Still, it does not follow that these 'local' factors fully explain student performance. Teacher and classroom quality, teaching times, reading materials, libraries, and other 'global' factors may also play an important role. Dramatic contrasts of success and failure, amongst students or amongst less-developed countries, do not then show global factors to be causally inert. In the former case, such global factors can greatly influence the overall progress of a class; they can influence the distribution of progress by being differentially appropriate to the needs and interests of different students; and they can affect the student-specific factors, as when a sexist teacher causes or aggravates motivational deficits in his female students. Analogous to these three possibilities, global institutional factors may greatly influence the evolution of severe poverty world-wide.

Exposure of the popular fallacy does not settle the issue. Dramatic divergences in national poverty trajectories do not disprove that decisions about the design of global institutional arrangements exert a powerful influence on the evolution of severe poverty world-wide. But is there such an influence? It is hard to doubt that there is. In the modern world, the traffic of transnational and even intra-national economic transactions is profoundly shaped by an elaborate system of treaties and conventions about trade, investments, loans, patents, copyrights, trademarks, double taxation, labour standards, environmental protection, use of seabed resources and much else. Structuring and enabling, permitting and constraining, these different parts of the present global institutional order realise highly specific design decisions within a vast space of alternative design possibilities. It is incredible on its face that all these alternative ways of structuring the world economy would have produced the same evolution in the overall incidence and geographical distribution of severe poverty.

II The Panglossian view of the present global order

If the design of the global institutional order makes a difference, then what has been the impact of the actual design of this order on the evolution of severe poverty world-wide? Here it is often claimed that we live, in this regard, in the best of all possible worlds: that the present global order is nearly optimal in terms of poverty avoidance.

A commonsense way of questioning this claim might develop a counterhypothesis in four steps. First, the interest in avoiding severe poverty is not the only interest to which those who negotiate the design of particular aspects of the global institutional order are sensitive. Such negotiators also care about their home government's political success and therefore about the interests of powerful corporations and other organisations on which such success depends. Second, these domestic interests are often in tension with the interest in global poverty avoidance. Third, when faced with such conflicts, negotiators generally give precedence to the interests of their own country's government, corporations and citizens over the interests of the global poor. Fourth, with 73 per cent of the world's social product (World Bank 2010, 379), the high-income countries enjoy great advantages in bargaining power and expertise, which enable their negotiators to deflect the design of the global order from what would be best for poverty avoidance. Given these four steps, we should expect the design of the global institutional order to reflect the shared interests of the governments, corporations and citizens of the affluent countries more than the interest in global poverty avoidance, insofar as these interests conflict.

There is much evidence that this counter-hypothesis is true. The present rules favour the affluent countries by allowing them to continue protecting their markets through quotas, tariffs, anti-dumping duties, export credits and subsidies to domestic producers in ways that poor countries are not permitted, or cannot afford, to match.[1] Other important examples include the World Trade Organisation regulations on cross-border investment and the Trade-Related Aspects of Intellectual Property Rights (TRIPs) Treaty of 1995 (see Pogge 2009; www.cptech.org/ip).

Such asymmetrical rules increase the share of global household income going to the affluent and decrease the share going to the poor relative to what these shares would be under symmetrical rules of free and open competition. The asymmetries thus reinforce the very inequality that enables the more powerful governments and their most influential constituents to impose these asymmetries in the first place. Table 17.1 documents this self-reinforcing trend.[2]

[1] The monstrosity of these subsidies is frequently lamented by establishment economists such as former World Bank chief economist Nicholas Stern (2002). But massive subsidies continue unabated. See *The Economist* (2010).

[2] Data kindly supplied by Branko Milanovic of the World Bank: e-mail, 25 April 2010. For earlier data, see Milanovic (2005, 107–108). Table 17.1 is based on currency exchange rates rather than purchasing power parities (PPPs) because the former are the more appropriate measure for estimating the influence (bargaining power and expertise) parties can bring to bear. Currency exchange rates are also the appropriate measure for assessing the *avoidability*

Table 17.1 Global distribution of income

Segment of world population	Share of global household income 1988	Share of global household income 2005	Absolute change in income share	Relative change in income share (%)
Richest ventile	42.87	46.36	+3.49	+8.1
Second ventile	21.80	22.18	+0.38	+1.8
Next three ventiles	24.83	21.80	−3.03	−12.2
Second quarter	6.97	6.74	−0.23	−3.3
Third quarter	2.37	2.14	−0.23	−9.8
Poorest quarter	1.16	0.78	−0.38	−32.9

Table 17.1 helps us understand how the number of chronically malnourished could break above 1 billion recently, for the first time in human history (FAO 2009). It also shows the proportions of the world poverty problem. In just seventeen years, the top tenth of humankind managed to capture an additional 4 per cent of global household income. Half of this gain would easily have sufficed to end all severe poverty in the bottom half, which instead sustained massive losses that reduced them to well under 3 per cent of global household income, also for the first time ever. Falling further and further behind, the global poor become ever more marginalised, with their interests ignored in both national and international decision-making. Annual spending power around $200 per person does not command much attention in international negotiations when *per capita* incomes in the affluent countries are some 200 times higher. And the interests of poor African countries do not carry much weight when the combined gross national incomes of twenty-six of them, representing over 400 million people, fall short of the annual sales volumes of the world's largest corporations.

Increasing income inequalities accumulate into even larger inequalities of wealth. A World Institute for Development Economics Research (WIDER) study estimated that in 2000 the bottom 50 per cent of the world's adults together had 1.1 per cent of global wealth, while the top 10 per cent had 85.1 per cent and the top 1 per cent had 39.9 per cent (Davies *et al.* 2006, Table 10a).

of poverty. For comparing standards of living, market exchange rates are indeed inappropriate. But PPPs are also problematic for assessing very low incomes because the poor must concentrate their consumption on basic necessities, which are cheaper in poor countries but not as cheap as PPPs would suggest. See Pogge (2010a, 80–85, 213–214, n. 127).

The authors stress that their study may understate global wealth inequality because the super-rich are typically not captured in household surveys (*ibid.*, 31).

These data should suffice to refute the Panglossian view: the present design of the global order is not optimal in terms of poverty avoidance. It is clear how this value could be better served: the poorest countries should receive financial support toward hiring experts to advise them how to articulate their interests in WTO negotiations, toward maintaining missions at WTO headquarters in Geneva, toward bringing cases before the WTO, and toward coping with all the regulations they are required to implement. Poor countries should face reduced barriers to their exports and should not have to pay for market access by collecting billions in economic rents for 'intellectual property'. The WTO Treaty should specify a global minimum wage and minimal global constraints on working hours and working conditions in order to halt the current 'race to the bottom' where poor countries competing for foreign investment must outbid one another by offering ever-more exploitable workforces. The affluent countries should be required to pay for the negative externalities we impose on the poor: for the pollution we have produced over many decades and the resulting effects on their environment and climate, for the rapid depletion of natural resources, and for the violence caused by our demand for drugs and our war on drugs. Examples could be multiplied. There clearly are feasible variations to the present global order that would dramatically reduce severe poverty world-wide, far below the current, staggering figures. This order is *not* optimal in terms of poverty avoidance. (For a more detailed discussion, see Pogge 2010b, Section 1).

III Is the present global order merely less beneficial than it might be?

Can one say that the global institutional order, though clearly and greatly sub-optimal in terms of poverty avoidance, is nonetheless not harming the global poor, nor violating their human rights? This third defence strategy appeals to something like the distinction between acts and omissions. It seeks to diminish the moral significance of the affluent states' decision to impose the present design of the global order rather than a foreseeably more poverty-avoiding alternative by assigning this decision the status of a mere omission. Now the affluent countries are clearly active in formulating the global economic rules they want, in pressing for their acceptance, and in pursuing their enforcement. The defence strategy must then apply the act/omission distinction at another place: not to how the relevant governments are related to the global rules, but to how these global rules are related to avoidable poverty. The idea must be that the rules governing the world economy are not actively causing excessive poverty, thus harming and killing people, but merely passively failing to prevent severe poverty, failing to protect people from harm.

The distinction between acts and omissions is difficult enough when applied to individual and collective agents. Its application to social institutions and rules is at first baffling. When more premature deaths occur under a system of rules than would occur under some feasible alternative, we might say that there are excessive deaths under the existing regime. But how can we distinguish between excessive deaths that the existing rules *bring about* and ones that these rules merely *fail to prevent*? Let us examine three ideas for how this defence strategy can be made to work.

First idea: invoking baseline comparisons

There is much debate about the apparently empirical question of whether WTO globalisation is harming or benefiting the global poor. Harm and benefit are comparative notions, involving the idea of people being worse or better off. But what is the implied baseline here – the alternative state compared to which the global poor are either worse off (and therefore harmed) or better off (and therefore benefited by globalisation)?

In most cases, it turns out, the popular debate is about whether poverty world-wide has been rising or falling since the latest globalisation push began in the 1980s. Yet, this debate is morally irrelevant. The charge is that governments, by imposing a global institutional order under which great excesses of severe poverty and poverty-related deaths persist, are violating the human rights of many poor people. The plausibility of this charge is unaffected by whether severe poverty is rising or falling. To see this, consider the parallel charges that slave-holding societies harmed and violated the human rights of those they enslaved, or that the Nazis violated the human rights of those they confined and killed in their concentration camps. These charges can certainly not be defeated by showing that the rate of victimisation was in decline. Of course, the words 'harm' and 'benefit' are sometimes appropriately used with implicit reference to an earlier state. But such a historical baseline is irrelevant here. For even if there were less severe poverty today than there was twenty-five years ago, we could not infer that the present global order is (in a morally significant sense) *benefiting* the global poor. This inference would beg the whole question by simply assuming the incidence of severe poverty twenty-five years ago as the appropriate no-harm baseline. Just as the claim that the United States violated the human rights of black slaves in the 1850s cannot be refuted by showing that such slaves were better off than in earlier decades, so the claim that the imposition of the present global order violates the human rights of the poor cannot be refuted by showing that their numbers are falling (see Pogge 2005, 55–58).

No less inconclusive than such *diachronic* comparisons are *subjunctive* comparisons with a historical baseline. Even if severe poverty were below what it now would be if the preceding regime had continued, we cannot infer that the present regime is benefiting the poor. This inference would again beg the question by assuming the incidence of severe poverty as it would have evolved under the preceding rules as the appropriate no-harm baseline. By the same reasoning, the military *junta* under Than Shwe could be said to be benefiting the Burmese people provided that they are better off than they would now be if the earlier *junta* under Ne Win were still in power. Sometimes subjunctive comparisons are presented with a historical baseline defined by reference to a much earlier time. Thus it is said that Africans today are no worse off than they would now be if there had never been significant contacts with outsiders. In response, we should question whether there are knowable facts about such a remote alternate history. We should also, once again, question the moral relevance of this hypothetical baseline involving continued mutual isolation: if world history had transpired without colonisation and enslavement, then there would – *perhaps* – now be affluent people in Europe and very poor ones in Africa. But these would be persons and populations entirely different from those now actually living there, who in fact are very deeply shaped and scarred by their continent's involuntary encounter with European invaders. So we cannot tell starving Africans that *they* would be starving and *we* would be affluent even if the crimes of colonialism had never occurred. Without these crimes there would not be the actually existing radical inequality which consists in *these* persons being affluent and *those* being extremely poor.

Similar considerations refute the moral relevance of subjunctive comparison with a *hypothetical* baseline – the claim, for instance, that even more people would live and die even more miserably in some fictional state of nature. Many such states have been described, and it is unclear how one can be singled out as the uniquely appropriate specification. Moreover, it is doubtful that *any* coherently describable state of nature on this planet would be able to match our globalised civilisation's record of sustaining a stable death toll of 18 million premature deaths per year from poverty-related causes (see Pogge 2008, 142–145). If no such state of nature can be described, then the present global order cannot be said to benefit the global poor by reducing severe poverty below a state-of-nature baseline. Finally, how can the claim that some people are being harmed *now* be undermined by pointing out that people in a state of nature would be even worse off? If such an argument succeeded, would it not show that *anything* done to another counts as harm only if it reduces the latter below the state-of-nature baseline? If we are not harming the billions we are keeping in severe poverty, then enslavement did not harm the slaves either, if only they were no worse off than people would be in the relevant state of nature.

I conclude that baseline comparisons of the three kinds we have considered are unsuitable for defending any institutional scheme from the charge that it harms or violates human rights. The severe burdens and disadvantages people suffer under some institutional scheme cannot be justified by any diachronic comparison with how such people had fared before or by any subjunctive comparison with how such people would have been faring under some (hypothetically continued) preceding regime or in a state of nature. What matters is whether the institutional order in question foreseeably leads to severe burdens that are reasonably avoidable (see Pogge 2005, 61).

Second idea: invoking the consent of the global poor

Another common way of denying that the present global order is harming the poor invokes the venerable precept *volenti not fit iniuria* – no injustice is done to the consenting. Supranational institutional arrangements cannot be harming the poor when participation in them, such as WTO membership, is voluntary.

This line of argument is refuted by four mutually independent considerations. First, appeal to consent cannot defeat a charge of human rights violation given that, on the usual understanding of moral and legal human rights, they are inalienable and thus cannot be waived by consent. Second, an appeal to consent cannot justify the severe impoverishment of children who are greatly over-represented amongst those suffering severe poverty and its effects. Third, most of the severely impoverished live in countries that lack meaningful democracy. Thus Nigeria's accession to the WTO was effected by its military dictator Sani Abacha, Myanmar's by the notorious SLORC *junta*, Indonesia's by Suharto, Zimbabwe's by Robert Mugabe and the Congo's by dictator Mobutu Sese Seko. These rulers' success in subjecting people to their rule does not give them the moral authority to consent on behalf of those whom they are oppressing. Fourth, insofar as very poor people do consent, through a meaningfully democratic process, to some global institutional arrangements, the justificatory force of such consent is weakened by their having no other tolerable option, and weakened even further by the fact that their calamitous circumstances are partly due to those whose conduct this consent is meant to justify. Poor countries need trade for development. They do not get fair trading opportunities under the WTO regime; but a country that failed to sign up would find its trading opportunities even more severely curtailed. Any poor country must decide about whether to accept the WTO rules against the background of other rules that it cannot escape and that make it extremely costly to decline.[3]

Third idea: invoking the flaws of the poor countries' social institutions and rulers

A further, popular way of denying that the present global institutional order is harming the poor invokes the success stories – the Asian tigers and China – to show that any poor country can defeat severe poverty under the existing global order.

This reasoning involves a some–all fallacy. The fact that *some* individuals born into poverty become millionaires does not show that *all* such persons can do likewise (see Cohen 1989, 262–263). The reason is that the pathways

[3] It is worth mentioning in this context another popular fallacy often adduced in defence of the status quo. As empirical research shows, poor countries embracing the new global rules perform better, economically, than countries that do not. This is taken to prove that the new global rules benefit the poor countries. This inference depends on conflating two claims: (A) *Given* the dominance of the affluent countries and their rules and organisations, it is better for a poor country to cooperate. (B) The dominance of these rich-country rules and organisations is better for the poor countries than alternative institutional arrangements. Once these claims are properly distinguished, it is obvious that (B) does not follow from (A).

to riches are sparse. They are not rigidly limited, but it is clearly impossible to achieve the kind of economic growth rates needed for everyone to become a millionaire. The same holds for formerly poor countries. The Asian tigers achieved impressive rates of economic growth and poverty reduction through a state-sponsored build-up of industries that mass produce low-tech consumer products. These industries were globally successful by using their considerable labour-cost advantage to beat competitors in the developed countries and by drawing on greater state support and/or a better-educated workforce to beat competitors in other poor countries. Building such industries was hugely profitable for the Asian tigers. But if many more poor countries had adopted this same developmental strategy, competition amongst them would have rendered it much less profitable.

Over the last two decades, China has been the great success story, achieving phenomenal growth in exports and *per capita* income. So China's example is now often used to argue that the rules of the world economy are favourable to the poor countries and conducive to poverty eradication. These arguments commit the same some–all fallacy. Exporters in the poorer countries compete over the same heavily protected rich-country markets. Thanks to its extraordinary ability to deliver quality products cheaply in large quantities, China has done extremely well. But this great success has greatly reduced market share and export prices for firms in many poorer countries. To be sure, the world economy as presently structured is not a constant-sum game, where any one player's gain must be another's loss. Yet, outcomes are strongly interdependent. We cannot conclude, therefore, that the present global institutional order, though less favourable to the poor countries than it might be, is still favourable enough for all of them to do as well as the Asian tigers and then China have done in fact.

This is not to deny that most severe poverty could be avoided, despite the current unfair global order, if the national governments and elites of the poor countries were genuinely committed to good governance and poverty eradication. But this claim provides no moral defence of the affluent countries and their present globalisation project if it is also true that most severe poverty could be avoided, despite the corrupt and oppressive regimes holding sway in so many less-developed countries, if the global institutional order were designed with more attention to this purpose. If we acquit causal factor A because of the necessary contribution made by B, we must acquit B as well because of the necessary contribution by A. But since we cannot acquit both for harm they knowingly produce together, we must conclude that each is responsible for much of the harm (see Pogge 2005, 62–64).

Still, by assuming symmetry between the two sets of causal factors, this response is too simple, failing to fully expose the responsibility of the affluent countries and of their globalisation project. There is an important asymmetry. While domestic institutional arrangements and policies in the poor countries have very little influence on the design of the global order, the latter has a great deal of influence on the former. The global institutional order exerts its pernicious influence on the evolution of world poverty not only directly, in the ways already discussed, but also indirectly through its influence on the domestic institutions and policies of the poorer countries. Oppression and corruption, so prevalent in many poor countries today, are themselves very substantially produced and sustained by central features of the present global order.

It was only in 1999, for example, that the developed countries finally agreed to curb their firms' bribery of foreign officials by adopting the Organisation for Economic Cooperation and Development (OECD) Convention on Combating Bribery of Foreign Public Officials in International Business Transactions. Until then, most developed states did not merely legally authorise their firms to bribe foreign officials, but even allowed them to deduct such bribes from their taxable revenues, thereby providing financial incentives and moral support for the practice of bribing politicians and officials in the poor countries. This practice diverts the loyalties of officials in these countries and also makes a great difference to which persons are motivated to stand for public office in the first place. Poor countries have suffered staggering losses as a result, most clearly in the awarding of public contracts. Preliminary evidence suggests that the new Convention is ineffective in curbing bribery by multinational corporations. And banks in the affluent countries continue to invite corrupt rulers and officials in the poorer countries to deposit their earnings from bribery and embezzlement. Supplemented by tax avoidance through transfer pricing and other schemes, such illicit financial flows are estimated to cost poor countries between \$850 billion and \$1 trillion, some ten times the official development assistance supposedly flowing the other way (Kar and Cartwright-Smith 2008, iv and 21–22). Such practices have created a pervasive culture of corruption now deeply entrenched in many poor countries.

Bribery and embezzlement are part of a larger problem. The political and economic elites of poor countries interact with their domestic inferiors, on the one hand, and with foreign governments and corporations, on the other. These two constituencies differ enormously in wealth and power. The former are mostly poorly educated and heavily preoccupied with the daily struggle to survive. The latter have vastly greater rewards and penalties at their disposal. Politicians with a normal interest in their own political and economic success thus cater to the interests of foreign governments and corporations rather than to the competing interests of their much poorer compatriots. There are plenty of poor-country governments that have come to power or remained in office solely as a result of foreign support. And there are many poor-country politicians and bureaucrats who, induced or even bribed by foreigners, work against the interests of their people: *for* the development of a tourist-friendly sex industry with forced exploitation of children and women, *for* the importation of unnecessary, obsolete, or overpriced products at public expense, *for* the permission to import hazardous products, wastes, or factories, *against* laws protecting employees or the environment, and so on.

In most poor countries, these incentive asymmetries are aggravated by the lack of genuine democracy. This democratic deficit also has global roots. It is a central feature of our global institutional order that any group controlling a preponderance of the means of coercion within a country is internationally recognised as the authoritative agent for the country's territory and people – regardless of how this group came to power, of how it exercises power and of how much popular support it has. International recognition means not merely that we engage such a group in negotiations, but also that we accept its right: to act for the people it rules and thereby authorise it to borrow in the country's name and thereby to impose debt service obligations upon it; to sell the country's resources and to dispose of the proceeds of such sales; to sign treaties on the country's behalf and thus to bind its present and future population; and to use state revenues to buy the means of internal repression. The conferral of these four important privileges on the basis of effective power alone goes a long way toward explaining why so many countries are so badly governed.

The *borrowing privilege* we confer upon *de facto* rulers includes the power to impose internationally valid debt service obligations upon the whole country. A later government that refuses to honour debts incurred by a predecessor will be severely punished by the banks and governments of other countries. At a minimum, it will lose its own borrowing privilege by being excluded from the international financial markets. Such refusals are therefore very rare, as governments, even when newly elected after a dramatic break with the past, are compelled to pay the debts of their predecessors, no matter how corrupt, brutal, undemocratic, unconstitutional, repressive and unpopular they may have been.

The international borrowing privilege makes three important contributions to the high prevalence of oppressive and corrupt regimes in less-developed countries. First, it facilitates borrowing by destructive rulers, who can borrow more money and can do so more cheaply than they could do if they alone were obliged to repay it, and thereby helps such rulers maintain themselves in power even against near-universal popular opposition. Second, the international borrowing privilege imposes the often huge debts of their corrupt predecessors upon democratic successor regimes. It thereby saps the capacity of democratic governments to implement structural reforms and other political programmes, thus rendering such governments less successful and less stable than they would otherwise be. (It is small consolation that *putschists* are sometimes weakened by being held liable for the debts of their democratic predecessors.) Third, the international borrowing privilege strengthens incentives toward *coup* attempts and civil war: whoever succeeds in bringing a preponderance of the means of coercion under his control gets the borrowing privilege as an additional reward.

The *resource privilege* we confer upon *de facto* rulers includes the power to effect legally valid transfers of ownership rights over resources. A corporation that has purchased resources from a tyrant thereby becomes entitled to be – and actually *is* – recognised anywhere as their legitimate owner. This is a remarkable feature of our global order. A group that overpowers the guards and takes control of a warehouse may be able to give some of the merchandise to others, accepting money in exchange. But the fence who pays them becomes merely the possessor, not the owner, of the loot. Contrast this with a group that overpowers an elected government and takes control of a country. Such a group, too, can give away some of the country's natural resources, accepting money in exchange. In this case, however, the purchaser acquires not merely possession, but all the rights and liberties of ownership, which are supposed to be – and actually *are* – protected and enforced by all other states' courts and police forces.

This international resource privilege has a disastrous impact in poor countries whose resource sector constitutes a large segment of the domestic economy. Whoever can take power in such a country by whatever means can maintain his rule, even against broad popular opposition, by buying the arms and soldiers he needs with revenues from the export of natural resources and with funds borrowed against future resource sales. The resource privilege thus gives insiders strong incentives toward the violent acquisition and exercise of political power, thereby causing *coup* attempts and civil wars. And it gives outsiders strong incentives to corrupt the officials of such countries who, no matter how badly they rule, continue to have resources to sell and money to spend.

The incentives arising from the international resource privilege help explain the significant *negative* correlation between resource wealth (relative to Gross Domestic Product) and economic performance. This 'resource curse' is exemplified by many less-developed countries that, despite great natural wealth, have achieved little economic growth or poverty reduction. This is so because they are more likely to experience civil wars, *coups*, and oppressive rule. And even an elected and well-intentioned government in such a country is often obliged to tolerate massive embezzlement by its military officers in order to counter-balance their incentive to take power for the sake of acquiring the lucrative privileges (see Lam and Wantchekon 1999, 31, 35; Wenar 2008).

Like the formerly tax-deductible bribery of poor-country officials and the complicity by banks in the embezzlement of public funds, the four privileges just discussed are significant features of our global order, greatly benefiting the governments, corporations and citizens of affluent countries and the political–military elites of poor countries at the expense of the vast majority of ordinary people in poor countries. Thus, while the present global institutional order indeed does not make it strictly impossible for poor countries to achieve genuine democracy and sustained economic growth, central features of this order greatly contribute to poor countries' typically failing on both counts. These features are crucial for explaining the inability and particularly the unwillingness of these countries' leaders to eradicate poverty more effectively. And they are crucial, therefore, to explaining why global inequality is increasing so rapidly that substantial global economic growth since the end of the Cold War has not reduced income poverty and malnutrition – *despite* substantial technological progress and global economic growth, *despite* huge reported poverty reductions in

China,[4] *despite* the post-Cold-War 'peace dividend',[5] *despite* substantial declines in real food prices,[6] *despite* official development assistance, and *despite* the efforts of international humanitarian and development organisations.

None of the three defence strategies, then, succeeds in showing that the imposition of the current global order, on the background of feasible alternatives, does no harm to the poor. Given that the present global institutional order is foreseeably associated with such massive incidence of avoidable severe poverty, its (uncompensated) imposition manifests an ongoing human rights violation – arguably the largest such violation ever committed in human history.[7] In just twenty years since the end of the Cold War, some 360 million human beings have died prematurely from poverty-related causes. Much larger numbers must live in conditions of life-threatening poverty that make it very difficult for them to articulate their interests and effectively to fend for themselves and their families. This catastrophe was and is happening, foreseeably, under a global institutional order designed for the benefit of the affluent countries' governments, corporations and citizens and of the poor countries' ruling elites. There are feasible alternative designs of the global institutional order, feasible alternative paths of globalisation, under which this catastrophe would have been largely avoided. Even now severe poverty could be rapidly reduced through feasible reforms that would modify the more harmful features of this global order or mitigate their impact.

This conclusion is quite distinct from the usual calls for more aid to the poor. There is still so much severe poverty, and so much need for aid, only because the poor are systematically impoverished by present institutional

[4] The number of Chinese living on less than $2.50 per day (2005 PPP) decreased by 36 per cent, or 356 million, between 1987 and 2005. See Chen and Ravallion (2008, Table 7).

[5] Thanks to the end of the Cold War, military expenditures world-wide have declined from 4.7 per cent of aggregate GDP in 1985 to 2.9 per cent in 1996 (UNDP 1998, 197) and to about 2.6 per cent or $1,531 billion in 2009 (SIPRI 2010). Today, this global peace dividend is worth over $1.2 trillion *per annum*.

[6] The World Bank's Food Price Index fell (in constant 1990 dollars) from 176.7 in 1980 to 100 in 1990 and then to 96.9 in 2002. See World Bank (2003, 277, row 18). Food prices rose substantially in 2006–2008.

[7] It is not the *gravest* human rights violation, in my view, because those who commit it do not intend the death and suffering they inflict either as an end or as a means. They merely act with wilful indifference to the enormous harms they cause in the course of advancing their own ends while going to great lengths to deceive the world (and sometimes themselves) about the impact of their conduct. But it is still the *largest* such human rights violation.

arrangements and have been so impoverished for a long time during which our advantage and their disadvantage have been compounded. True, eradicating severe poverty at a morally acceptable speed would impose costs and opportunity costs on the affluent countries. However acceptance of such costs is not generous charity, but required compensation for the harms produced by unjust global institutional arrangements whose past and present imposition by the affluent countries brings great benefits to their citizens.

IV The promise of global institutional reform

Human rights impose on us a negative duty not to contribute to the imposition of an institutional order that foreseeably gives rise to an avoidable human rights deficit without making compensatory protection and reform efforts for its victims. Analogous to the negative duties not to break a promise or contract and not to make emergency use of another's property without compensation, this negative institutional duty may impose positive obligations on advantaged participants: obligations to compensate for their contribution to the harm. Such compensation can take the form of individual efforts (donations to efficient non-governmental organisations) or of bilateral or multilateral government aid programmes. Or it can focus on institutional reform. I close with some comments on this latter option.

In the modern world, the rules governing economic transactions – both nationally and internationally – are the most important causal determinants of the incidence and severity of human rights deficits. They are most important because of their great impact on the economic distribution within the jurisdiction to which they apply. Thus, even relatively minor variations in a country's laws about tax rates, labour relations, social security, and access to health care and education can have a much greater impact on poverty than large changes in consumer habits or in the policies of a major corporation. This point applies to the global institutional order as well. Even small changes in the rules governing international trade, lending, investment, resource use, or intellectual property can have a huge impact on the global incidence of life-threatening poverty.

Rules governing economic transactions are important also for their greater visibility. To be sure, rule changes, like specific projects and initiatives, can have unintended and even unforeseeable effects. But with rules it is easier to diagnose such effects and to make corrections. This point is not threatened, I believe, by recent critiques that international lawyers have set forth of 'formalism', claiming that it is exceedingly difficult to tailor international rules to promote moral and political goals. The argument given for this claim is that rule-makers cannot anticipate every possible case that will be covered by a rule and therefore cannot ensure that the rule will always prescribe the best settlement (see Koskenniemi 2007, 9). This is a familiar problem with the efficacy of rules generally, applying to both domestic and international contexts (see Schauer 1991, cited in Koskenniemi 2007, 9, n. 37). But the problem is said to be further compounded by the 'fact-intensiveness' of international context. As Martti Koskenniemi writes:

> International situations tend to be seen as idiosyncratic and fact-intensive. Any single rule might spell injustice in some of the future cases where it will be applied. Thus the failure of international efforts to find universal 'criteria' for humanitarian intervention, for the identifying of 'aggression', or for singling out human groups that ought to be treated as 'terrorists'. (*Ibid.*, 10)

Fortunately, these points have limited application to the goal of poverty reduction. The objective here is not to design institutional reforms that will deliver the desired effect in every case, that is, will raise the income of every poor person. Rather, institutional reforms should aim at a statistical objective: at reductions in the depth and incidence of poverty as reflected in a substantial increase in the share of global household income going to the bottom half of humankind. Such effects may not be easy to predict with precision. But there are sophisticated econometric techniques that show considerable convergence – for example in regard to the harm done by the affluent countries' continued protectionism (see Pogge 2010b, 183–184). Such techniques of causal analysis have played a key role in successful national efforts at poverty eradication, and I see no reason why they should fail in the assessment of global measures such as a world-wide minimum wage or a modification of the international borrowing privilege, for example. In any case, such assessments of the statistical effects of global institutional reforms are far easier than assessments of the relative impact of variations in the conduct of individual or collective agents. The latter assessment can be confined to the persons immediately affected – for example, to the employees of a corporation or to the inhabitants of a town in which an aid agency is running a project. But such a confined assessment is always vulnerable to the charge of ignoring indirect effects upon outsiders or future persons.

In addition to fact-intensiveness, the global institutional order, unlike (at least some) domestic institutional orders, is also marked by extensive 'fragmentation', defined by international lawyers as the 'proliferation of international regulatory institutions with overlapping jurisdictions and ambiguous boundaries' (Benvenisti and Downs 2007, 596). Benvenisti and Downs discuss a number of problems with increased institutional fragmentation, but most threatening to the prospects of significantly reducing world poverty through institutional reform are the following: first, the rise of issue-specific treaties and legal fora only serves to increase the bargaining power of wealthier and more powerful states by preventing logrolling tactics amongst their poorer, less powerful, and more diverse and numerous counterparts; and second, the existence of multiple possible fora for dispute resolution allows the more powerful states to engage in 'forum-shopping' as a means to pursue their own interests at the expense of the poor and lesser advantaged.[8]

These concerns are real and important. Affluent countries and their constituents have designed our global institutional order in a way that is very harmful to the poor and they can find ways to continue to do this. And they have an incentive to do so: to avoid the slight loss they would incur if the poorer half's share of global household income increased, say, from 3 to 4 per cent. Institutional reform that imposes some opportunity cost on the affluent is thus indeed difficult to achieve. And yet, such reform is much easier to achieve than equally effective unilateral changes in the conduct of states, corporations, and individuals. This is so, because individual and collective agents are under continuous counter-moral pressures not merely from their ordinary self-interested concerns, but also from their competitive situation as well as from considerations of fairness. These phenomena are illustrated by the case of competing corporations, each of which may judge that it cannot afford to pass up immoral opportunities to take advantage of its employees and customers because such unilateral self-restraint would

[8] Benvenisti and Downs (2007, 597). See also Koskenniemi (2007, 4); Chimni (2005) (arguing that emerging global administrative institutions have an 'imperial' character and are effectively harnessed to further the interests of the transnational capitalist class). For a contrary view, see Charney (1996, 73–75), cited at Benvenisti and Downs (2007, 600–601) (defending the multiplicity of fora as a step in the right direction towards increasing acceptance of peaceful means of international arbitration and dispute resolution).

place it at an unfair competitive disadvantage vis-à-vis its less scrupulous competitors. Domestically, this sort of problem can be solved through changes in the legal rules that require all corporations, on pain of substantial penalties, to observe common standards in their treatment of customers and employees. Corporations are often willing to support such legislation even while they are unwilling to risk their competitive position through unilateral good conduct.

Similar considerations apply in the international arena, where corporations and governments compete. Given their concern not to fall behind in this competition and not to be unfairly handicapped through unilateral moral efforts and restraints, it is perhaps not surprising that individuals, corporations and governments have been so reluctant to make meaningful efforts toward eradicating global poverty.[9] Again, it is possible that affluent governments and corporations could be brought to do much more by accepting and honouring legal rules that apply to them all and thereby relieve each of the fear that its own good conduct will unfairly disadvantage it and cause it to lose ground against its competitors. Successful efforts to reduce poverty within states exemplify this model of structural reform rather than individual moral effort.

To be sure, this thought is not new, and governments have been very reluctant to commit themselves, even jointly, to serious global anti-poverty measures. Their solemn promise to halve global poverty by 2015 has been reiterated – in cleverly weakened formulations – but has yet to result in serious implementation efforts (see Pogge 2010a, Chapter 3). Official development assistance (ODA) from the affluent countries, once supposed to reach 1 per cent, then 0.7 per cent of their combined gross national products, actually shrank throughout the 1990s, from 0.33 per cent in 1990 to 0.22 per cent in 2000 (UNDP 2002, 202). With the 'war on terror', ODA is reported to have grown back to 0.31 per cent in 2009 due in part to dramatic growth in spending on post-occupation Afghanistan and Iraq (OECD 2010).

[9] Their current effort amounts to about $22.5 billion annually – 0.05 per cent of the gross national incomes of the affluent countries – consisting of $7 billion annually from individuals and corporations (UNDP 2003, 290) and another $15.5 billion (2008) annually from governments in official development assistance for basic social services (Millennium Development Goals Indicators). Aggregate official development assistance is some eight times higher, but most of it is spent for the benefit of agents more capable of reciprocation: domestic exporters or 'friendly' regimes (such as those in Iraq, Afghanistan, or Egypt).

Yet, even this new $120 billion level is not enough to eradicate severe poverty – and only one eighth of this ODA is actually spent on basic social services.

This discouraging evidence suggests that reform in the global institutional order will be difficult to achieve. However, this fact does not undermine my hypothesis that such structural improvements are *easier* to achieve and much *easier* to sustain than equally significant unilateral improvements in the conduct of individual and collective agents. We know how much money individuals, corporations and the governments of affluent countries are now willing to spend on global poverty eradication: about $22.5 billion annually (see n. 9). This amount is very small in comparison to the harms inflicted on the global poor by evident injustices in the present global order. It is also very small in comparison to what would be required to achieve substantial progress: the amount needed in the first few years of a serious offensive against poverty is closer to $300 billion annually.[10] It is not realistic to hope that we can achieve such a thirteen-fold increase in available funds through appeals to the morality of the relevant agents: affluent individuals, corporations and the governments of affluent countries. It is *more* realistic – though admittedly still rather unrealistic – to achieve substantial progress on the poverty front through institutional reforms that make the global order less burdensome on the poor. Accepting such reforms, affluent countries would bear some opportunity costs of making the international trade, lending, investment and intellectual property regimes fairer to the global poor as well as some costs of compensating for harms done – for example by helping to fund basic health facilities, vaccination programmes, basic schooling, school lunches, safe water and sewage systems, basic housing, power plants and networks, banks and micro-lending, road, rail and communication links where these do not yet exist.

Of course, if such a reform programme is to gain and maintain support from citizens and governments of affluent countries, it must distribute such costs and opportunity costs fairly amongst them. Transparency will be required in order to assure each of these actors that their competitive position will not be eroded by the non-compliance of others. It is also

[10] See Pogge (2008, 202–221). Amazingly, $300 billion is only 0.5 per cent of the global product or 0.7 per cent of the combined gross national incomes of the affluent countries. See World Bank (2010, 379).

important to tailor specific institutional proposals so that they are not easily circumvented through the usual institutional and bargaining manoeuvres employed by these countries. This is a problem I have been sensitive to throughout my work.[11] For instance in my advocacy of the Health Impact Fund, I supplement moral arguments with arguments about *feasibility* (that reform, once implemented, must be able to generate its own support amongst those with the power to uphold it) and *realism* (that reform-proposals must enjoy support of key stake-holders under existing institutions).[12]

A final point in favour of global institutional reform is that the path of such reform is far more realistic and sustainable than individual giving for ordinary citizens who, in democratic societies, hold the ultimate power to effect political change in the wealthy countries. This is so for three obvious reasons. First, the costs and opportunity costs each affluent citizen imposes on herself by supporting structural reform is extremely small relative to the contribution this reform makes to avoiding severe poverty. The reform may lower your family's standard of living by $900 annually, say, while improving by $300 annually the standard of living for hundreds of millions of poor families. By contrast, a unilateral donation of the same amount would lower your family's standard of living by $900 annually while improving by $300 annually the standard of living of only three poor families. Given such pay-offs, rational agents with some moral concern for the avoidance of severe poverty will be far more willing to support structural reform than to sustain donations. Second, structural reform assures citizens that costs and opportunity costs are fairly shared amongst the more affluent, as already discussed. And third, structural reform, once in place, need not be repeated, year after year, through painful personal decisions. Continual alleviation of poverty leads to fatigue, aversion, even contempt. It requires affluent citizens to rally to the cause again and again while knowing that most others similarly situated contribute nothing or very little, that their own contributions are legally optional and that, no matter how much they give, they could for just a little more always save yet further children from sickness or starvation. Today, such fatigue, aversion and contempt are

[11] See for instance Pogge (2008, 20–21). I take note of the vastly unequal bargaining power in WTO trade negotiations between rich and poor countries.

[12] *Ibid.*, Chapter 9. The proposed Health Impact Fund has the further advantage that much of its cost is balanced by the aversion of deadweight losses arising from the present regime that rewards pharmaceutical innovation with monopoly patents. *Ibid.*, 237–238.

widespread attitudes amongst citizens and officials of affluent countries toward the 'aid' they dispense and its recipients.

Conclusion

The ability of affluent countries to take advantage of the fragmentation of the current global order is likely to be a long-lasting, if not permanent, feature of our world. These countries will probably continue to exploit this and other loopholes to further their ends. But given that the eradication of severe poverty requires only a small shift in the distribution of global household income, I believe that carefully crafted and targeted institutional reforms such as the Health Impact Fund are nonetheless achievable and offer the most promising opportunities for attaining lasting progress. Relatively small reforms of little consequence for the world's affluent would suffice to eliminate most of today's vast human rights deficit, whose magnitude makes such reforms the most important moral task of our age.

Bibliography

Benvenisti, E. and G. Downs, 2007. 'The Empire's New Clothes: Political Economy and the Fragmentation of International Law', *Stanford Law Review*, 60, 595–632

Charney, J., 1996. 'The Implications of Expanding International Dispute Settlement Systems: The 1982 Convention on the Law of the Sea', *American Journal of International Law*, 90, 69–75

Chen, S. and M. Ravallion, 2008. 'The Developing World is Poorer than We Thought, but No Less Successful in the Fight against Poverty', *World Bank Policy Research Working Papers*, WPS 4703

Chimni, B., 2005. 'Global Administrative Law: Winners and Losers', NYU Global Administrative Law Conference, 22–23 April

Cohen, G., 1989. *History, Labour, and Freedom*, Oxford: Clarendon Press

Davies, J. B., S. Sandstrom, A. Shorrocks and E. N. Wolff, 2006. *The World Distribution of Household Wealth*, 5 December

FAO (Food and Agriculture Organization of the United Nations), 2009. '1.02 Billion People Hungry', *News Release*, 19 June

Kar, D. and D. Cartwright-Smith, 2008. *Illicit Financial Flows from Developing Countries 2002–2006*, Washington, DC: Global Financial Integrity

Koskenniemi, M., 2007. 'The Fate of Public International Law: Between Technique and Politics', *The Modern Law Review*, 70, 1–30

Lam, R. and L. Wantchekon, 1999. 'Dictatorships as a Political Dutch Disease', Yale University Economic Growth Center Working Papers, No. 795

Milanovic, B., 2005. *Worlds Apart: Measuring International and Global Inequality*, Princeton University Press

OECD (Organisation for Economic Cooperation and Development), 2010. 'Development Cooperation Directorate, Development Aid Rose in 2009 and Most Donors Will Meet 2010 Aid Targets', *Aid Statistics*, 14 April

Pogge, T., 2005. 'Severe Poverty as a Violation of Negative Duties', *Ethics and International Affairs*, 19, 55–83

Pogge, T., 2008. *World Poverty and Human Rights, Cosmopolitan Responsibilities and Reforms*, 2nd edn., Cambridge: Polity Press

Pogge, T., 2009. 'The Health Impact Fund and its Justification by Appeal to Human Rights', *Journal of Social Philosophy*, 40, 542–569

Pogge, T., 2010a. *Politics as Usual: What Lies behind the Pro-poor Rhetoric*, Cambridge: Polity Press

Pogge, T., 2010b. 'Responses to the Critics', in A. Jaggar (ed.), *Thomas Pogge and His Critics*, Cambridge: Polity Press, 175–250

Rawls, J., 1993. 'The Law of Peoples', in S. Shute and S. Hurley (eds.), *On Human Rights: The Oxford Amnesty Lectures 1993*, New York: Basic Books, 41–82

Rawls, J., 1999. *The Law of Peoples, With 'The Idea of Public Reason Revisited'*, Cambridge, MA: Harvard University Press

Schauer, F., 1991. *Playing by the Rules: A Philosophical Examination of Rule-based Decision-making in Law and in Life*, Oxford University Press

SIPRI (Stockholm International Peace Research Institute), 2010. Press Release on the Launch of its Yearbook for 2010

Stern, N., 2002. 'Making Trade Work for Poor People', speech delivered at National Council for Applied Economic Research, New Delhi, 28 November

The Economist, 2010. 'Ploughing on', 1 July

UNDP (United Nations Development Programme), 1998. *Human Development Report 1998*

UNDP, 2002, *Human Development Report 2002*

UNDP, 2003, *Human Development Report 2003*

Wenar, L., 2008. 'Property Rights and the Resource Curse', *Philosophy and Public Affairs*, 36, 2–32

WHO (World Health Organisation), 2008. *The Global Burden of Disease: 2004 Update*

World Bank, 2003. *Global Economic Prospects 2004*

World Bank, 2010. *World Development Report 2010*

18 Conserving the world's resources?

Sundhya Pahuja[*]

Introduction

Central to the question of how we live is how we share the earth. From conflict over territory, to passage over the high seas, to the quest for raw materials, to disputes over water and oil, to dams and development, to methods of agriculture, food security and to negotiations over climate change, the question of resources lies at the heart of many international events. The struggle for the use, control and distribution of the earth and its riches has been the impelling force behind a great deal of international legal doctrine, including much which might, at first glance seem unrelated to that issue. From the *River Oder* case at the Permanent Court of Justice in 1929, to the judgments of the International Court in *Corfu Channel* in 1949 and the *Gabčíkovo-Nagymaros Project* case in 1997, many landmark decisions of international courts and tribunals, cited for a range of legal principles involving sources, jurisdiction, nationality, etc. involve at base disputes over scarce resources.

But if the struggle for control over resources lurks under the surface of international law, international law lies in the background of how we understand and define them in the first place. The idea of background reiterates the importance, highlighted by other chapters in this volume, of an appreciation of historical context in understanding international law. In this instance, the 'background' is closely connected to international law's imperial origins (Anghie 2005; Chimni 1987).

International law backgrounds the way we share the earth in two key ways; first as land appropriation, and second as the way in which the conceptual transformation of nature, and some kinds of knowledge, *into* 'resources' is institutionalised. Land is amongst the most basic of all

* Thanks to Luis Eslava for help with research on this chapter, and to him, Shaun McVeigh and Jeremy Baskin for several clarifying conversations, as well as to Ruth Buchanan, Anne Orford, Fiona Macmillan and Hilary Charlesworth for comments on an earlier version.

resources. It represents the name we give to the utility function of the earth itself. When a community takes the land as its own, it is creating the conditions for 'property' to exist. That act, which makes property rights possible, is also in a sense, the 'ground' of law. Land appropriation is what German jurist Carl Schmitt called 'the primeval act in founding law' (Schmitt 1950 [2003], 45).

For international lawyers, this appropriation is neither myth nor 'mere' jurisprudence, but history and doctrine. As Immanuel Kant and John Locke remind us, externally sovereignty is the jurisdictional consequence of the appropriation of land (see Crawford, Chapter 5). The Enlightenment also emphasised man's mastery over nature; the use of nature 'in the services of humane life' was one of its central ideas (Porter 2001, 305). Indeed, according to Locke, a key function and source of internal legitimacy of the state is to ratify that god-given link between man and nature through a system of property rights. Property rights, whether public or private, are the institutional form of the transformation of nature into a resource for human use. The division of the world into nation-states is thus both an apportionment of the earth, and the foundation of property rights.

In the foreground of the use and regulation of resources, international law has long been an arena for the struggle between the imperative to harness and exploit the earth's resources in the service of mankind, with the equally ancient ethical duty of stewardship to conserve and protect the earth. This chapter will focus largely on tracing the way this tension has taken shape in international law over the last half-century.

In general, the formal structure of international law and its regulatory baseline of the unconstrained sovereign state (*Lotus* case, PCIJ 1927, Series A. No. 10) has meant that the tension between the exploitation and conservation of the earth has largely been translated into a jurisdictional dispute; the sovereign nation's right to exploit its own resources, versus an internationally defined responsibility not to cause harm to other states (*Corfu Channel* case, ICJ Reports 1949, p. 4; *Trail Smelter* arbitration, RIAA 1941, 1905; Birnie, Boyle and Redgwell 2009). The legacy of imperialism and its historical intimacy with international law has overwritten these jurisdictional battle lines, transforming the tension between the competing imperatives of exploitation and conservation into a contest between promoting 'development' and protecting the environment. This opposition has tended to revolve around the metaphorical axis of 'North' and 'South'.

These formal oppositions have been complicated by the permeability of the sovereignty of states in the South to developmental interventions, and by the rhetorical deployments of a notion of the 'common interest' by both North and South. The sovereign 'right' to exploit resources is thus sometimes merely the form of argumentation taken by a different set of international imperatives. So while the terrain of negotiation over resources certainly includes those fields that derive overtly from the contest between the right to exploit one's resources and the responsibility to protect the environment, in the regulatory foreground of the resource question is also the flipside of those rules and claims. On the 'verso' side of the rules that might immediately spring to mind are the international law of development, foreign investment law, trade rules and intellectual property. Indeed, the way we share the earth and its 'resources' is encapsulated in many different ways in international legal theory and doctrine, some of which do not appear to be about resources at all. And the resources themselves can look quite different, depending on where you are speaking from.

Notwithstanding this regulatory variety, the way the opposition between exploitation and conservation plays out in international law makes it seem difficult to reconcile a desire for greater equity between North and South with a concern for the environment. In international law and institutions, 'sustainable development' has become the received way to square the circle of development and environment, but has been shown by many commentators to hold out little promise in ecological terms, especially when confronted by contemporary resource challenges such as climate change.

Instead, activists and grass-roots social movements are increasingly mobilising around a reconceived notion of the 'global commons' as a way to think simultaneously about both economic and environmental 'justice'. The commons as a resurgent political and philosophical concept is a broad idea, denoting at its most expansive, 'the common wealth we share' (Hardt 2009). This wealth would encompass the 'resources' shared by a common law, custom or necessity. In descriptive understandings of the commons, it usually denotes that which has not (yet) been brought within a regime of private property. But in more radical normative versions the commons includes everything we share *a priori*, and the creation of property rights is understood as the conceptual removal of goods from the commons.

In contrast to richer understandings, in international law doctrine the 'global commons' is a residual category denoting territory or resources beyond the limits of national jurisdiction. As we shall see, this has not in itself precluded collective action in common areas, though the record is mixed at best. The key problem of the vestigial status of the commons is that it encourages us to forget the way international law 'backgrounds' our relationship to resources through property rights. One effect of this is arguably to encourage a certain complicity of international lawyers in a new wave of 'enclosures' of the commons and the dispossession and destruction that entails, particularly in relation to cultural 'resources' such as indigenous knowledge and the laws of indigenous peoples. On the other hand, the emergent idea of the 'common concern', though different again from activists' understandings of the global commons, is an attempt within the framework of international law and institutions to overcome some of the limitations of a jurisdictional understanding of the commons, and may hold some promise for the creative function of international law.

Conservation versus exploitation

International environmental law is, almost by definition, concerned with the global interest in a way that transcends the nation-state. Tracking the environment as their subject matter, international environmental lawyers are obliged to think more in terms of ecosystems and watercourses than state boundaries and sovereign territories. Because of this global imperative, chronologies of international environmental law are often produced to evince the emergence of a more genuine international community, demonstrating that we are finally finding some values we can share and learning to live together on one small planet (Brunnée 2007, 552). Particularly during the optimistic 1990s, the rapid expansion of international environmental law was said by more than one commentator to evidence 'the international community's learning curve' (Brown-Weiss 1992, 684), the vertiginous gradient of which should give us hope that we can address global environmental challenges in the future.

Indeed, if sheer volume is indicative, there is cause for some optimism on that score, with over 480 international agreements, amendments and protocols concluded in the twenty years between 1990 and 2009 alone (Mitchell 2010). This is a far cry from the position before the 1970s, in which there were just a handful of treaties protecting, for example, species of commercial value such as fur seals (North Pacific Fur Seal Convention 1911) and birds useful to agriculture (Convention for the Protection of Birds

Useful to Agriculture 1906) as well as a handful of colonial conservation treaties (such as the Convention for the Preservation of Wild Animals, Birds and Fish in Africa 1900 and the Forest Regulations of British India, starting in 1865 (Ribbentrop 1900 [1989])).

International environmental lawyers themselves also tend to be cosmopolitan in orientation, seeing the international as the necessary level of governance for the issues at hand, and themselves as critics of the classical emphasis on sovereignty. Within the idiom of international law, the dramatic expansion of international environmental law in the 1970s emerged precisely as a critique of what many would call 'traditional' international law with its emphasis on the right of states to exercise unfettered sovereignty within territorial boundaries.

The particular assertion of sovereignty to which the nascent field of international environmental law was responding was the claim to *Permanent Sovereignty over Natural Resources* (PSNR) (General Assembly Resolution 1803, 19 December 1962). This claim was launched by the Non-Aligned Movement in the 1950s and 1960s as part of a broader attempt to renew the international economic order after the end of imperialism; it took institutional form in the claim to a *New International Economic Order* (NIEO Declaration, General Assembly Resolution 3201, 1 May 1974). Demands for the NIEO briefly took flight on the international stage due to a moment of Third-World unity arising from a jump in commodity prices (brought on by an economic boom in the North) and the oil crisis of 1973 precipitated by the Yom Kippur War fought between Israel and a coalition of Arab states backing Egypt and Syria from 6 to 26 October of that year. These factors gave rise to a certain sense of vulnerability in the North, particularly in Europe.

Within that movement, the claim to PSNR was an attempt to mobilise sovereignty in the name of economic and political independence. In a world in which international law had successfully universalised itself as 'law' during the imperial period, and consequently acquired a 'monopoly of process' (Crawford, Chapter 5), becoming a state was the only way for a decolonising entity to claim legal personality. The barely complete struggle for decolonisation therefore took the form of self-determination as a nation-state almost by necessity. Because sovereignty, and the attendant principle of formal legal equality (Simma and Müller, Chapter 6), were hard-won prizes, and for some quite newly acquired, it made sense to try use international law and all its post-war promise to begin to redress the perceived injustices of the imperial era. In the quest for more substantive equality, the combination of sovereignty and natural resources seemed to hold the key (Bedjaoui 1979).

The way the claim to PSNR tried to leverage a state's resource endowment to bring about greater economic equality, largely involved the nationalisation of various natural resource interests (usually known then as 'concessions') that had been sold to foreign investors, either under imperial occupation, or by more or less coercive means (Anghie 2005, 211–244). The resources in question were varied, including tin (Bolivia), farmland (Guatemala), copper (Chile) and oil (Iran, Argentina and Sri Lanka). The nationalisations were an overt reaction to the experience of colonialism in the form of a rejection of what was perceived as ongoing domination by foreign interests. A series of UN resolutions accompanied the nationalisations during the 1950s and early 1960s, evincing the sense of promise the new international institutions seemed to engender. But the issue was highly contested by the North, and when commodity prices came down, the solidarity between oil producers and non-oil producers dissolved. The North began to feel less vulnerable, and the shouts of discontent from the South became commensurately less audible. Once the debt crisis broke out in Latin America by the 1980s, the last few voices were drowned out altogether.

But although flurry and failure is one way of understanding the resolution of that story, another is that the claims were deflected by the principle of compensation. Once mandatory compensation was agreed upon in principle, the private ownership of natural resources was normalised on the international plane. This normalisation meant that even though the measure of compensation to be paid upon nationalisation remains doctrinally unresolved (Sornarajah 2004, 336), in practice the question is resolved by reference to functional jurisdictions dealing with the protection of foreign investors (Ratner 2008). In particular, this includes arbitrations, investment treaties and conditionalities imposed by the International Financial Institutions (Pahuja 2011).

But if some feel that in the environmental sphere, the international is more likely to be generative of the right values than national governments, others might suggest that like the 'export theory' of human rights, faith in the international is rather more tenacious when 'domestic' means states in the South, rather than the North (Simpson 2001, 347–348). And in one version of the story, notwithstanding their anti-imperial impetus, these 'sovereigntist' claims catalysed the expansion of international environmental law (Rajagopal 2006; Schrijver 2008). The background to this was an increased sensitivity to the environment in the rich countries of the North, and particularly within the United States (Brown-Weiss 1992). The nascent field was particularly critical of claims that states have a right to exploit resources without regard for the environmental consequences. Several international environmental institutions arose in this period including the UN Environment Programme (UNEP, 1972), the International Tropical Timber Organisation (1987), and the Basel hazardous waste regime (1989). UNEP was set up to help coordinate the international response to environmental concerns, particularly, and perhaps predictably, in developing countries. It has been instrumental in the evolution of many environmental law conventions, as well as a great deal of 'soft law', such as declarations, recommendations, guidelines, codes and other non-binding instruments. Amongst the best known examples are the Convention on International Trade in Endangered Species (CITES, 1973), the Vienna Convention for the Protection of the Ozone Layer (1985), the Intergovernmental Panel on Climate Change (IPCC, 1988), and the Convention on Biological Diversity (1992).

Before this time, environmental problems were dealt with on a bilateral basis. Whilst the *Trail Smelter* arbitration is the paradigmatic example of this, bilateralism did facilitate a cooperative approach to many trans-boundary issues, such as boundary rivers and the protection of frontier areas. But once the environment was 'internationalised', environmental problems translated into international law only by virtue of being a sovereignty problem.

By the late 1970s, international attempts to regulate the environment were focused in part on common resources, but significant attempts were also being made within the emergent field to inscribe limits around the right of states to exploit resources which were avowedly within their respective sovereign territories, but which touched on what we would now think of as the common interest. In terms of customary international law, this attempt consolidated the 'no-harm' principle (Bastmeijer and Koivurova 2008, 1–26). Under this principle, a state's right to use its territory is limited by the obligation to avoid causing serious trans-boundary damage. On the flipside, a state affected by another state's use of its territory can only complain in law about damage that is defined as 'serious'. Widely regarded as a foundational principle of international environmental law, this principle is a good example of the way international legal doctrine is frequently balanced at the fulcrum of competing sovereign interests. The origins of the no harm principle lie in the *Corfu Channel* case; it was consolidated in the Stockholm Declaration of 1972. Principle 21 of that Declaration captures this delicate balance of tensions, between abstract sovereign interests, but also the political balance between North and South, with its qualification of 'the sovereign right to exploit [a state's] own resources ... and the responsibility to ensure that activities within [the state's] jurisdiction and control do not cause damage to ... other states'. The 1992 Rio Declaration on Environment and Development updated the principle in terms of precaution. Principle 15 states: '[w]here there are threats of serious or irreversible damage, lack of full scientific evidence shall not be used as a reason for postponing cost-effective measures to prevent environmental degradation.' In treaty terms, a multitude of conventions relevant to resources were concluded during this time, including the Ramsar Convention on Wetlands of International Importance (1971), the Convention for the Conservation of Antarctic Seals (1972) and the Convention on Long-range Transboundary Air Pollution (1979).

We can thus see that on one level the tension between the imperative to exploit, develop and grow, and the counter-imperative to preserve and protect the earth was jurisdictionalised into a contest between the right of a sovereign state to exploit its resources on one hand, and the interests of the 'international community' in the protection of the global environment on the other. But it is here that 'locating the international' (Orford 1997) becomes perhaps less straightforward. Because if the right being asserted by states in the South to control their own resources could be said to have catalysed the expansion of international environmental law from one perspective, it was attended by an equally fertile regime on the other – the international law of foreign investment. Just as the 'sovereigntist' claims of the 'Third World' were met on one side by those who favoured the 'common interest' of the world understood in terms of the earth, so were those claims met on the other side by those who favoured the common interests of the world understood in terms of the 'world economy'.

Foreign investment rules are a significant element in the political economy of global resource regulation in the same way that private law, and not only public law, structures economic relations between parties in domestic legal systems. Efforts to regulate foreign investment have produced a network of multilateral and, increasingly, bilateral investment treaties (BITs), of which there are now more than 2,400 in force (UN Conference on Trade and Development 2006). These treaties aim to structure North–South investment relations on the basis of mutual trade and sovereign concessions, though the South in fact gives most concessions.[1] Such treaties usually establish the principle of fair and equitable treatment for investors, protection from expropriation (in contrast to the sovereign right to nationalise resources asserted in the 'public' sphere), free transfer of capital and full protection and security of investment. They also establish dispute resolution procedures that dramatically restrict the jurisdiction of national courts. Creating a separate normative and jurisdictional environment for the effective operation of foreign investment, these treaties rearticulate the natural and human resources of the host nation in terms of their availability for trade. Importantly, this rearticulation takes form in the language of comparative advantage: namely the investor state's superior technological capacity to exploit the excess of resources of the receiving (developing) country (Vandevelde 2000). In this context, resource-rich states in the South thus approach their forests, seas, earth and lands as commodities. The nature of the functional jurisdiction of foreign investment means that this rearticulation takes place in a regulatory frame removed from public attention at both the international and domestic levels.

In one account, the combined flourishing of environmental law and foreign investment law is read as the 'progressive development' of international law, in which international law expands because of an increasing sense of global interconnectedness. In this story, signs of convergence between different fields, such as the economic and the environmental, are taken as positive indications of international law's increasing coherence, if not 'constitutionalisation'. And as mentioned above, international environmental law itself is often held up as an example of the way in which shared global values and a new focus on 'people' are softening what was once a purely inter-state system. But even if the two fields of environment and investment are seen as operating in parallel yet touching the same subject matter, the diagnosis of progressive development is usually robust enough to survive some symptomatic 'fragmentation' into different regulatory regimes.

A powerful counter-narrative to this optimistic story of progress is that the expansion of both the environmental and investment regimes could be read as a version of what Rajagopal has diagnosed, following Foucault, as

[1] Although an increasing number of BITs are South–South agreements (UNCTAD 2005).

the 'instrument effect' of international law (Rajagopal 2003, 76). According to that account, since the post-war settlement and the establishment of contemporary international law, claims for global justice made by states in the South have more often than not resulted in the incorporation of uncomfortable claims into the body of international law, usually through the proliferation of institutions. This incorporation and proliferation has been a 'success' of sorts, expanding the domain of international law, and ostensibly increasing its responsiveness to the concerns of 'the people'. But it has also de-radicalised the respective claims, and resulted in the subjection of the South to ever-more international institutional scrutiny and intervention.

A key site of institutional expansion in this regard is the World Bank. Although the Bank is not a typical character in treatises about public international law, a discussion of the international regulation of resources would not be complete without mention of it. Through the conditions attached to loans by both the Bank and its sister organisation the International Monetary Fund (IMF), and in keeping with colonial formulations of land use, states in the South are obliged to exploit the natural resources within their territory to their fullest extent and usually to privatise their ownership and extraction, in order to foster economic growth (Bayliss and Cramer 2001). Resources which straddle the line of public utilities, such as water, are also often subject to the orthodoxy of privatisation to effect distribution, frequently causing social activism in response, such as occurred in La Paz and Cochabamba, Bolivia in 2008 (Perreault 2008; Shiva 2002, 102). These obligations may not be unwelcome to the ruling elites of borrower states, who often grow rich in the process of exploitation and privatisation. Instead, it is the poorest people who pay the price for the environmental damage, dislocations, forced migrations and violence that such 'development' causes.

So although the tension between exploitation and conservation plays out on one level in formal terms as a divide between the national and the international, this jurisdictional divide is belied by the internationalisation of the development project (Nesiah 2006). In other words, the 'international' penetrates the 'developing' state in a way which traditional public international law cannot account for, 'internationalising' state actions in that context. The development imperative also seems to create a problem for the international lawyer who wishes to combine a concern for 'justice' between North and South with a concern for the environment (see also

Pogge, Chapter 17). For how can poor countries rise up from poverty unless they are allowed to develop? But how can we protect the environment from the poor countries' desire for development?

This seeming tension – between a desire for economic justice between North and South and a concern for the environment – arises in large measure because within international law and institutions we treat development as a *proxy* for questions of inequality. In other words within international law, issues of global justice and the distribution of wealth are framed, whether explicitly or implicitly, in terms of development. This equivalence is problematic for several reasons. The development construct remains tied to ideologies of progress (Beard 2007), and comes at the cost of broader political conceptions of 'justice' which international law might otherwise facilitate (Pahuja 2011). But crucially in this context, despite the many and varied attempts to reinvent it, development also remains centred on the notion of economic growth as the only way to improve material well-being.

Economic growth is of course, the classic discourse of the extrinsic use value for resources. It is true that Gross Domestic Product (GDP) growth and technological change (including the 'green revolution') have enabled many to improve their living standards and especially to have better nutrition. In this sense the Malthusian argument has proved too limited, unable to factor in human ingenuity and adaptability. However, this time around we are arguably facing real biophysical limits and disrupting the earth's capacity to act as both 'source' and 'sink'. In the face of estimates that we are already using around one-and-a-half planets worth of resources (Millennium Ecosystem Assessment Board 2005; WWF 2008), there are clearly physical limits to growth. The dominant model of growth as the means to bring about development therefore becomes unconvincing. Absent unprecedented technological change able to completely de-link economic growth from 'throughput' growth (that is to increase output by using less input in absolute terms, and generating little or no waste), more growth and a sustainable biosphere are incompatible (Jackson 2009). There is simply not world enough. Translated into the idiom of international law, this means that, on the face of it, there would seem to be no compatible way to be both for the environment – understood as the preservation of the biosphere – and for global justice – understood as increased (economic) development in the South. Or would there?

Within a significant section of the international legal community (and beyond), 'sustainable development' is seen as the way to square this particular circle. As expressed in the 1987 Report of the World Commission on Environment and Development (the Brundtland Commission), sustainable development is 'development that meets the needs of the present without compromising the ability of future generations to meet their own needs'.

Sustainable development was understood even at the time as a political compromise between North and South, rather than a genuine 'balance' between ecological conservation and capitalist development. It has been criticised most harshly as being concerned primarily with sustaining capitalism, rather than emphasising ecological sustainability. However, despite the problems, and perhaps because of its capaciousness as a concept and its place in North–South diplomacy, international institutions have embraced the concept of sustainable development. In this embrace, the inherent contradiction between an awareness of the limits of the biosphere, and an approach to alleviating poverty that relies primarily on unlimited growth, continues to haunt attempts to make good the promise of the globalisation of prosperity. A good example of the way the spectre of limit stalks the development promise is contained in the World Bank's *World Development Report 2010: Development and Climate Change* (World Bank 2009). With a certainty about its means and authority, the World Bank declares:

> High-income countries can and must reduce their carbon footprints. They cannot continue to fill up an unfair and unsustainable share of the atmospheric commons. But developing countries – whose average per capita emissions are a third those of high-income countries – need massive expansions in energy, transport, urban systems, and agricultural production. If pursued using traditional technologies and carbon intensities, these much-needed expansions will produce more greenhouse gases and, hence, more climate change. The question, then, is not just how to make development more resilient to climate change. It is how to pursue growth and prosperity without causing 'dangerous' climate change.

The commons

But if the international environmental lawyer's fantasy is cosmopolitan in orientation, including understanding a move beyond the nation-state as crucial to the preservation, protection and regulation of the environment, she is yet bound to nation-states if only to transcend them. This is the triumph and tragedy of international law. If you do not like the national sphere, there is nowhere else to go but the inter-national. But at least that is somewhere. The limitations and possibilities of this constitutive feature of international law are evident in the approach of international law to the idea of the global commons.

In keeping with international law's formal structure, and its earthly attachment, 'the commons' as a category in international law is defined by where it is; the 'global commons' in international law denotes what many have called 'common areas' (Brunnée 2007, 552). These are areas located beyond the jurisdiction of nation-states. Given that the earth is now blanketed with nation-states, there are very few (but admittedly very vast) areas left which are usually said to fall into this category: outer space, the high seas and Antarctica. Some people would include the atmosphere in this category, though it is arguably preferable to think of it as a 'common concern' to which we shall turn shortly.

Outside international legal doctrine, as a concept the 'commons' at its broadest means 'the common wealth we share' (Hardt 2009). This wealth may be both natural and man-made, though the distinction between the two is not always clear-cut. In this politically resurgent understanding, the commons comes conceptually *before* state and international law. The application of modern (state and international) law to the commons is understood as a process of the progressive appropriation of that wealth in the name of the 'nation', through the mechanism of property rights enforced by state violence and resulting in the dispossession of the many (e.g. Witbooi 2008). This classic gesture of imperial law returns us to the way international law 'backgrounds' our relationship to resources. In this story, capitalist development can be read as a series of enclosures and the commodification of an ever-expanding sphere of life, aided by modern law.

Within a different tradition, the 'commons' is represented as an area bereft of law. This absence of law creates a potential 'tragedy' which only law can solve. The commons here does not relate to everything shared, but only to 'rival' goods, which are both finite, and 'subtractable' in the sense that any amount used by one person is no longer available to another person: so, for example, a pond full of fish as opposed to a book full of ideas. In this strand of thought, the tragic potential for over-exploitation looms over all rival goods for which no individual or entity has direct responsibility. The only way to avert the tragedy is by the *intervention* of modern law through the commodification of the resource, i.e. the creation of property rights over it, whether public or private (Hardin 1968).

The delineation of the 'global commons' in international law in a sense admits of both understandings. It is usual to contrast two meanings of 'common' as '*res nullius*' subject to appropriation by anyone and '*res communis*', that which can only be managed internationally. In doctrinal terms, the global commons denotes those areas not subject to any one state's sovereignty. According to customary international law, the commons is not open to appropriation by any state, but may freely be used by everyone. This freedom encompasses both passage over the commons and the exploitation of the 'common pool resources' found there.

The oldest recognised commons are the high seas, dating back to Grotius' *Mare Liberum* and the assertion of the notion of the 'freedom of the sea' (Grotius 1608 [1972]). On the one hand, this freedom alludes to a very different kind of sharing envisaged in the apportionment of the land, and suggests an inherent form of ordering 'natural' to the sea (Schmitt 1950 [2003]). On the other, the high seas have, like land, been subject to a logic of appropriation. The oceans too are criss-crossed with a history of progressive enclosures, both attempted and successful, in which papal and other empires and then modern nation-states have claimed more and more of the oceans via the assertion of sovereign rights over them.

But although the size of a state's territorial sea has been a source of controversy that has impacted on the delineation of the commons for hundreds of years (Freestone and Salman 2007), for our purposes the potential for 'tragedy' has increased commensurately with the technological capacity for the exploitation of the ocean's resources. In customary international law, the combination of the emphasis on the sovereign state and the default position of the commons as an area of 'freedom' in relation to the exploitation of resources has set the conditions for this tragedy, offering a very limited capacity for a 'community' interest to take regulatory shape. And indeed, although attempts have periodically been made to argue that in customary international law, the no-harm rule implies an obligation owed to the international community at large, questions of 'standing', or the right to bring an action before a court on that basis, remain unresolved (Fitzmaurice 2007).

Beginning with the relatively low-tech developments in whaling – which nonetheless brought almost all commercially exploited species to the brink of extinction by the 1980s (Vogler 1995, 52) – and continuing through seal hunting, the potential for a modern resource tragedy really began to take flight in the 1940s when resource exploitation in the form of both seabed mining and distant-water fishing became technically possible (e.g. Lynch 2002). Besides fish, oil and gas, other resource dimensions of the oceans include seabed minerals, living marine resources and the sea as waste dump and carbon sink.

Various attempts have been made to regulate the global oceanic commons through treaties, but with very mixed results. In the late nineteenth and early twentieth centuries a number of conventions, regional fisheries commissions and scientific bodies came into being, in part in response to changing understandings about the finitude of ocean resources and in some cases, as an expression of nascent thinking in Europe about what we would now call conservation. As Kaye points out, it was around this time that scientific knowledge emerged as an important way to ground the normative basis of management regimes over areas such as the oceanic commons, where jurisdiction based regimes were impossible (Kaye 2001, 45–47).

As it circulates within international law, science is an idiom that appears to transcend both the appropriative language of capitalism and the normative reliance on the inheritance of natural law, through its positioning as 'technical' or 'expert' knowledge. It is a significant counterpoint to enclosure and commodification as the appropriate way to forestall the tragedy of the commons, and continues to play an important strategic role in conservation efforts more broadly, including in relation to climate. However, the enclosure of large tracts of the ocean and seabed was precisely the outcome of the tortuous negotiations over the third Law of the Sea Convention (1982), which codified the removal of much of the world's fisheries from the global commons through the adoption of the 'exclusive economic zone'.

But despite these enclosures, and efforts to regulate the oceanic commons, current reports on the state of the oceans suggest that the situation is grave in almost all respects. World fisheries, for instance, are in crisis (Kaye 2001). No fishery remains unexploited. Two-thirds of all fisheries fall into the category of fully or over-exploited, and one-quarter are said to have 'crashed' (Cramer 2008, 271). With this, ocean biodiversity is declining rapidly (Secretariat of the Convention on Biological Diversity 2010). Scientific studies estimate that over 90 per cent of large predatory fish are gone (The Economist 2010, 3) and the population of jellyfish has exploded. Marine ecosystems remain virtually unprotected in the open ocean

(Secretariat of the Convention on Biological Diversity 2010, 49). And pollution from both ocean- and land-based activities has reached critical dimensions: most human contaminants eventually end up in the sea. Added to this mix are climatically induced changes such as ocean acidification, increasing water temperatures and thermal expansion (UN Intergovernmental Panel on Climate Change (IPCC) 2007). The state of the oceans is indeed a contemporary tragedy, the full implications of which are yet to be felt.

The United Nations has been the site for the negotiation of three rounds of 'Law of the Sea' conferences since the 1950s (1958, 1960, 1973–1982). These and many other treaty negotiations around the oceans, including those around whaling and marine pollution, are in themselves important sites for a contest between competing approaches to resources, and the tension between conservation and exploitation. As well as being of direct relevance to the resource question, the negotiations may also be understood as offering object studies in the formation of contemporary international law. Indeed, much of the recent literature on the global commons from within the idiom of international law takes an empirical approach to understanding the regulatory frameworks that have emerged under the rubric of 'regime formation'. 'Epistemic communities' of technocrats and experts feature large in these thick descriptions, as do non-governmental organisations (NGOs) usually pushing for the protection of the environment (Spiro 2007). Reading with critically inclined scholars here, we feel the discursive weight of scientific knowledge and understandings of risk in international law (Godden 2009). Thinking with the mainstream, we learn of the relevance of 'non-state actors', who figure in a burgeoning literature dedicated to showing why nation-states are (analytically) no longer, nor should they (normatively) be any longer, considered the sole, or chief actors in creating international law. International negotiations over the oceans offer us a particularly rich case through which to study these empirical and reflexive concerns, and for showing how competing approaches to both resources and to the commons have taken shape and played out in international law over a long period of time.

The rhetorical use of an idea of what should rightfully be shared was not confined to the North. Coming before the NIEO, but ultimately subsumed within it was also the principle of Common Heritage of Mankind. That principle was an attempt to assert shared control over resources beyond the jurisdiction of any one state. In accordance with Arvid Pardo's original proposal in 1967, the deep seabed was where the origin of the principle lay, but the same principle was extended to the moon in the 1979 Moon Treaty. Despite the language of 'heritage', the thrust of the principle was the exploitation of resources and the redistribution of the proceeds, not conservation for future generations. Given that any state could freely access 'common pool resources,' at the time of the push for a Common Heritage principle it seemed inevitable that the states best equipped to exploit them would do so at the expense of the poorer nations. This suspicion was especially acute on the part of the large number of states just emerging from the extractive embrace of empire.

But although the principle was included in both the Law of the Sea Convention (LOSC) and the Moon Treaty, it has never become a principle of customary international law, and even the LOSC has since been watered down (Brunnée 2007, 563) through the removal in 1994 of the mandatory technology transfer provisions of earlier versions, and by changing the voting rules in ways which are likely to favour the exploitation of the seabed for private profit. Outer space in general remains jurisdictionally part of the global commons (Outer Space Treaty 1966; Moon Treaty). As with the high seas, this status brings collective benefits in the shape of free passage, access to the geostationary orbit (Vogler 1995),[2] and in preventing the appropriation (of planets, for example) by any one state. On the other hand, it opens outer space to unilateral (and corporate) exploitation (Rowlands 2007) and to the problem of responsibility for damage to the commons, an issue especially likely to generate conflict as geo-engineering is added to the suite of measures to tackle climate change.

It may, however, be too quick to say that the common heritage principle is moribund: some rich countries have recently argued for a common heritage principle over plant knowledge and biodiversity (Mgbeoji 2003). Like the invocation of the needs of the 'world economy' in response to the claim to PSNR, such a construction of the 'common heritage' would have the effect of internationalising something that is currently within the domestic jurisdiction of states. But like the tension between international environmental law and the law regulating foreign investment, internationalisation as such would not resolve the struggle between exploitation and conservation. It simply changes the way it is played out.

[2] Although arguably part of the commons, the geostationary orbit is subject to a great deal of regulation.

Despite attempts, the common heritage principle has never been successfully asserted in relation to Antarctica that, although usually grouped taxonomically within the commons, operates under a *sui generis* and perhaps unrepeatable treaty system – the 1959 Antarctic Treaty. Under that system, the conflicting territorial claims of Australia, Chile, France, New Zealand, Norway and the United Kingdom have all been 'suspended'. Attempts to bring Antarctica within the UN system have been unsuccessful. Given the emphasis on resource exploitation of the Common Heritage principle, and the 'development' pressures, both political and material, which press upon the United Nations, avoiding both has perhaps assisted in conservation taking priority. To date, Antarctica has largely been the domain of scientists who have managed to direct the focus of collective concern to the preservation of that delicately balanced ecosystem. This has resulted in a successful mining ban, but has been less successful in preventing the decline in fish stocks.

However, resource struggles will undoubtedly resurface in the future. Some, including some states, continue to push for the transformation of Antarctica into a world conservation area. On the other hand, the fresh water captured in the polar ice caps (around three-quarters of the world's total supply) may become an exploitable resource and, if it does, may become the subject of conflict. And if Antarctica's mineral resources become easier to access, the fifty-year ban will come under great pressure. Meanwhile Antarctica continues to be both crucial to the global climate and an important source of information about it in the form of ice cores, which reveal the secrets of 100,000 years of atmospheric change (World Data Centre for Glaciology, University of Cambridge).

Climate change and 'common concern'

The most critical resource challenge facing the world today is not a shortage of any resources we take from the earth, but rather something we have until quite recently taken for granted – that is the earth's atmosphere and its capacity to absorb carbon. The crisis that confronts us is the limitation of the carbon 'sink'. This time the challenge is not to think 'outside the box', but to think 'inside the box' of the earth's resources, for we are nearing its limits (Baskin 2009). Although climate change presents a collective action problem *par excellence*, the danger is not that we are all in the same boat, but that the undoubtedly global effects of climate change will have grossly disparate outcomes. The exacerbation of inequality likely to result from climate change could encourage the wealthy to insulate themselves in fortress states, leaving others (literally in some instances) to sink. If the struggle over resources has in some ways been generative of international law, the ramifications of climate change and the resource pressures on a finite earth are likely to be another tragic catalyst for disciplinary activity as it feeds feverishly on famine, wars, migration, refugee flows and water shortages (Charlesworth 2002).

Some have little faith in international law and diplomacy as likely fora for addressing the problem of reconciling environmental and material justice. The 2009 Copenhagen conference was in some ways a redux of the claim to permanent sovereignty over natural resources. Many of the same old problems were thrown up – the tension between development and the environment, historical responsibility (this time for past emissions), and the idea that the South continues to pay the price for the North's prosperity. Added to this were more and newer tensions between more and less industrialised nations in the South, an alliance of small island states, and unstable coalitions of richer states. International legal responses have so far continued to hold on to the apron strings of sustainable development, as well as to dealing with the equity question through notions of common and differentiated responsibility.

But others have more hope for international law. The notion of 'common concern', distinct from both common heritage and the jurisdictionally defined global commons, is one source of possibility. Essentially an idea which targets problems and processes rather than resources or areas, the principle has recently gained currency in relation both to climate change and the loss of biodiversity, but it is also homologous to similar principles in earlier treaties which it may build on (Brunnée 2007, 565). Its much older roots draw on what we might call the 'communitarian' strain within international law. Usually manifest in fields like human rights, this strain may also be thought of as the ethic of the commons as community, or as 'law-full' space. Although the status of the principle is subject to many uncertainties, it potentially offers a vocabulary that offers a counterweight to the nation-state and the centripetal pull of the either/or logic it seems to offer (Brunnée 2007; Cottier and Matteotti-Berkutova 2009; Toope 2007).

Conclusion

The crucial question which remains is what the future role of international law might be in the face of the major challenges of the coming decades, including anthropogenically-induced climate change, pressure on ecosystems, ecological disasters and an unprecedentedly rapid decline in biodiversity. The political battle between those who regard nature and knowledge as having inherent worth versus those who 'regard the earth as a collection of "resources" having an intrinsic value no larger than their usefulness at the moment' (Gore 1992, 225) will continue to be waged in international law and institutions. In a larger sense, the oscillations within international law that have surfaced in several chapters in this book, between its technical function and political orientation, between its imperial urge and emancipatory dimension, will not disappear, nor could we wish them gone. But for those interested in both equity and environment, or in the question of the responsibility of the international lawyer, rethinking the idea of the commons and international law's relation to it may be useful. In particular, the recuperation from within international law of the commons as a political rather than jurisdictional idea may draw out the way international law is *creative*, though as we have seen from our exploration here, not necessarily in ways we might expect or want. In the face of that creativity, the international lawyer has a responsibility to be vigilant about what she is involved in creating (and destroying) in and through international law.

Bibliography

Anghie, A., 2005. *Imperialism, Sovereignty and the Making of International Law*, Cambridge University Press

Baskin, J., 2009. 'The Impossible Necessity of Climate Justice?', *Melbourne Journal of International Law*, 10, 424–438

Bastmeijer, K. and T. Koivurova, 2008. *Theory and Practice of Transboundary Environmental Impact Assessment*, Boston: Martinus Nijhoff

Bayliss, K. and C. Cramer, 2001. 'Privatisation and the Post-Washington Consensus: Between the Laboratory and the Real World', in B. Fine, C. Lapavitsas and J. Pincus (eds.), *Development Policy in the 21st Century: Beyond the Post-Washington Consensus*, London Routledge, 52–79

Beard, J., 2007. *The Political Economy of Desire: International Law, Development and the Nation State*, London: Routledge

Bedjaoui, M., 1979. *Towards a New International Economic Order*, New York: Holmes & Meier

Birnie, P., A. Boyle and C. Redgwell, 2009. *International Law and the Environment*, 3rd edn., Oxford University Press

Brown-Weiss, E., 1992. 'International Environmental Law: Contemporary Issues and the Emergence of a New World Order', *Georgetown Law Journal*, 81, 675–710

Brunnée, J., 2007. 'Common Areas, Common Heritage, and Common Concern', in D. Bodansky, J. Brunnée and E. Hey (eds.), *The Oxford Handbook of International Environmental Law*, Oxford University Press

Charlesworth, H., 2002. 'International Law: A Discipline of Crisis', *Modern Law Review*, 65, 377–392

Chimni, B., 1987. *International Commodity Agreements: A Legal Study*, London: Croom Helm

Cottier, T. and S. Matteotti-Berkutova, 2009. 'International Environmental Law and the Evolving Concept of "Common Concern of Mankind"', in T. Cottier, O. Nartova and S. Bigdeli (eds.), *International Trade Regulation and the Mitigation of Climate Change: World Trade Forum*, Cambridge University Press

Cramer, D., 2008. *Smithsonian Ocean: Our Water, Our World*, New York: HarperCollins

Fitzmaurice, M., 2007. 'International Responsibility and Liability', in D. Bodansky, J. Brunnée and E. Hey (eds.), *The Oxford Handbook of International Environmental Law*, Oxford University Press

Freestone, D. and M. Salman, 2007. 'Ocean and Freshwater Resources', in D. Bodansky, J. Brunnée and E. Hey (eds.), *The Oxford Handbook of International Environmental Law*, Oxford University Press

Godden, L., 2009. 'Death, Desire, Modernity and Redemption: Climate Change and Public International Law', *The Melbourne Journal of International Law*, 10, 543–578

Gore, A., 1992. *The Earth in the Balance: Ecology and the Human Spirit*, Boston: Houghton Mifflin

Grotius, H., 1972. *The Freedom of the Seas, Or, The Right Which Belongs to the Dutch to Take Part in the East Indian Trade*, reprint New York: Arno Press

Hardin, G., 1968. 'The Tragedy of the Commons', *Science*, 162, 1243–1248.

Hardt, M., 2009. 'Politics of the Common', Remaining Society Project, Z Net, 6 July

Jackson, T., 2009. *Prosperity Without Growth: Economics for a Finite Planet*, London: Earthscan

Kaye, S., 2001. *International Fisheries Management*, Boston: Kluwer Law International

Lynch, M., 2002. *Mining in World History*, London: Reaktion

Mgbeoji, I., 2003. 'Beyond Rhetoric: State Sovereignty, Common Concern, and the Inapplicability of the Common Heritage Concept to Plant Genetic Resources', *Leiden Journal of International Law*, 16, 821–837

Millennium Ecosystem Assessment Board, 2005. *Ecosystems and Human Well-being*, Washington, DC: Island Press

Mitchell R., 2010. International Environmental Agreements Database Project, Version 2010.2, http://iea.uoregon.edu

Nesiah, V., 2006. 'Resistance in the Age of Empire', in R. Falk (ed.), *Third World Quarterly – Special Issue: Reshaping Justice: International Law and the Third World*, 27, 903–922

Orford, A., 1997. 'Locating the International: Military and Monetary Interventions after the Cold War', *Harvard International Law Journal*, 38, 443–485

Ostrom, E., 1990. *Governing the Commons: The Evolution of Institutions for Collective Action*, Cambridge University Press

Pahuja, S., 2011. *Decolonising International Law: Development, Economic Growth and the Politics of Universality*, Cambridge University Press

Perreault, T., 2008. 'Popular Protest and Unpopular Policies: State Restructuring, Resource Conflict, and Social Justice in Bolivia', in D. Carruthers (ed.), *Environmental Justice in Latin America: Problems, Promise, and Practice*, Cambridge, MA: MIT Press

Porter, D., 2001. *The Enlightenment*, Basingstoke: Palgrave

Rajagopal, B., 2003. *International Law From Below: Development, Social Movements, and Third World Resistance*, Cambridge University Press

Rajagopal, B., 2006. 'Counter-hegemonic International Law: Rethinking Human Rights and Development as a Third World Strategy', *Third World Quarterly*, 27(5), 767–783

Ratner, S., 2008. 'Regulatory Takings in Institutional Context: Beyond the Fear of Fragmented International Law', *American Journal of International Law*, 102, 475–528

Ribbentrop, B., 1989. *Forestry in British India*, reprinted Calcutta: Office of the Superintendent of Government Printing

Rowlands, I., 2007. 'Atmosphere and Outer Space', in D. Bodansky, J. Brunnée and E. Hey (eds.), *The Oxford Handbook of International Environmental Law*, Oxford University Press

Schmitt, C., 2003. *The Nomos of the Earth in the International Law of the Jus Publicum Europaeum*, Ulmen, G. L. (trans.), New York: Telos Press

Schrijver, N., 2008. *The Evolution of Sustainable Development in International Law: Inception, Meaning and Status*, Leiden: Martinus Nijhoff

Secretariat of the Convention on Biological Diversity, 2010. *Global Biodiversity Outlook 3*

Shiva, V., 2002. *Water Wars: Privatisation, Pollution and Profit*, Cambridge, MA: South End Press

Simpson, A. W. B., 2001. *Human Rights and the End of Empire: Britain and the Genesis of the European Convention*, Oxford University Press

Sornarajah M., 2004. *The International Law of Foreign Investment*, 2nd edn., Cambridge University Press

Spiro, P., 2007. 'Non-governmental Organisations and Civil Society', in D. Bodansky, J. Brunnée and E. Hey (eds.), *The Oxford Handbook of International Environmental Law*, Oxford University Press

The Economist, 2010. *Ploughing On*, 1 July

Toope, S., 2007. 'Formality and Informality', in D. Bodansky, J. Brunnée and E. Hey (eds.), *The Oxford Handbook of International Environmental Law*, Oxford University Press

UNCTAD, 2005. *South–South Cooperation in International Investment Agreements*

UNCTAD, 2006. *International Investment Arrangements: Trends and Emerging Issues*

United Nations Intergovernmental Panel on Climate Change (IPCC), 2007. *Fourth Assessment Report of the Intergovernmental Panel on Climate Change*

Vandevelde, K., 2000. 'The Economics of Bilateral Investment Treaties', *Harvard International Law Journal*, 41, 469–502

Vogler, J., 1995. *The Global Commons: A Regime Analysis*, Sussex: Wiley & Sons

Witbooi, E., 2008. 'Governing Global Fisheries: Commons, Community Law and Third-country Coastal Waters', *Social & Legal Studies*, 17, 369–386

World Bank, 2009. *World Development Report 2010: Development and Climate Change*

World Commission on Environment and Development, 1987. *Our Common Future*

World Data Centre for Glaciology, University of Cambridge www.wdcgc.spri.cam.ac.uk

WWF, 2008. *Living Planet Report*, World Wildlife Fund

Guide to electronic sources of international law

Lesley Dingle*

Introduction

Several fundamental problems confront those seeking to find the sources of international law. First and foremost, at the conceptual level, there is no constitutional 'machinery for the creation of rules of international law' so that the notion of 'formal sources' is misleading (Brownlie 2008, 3). Additionally there is the phenomenon of 'fragmentation' of international law (see, e.g., Koskenniemi 2007; Shaw 2008, 65). What we can search for is evidence of 'general consent of states [that] creates rules of general application'; sources that may provide such evidence are, for example, decisions of the International Court of Justice (ICJ), United Nations General Assembly resolutions and various 'law-making' multilateral treaties (Brownlie 2008, 3–4). But these 'sources and evidences' are extensive, diffuse and decentralised. Even locating them is a challenge.

Although there is still no substitute for a fully equipped law library, this vast range of potentially relevant materials is increasingly accessible on the internet. This account of electronic sources conforms to the categories of article 38(1) of the ICJ's Statute (see Charlesworth, Chapter 8), but adds some additional materials, not specifically identified in the Statute. These are: Section 5 which deals with 'Other Sources', such as UN Resolutions and 'soft law'; and Section 6, listing 'Guides, Encyclopaedias and Digests' which are useful as starting points for searches on particular problems or topics.

Particular topics (e.g. human rights, environmental law, and specialised aspects therein) are sometimes viewed as generating independent bodies of

* Foreign and International Law Librarian Squire Law Library, University of Cambridge. I am indebted to Mary Rumsey (University of Minnesota Law Library) and Jonathan Pratter (Tarlton Law Library) for their constructive criticism of the manuscript.

law, but they are still part of the general corpus of public international law. Thus materials relevant to such topics are nested within several of the main categories outlined here. Researchers will need to adopt systematic strategies for tracking down required items: a good guide to formulating plans for such cross-referencing can be found in Hoffman and Rumsey (2008, Chapter 9).

Tips for searching will be shown [within square brackets, in smaller font, thus].

1 International conventions

According to article 38(1) of the ICJ Statute, international conventions are agreements 'general or particular' that establish 'rules expressly recognised by the contesting states'. They take the form of written bilateral or multilateral treaties (agreements, conventions, protocols, covenants, etc.) between states and/or international organisations.

A few general comments as to the location and arrangement of treaty materials should be made (for a useful guide, see Gardiner 1997, Gardiner 2008):

- Finding the complete and authentic text of a particular treaty may depend on correctly citing its full title, and its date and place of signature.
- There is no central register for the recording, publication and indexing of treaty texts or related materials (in contrast to courts and other bodies such as the United Nations, European Union, etc.).
- The public may have no right to access materials relating to a particular treaty and there is no rule of international law requiring a state to publish a treaty (on this point, see Aust 2007, 346).
- There is no uniform source of current data on the parties to a particular treaty (i.e. no uniform source of 'status lists').
- The *travaux préparatoires* (i.e. preparatory work) for treaties may not be published, in full or at all.

1.1 General treaty sources

1.1.1 United Nations Treaty Collection (UNTC)

This is the most comprehensive treaty repository of image-based texts, which includes status information, reservations and declarations. Useful compilations on UN treaty procedures and terms are the Treaty Handbook[1] and the Glossary.[2] In addition, there is a Cumulative Index and a Handbook of Final Clauses. [Not possible to search by treaty citation, but there is a helpful guide.][3]

The two most important databases in the UNTC are:

(a) *United Nations Treaty Series (UNTS).* Comprises treaties registered or filed with the United Nations since 1946. Includes over 158,000 treaties and related subsequent actions. Also contains current status lists. [Use the 'Advanced Search' function. Beneath each link to a treaty text, there is a table with a variety of information on the circumstances of signature/ratification/accession by individual member states. UNTS registration number and date facilitate searching. Delays in translation into English and/or French mean that UNTS publication can be delayed, so for recent treaties, first try International Legal Materials.]

   UNTS also includes the *League of Nations Treaty Series.* [Much of the metadata (e.g. title, date, parties, etc.) are missing so use Full Text tab to search.]

(b) *Status of Multilateral Treaties Deposited with the Secretary-General.* Gives current status (signatures, ratifications, reservations, etc.) of over 500 multilateral treaties for which the United Nations is the depositary. There are also sections on Depositary Notifications and Certified True Copies. [In the Status Table, countries underlined are those that registered reservations, declarations, etc. at the time of signing or ratifying.]

1.1.2 Consolidated Treaty Series

Includes texts of bilateral and multilateral treaties concluded between 1648 and 1919 (some only in the vernacular). Comprises 231 volumes with Party Index and chronological list. There is no electronic version.[4]

1.1.3 Council of Europe

Produces the *Council of Europe Treaty Series*[5] with over 200 treaties, including the European Convention on Human Rights (ECHR). Timely posting of new protocols as well as status information on all treaties.

1 http://treaties.un.org/doc/source/publications/THB/English.pdf
2 http://treaties.un.org/Pages/Overview.aspx?path=overview/glossary/page1_en.xml
3 http://treaties.un.org/doc/source/guide_en.doc
4 Published by Oceana Publications, Dobbs Ferry, NY.
5 http://conventions.coe.int. See http://ials.sas.ac.uk/library/guides/research/res_council_of_europe.htm

1.1.4 European Union

The Europa website is a useful resource.[6] Treaties and other documentation can also be found on the EURLex portal.[7] N-Lex[8] links to legislation in national databases of 24 member states. See guides from University of Exeter[9] and American Society of International Law.[10]

1.1.5 National Treaty Collections

Many states publish their treaties in government gazettes, journals or official treaty series. In the United Kingdom, treaties need to be enacted into law by Parliament to be effective domestically. They are then published as Command Papers (in .pdf since 1997 on the Foreign and Commonwealth Office website).[11] [Note: treaties that have come into force 'on signature' generally do not appear as Command Papers, and need to be sought in the UK Treaty Series (Aust 2007, 349).]

The FCO *UK Treaties Online*[12] provides access to over 14,000 UK treaties, from 1832 to the present. It includes .pdf versions of original maps. It also includes some translations of treaties from original languages. [Place of signature can be useful for finding treaties, e.g. 'Trianon' produces the 1920 Treaty of Peace between the Allied and Associated Powers and Hungary and Protocol and Declaration.]

Recent materials on US treaties can be found on the US State Department's website, on the Treaty Affairs page.[13] Lexis,[14] Westlaw[15] and HeinOnline[16] are useful. For a general overview of US treaty collections see Hoffman and Rumsey (2008, 82–97) and Pratter (2009, 423–432). See Harvard University Law Library for a listing of other national collections online.[17]

If a particular treaty in the UNTC or a national treaty collection cannot be found, websites or sponsoring international organisations should be consulted,

[6] http://europa.eu/index_fn.htm. Within Publications & Documents, see Legislation & Treaties.

[7] http://eur-lex.europa.eu/en/index.htm

[8] http://eur-lex.europa.eu/n-lex/index_en.htm

[9] www.nyulawglobal.org/globalex/European_Union_Travaux_Preparatoires1.htm

[10] www.asil.org/eu1.cfm

[11] www.fco.gov.uk/en/about-us/publications-and-documents/treaty-command-papers-ems

[12] www.fco.gov.uk/en/about-us/publications-and-documents/treaties/uk-treaties-online

[13] www.state.gov/s/l/treaty Reporting International Agreements to Congress under Case Act (Text of Agreements). [At the Case Act page, find a sidebar with links from 2006 onwards.]

[14] Contains full text US treaties from 1776, including treaties no longer in force.

[15] Within 'USTREATIES'.

[16] Treaties & Agreements Library contains, *inter alia, Treaties in Force, International Legal Materials [ILM] and Hertslet's Commercial Treaties*

[17] www.law.harvard.edu/library/research/guides/int_foreign/web-resources/treaties.html

while foreign ministries may also be able to provide data, particularly status information. The FLARE Index to Treaties (see below) may also be useful.

1.1.6 Treaty portals, sources and guides

EISIL[18] is an open database of annotated links to authenticated primary and other materials.

Minnesota Human Rights Library[19] is an open database of treaties and other documents related to human rights.

Avalon[20] contains documents in the fields of Law, History, Economics, Politics, Diplomacy, Government. Includes some treaties.

International Legal Materials[21] **(ILM)** prints selected current international and foreign documentation including selected treaties and cases. More current than UNTS (but much less comprehensive).

Scholarly Treaty Guides[22] are mainly by law librarians.

1.1.7 Indexes

FLARE Index to Treaties.[23] Details of over 1,500 multilateral treaties from 1856 to the present. [Also directs users to *original* sources of older treaties when only the text of later, amended versions is available on a depository website.] Treaties selected from *Multilateral Treaties: Index and Current Status*, compiled and annotated by Bowman and Harris (1992), as well as *ILM*.

Oceana Free Treaties Index.[24] Covers more than 17,000 treaties and international agreements in over forty categories. Up-to-date source for US treaties.

World Treaty Index.[25] Documents bilateral and multilateral treaties entered into during the twentieth century. Not full text, but citation data allow statistical analysis of treaty topics etc. Contains more than 69,000 treaty citations.

18 www.eisil.org 19 www1.umn.edu/humanrts 20 http://avalon.law.yale.edu

21 Tables of Contents available at www.asil.org/ilm.cfm. Also accessible via Westlaw, Lexis and HeinOnline.

22 http://library.law.umn.edu/researchguides/most-cited.html; www.llrx.com/features/non_ustreaty.htm; www.nyulawglobal.org/globalex/treaty_research.htm; http://library.law.umn.edu/researchguides/treatysources.html.

23 http://193.62.18.232/dbtw-wpd/textbase/treatysearch.htm.

24 www.oceanalaw.com/default.asp. Click Free Treaties Index

25 http://worldtreatyindex.com Originally founded in 1974 by Peter Rohn, University of Washington, currently maintained by Michael Bommarito, Daniel Martin Katz and Paul Poast, University of Michigan.

1.2 Specific areas

International and regional organisations publish treaties for which they are depositaries, e.g. the International Labour Organisation (ILO) in the area of labour law or the International Committee of the Red Cross (ICRC) for humanitarian law. If such organisations do not carry the original text, consult one of the older print collections (e.g. Martens[26] or British and Foreign State Papers[27]). [Older treaty series may be located through the FLARE Index.] See also the ASIL guide[28] for lists of treaty sources.

1.3 Treaty interpretation

An important aspect of treaty interpretation is the preparatory material (*travaux préparatoires*) which includes 'written material such as successive drafts of the treaty, conference records, explanatory statements by an expert consultant at a codification conference, interpretative statements by the chairman of a drafting committee and ILC Commentaries' (Aust 2007, 246–247). Useful starting points include the comprehensive review by Pratter,[29] and – for the legislative history of many UN instruments – the International Law Commission (ILC).[30]

2 International custom

Customary international law is extracted from state practice informed by *opinio juris*. Sources include diplomatic correspondence, policy statements, official manuals, state legislation, international and national decisions (Brownlie 2008, 6). Shaw draws attention to General Assembly (GA) resolutions, the work of the International Law Commission, treaties and other general practice of international organisations (Shaw 2008, 82).

[26] *Nouveau recueil general de traites*. By Karl von Martens *et al.* Series 1, Leipzig: Dietrich, 1902; Series 2, Leipzig: Dietrich, 1910; Series 3, Leipzig: Weicher, 1922–1975. Includes materials from 1840–1969 in original languages.

[27] London: James Ridgway & Sons, 1841–1977. Published by the FCO. Includes materials from 1373 to 1974. See also *Law Librarian*. 1986, 17(2), 64–66.

[28] www.asil.org/treaty1.cfm

[29] www.nyulawglobal.org/globalex/Travaux_Preparatoires1.htm

[30] www.un.org/law/ilc [Click Analytical Guide]

Useful guides are produced by the University of California, Berkeley Law Library and Globalex.[31]

2.1 Foreign Ministry websites

Such websites provide information on states' foreign policy and positions on specific issues. The Foreign and Commonwealth Office (FCO) has manuals on diplomatic law (e.g. Consular Services[32] [Click 'Travelling & Living Abroad', 'When Things go Wrong', or 'Our Publications']. The US State Department produces Guidelines[33] and its online *Digest of International Law* supplements the print *Digest of United States Practice in International Law*. For sites world-wide see Lauterpacht Centre for International Law,[34] and US Institute of Peace.[35]

2.2 State legislation

2.2.1 UK House of Commons Parliamentary Papers[36]

Database of over 200,000 sessional papers from 1715 to the present, with supplementary material such as journals and private acts, published by the House of Commons and – from 1688 to 1834 – the House of Lords.

2.2.2 FLAG Foreign Law Guide[37]

Internet gateway providing descriptions of primary materials from foreign jurisdictions held in UK libraries. Includes holdings for obscure jurisdictions with no official government websites.

2.2.3 Foreign Law Guide[38]

Subscription database compiled at University of California, Berkeley. Includes materials from 189 jurisdictions and scholarly accounts of constitutional legal histories and comments on legislative and judicial systems.

[31] www.law.berkeley.edu/library/classes/iflr/customary.html; See also: www.nyulawglobal.org/globalex/Customary_International_Law.htm

[32] www.fco.gov.uk/en [33] http://travel.state.gov/law/law_1734.html

[34] www.lcil.cam.ac.uk/research_links/state_practice.php

[35] www.usip.org/resources/foreign-affairs-ministries-web

[36] http://parlipapers.chadwyck.co.uk/home.do

[37] http://193.62.18.232/dbtw-wpd/textbase/collsearch.htm. [38] www.foreignlawguide.com

Also cites English translations or digests of particular laws. For further useful guides see: Harvard Law Library,[39] GLIN,[40] Globalex,[41] LLRX Country Guides[42] and WorldLII.[43]

2.3 Yearbooks and equivalents

Produced annually by scholarly committees, law societies and universities. They summarise developments in international law and government practice, including decisions of international tribunals and digests of national cases. One of the most prestigious is the *British Yearbook of International Law*.[44] There is no American equivalent yearbook but the *American Journal of International Law* fulfils a similar function. Several yearbooks are available electronically from HeinOnline.[45]

3 General principles of law

See the research guides published by the Law Libraries of Columbia University[46] and Oklahoma City University.[47]

4 Judicial decisions and teachings of publicists

In accordance with article 59 of the ICJ Statute, ICJ decisions have no force except between the parties and in relation to the particular case. More generally, there is no doctrine of binding precedent in international courts and tribunals. The writings and opinions of jurists play some role in judicial decision-making, but the ICJ, for its part, does not cite individual writers even when it may have relied on them.

[39] www.law.harvard.edu/library/research/guides/int_foreign/web-resources/metapages.html
[40] www.glin.gov/search.action
[41] www.nyulawglobal.org/globalex/Foreign_Law_Research1.htm gives useful overview of strategies, concentrating on codes and laws.
[42] www.llrx.com/comparative_and_foreign_law.html [43] www.worldlii.org
[44] http://bybil.oxfordjournals.org
[45] www.heinonline.org/HOL/Index?collection=intyb&set_as_cursor=clear
[46] http://library.law.columbia.edu/guides/Researching_Public_International_Law#General_Principles_of_Law
[47] www.okcu.edu/law/lawlib/pdfs/guide_custom.pdf

4.1 Judicial decisions

There are very many international adjudicatory bodies and in the absence of any systemic hierarchy between them sources are widely scattered. National courts, too, deal with international law in different ways. No single text encapsulates the work of all these bodies, but the Project on International Courts and Tribunals (PICT) attempts to keep abreast of the main developments (see below). The following account is merely a summary and is loosely based on the classification used in Mackenzie *et al.* (2010), which presents the work of PICT.[48]

4.1.1 Global courts

International Court of Justice (ICJ).[49] Established in 1945. Succeeded the Permanent Court of International Justice (PCIJ). Judicial arm of the United Nations with general jurisdiction over inter-state disputes. The basis for jurisdiction is consensual. Also entitled to give Advisory Opinions to the United Nations and authorised institutions. The Court's website is timely, comprehensive and includes briefs, transcripts, final judgments, dissenting and separate opinions, and complete PCIJ documentation from 1922 gto 1946. Further sources include *ILM*, Westlaw, LexisNexis.

International Tribunal for the Law of the Sea (ITLOS).[50] Operational since 1996. A permanent UN court with compulsory jurisdiction over certain areas, in accordance with articles 287 and 288 of the UN Convention on the Law of the Sea (UNCLOS). The Seabed Disputes Chamber can also exercise jurisdiction over disputes which involve private parties. Authorised to give advisory opinions. Had heard fifteen cases to the end of 2007.

World Trade Organisation Dispute Settlement (WTO).[51] Established in 1994. Comprises the Dispute Settlement Body (DSB), *ad hoc* panels and a standing Appellate Body. Proceedings initiated by request for consultation or dispute settlement. Decisions are available on Westlaw and Lexis. Subscription databases providing summaries and analysis include Trade LawGuide[52] and WorldTradeLaw.net.[53] See also Hoffman and Rumsey (2008, 257–265) and the ASIL guide.[54]

48 www.pict-pcti.org 49 www.icj-cij.org 50 www.itlos.org
51 www.wto.org See also ASIL Research Guides. www.asil.org/iel1.cfm.
52 www.tradelawguide.com/index.asp 53 www.worldtradelaw.net/dsc/main.htm
54 www.asil.org/iel1.cfm

4.1.2 Arbitration institutions

Permanent Court of Arbitration (PCA).[55] Established in 1899. Supports *ad hoc* arbitral proceedings, particularly in investor–state matters, for which it provides registry support and hosts oral proceedings. Selected cases available from court website and from *Reports of International Arbitral Awards* (section 4.1.5).

International Centre for Settlement of Investment Disputes (ICSID).[56] Established 1965. Creates institutional framework for arbitral tribunals and disputes between host states and foreign investors. See ICSID website for selected awards.

Other sources. ITA,[57] UNCTAD,[58] ICC,[59] TDM,[60] KluwerArbitration,[61] Investor-State LawGuide,[62] Westlaw.[63] Further useful guide from ASIL.[64]

4.1.3 European courts

European Court of Justice (ECJ).[65] Established in 1951 by the European Community Treaty. Since 2009 it has been known as the Court of Justice of the European Union (CJEU) Its role (article 220) is to 'ensure that in the interpretation and application of this treaty, the law is observed'. It reviews the legality of the acts of EU institutions, compliance by member states of their obligations; and ensures uniform interpretation and implementation of EU law. The court's website (Curia) provides access to case law since 1953. See Institute of Advanced Legal Studies guide.[66]

For Courts of Justice of other Economic Communities, see Mackenzie *et al.* (2010, 278–328).

55 www.pca-cpa.org/showpage.asp?pag_id=363

56 http://icsid.worldbank.org/ICSID/Index.jsp [Click 'Cases', then 'Search Online Decisions and Awards'.]

57 http://ita.law.uvic.ca Investment Treaty Arbitration. University of Victoria (Canada) Law Faculty.

58 www.unctad.org/iia-dbcases UN Conference on Trade & Development.

59 www.iccwbo.org/court By subscription

60 www.transnational-dispute-management.com Transnational Dispute Management. By Subscription, providing analysis, commentary, national legislation and case-law.

61 www.kluwerarbitration.com/arbitration Full text by subscription, but searching and citation are free.

62 www.investorstatelawguide.com By subscription. Includes archive of decisions with cross-referencing facility, tribunal interpretations, texts of legal instruments and directory of investment treaty law.

63 For coverage by *Westlaw*, See item D of Asil Guide www.asil.org/arb1.cfm

64 www.asil.org/arb1.cfm

65 http://curia.europa.eu

66 http://ials.sas.ac.uk/library/guides/research/res_eu.htm#reports

European Court of Human Rights (ECtHR).[67] Established by European Convention on Human Rights 1950 (ECHR). Handles complaints from states and individuals in the forty-seven states party to the ECHR. Applications initially assessed for admissibility, then subjected to 'friendly settlement' in line with the Convention and its protocols before being passed on to a hearing. Judgements are binding. Has the largest number of pending cases before a single international tribunal (90,000, according to Lowe 2007, 127). Case law is contained in HUDOC,[68] which provides Decisions and Judgments from both the Court and the Commission (the latter only pre-1998). [When using HUDOC for subject searches, identify the Article of the Convention at issue. Key this number into the relevant search facility. E.g. to find inter-state cases, key in '33'.] See Institute of Advanced Legal Studies guide.[69]

For further information on Human Rights bodies see Mackenzie *et al.* (2010, 334–542).

4.1.4 International criminal courts and tribunals

International Criminal Court (ICC).[70] Became operational in 2002. A permanent Court, with jurisdiction over four categories of international crimes committed by individuals after July 2002: genocide, crimes against humanity, war crimes and crimes of aggression. The Court's website gives access to its activities and documentation.

***Ad hoc* International Criminal Tribunals.** UN bodies created to deal with specified international crimes with scope limited to specified territories. Currently limited to International Criminal Tribunal for the Former Yugoslavia (ICTY),[71] and International Criminal Tribunal for Rwanda (ICTR).[72] Websites contain case materials and judgment details. For information on similar tribunals, e.g. military and hybrid criminal, see Mackenzie *et al.* (2010, 154) and PICT synoptic chart.

4.1.5 Collections

Reports of International Arbitral Awards (RIAA).[73] The United Nations publishes selected arbitration awards of international decisions, (a) between states and (b) between states and international organisations.

67 www.echr.coe.int/echr/Homepage_EN
68 www.echr.coe.int/ECHR/EN/Header/Case-Law/Hudoc/Hudoc+database/
69 http://ials.sas.ac.uk/library/guides/research/res_council_of_europe.htm
70 www.icc-cpi.int 71 www.icty.org 72 www.ictr.org
73 http://untreaty.un.org/cod/riaa/index.html. Available from Vol. I (1948) to Vol. XXVIII (2007).

International Law Reports (ILR).[74] The only publication devoted to systematic reporting (in English) of full decisions from international courts and arbitrators, as well as judgments of national courts, from 1919 to the present. Citations to treaties in decisions of courts and tribunals can also be found in the Index to the ILRs. Available online from *Justis*.

4.1.6 Decisions of municipal courts

International law issues are frequently raised in domestic courts. Useful sites for domestic law in Common Law jurisdictions include BAILLI,[75] Austlii,[76] US Supreme[77] and Federal Courts.[78] There is no systematic reporting of cases in civil jurisdictions where journals often document cases, but see Globalex country guides.[79] For both common and civil jurisdictions see *Oxford Reports on International Law*[80] and WorldLII.[81]

4.2 Teachings of publicists

4.2.1 Textbooks, monographs and journals

Use Library catalogues such as COPAC, WorldCat, Harvard Law School Library, Peace Palace Library. Some of the more important journals include:

Academie de Droit International de la Haye, Recueil des Cours (Collected Courses of the Hague Academy of International Law). Starting in 1923, courses cover both public and private international law. Available online from Nijhoff/Brill.

American Journal of International Law
European Journal of International Law
International & Comparative Law Quarterly
Zeitschrift für Ausländisches öffentliches Recht und Völkerrecht.[82]

4.2.2 Journal indices

Index to legal periodicals. Started in 1908. Indexes ~1,000 mainstream journals with permanent reference value from common law jurisdictions. Electronic access from 1980 via Westlaw or LexisNexis (~500 titles).

[74] Lauterpacht, E., C. Greenwood and K. Lee (eds.), Cambridge University Press.
[75] www.bailii.org [76] www.austlii.edu.au [77] www.supremecourtus.gov
[78] www.findlaw.com/11stategov [79] www.nyulawglobal.org/globalex
[80] http://www.oxfordlawreports.com [81] http://www.worldlii.org/
[82] www.hjil.de. Non-fee-based digitised content from Vol. 1 (1929) to Vol. 67 (2008). In later volumes, many articles are in English.

Index to foreign legal periodicals. Started in 1960, online access via Ovid Technologies since 1980. Multilingual index covering 470 legal journals including from lesser-known jurisdictions.

5 Other sources

5.1 International organisations

Primarily involves the United Nations but also includes various regional economic organisations, IGOs and NGOs.

5.1.1 UN bodies

UN competence includes rule-making, adjudication, monitoring state compliance and policy formulation (Lowe 2007, 12–14). The documentation is vast. Official records comprise meeting records, resolutions and decisions and reports of major committees. Accessed via UN Documentation Centre.[83] Several useful guides (see section 5.1.2) describe the structure of the United Nations, the system of document notation and the reporting route (e.g. the ILC reports to the GA).

UN General Assembly (GA).[84] Articles 24 and 25 of the UN Charter state that Resolutions of the GA are recommendatory. However where states 'consistently vote for resolutions and declarations on a topic, that amounts to a state practice and a binding rule may very well emerge provided that the requisite *opinio juris* can be proved' (Shaw 2008, 115).

There are seven specialised GA committees; the 6th Committee[85] considers legal matters, which include: GA questions, reviewing work of *ad hoc* GA committees, and approving the codification programme of the ILC (see below). Its website has material from 1977. Summary records of meetings in the 6th Committee can be retrieved through UNBISNET or the ODS (see section 5.1.2).

UN Security Council (SC).[86] Articles 24 and 25 of the UN Charter state that SC Resolutions are binding on all member states of the organisation. In recent years the SC has been willing to lay down rules and principles of general application including use of its power to override customary law and treaty

[83] www.un.org/en/documents/index.shtml

[84] www.un.org/ga/64/resolutions.shtml. Search by General Assembly session number and then by agenda items.

[85] www.un.org/ga/sixth [86] www.un.org/Docs/sc/unsc_resolutions.html

obligations (Boyle and Chinkin 2007, 109–110). Documents on its website include voting records, and are arranged by year and resolution number.

International Law Commission (ILC).[87] Established by the UN GA in 1947 to develop and codify international law. In addition to draft treaties and guidelines, also prepares reports and studies on topical issues of international law. ILC records can be retrieved using UNBISNET or the ODS (section 6.1). ILC Yearbooks accessible online from 1949.

Other UN bodies. International law is also developed during the work of:

UNCITRAL (United Nations Commission on International Trade Law), whose work is scrutinised by the GA 6th Committee.

UNHCR (United Nations High Commissioner for Refugees), whose recommendations have been adduced before some national courts (see Gardiner 1997, 660).

UNCTAD (United Nations Conference on Trade and Development), whose reports include, *inter alia*, the harmonisation of trade and development policies and cases of investor-state dispute settlement.[88]

Specialised Agencies, e.g. ILO,[89] UNESCO.

5.1.2 Guides, repositories and catalogues for UN materials

Overviews of documents and publications issued by the United Nations[90] (e.g. reports, resolutions, meeting records, press releases) and guidance on how to work with them.[91]

Audiovisual Library of International Law (AVL).[92] A unique resource of (a) Historic Archives, (b) Lecture Series, (c) Research Library.

Official Documents System (ODS).[93] All types of official UN documentation. Includes resolutions of the GA, SC, ECOSOC and the Trusteeship Council from 1946. Excludes press releases, sales publications, UNTS and brochures issued by Department of Public Information. Indexed according to UNBIS.

[87] www.un.org/law/ilc [Click on Analytical Guide to the Work of the International Law Commission.]

[88] www.unctad.org/Templates/Page.asp?intItemID=1397&lang=1

[89] www.ilo.org/global/lang–en/index.htm [For Meeting Documents, click on Publications & Research, Official Reports.]

[90] www.un.org/Depts/dhl/resguide See for UN Document notation and reporting routes.

[91] www.nyulawglobal.org/globalex/UN_Resources_Research_Tools.pdf www.asil.org/un1.cfm See for structure of United Nations. www.un.org/en/law; www.law.duke.edu/lib/researchguides/un.html

[92] www.un.org/law/avl [93] http://documents.un.org/welcome.asp?language=E

UNBISNET.[94] Catalogues UN material indexed by the Dag Hammarskjöld Library (including commercial publications and non-UN sources) and the UN Geneva Office library. Mainly focuses on the period after 1979, but does have older documents. Includes many full-text resources in the six official languages of the United Nations. Also includes voting records for all resolutions of the GA and SC back to 1946, and citations to speeches in the GA and SC from 38th session (1983), ECOSOC (from 1983) and Trusteeship Council (from 1982).

5.1.3 Other bodies outside the United Nations

Regional Organisations (EU,[95] Council of Europe,[96] OAS,[97] OAU,[98] League of Arab States[99]), IGOs,[100] NGOs[101] (e.g. Amnesty International, International Committee Red Cross, GATT and WTO).

5.2 Soft law

Soft law is a convenient term for a variety of non-binding instruments used in contemporary international relations (e.g. inter-state conference declarations), common international standards of transnational regulatory bodies, NGOs and professional and industrial associations (Boyle and Chinkin 2007, 212–213). There is no centralised list – researchers have to look up the particular statements, standards and declarations as required.

6. Encyclopaedias, digests, research guides, etc.

Useful 'first bases' from which to launch searches on particular problems or for specific topics.

6.1 Encyclopaedias

Several encyclopaedias deal with international law (e.g. **Parry & Grant Encyclopaedic Dictionary of International Law, 2009**), but by far the

[94] http://unbisnet.un.org [95] www.asil.org/eu1.cfm;
[96] www.coe.int/lportal/web/coe-porta
[97] www.oas.org/en/information_center/default.asp
[98] www.africa-union.org/root/au/index/index.htm
[99] www.arableagueonline.org/las/index.jsp
[100] www.library.northwestern.edu/govinfo/resource/internat/igo.html
[101] www.asil.org/intorg1.cfm; www.ll.georgetown.edu/guides/IGOsNGOs.cfm

most comprehensive online is the **Max Plank Encyclopedia of Public International Law (MPEPIL)** (general editor, R Wolfrum).[102] A feature is the avoidance of purely Eurocentric perspectives, with contextualisation of each topic and the maintenance of a focus on the mainstream/majority view, and with hyperlinks to primary sources. Citator record links to *Oxford Reports on International Law*. Authors are international legal scholars and practitioners. Articles reviewed by the Members of the MPEPIL Advisory Board.

6.2 Digests

Keesing's World News Archive[103] is a comprehensive online archive including political, constitutional and legal topics. Access to a seventy-nine-year archive, with 95,000 searchable articles. Cross-referencing is incremental and citations lead directly to earlier articles.

6.3 Research guides, etc.

Useful websites include: ASIL guides,[104] LLRX,[105] Globalex,[106] Academic Library guides,[107] Legal Citation guides,[108] Current Awareness sites,[109] blogs.[110]

Bibliography

Aust, A., 2007. *Modern Treaty Law and Practice*, Cambridge University Press

Bowman, M.I. and D.J. Harris, 1992. *Index and Current Status/Compiled and Annotated within the University of Nottingham Treaty Centre*, London: Butterworths, St. Paul, MN: Mason Publishing

Boyle, A. and C. Chinkin, 2007. *The Making of International Law*, Oxford University Press

102 www.mpepil.com 103 www.keesings.com 104 www.asil.org/erghome.cfm
105 www.llrx.com 106 www.nyulawglobal.org/globalex/index.html
107 http://ials.sas.ac.uk/library/guides/research_guides.htm; www.ouls.ox.ac.uk/law/guides; http://library.law.umn.edu/researchguides.html#FCIL; www2.lib.uchicago.edu/~llou/forintlaw.html
108 E.g. The Bluebook (www.legalbluebook.com), OSCOLA (www.competition-law.ox.ac.uk/published/oscola.shtml)
109 www.biicl.org BICL, www.asil.org/electronic-publications.cfm ASIL Insights
110 Blogs www.opiniojuris.org, http://ilreports.blogspot.com, http://intlawgrrls.blogspot.com

Brownlie, I., 2008. *Principles of Public International Law*, 7th edn., Oxford University Press

Gardiner, R. K., 1997. 'Treaties and Treaty Materials: Role, Relevance and Accessibility', *International and Comparative Law Quarterly*, 46, 643–662

Gardiner, R. K., 2003. *International Law*, Harlow: Pearson-Longman

Gardiner, R. K., 2008. *Treaty Interpretation*, Oxford University Press

Hoffman, M. and M. Rumsey, 2008. *International and Foreign Legal Research: A Coursebook*, Leiden: Martinus Nijhoff

Koskenniemi, M., 2007. 'The Fate of Public International Law: Between Technique and Politics', *Modern Law Review*, 70 (1), 1–30

Lowe, V. 2007, *International Law*, Oxford University Press

Mackenzie, R., C. Romano, Y. Shany and P. Sands, 2010. *Manual on International Courts and Tribunals*, Oxford University Press

Pratter, J., 2009. 'International Law', in S. M. Barkan, R. M. Mersky and D. J. Dunn (eds.), *Fundamentals of Legal Research*, New York: Foundation Press

Shaw, M., 2008. *International Law*, Cambridge University Press

International law chronology

(With emphasis on the twentieth and twenty-first centuries)

Diplomatic and other legally relevant events	Doctrinal developments
1494 'Discovery' of the Indies	Natural law and *ius gentium*: The theologians: – Francisco de Vitoria (c. 1480 – 1546) – Francisco Suárez (1548 – 1617)
1555 Peace of Augsburg – *Cuius regio eius religio* 1559 Peace of Cateau-Cambresis	Protestant natural law: – Alberico Gentili (1552 – 1608) – Hugo Grotius (1583 – 1645) *Mare Liberum* (1609) *De Jure Belli ac Pacis* (1625)
1648 Peace of Westphalia – German settlement, religious peace	
1713 Peace of Utrecht – balance of power – British colonial world begins – *Ancien régime* diplomacy	Rationalism and balance of power: – Christian Wolff (1679 – 1754) – Emer de Vattel (1714 – 1767) *Droit public de l'europe* (1758) – Abbé de Mably (1709 – 1785)
1775 – 1783 American War of Independence 1789 French Revolution – *Déclaration des droits de l'Homme et du Citoyen* (1789) – *Déclaration des droits des nations* (1795) – Revolutionary wars	Peace plans: – Abbé de St. Pierre (1658 – 1743) – Jean-Jacques Rousseau (1712 – 1778) – Immanuel Kant (1724 – 1804) Into positivism: – Jeremy Bentham (1748 – 1832) *Principles of International Law* (1798) – Georg Friedrich de Martens (1756 – 1821) – John Austin (1790 – 1859) *Province of Jurisprudence Determined* (1832)

Diplomatic and other legally relevant events	Doctrinal developments
1809–1810 First declarations of independence of Spanish American colonies	
1815 Congress of Vienna – 'The congress System': legitimacy – Diplomatic precedence	Treaty law, diplomatic forms, intervention
Central Commission for Navigation on the Rhine (est. 1815)	
1826 Congress of Panama, Organisation of American States	Anti-slavery campaigns
1837 *Caroline* incident	
1863–1864: International Committee of the Red Cross (ICRC), First Geneva Convention for the Amelioration of the Condition of the Wounded in Armies in the Field	
1865–1874: establishment of the International Telegraphic and Postal Unions	
1870–1871: Franco-Prussian War	
1871 *Alabama Arbitration* (*USA* v. *UK*)	1873: establishment of the *Institut de droit international* and the International Law Association (ILA)
1878 Congress of Berlin	
1884–1885 Berlin West Africa Conference	The 'civilising mission', sovereignty and protectorates; territorial acquisition.
1899/1907 Hague Conferences and Convention for the Pacific Settlement of International Disputes (establishing Permanent Court of Arbitration); Convention on the Laws and Customs of War	Professionalisation of international law; establishment of chairs at European universities; collaboration with peace movement. – Lassa Oppenheim (1858–1919) *International Law* (2 vols., 1905)
1914–1918 First World War	
1919 League of Nations, Peace Treaty of Versailles, etc.	
1922 Permanent Court of International Justice (PCIJ)	Hague Academy of International Law (1923)
1928 Kellogg–Briand Pact	The 'turn to institutions', collective security, sanctions, peaceful

Diplomatic and other legally relevant events	Doctrinal developments
	settlement of disputes, critique of 'excessive' sovereignty, minority regimes, trusteeship. Functional integration
1930 Hague Codification Conference, conventions on conflict of laws, statelessness and double nationality	International law as 'science': formalism/sociological approaches/ international courts – Hans Kelsen (1881 –1973) – Georges Scelle (1878 –1961) – Hersch Lauterpacht (1897 –1960) *The Function of Law in the International Community* (1933)
1938 Munich Accord	
1939 –1945 Second World War	
1944 Bretton Woods Conference: Establishment of IMF and IBRD (World Bank)	
1945 United Nations	Into pragmatism; against 'idealism' Separation of inter-bloc and intra-bloc cooperation
1945 –9 Nürnberg Trials	
1946 –1948 International Military Tribunal for the Far East, Tokyo Trials	
1947 Havana Conference – General Agreement on Tariffs and Trade (GATT)	
1947 establishment of the International Law Commission (ILC) by the UN General Assembly	German question Cooperation in humanitarian and trade issues: – West: human rights and economic cooperation, Western European integration – East: cooperation in the socialist bloc; 'peaceful coexistence'; disarmament, limited economic cooperation – South: calls for decolonisation, development – externalised war
1948 Universal Declaration of Human Rights (UDHR)	
Genocide Convention	
1949/1955 North Atlantic Treaty and Warsaw Pact	
1949 Council of Europe	

Diplomatic and other legally relevant events	Doctrinal developments
1949 Four Geneva Conventions on the Laws and Customs of War (under auspices of ICRC)	
1950 European Convention on Human Rights	
1950–1953 Korean war	
1955 Bandung Declaration	
1957 EC Treaty	
1958 Four Geneva Conventions on the Law of the Sea	
1960–1970 Decolonisation	Decolonisation – State succession – peacekeeping UN General Assembly plays greater role
1961–1963 Vienna Conventions on Diplomatic and Consular Relations	UN Declaration on Permanent Sovereignty over Natural Resources (1962)
1962 Cuban Missile Crisis	– Wolfgang Friedmann (1907–1972) *The Changing Structure of International Law* (1964)
1966 UN Human Rights Covenants: International Covenant on Economic, Social and Cultural Rights (ICESCR) and International Covenant on Civil and Political Rights (ICCPR)	Cooperation in humanitarian, economic, environmental and technical fields
1966 International Convention on the Settlement of Investment Disputes between States and Nationals of Other States (ICSID)	The law of outer space The law of the sea Civil and political rights versus economic, social and cultural rights
1967 Association of Southeast Asian Nations (ASEAN)	
1968 Non-Proliferation Treaty	
1969 Vienna Convention on the Law of Treaties (VCLT)	
1970 UN Declaration on Principles of International Law concerning Friendly Relations and Cooperation among States	Third world themes: – UN General Assembly resolutions – Commodity Agreements – Regulation of transnational corporations international environmental law
1972 UN Stockholm Conference on the Human Environment (Stockholm Declaration), UNEP	

Diplomatic and other legally relevant events	Doctrinal developments
1974 New International Economic Order (NIEO), Charter of Economic Rights and Duties of States	– Mohammed Bedjaoui (b. 1929) *Towards a New International Economic Order* (1979)
1973 –1982 UN Conference on the Law of the Sea (UNCLOS)	– Law and development
1981 establishment of the Iran–US Claims Tribunal after the Islamic Revolution in Iran	
1981 African Charter on Human and Peoples' Rights	
1989 Fall of the Berlin Wall. Breakup of Soviet Union	State succession and continuity; human rights; liberal economics
1990 OSCE Paris Charter for a New Europe	
IMF Structural Adjustment Programs (SAPs), OECD	
1990 –1991 Kuwait crisis, the first Iraq War 1991 Mercosur Trade Agreement 1992 North American Free Trade Agreement (NAFTA)	'Reinvigorated collective security'; the powers of the UN Security Council; economic sanctions; 'authorisations for the use of force'
1992: Rio Conference on Environment and Development (Rio Declaration) Framework Convention on Climate Change Convention on Biological Diversity	The international law of sustainable development
1992 –1997. The Yugoslavian wars; ICTY 1994 Genocide in Rwanda; ICTR	Humanitarian intervention; crisis of peace-keeping
1994 Energy Charter Treaty	
1994 Implementation Agreement on Part X of UNCLOS; UNCLOS enters into force	
1995 WTO enters into force following Uruguay Round of multilateral negotiations	WTO Dispute Settlement Understanding (DSU); work of the Appellate Body ('constitutionalisation of international trade law')
1998 International Criminal Court (ICC) Statute (in force 2002)	'The fight against impunity'

Diplomatic and other legally relevant events	Doctrinal developments
1999 Bombing of Kosovo 1999 East Timor	'illegal but legitimate'; peace enforcement; transitional justice, international territorial administration; 'responsibility to protect'
UN Millennium Meeting and Declaration	UN Millennium Development Goals (MDGs) 2000 ILC Articles on State Responsibility 2001
2001 World Trade Centre (New York) attacks	international law and terrorism; terrorism and human rights; 'unlawful combatants'; 'new wars'
2001 War in Afghanistan 2003 War on Iraq	
2002 African Union	Fragmentation of international law
2005 UN World Summit and Outcome	'Constitutionalisation of international law'
2007 Lisbon Treaty amending EU Treaties (in force 2009) 2009 ICC issues arrest warrant against President Al-Bashir (Sudan) 2011 'Arab Spring'; Security Council authorises use of force against Libya	

Select guide to further reading

[*See also the bibliographies to individual chapters*]

Chapter 1 International law in diplomatic history

Black, J., 2010. *A History of Diplomacy*, London: Reaktion Books
Butterfield, H. and M. Wight, 1966. *Diplomatic Investigations*, London: Allen & Unwin
Craven, M., 2008. *The Decolonisation of International Law*, Oxford University Press
Grotius, H. 1625, *De jure belli ac pacis*
Hobbes, T., 1985. *Leviathan*, London: Penguin Classics
Johns, F., R. Joyce and S. Pahuja, 2010. *Events: The Force of International Law*, London: Routledge
Kennedy, D., 1987. 'The Move to Institutions', *Cardozo Law Review*, 8, 841–988
Niebuhr, R., 2008. *The Irony of American History*, University of Chicago Press
Pufendorf, S., 1927. *On The Duty of Man and Citizen According to the Natural Law*, Oxford University Press
Tuck, R., 1999. *The Rights of War and Peace: Political Thought and the International Order from Grotius to Kant*, Oxford University Press
Westlake, J., 1894. *Chapters on the Principles of International Law*, Cambridge University Press

Chapter 2 International law in the world of ideas

Allott, P., 1990. *Eunomia: A New Order for a New World*, Oxford University Press
Armstrong, D. (ed.), 2009. *Routledge Handbook of International Law*, London: Routledge
Berman, N., 2008. *Passions et ambivalences: Le colonialisme, le nationalisme et le droit international*, Paris: Pedone
Carty, A., 2007. *Philosophy of International Law*, Edinburgh University Press
Daillier, P., M. Forteau and A. Pellet, *Le droit international public*, 8th edn., Paris: LGDJ
Evans, M. (ed.), 2010. *International Law*, 3rd edn., Oxford University Press
Franck, T., 1990. *The Power of Legitimacy Among Nations*, Oxford University Press
Grewe, W., 2000. *The Epochs of International* Law, Berlin: De Gruyter

Kennedy, D., 2004. *The Dark Sides of Virtue: Reassessing International Humanitarianism*, Princeton University Press
Max Planck Encyclopaedia of Public International Law, online

Chapter 3 International law as law

Anghie, A., 2005. *Imperialism, Sovereignty and the Making of International Law*, Cambridge University Press
Klabbers, J., A. Peters and G. Ulfstein, 2009. *The Constitutionalisation of International Law*, Oxford University Press
Koskenniemi, M., 2001. *The Gentle Civilizer of Nations: The Rise and Fall of International Law 1870–1960*, Cambridge University Press
Lauterpacht, H., 1932. 'The Nature of International Law and General Jurisprudence', *Economica*, 37, 301–320
Mégret, F., 2008. 'Globalisation', in R. Wolfrum (ed.), *Max Planck Encyclopedia of Public International Law, online*
Rajagopal, B., 2006. 'Counter-hegemonic International Law: Rethinking Human Rights and Development as a Third World Strategy', *Third World Quarterly*, 27(5), 767–783
Simma, B. and A. Paulus, 1998. 'The "International Community": Facing the Challenge of Globalisation', *European Journal of International Law*, 9(2), 266–277
Vagts, D. F., 2001. 'Hegemonic International Law', *American Journal of International Law*, 95, 843–848
Weil, P., 1992. 'Le Droit international en quête de son identité: Cours général de droit international public', *Recueil des cours de l'Académie de droit international*, 237, 11–370
Williams, G., 1945. 'International Law and the Controversy Concerning the Word Law', *British Yearbook of International Law*, 22, 146–163

Chapter 4 Statehood: territory, people, government

Anaya, S., 2004. *Indigenous Peoples in International Law*, Oxford University Press
Berman, N., 2008. *Passions et ambivalences: Le colonialisme, le nationalisme et le droit international*, Paris: Pedone
Crawford, J., 2006. *The Creation of States in International Law*, Oxford: Clarendon
Johns, F. (ed.), 2010. *International Legal Personality*, Farnham: Ashgate
Simpson, G. (ed.), 2002. *The Nature of International Law*, Aldershot: Ashgate Dartmouth

Chapter 5 Sovereignty as a legal value

Chayes, A. and A.H. Chayes, 1995. *The New Sovereignty: Compliance with International Regulatory Agreements*, Cambridge, MA: Harvard University Press

Endicott, T., 2010. 'The Logic of Freedom and Power', in S. Besson and J. Tasioulas (eds.), *The Philosophy of International Law*, Oxford University Press, 245–259

Jackson, J., 2003. 'Sovereignty – Modern: A New Approach to an Outdated Concept', *American Journal of International Law*, 97, 782–802

Kalmo, H. and Q. Skinner (eds.), 2010. *Sovereignty in Fragments: The Past, Present and Future of a Contested Concept*, Cambridge University Press

Kokott, J., 2007. 'States, Sovereign Equality', in R. Wolfrum (ed.), Max Planck Encyclopedia of Public International Law, online

Krasner, S., 1999. *Sovereignty: Organized Hypocrisy*, Princeton University Press

MacCormick, N., 1999. *Questioning Sovereignty: Law, State and Nation in the European Commonwealth*, Oxford University Press

Raustiala, K., 2003. 'Rethinking the Sovereignty Debate in International Economic Law', *Journal of International Economic Law*, 6, 841–878

Chapter 6 Exercise and limits of jurisdiction

Capps, P., M. Evans and S. Konstadinidis (eds.), 2003. *Asserting Jurisdiction: International and European Legal Perspectives*, Oxford: Hart

Restatement of the Law, 3d, 1987. *The Foreign Relations Law of the United States*

Ryngaert, C., 2008. *Jurisdiction in International Law*, Oxford University Press

Verdross, A. and B. Simma, 1984. *Universelles Völkerrecht: Theorie und Praxis*, Berlin: Duncker & Humblot Gmbh

Chapter 7 Lawfare and warfare

Byers, M., 2007. *War Law: Understanding International Law and Armed Conflict*, New York: Grove Press

Clausewitz, C. von, 1984. *On War*, M. Howard and P. Paret (eds.), Princeton University Press

Dinstein, Y., 2010. *The Conduct of Hostilities under the Law of International Armed Conflict*, Cambridge University Press

Foucault, M., 2003. *'Society Must Be Defended': Lectures at the College de France 1975–1976*, D. Macey (trans.), New York: Picador

Fussell, P. (ed.), 1991. *The Norton Book of Modern War*, New York and London: W.W Norton

Gray, C., 2008. *International Law and the Use of Force*, 3rd edn., Oxford University Press

Howard, M., 1997. *The Laws of War: Constraints on Warfare in the Western World*, G. Andreopoulos and M. Shulman (eds.), New Haven: Yale University Press
Kennedy, D., 2006. *Of War and Law*, Princeton University Press
Neff, S., 2005. *War and the Law of Nations: A General History*, Cambridge University Press
Roberts, A., and R. Guelff, 2000. *Documents on the Laws of War*, Oxford University Press
Sassoli, M. and A. Bouvier, 1999. *How Does Law Protect in War? Cases, Documents and Teaching Materials on Contemporary Practice in International Humanitarian Law*, Geneva: International Committee of the Red Cross
Solis, G., 2010. *The Law of Armed Conflict: International Humanitarian Law in War*, Cambridge University Press

Chapter 8 Law-making and sources

Abi-Saab, G., 1987. 'Cours général de droit international public', *Recueil des cours*, 207(VII), 9–463
Byers, M., 2000. *Custom, Power and the Power of Rules*, Cambridge University Press
Gowlland-Debbas, V. (ed.), 2000. *Multilateral Treaty-making*, The Hague: Kluwer
Higgins, R., 1994. *Problems and Process: International Law and How We Use It*, Oxford University Press
Kennedy, D., 1987. 'The Sources of International Law', *American University Journal of International Law and Politics*, 2, 1–96
Rajagopal, B., 2003. *International Law from Below: Developments, Social Movements, and Third World Resistance*, Cambridge University Press
Weiler, J., 2004. 'The Geology of International Law: Governance, Democracy, and Legitimacy', *Heidelberg Journal of International Law*, 64, 547–562

Chapter 9 International courts: uneven judicialisation in global order

Alvarez, J., 2005. *International Organisations as Law-makers*, Oxford University Press
Ascensio, H., E. L. Abdelgawad and J.-M. Sorel (eds.), 2006. *Les juridictions pénales internationalisées (Cambodge, Kosovo, Sierra Leone, Timor Leste)*, Paris: Société de législation comparée
Brown, C., 2007. *A Common Law of International Adjudication*, Oxford University Press
Cassese, S., 2009. *I Tribunali di Babele: I giudici alla ricerca di un nuovo ordine globale*, Rome: Donzelli Editore
French, D., M. Saul and N. D. White (eds.), 2010. *International Law and Dispute Settlement: New Problems and Techniques*, Oxford: Hart
Mackenzie R., K. Malleson, P. Martin and P. Sands, 2010. *Selecting International Judges: Principle, Process, and Politics*, Oxford University Press

Rosenne, S. and Y. Ronen, 2006. *The Law and Practice of the International Court, 1920–2005*, Leiden and Boston: Martinus Nijhoff

Ruiz Fabri, H. and J.-M. Sorel, 2003. *Le contentieux de l'urgence et l'urgence dans le contentieux devant les juridictions internationales: regards croisés*, Paris: Pedone

Ruiz Fabri, H. and J.-M. Sorel, 2004. *Le principe du contradictoire devant les juridictions internationals*, Paris: Pedone

Ruiz Fabri, H. and J.-M. Sorel, 2005. *Le tiers à l'instance devant les juridictions internationals*, Paris: Pedone

Ruiz Fabri, H. and J.-M. Sorel, 2006. *La saisine des juridictions internationals*, Paris: Pedone

Ruiz Fabri, H. and J.-M. Sorel, 2007. *La preuve devant les juridictions internationals*, Paris: Pedone

Ruiz Fabri, H. and J.-M. Sorel, 2008. *La motivation des décisions des juridictions internationales* Paris: Pedone

Santulli, C., 2005. *Droit Du Contentieux International*, Paris: Montchrestien

Schill, S. W. (ed.), 2010. *International Investment Law and Comparative Public Law*, Oxford University Press

Shany, Y., 2003. *The Competing Jurisdictions of International Courts and Tribunals*, Oxford University Press

Zimmermann, A., C. Tomuschat and K. Oellers-Frahm (eds.), 2006. *The Statute of the International Court of Justice: A Commentary*, Oxford University Press

Chapter 10 International institutions

Amerasinghe, C., 2005. *Principles of Institutional Law of International Organisations*, Cambridge University Press

Klabbers, J., 2009. *An Introduction to International Institutional Law*, 2nd edn., Cambridge University Press

Reinisch, A., 2010 *International Organisations before National Courts*, Cambridge University Press

Sarooshi, D., 2005, *International Organisations and their Exercise of Sovereign Powers*, Oxford University Press

Chapter 11 International law and the relativities of enforcement

Alland, D., 2002. 'Counter-measures of General Interest', *European Journal of International Law*, 13, 1221–1239

Bederman, D., 2002. 'Counterintuiting Counter-measures', *American Journal of International Law*, 96, 817–832

Brown-Weiss E., 2002. 'Invoking State Responsibility in the Twenty-first Century', *American Journal of International Law*, 96, 798–816

Charney, J., 1989. 'Third State Remedies in International Law', *Michigan Journal of International Law*, 10, 57–101

Charnowitz, S., 2001. 'Rethinking WTO Sanctions', *American Journal of International Law*, 95, 792–732

Chayes, A. and A.H. Chayes, 1995. *The New Sovereignty: Compliance with International Regulatory Agreements*, Cambridge, MA: Harvard University Press

Fisler Damrosch, L., 1997. 'Enforcing International Law Through Non-forcible Measures', *Recueil des cours de l'Académie de droit international*, 269, 9–250

Gordan, J., 2010. *Invisible War: The United States and the Iraq Sanctions*, Cambridge, MA: Harvard University Press

Gray, C., 2008. *International Law and the Use of Force by States*, 3rd edn., Oxford University Press

Katselli Proukaki, E., 2010. *The Problem of Enforcement in International Law: Counter-measures, the Non-injured State and the Idea of International Community*, London and New York: Routledge

Koskenniemi, M., 2001. 'Solidarity Measures: State Responsibility as a New International Order?', *British Yearbook of International Law*, 71, 337–355

Kritsiotis, D., 2004. 'Arguments of Mass Confusion', *European Journal of International Law*, 15, 233–278

O'Connell, M.E., 2008. *The Power and Purpose of International Law: Insights from the Theory and Practice of Enforcement*, Oxford University Press

Ulfstein, G., T. Marauhn and A. Zimmermann (eds.), 2007. *Making Treaties Work: Human Rights, Environment and Arms Control*, Cambridge University Press

Chapter 12 Constituting order

Beard, J., 2007. *The Political Economy of Desire: International Law, Development and the Nation State*, Oxford: Routledge-Cavendish

Bell, D. (ed.), 2007. *Victorian Visions of Global Order: Empire and International Relations in Nineteenth-century Political Thought*, Cambridge University Press

Bull, H., 2002. *The Anarchical Society: A Study of Order in World Politics*, New York: Columbia University Press

Carty, A., 2007. *The Philosophy of International Law*, Edinburgh University Press

Foote, W. (ed.), 1962. *The Servant of Peace: A Selection of the Speeches and Statements of Dag Hammarskjöld*, London: The Bodley Head

Koskenniemi, M., 1995. 'The Police in the Temple: Order, Justice and the UN. A Dialectical View', *European Journal of International Law*, 6, 325–348

Orford, A., 2010. 'International Territorial Administration and the Management of Decolonisation', *International and Comparative Law Quarterly*, 59, 227–249

Schmitt, C., 2003. *The Nomos of the Earth in the International Law of the Jus Publicum Europaeum*, G.L. Ulmen (trans.), New York: Telos Press

Schwebel, S., 1951. 'The Origins and Development of Article 99 of the Charter', *British Year Book of International Law*, 28, 371–382 van Ittersum, M. J., 2010. 'The Long Goodbye: Hugo Grotius and the Justification of Dutch Expansion Overseas (1604–1645)', *History of European Ideas*, 36, 386–411

Chapter 13 Legitimating the international rule of law

Chimni, B. S., 1993. *International Law and World Order: A Critique of Contemporary Approaches*, New Delhi: Sage

Koskenniemi, M., 2001. *The Gentle Civilizer of Nations: The Rise and Fall of International Law 1870–1960*, Cambridge University Press

Marx, K., 1968. *The German Ideology, Chapter I (1846)*, Moscow: Progress Publishers

Mattei, U. and L. Nader, 2008. *Plunder: When the Rule of Law is Illegal*, Malden, MA: Blackwell

Nandy, A., 1983. *The Intimate Enemy*, Oxford University Press

Nardin, T., 1983. *Law, Morality, and the Relations of States*, Princeton University Press

Onuma, Y., 2010. *A Transcivilisational Perspective on International Law*, Leiden: Martinus Nijhoff

Ramanujan, A. K., 1990. 'Is there an Indian Way of Thinking? An Informal Essay', in M. Marriot (ed.), *India through Hindu Categories*, New Delhi: Sage, 41–58

Ratner, S. and A.-M. Slaughter (eds.), 2004. *The Methods of International Law*, Washington, DC: The American Society of International Law

Teubner, G. (ed.), 1997. *Global Law Without a State*, Sudbury, MA: Dartmouth

Chapter 14 Human rights in disastrous times

Baxi, U., 2002. *The Future of Human Rights*, Oxford University Press

Clapham, A., 2006. *Human Rights Obligations of Non-state Actors*, Oxford University Press

Douzinas, C., 2000. *The End of Human Rights*, Oxford: Hart

Gordon, N. (ed.), 2004. *From the Margins of Globalisation: Critical Perspectives on Human Rights*, Lanham: Lexington Books

Kennedy, D., 2004. *Dark Sides of Virtue: Reassessing International Humanitarianism*, Princeton University Press

Marks, S. and A. Clapham, 2005. *International Human Rights Lexicon*, Oxford University Press

Meckled-Garcia, S. and B. Cali (eds.), 2006. *The Legalisation of Human Rights: Multidisciplinary Perspectives on Human Rights and Human Rights Law*, London: Routledge

Mutua, M., 2002. *Human Rights: A Political and Cultural Critique*, University of Pennsylvania Press

Steiner, H., P. Alston and R. Goodman, 2007. *International Human Rights in Context: Law, Politics, Morals*, Oxford University Press

Twining, W., 2009. *Human Rights: Southern Voices*, Cambridge University Press

Chapter 15 Justifying justice

Aukerman, M. J., 2002. 'Extraordinary Evil, Ordinary Crime: A Framework for Understanding Transitional Justice', *Harvard Human Rights Journal*, 15, 39–97

Cassese, A., 2008. *International Criminal Law*, Oxford University Press

Cryer, R., H. Friman, D. Robinson and E. Wilmshurst, 2010. *Introduction to International Criminal Law and Procedure: Principles, Procedures, Institutions*, Cambridge University Press

Drumbl, M. A., 2007. *Atrocity, Punishment, and International Law*, Cambridge University Press

Robinson, D., 2008. 'The Identity Crisis of International Criminal Law', *Leiden Journal of International Law*, 21, 925–963

Schabas, W., 2007. *An Introduction to the International Criminal Court*, Cambridge University Press

Simpson, G., 2007. *Law, War and Crime: War Crimes Trials and the Re-invention of International Law*, Cambridge: Polity Press

Chapter 16 Regulating trade, investment and money

Carreau, D. and P. Juillard, 2010. *Droit International Économique*, Paris: Dalloz-Sirey

Howse, R., 2007. *The WTO System: Law, Politics and Legitimacy*, London: Cameron May

Lowenfeld, A. F., 2008. *International Economic Law*, Oxford University Press

Newcombe, A. and L. Paradell, 2009. *Law and Practice of Investment Treaties: Standards of Treatment*, Aalphen aan den Rijn: Kluwer Law International

Picker, C., I. Bunn and D. Arner (eds.), 2008. *International Economic Law: The State and Future of the Discipline*, Oxford: Hart

Trebilcock, M. and R. Howse, 2005. *The Regulation of International Trade*, London: Routledge

Chapter 17 Divided against itself: aspiration and reality of international law

Beitz, C., 1999. *Political Theory and International Relations*, Princeton University Press

Caney, S., 2005. *Justice Beyond Borders: A Global Political Theory*, Oxford University Press

Cohen, J., 2010. 'Philosophy, Social Science, Global Poverty', in A. Jaggar (ed.), *Pogge and His Critics*, Cambridge: Polity Press, 18–45.

Hollis, A. and T. Pogge, 2008. *The Health Impact Fund: Making New Medicines Accessible to All*, Oslo and New Haven: Incentives for Global Health

Howse, R. and R. Teitel, 2010. 'Global Justice, Poverty, and the International Economic Order', in S. Besson and J. Tasioulas (eds.), *The Philosophy of International Law*, New York: Oxford University Press, 437–449

Pogge, T., 1989. *Realizing Rawls*, Ithaca, NY: Cornell University Press

Pogge, T., 1994. 'An Egalitarian Law of Peoples', *Philosophy and Public Affairs* 23, 195–224.

Pogge, T., 2011. 'The Achilles Heel of Competitive/Adversarial Systems', in N. Dobos, C. Barry and T. Pogge (eds.), *Global Financial Crisis: The Ethical Issues*, Basingstoke: Palgrave Macmillan, 120–131

Pogge, T. and D. Moellendorf (eds.), 2008. *Global Justice: Seminal Essays*, St. Paul, MN: Paragon House

Salomon, M. E., 2007. *Global Responsibility for Human Rights: World Poverty and the Development of International Law*, Oxford University Press

Shue, H., 1996. *Basic Rights: Subsistence, Affluence, and US Foreign Policy*, Princeton University Press

Tan, K.-C., 2004. *Justice without Borders: Cosmopolitanism, Nationalism, and Patriotism*, Cambridge University Press

Chapter 18 Conserving the world's resources?

Benvenisti, E., 2002. *Sharing Transboundary Resources*, Cambridge University Press

Bodansky, D., J. Brunnée and E. Hey (eds.), 2007. *The Oxford Handbook of International Environmental Law*, Oxford University Press

Hardt, M. and A. Negri, 2009. *Commonwealth*, Cambridge, MA: Harvard University Press

Radin, M. J., 1996. *Contested Commodities*, Cambridge, MA: Harvard University Press

Rist, G., 1997. *The History of Development: From Western Origins to Global Faith*, Atlantic Highlands, NJ: Zed Books

Index